N

ESCAPE TO FREEDOM

A FREEDOM HOUSE BOOK

Strategies for the 1980s: Lessons of Cuba, Vietnam, and Afghanistan
Philip van Slyck
STUDIES IN FREEDOM, NUMBER 1

ESCAPE TO FREEDOM

The Story of the International Rescue Committee

AARON LEVENSTEIN

Studies in Freedom, Number 2

GREENWOOD PRESS
Westport, Connecticut • London, England

Acknowledgments

The following publishers and sources have generously given permission to use extended quotations from copyrighted works: From *The Lost Crusade: America in Vietnam*, by Chester L. Cooper. Copyright 1970 by Chester L. Cooper. Reprinted by permission of the publisher, Dodd, Mead & Company. From *Britannica Book of the Year, 1976 through 1980*, "Cambodia." Copyright by the Encyclopaedia Britannica, 1976, 1977, 1978, 1979, 1980. Reprinted by permission of the publisher, Encyclopaedia Britannica. From *From Russia With Love: One Woman's Experience in the Premigration Counseling of Soviet Refugees*, by Laraine Lippe, unpublished master's thesis. Reprinted by permission of the author. From *Indochinese Refugees*, MacNeil-Lehrer Report. Copyright 1979 by Educational Broadcasting Corporation and GWETA. Reprinted by permission of the publisher, the MacNeil-Lehrer Report.

Library of Congress Cataloging in Publication Data

Levenstein, Aaron, 1910-
 Escape to freedom.

 (Studies in freedom, ISSN 0273-1231 ; no. 2)
 Bibliography: p.
 Includes index.
 1. International Rescue Committee — History. I. Title.
II. Series.
HV640.L4   1983   362.8'7   82-21078
ISBN 0-313-23815-4 (lib. bdg.)

Library of Congress Catalog Card Number: 82-21078
ISBN: 0-313-23815-4
ISSN: 0273-1231

First published in 1983

Greenwood Press
A division of Congressional Information Service, Inc.
88 Post Road West
Westport, Connecticut 06881

Printed in the United States of America

10 9 8 7 6 5 4 3 2 1

To the Staff and Volunteers
of the
International Rescue Committee

But they shall sit every man under
his vine and under his fig tree;
and none shall make him afraid.

—Micah, 4:4

Contents

Illustrations

Preface

It is a commonplace of American demography that, except for those whose ancestors greeted Columbus as he disembarked, all of us are either immigrants or the descendants of immigrants. Yet, among the paradoxes of our national history is the coolness with which each ethnic group, on settling in, has regarded the later arrivals. Newcomers have always been greeted with ambivalence. Doctrines of the melting pot and of cultural pluralism have wrestled with know-nothing xenophobia. The outcome, in any given era, has depended on the state of the economy, the level of psychological security, the fears of foreign expansionism, and other adversities to which societies succumb.

As this is written, the mood is depressed. We wallow in the trough. Retrenchment restrains the putative traditional spirit of American generosity. The nation has come through a period of almost intolerable stress. Prominent among the debilitating events has been the need to admit hundreds of thousands of Vietnamese and Cubans, not to mention lesser numbers of expatriates from Communist countries in Europe. In this period the American people have acquiesced, if not always with enthusiasm, at least with a sense of moral obligation, in opening the doors a little more widely to those who ask admission.

There is much in the record that is praiseworthy, but only an extreme chauvinist would insist that we are without fault. A nation's ultimate character is to be discerned not only in its behavior, which through the centuries is inevitably marked by inconsistencies, but by the mythology that preserves a continuing leitmotif. Significantly, the American self-image is that of a haven for the oppressed, a nation always extending a hand of welcome to those who seek freedom. The reality is that the gates have frequently clanged shut, though many of us, by our presence, bear witness to how often they have been kept open.

Few social analysts, however, would disagree: on balance, America has prospered because of the magnetic attraction it has had for those who seek a freer and better life. The benefits from admitting those who fled from tyranny have outweighed the social costs involved in absorbing them. The process has had its pain. Resources both material and emotional had to be invested. The dislocations attendant on migration — mental breakdown, festering centers of poverty, epidemics of disease and crime — had to be paid for by the host society.

One need not search far for substantial evidence of prejudicial passions directed at "foreigners" through the years. A typical example is a 1914 series of articles on each of the major ethnic groups in the United States. Written by Edward A. Ross, a leading American sociologist based at the University of Wisconsin, and published in the *Century Magazine*, a widely read, middle-brow monthly of the time, the articles added up to consistent denigration. For example, "the average German-American stands below the level of the average German at home."[1] Among the Scandinavians, Ross wrote, there was little "resourcefulness and intellectual initiative."[2] Rating the Italians "below even the Portuguese and the Poles," the sociology professor reported that "the Slavs are ferocious in their cups, but none is so ready with his knife when sober as the Southern Italian."[3] The Jews, in particular, seemed most threatening to America's domestic tranquility. Ross quoted with approval a statement by a Boston observer: "There are actually streets in the West End where, while Jews are moving in, negro (sic) housewives are gathering up their skirts and seeking a more spotless environment."[4] The prediction with which he concluded his study of "The Hebrews of Eastern Europe in America" has since been tested by history:

If the czar, by keeping up the pressure which has already rid him of two million undesired subjects, should succeed in driving the bulk of his six million Hebrews to the United States, we shall see the rise of a Jewish question here, perhaps riots and anti-Jewish legislation. No doubt thirty or forty thousand Hebrews from eastern Europe might be absorbed by this country every year without any marked growth of race prejudice; but when they come in two or three or even four times as fast, the lump outgrows the leaven, and there will be trouble.[5]

Such were the judgments of a prominent sociologist. But the actual outcome has been a triumph of the American myth. These characterizations are seen today as shocking. Certainly, no contemporary journal would dare to present such analysis to an audience with any kind of intellectual or literary pretensions. The very fact of such a revolutionary change of attitude is a measure of progress that justifies the pride with which most Americans read the record.

Consider what the "newcomers" themselves have to say about that record. Over the generations they have given us an invaluable literary legacy describing the alienation they suffered. Particularly illuminating are the commentaries of a group of writers fresh from the transition. With their sensitivities heightened by the need to work in a new setting, far from their native audience, they have been in a position both to appreciate and deprecate. In the late 1960s, when America was bracing itself against the impact of a war abroad and rebelliousness at home, Thomas C. Wheeler assembled an anthology entitled *The Immigrant Experience*. The essays describe "the anguish of becoming American."[6]

Among the authors is Czeslaw Milosz, the Polish poet, now teaching at the University of California, whose work has since won for him (and for his adopted country) a Nobel Prize in literature. In the 1950s when he chose exile, his book, *The Captive Mind*, written in France, presented the first profound analysis of what communism was doing to the intellectual. After witnessing America's growing doubts about herself—"the suffering of America, the violence of its nearly insoluble conflicts, the uncertainty of America"[7]—he perceives with an objective clarity denied to many of her native sons the ultimate good inherent in the democratic potential: "In spite of arguments to the contrary, in spite of the paradox, America is the legitimate heir to Judaeo-Christian civilization. . . ."[8] And of the uncertain future, he finds it possible to say: "Since self-accusation and the feeling of being lost are more out in the open in America than anywhere else, America is the testing ground for all mankind."[9] That is why the American response to the plea of the beleaguered in all lands is the ultimate measure of our national character.

To recount the role of the United States in meeting the challenge raised by the world's refugee population is an essential undertaking, particularly at this time when the quantum of human generosity seems to be at a low level. The objective situation is readily understood. The economy is in difficulty. Many Americans are wearied or numbed by the international tragedies that send hundreds of thousands to our embassies and consulates around the world. The number of "illegals" in the United States is now counted in the millions; their presence raises problems of legalization and social ethics. Even as this preface is being written, the Supreme Court of the United States has ruled that the children of illegal aliens are under the equal protection of the Constitution and the individual states must provide for their education.

No one would suggest that a blanket visa be issued to the peoples of the world. The consequence would be chaos. Even the severest critics of the United States must admit that if the planet's billions were given their choice of where to live, the resulting mass migration would flow predominantly toward this country. It would include Indians who now regularly denounce America's "materialism"; Chinese who have every reason to recall the brutal exploitation of the coolies in the nineteenth century; Eastern Europeans who have been told repeatedly that America is "imperialist" and exploits the poor; Latinos who have been the victims of "dollar diplomacy"; and Africans who know well the history of racism in this country.

It is estimated that there are now 17 million refugees stumbling around the globe. They dream of coming to rest where they can earn a decent livelihood in peace and freedom. Obviously, no one nation can resolve the problem. All governments have a responsibility to contribute to two ends: first, the victims must be kept alive, and second, they must be given access to places of resettlement. But the task also devolves on individuals. Many have found it possible to act in voluntary organizations. They have contributed funds to feed, clothe and house refugees in passage, to provide medical care and other necessities for them, and to serve as sponsors for their permanent resettlement.

This book tells the story of one such organization, the International Rescue Committee. My aim has been to present the drama of the refugees simultaneously on three stage levels, so to speak: the historical background that produced each major flow of refugees; the difficulties encountered on the route to freedom; and how IRC helped to overcome those difficulties.

My interest in the subject goes back to my own origins. At the turn of the century my parents and grandparents were among those who fled from Czarist Russia. With the advent of Hitler, I joined in efforts to rescue the victims of Nazism. In the postwar period the same logic that required assistance for the antifascists demanded action on behalf of those being oppressed by totalitarian communism and authoritarian regimes.

In 1963, I wrote a short history of the International Rescue Committee entitled *They Chose Freedom*, which provides much of the material in the early chapters of this book. I have not only had the opportunity to observe IRC at work but have participated in the field as the reader will find in these pages. In collecting data, my wife and I have visited IRC's installations in the United States, Europe, Africa, India, and Southeast Asia. We have seen its dedicated personnel, both professional and volunteer, functioning in headquarters and on the firing line.

My indebtedness to members of IRC's staff and others I have interviewed would involve a list too long to be enumerated here. In some instances, their names appear in the pages dealing with their specific activities. To the many others who have helped but who, because of space limitations, remain unnamed, I can only express regrets and thanks. But I must acknowledge specifically those who have read the manuscript in whole or in part and made invaluable suggestions—Leo Cherne, Alton Kastner, Charles Sternberg and Louis Wiesner. My greatest debt is to my wife, Margery, who served with me as codirector of the IRC program in West Bengal during the Bangladesh crisis and who in a real sense is coauthor of this book.

—Aaron Levenstein

ESCAPE TO FREEDOM

I

The Long Journey

In the years of your youth you were on the eve of a great career as a historian, with just enough of a reputation to attract the attention of the Fuehrer's Gestapo. Without time to pack a bag, you crossed the border — and lived to write the history of what Hitler did to Europe and the world. . . .

Or you were an established artist in Paris. Your pictures of cows and countryside had already brought crowds to the galleries. But you were Jewish. And when the jackboots reached the Arc de Triomphe in 1940 you fled to Marseilles, and then across the Pyrenees, ultimately reaching a haven in America from which eventually you could return to your studio in France. . . .

Or maybe in the fall of 1956 you were suddenly made mayor of Budapest for the ten days of freedom that Hungary enjoyed that year. You know what it means to have been a prisoner of the Nazis, and then of the Communists. Ultimately, when you reach freedom in America, you resume your career as an engineer in a Du Pont plant in Wilmington.

Perhaps a few short years ago you were in charge of all the pulmonary hospitals in Rumania. But you could not stand the stifling atmosphere of political and scientific repression. So now you are a doctor quietly practicing medicine in Cleveland. . . .

Or your curriculum vitae records that two decades ago you were an engineering student at the University of Stettin. You had won a place in the Polish Academy of Sciences in Warsaw. But the lack of freedom forced you to give up the honors, the status and the income. You made your way to America where you now work as a radio specialist — as a free man. . . .

Maybe you were once a lawyer in Havana. Today you earn your living in New York as an accountant. You will practice advocacy again only if the rule of law is ever restored in your country. Your friend who fled from Cuba in an open boat, however, is somewhat more fortunate: he was a carpenter and can wield a hammer in any language. . . .

Or you are a Ugandan housewife whose husband offended a bodyguard of the once mighty Idi Amin. You saw your man arrested; you heard he had been tortured; on a grim day you will never forget, he was brought home broken to be displayed to your family and then taken off to be executed. You gathered up the children and headed for Kenya. . . .

Or you have other memories. You were a schoolteacher in Cambodia, a country whose new masters pigeonholed you as an employee of the *ancien régime* because of your profession. Culture itself had became counter-revolutionary. Separated from your family, you were put to work like a water buffalo, dragging tree trunks in a jungle area euphemistically called a "new economic zone." You wandered for days through the forest until you reached Thailand. Now, lucky to be alive, you are an auto mechanic in Los Angeles where you learned a new trade — and a free way of life. . . .

You may be of any nationality — a Russian dissident, a Polish religionist, a Yugoslav teacher, a citizen of any nation where speech is costly, assembly is hazardous and publishing is a state monopoly. To exercise these "human rights" was an act of treason, so you fled to safety in a freer land.

Between then and now, how great a distance?

To those still en route, of whatever class or status, the path seems endless. The course each traveler takes twists and turns uniquely over the world's toughest terrain — the freedom road.

For one it means a sudden leap from a window to cross a wall; for another, a perilous trip on foot through a mine field; for still another, defection in a foreign city while on authorized official travel; for someone else, a quick dash over a border with bullets whistling around your ears; for others, a hazardous journey in a leaky, overcrowded tub, blown by the winds across the South China Sea or the Gulf of Siam, water and food supplies consumed a week ago.

Whatever the route, the journey is hard. But worthwhile. For your goal is to reach a place where you can breathe and think. In the process your life and work will enrich the society that welcomes you.

SUBSTANCE OF A DECISION

Nobody can say what alchemy of the spirit transforms discontent into decision. Millions never make the change. They let the days drift by, dreaming and hoping until the dreams are frayed and the hopes withered. Only the brave muster the courage to venture into the unknown.

The problems that await them are limitless and go to the heart of existence. How will they eat? Where will they sleep? Who will provide medical care in the inevitable days of illness that lie ahead? Will they be able to speak, communicate their simplest wants, in the alien tongue? What kind of xenophobic prejudices are they likely to encounter?

Look around at your familiar environs and try to imagine you are about to leave them forever. For the last time, finger the mementoes identified with home and family and life's continuity. Hiding in your heart the secret decision you have made, look at your friends and loved ones to etch their memory on your brain. You may never see them again.

How much must you forfeit? Not just the physical possessions you accumulated in a lifetime of work and effort. Now you must part with your daily habits, the routine that gave you stability, even the language in which you think. You will have to learn new ways of speech and thought in the foreign world you are about to enter. Like a craftsman abandoning his tools, you may have to leave behind the trade or profession you mastered at such great cost and with so much pride. To reach the goal of freedom, you must travel light.

But one thing you can take along with you — your love of liberty, coupled with the hope of a better life. That is your passport. As you choose freedom and plunge into an uncertain future, there is a thought to comfort you: outside, beyond the barbed wire and the watchtower where the machine-gunner keeps his vigil for tyranny, you will not be alone. At the border, others are keeping the watch and await your coming.

II

Escape from Hitler

Not since the Voelkerwanderung *of prehistoric and ancient times has* the earth so trembled under the impact of moving feet. Beginning with the 1930s, a rising tide has carried millions of human beings, principally westward, on the waves of war and dictatorship.

History has known few events comparable to the opening of the sluicegates that started on Monday, January 30, 1933, a few moments before noon. A man with a comical Chaplinesque moustache, but with the burning eyes of a fanatic, had just faced a senile old soldier to take the oath of office as Chancellor of the German Reich.

From that moment, the tragedy of twentieth-century man took on new and more horrible dimensions. The world had known refugees before. It had seen orderly emigrations, organized for the purpose of escaping religious and political persecution. In colonial days, America had been the destination of religious dissenters — Puritans, Quakers, Huguenots, Catholics, Jews. Throughout the nineteenth century, the United States was the haven of political refugees caught by the backlash of revolutions, civil conflicts and hunger, in Ireland and on the continent. Now in the twentieth century, would America again be the place of refuge?

Even before the explosion in Germany, the political refugee had become the symbol of our age. The Bolshevik revolution in Russia, preceding Hitler's by less than two decades, had already given notice of a new phenomenon in the world — totalitarian terror. Those who had hoped to make Russia a democracy were forced to flee in the early twenties; in the thirties, the purge-frenzy of the Soviet dictator caused a trickle of defectors to move West. Italy, too, was driving its best elements into flight as Mussolini postured at home and sought weaker nations to conquer in Africa.

In 1933 the people of the United States, preoccupied with their own economic problems, could spare few thoughts for events abroad. Only a comparative handful — political analysts, educators, clergymen, journalists — read the portents. Humanity was about to be put to the rack.

Already refugees were being flung on many shores like spume from the raging seas. Emergency action was required, but eventually it became clear that for the rest of our lives we would confront crisis. The stakes would be the values of civilization itself. From 1933 on, defending those who refused to be hitched to the chariots of the new Caesars became the continuing obligation of all lovers of freedom.

THE MODEST BEGINNINGS

On July 24, 1933, a brief item appeared in the *New York Times*. The 10-point heading said simply: "New German Relief Unit." A subhead explained: "American Branch Formed to Aid Work Headed by Einstein." As the first published reference to what was to become the International Rescue Committee, two paragraphs warrant recording here:

At the request of the International Relief Association, headed by Albert Einstein, an American committee has been formed to assist Germans suffering from the policies of Hitler.

Funds are being solicited to send to Mayor Charles Hueber of Strasbourg, in Alsace, France, who is treasurer of the European organization of the International Relief Association. The headquarters of the American committee, of which Amos Pinchot is chairman, is at 11 West 42nd Street.

The article noted that the international group had been in existence since 1931. "It aids victims of civil oppression in many lands without reference to religious or political faith."

In the next few years the International Relief Association branch based in New York would be busy educating the American people to the infamies being perpetrated inside Germany by the Nazi regime. In addition to facilitating the emigration, legal and illegal, of Hitler's victims, it threw itself into the task of mobilizing public opinion to press for the release of prisoners held by the Gestapo. Most notable among these was Carl von Ossietsky, the distinguished German pacifist. Charles A. Beard, the historian and honorary chairman of the International Relief Association, together with more than 900 other scholars and world figures, pressed successfully to have the Nobel Peace Prize awarded to Ossietsky. His resulting release from a concentration camp was celebrated in a mass meeting at New York's Cooper Union. In his speech, Einstein hailed Ossietsky as the "most admirable of the few outstanding personalities of Nazi Germany who have put the interests of humanity above that of national egotism." Sharing the platform, or sending messages of support, were the leaders of American secular and religious thought, including philosopher John Dewey, Columbia University president Nicholas Murray Butler, publicist Oswald Garrison Villard, clergymen Harry Emerson Fosdick and John Haynes Holmes. New York's feisty Mayor Fiorello LaGuardia contrasted the ease with which one could champion any cause in the United States and the burdens suffered by those defending the ideals of civilization in the shadow of the concentration camps. "It takes a real man to do it in Hitler Germany," he said.

It had become impossible in the Third Reich to express any dissent. Communists, socialists, unionists, liberals, traditional conservatives, were being rounded up by the Gestapo. By 1937, an incredulous world had to recognize the truth. Senator William E. Borah of Idaho, who had been America's leading isolationist in the years before and after World War I, told his colleagues that in Germany "there is no law — only the will of the master; there is no liberty, there is no freedom, there is no security. Men and women are hunted like wild beasts."

As Hitler moved on to new victories without resistance from his neighbors — marching troops into the demilitarized Rhineland, swallowing Austria in one gulp of *Anschluss*, snatching the Sudetenland from Czechoslovakia and finally taking over the whole country — the flight of East Europeans and Germans became a stampede. The International Relief Association struggled to provide the necessary funds to sustain them in France and to provide entry to the United States whose doors had been bolted years before by a xenophobic Immigration Act.

What at first had seemed an impossible task was somehow being reduced to the level of the very difficult. Escapes were occurring, and those fortunate enough to reach safety were being cared for. But the specter of total impossibility was to recur when war broke out in 1939. Hitler, in pursuit of Nazi domination, had cleared the way by signing a "nonaggression" pact with his supposed archenemy, his fellow-totalitarian Josef Stalin. What would enter the pages of history as the most unscrupulous deal ever made between nations was accompanied by a secret protocol that callously aimed at looting Europe and dividing the spoils into defined spheres of influence and territorial distributions. The cynics in the Kremlin assumed that they had won a respite for themselves and eventual superiority, for the ensuing war would debilitate the democracies and the Nazis alike. As for issues of justice or morality, the Soviet foreign minister Molotov shrugged off such bourgeois values with the statement that "fascism is merely a matter of taste." For the world, including the Russians themselves, it was to become a matter of blood.

AFTER THE FALL

The first months of World War II came to be known as the "Phony War" among the English-speaking allies and as the *"Sitz-krieg"* among the Germans. While the French troops sat passively behind the Maginot Line in the West, their Polish ally to the East was being ground between the invading forces of the Wehrmacht and the Red Army. Once this phase of the war was completed, the genocidal process could begin, even as Berlin prepared to woo Britain and France to accept peace on Nazi terms. When this failed, the full fury of the Stukas and Panzers was unleashed, and the Maginot Line was by-passed by an invasion of Belgium and the Netherlands, soon to be followed by the rape of Denmark and Norway.

For Americans, the fall of France was like the funereal tolling of a distant bell. In the United States, a stirring of political activism was felt. A small group, calling themselves the Emergency Rescue Committee, met in a hotel room in New York to see what could be done. The moving spirits included Karl Frank, a German refugee, his wife, Anna Caples, and the Viennese Joseph Buttinger. They had been active, together with Reinhold Niebuhr, in an anti-Hitler group called the American Friends of German Freedom. The crisis now required a new approach. Harold Oram, who had won his spurs raising support for the Loyalists in the Spanish Civil War, undertook fund-raising responsibilities. Participants in the program recall early meetings in the home of H. William Fitelson, a young attorney who was to become a prominent figure in theatrical and publishing law. He has remained through-out his career an active leader in refugee work.

Few in number and limited in resources, the group made no grandiose plans. Armed only with a sense of responsibility, they were determined to do what lay in their power to vindicate a belief in man's humanity to man. They had no idea then that out of their conversations and a merger with the International Relief Association would come the worldwide International Rescue Committee, whose representatives would eventually bring succor to the oppressed of Asia, Africa and Latin America as well as Europe, to people of all creeds, races and nationalities.

Before long they gathered to their ranks leading public figures: Frank Kingdon, who presided over the Committee, Elmer Davis, Robert Hutchins, Alvin Johnson, William Allan Neilson, David Seiferheld, George Shuster, Raymond Gram Swing and Dorothy Thompson.

Others were similarly moved to act. The brutal anti-Semitism of the Nazis had led organizations such as the American Jewish Committee and the American Jewish Congress to respond energetically from the first days of Hitler's accession to power. Special purpose groups now appeared. Thus the Jewish Labor Committee, with which the International Rescue Commit-tee would cooperate through the years, came into being. As a Jewish voice in the American labor movement and as a labor voice in the American Jewish community, it helped to rally the support of the American Federa-tion of Labor and the Congress of Industrial Organizations, then separate institutions, in behalf of those attempting to escape and seeking resettlement.

The International Relief Association, during the 1930s, had already at-tracted the nation's foremost intellectuals and labor spokesmen to its ranks. Among its leading spirits were John Dewey, America's best known philos-opher; Reinhold Niebuhr, the country's foremost Protestant theologian; Sterling Spero, political scientist and educator; David Dubinsky, president of the garment workers; Bryn Hovde, educator, later head of the New School for Social Research; Paul Brissenden, Columbia University's labor scholar. They had observed the decimation of Germany's most distinguished intellectuals. Hitler had dismembered the university faculties and had driven into exile the scientists who would ultimately give the Allies, and especially the United States, their most awesome weapons. The figures, when available after the war, not only revealed why flight became a major recourse of Germany's large intelligentsia, but demonstrated how a braindrain created by a short-sighted regime can prove to be its undoing. William L. Shirer writes:

After six years of Nazification the number of university students dropped by more than one half — from 127,920 to 58,325. The decline in enrollment at the institutes of technology, from which Germany got its scientists and engineers, was even greater — from 20,474 to 9,554. Academic standards fell dizzily. By 1937 there was not only a shortage of young men in the sciences and engineering but a decline in their qualifications. Long before the outbreak of the war the chemical industry, busily helping to further Nazi rearmament, was complaining through its organ, *Die Chemische Industrie*, that Germany was losing its leadership in chemistry. Not only the national economy but national defense itself was jeopardized, it complained. . . .

Nazi Germany's loss, as it turned out, was the free world's gain, especially in the race to be the first with the atom bomb. . . . It was one of the ironies of fate that the development of the bomb in the United States owed so much to two men who had been exiled because of race from the Nazi and Fascist dictatorships: Einstein from Germany and Fermi from Italy.[1]

The war had deepened the plight of those German refugees who had made their escape to other countries. If help was to be provided with some degree of effectiveness, union between the International Relief Association and the Emergency Rescue Committee was a clear necessity. A dynamic young woman, Sheba Strunsky (later Goodman), abandoned a promising career as an actress to become the first executive secretary of the merged International Rescue Committee on its establishment in 1942. For the first four years of her service, she refused to accept any compensation.

INITIAL GOALS

At the outset of the war, the objectives of the relief organizations had been clearly defined: to send financial assistance to the families of Hitler's victims; to resettle anti-Nazis who had made good their escape; whenever possible to further the dangerous work of smuggling democratic leaders out of the Gestapo's reach. First contacts with European centers of activity had been made through Albert Einstein and Käthe Kollwitz, the brilliant artist who in 1919 became the first woman ever elected to the Berlin Academy, only to be expelled by the Nazis in 1933.

In a little room provided by Oswald Garrison Villard in the offices of *The Nation*, overlooking the graveyard of New York's Trinity Church, Sheba Strunsky directed the command post. Her tasks were to enlarge the contacts, maintain communications, raise money, allocate aid, cut the international red tape, and guide individuals to safety and ultimate self-help. In those early years, the office considered itself fortunate if it raised an annual budget of six to eight thousand dollars. As of 1980, the annual budget of the organization, which funds activities on every continent of the globe, reached $26,913,425.

At first the refugees were a handful. Then, as the real nature of Nazism penetrated the incredulity of its potential victims, the stream became a torrent. In later years, survivors would recount events that once seemed utterly unlikely in a "modern" society. There was, for example, the successful German lawyer who, one day long before Hitler took over, had dared to respond to a Nazi's insult with a slap in the face. Two years later the Nazis threw him in jail, beat his teeth out and later sentenced him for attempted murder. While his appeal was pending he gathered his family together and left immediately for Paris. His son, Ralph M. Baruch, who has never forgotten the precipitate flight and the need to repeat it in 1940 with the fall of France, is today a major figure in America's broadcasting industry, chairman of Viacom, a leading communications company. He serves as a member of the Executive Committee of IRC, which had brought his family to the United States.

Various groups came into being. Jewish organizations rallied to aid their brethren who succeeded in emigrating. As the Nazis extended their attack to other faiths, the Catholic and Protestant churches assumed the care of their coreligionists. The labor groups concentrated on trade unionists. But the political refugees—those who had led the fight in defense of democratic institutions *per se*—had no existing organizations abroad to befriend them.

Their rescue, however, was of the utmost importance, not only for immediate humanitarian reasons but to encourage democrats who were yet to face the challenge in other places. Moreover, the time was bound to come when these stalwarts would be needed to rehabilitate their countries and lead their people back into democratic paths. Their survival could be a major factor in the ultimate redemption of the twentieth century.

NATURE OF THE CHALLENGE

To save the leadership remnants would be no easy task. European democracy, in the 1930s, was caught between giant pincers. Two forces, each thinking and planning in long-range terms, were intent on wiping out all potential cadres of democratic action that might fight them in the future.

On the one hand were the Nazis, well launched on their policy of exterminating all opposition in order to assure that the Third Reich, in Hitler's words, would "last a thousand years." None who might challenge it could be permitted to escape.

On the other hand were the Communists, also thinking in broad historical perspectives. On the eve of Hitler's triumph they had deliberately decided to pave the way for his victory by helping to plunge Germany into chaos. William L. Shirer, who was an eyewitness in the last days of the Weimar Republic, has written:

The Communists, at the behest of Moscow, were committed to the last to the silly idea of first destroying the Social Democrats, the Socialist trade unions and what middle-class democratic forces there were, on the dubious theory that although this would lead to a Nazi regime, it would be only temporary and would bring inevitably the collapse of capitalism, after which the Communists would take over and establish the dictatorship of the proletariat. Fascism in the Bolshevik Marxist view, represented the last stage of a dying capitalism; after that the Communist deluge![2]

The strategy was more sinister than silly, and came close to realization, as postwar history reveals. For part of the Kremlin's grand design was that the Nazis would eliminate any democratic leadership that might challenge the Communists in the aftermath.

The founders of the International Rescue Committee understood the nature of the gauntlet through which European democrats were being run. The best of Germany's anti-Nazi and anti-Communist leadership — thinkers, writers, labor leaders, educators, poets, artists, journalists — had to be saved from both the Nazi executioners and the Communist conspirators. The task would be fraught with dual dangers: Nazi discovery and Communist betrayal.

In the first months after Hitler's accession, the Communists had two advantages: an existing underground that could be used to bring out many of their leaders, and a haven in the Soviet Union where these leaders could be kept in reserve and trained for future use. When the war was over, Russia intended to have on its leash a band of leaders, like Ulbricht and Pieck for Germany and Bierut for Poland. The International Red Aid, set up by the Communist International in 1922, already had an established apparatus with more than a decade of underground experience. After 1933, it oriented itself to attracting refugees to Moscow's cause, frequently by merely proffering relief. Those who opposed the party's objectives were pushed aside. Among its assignments, the International Red Aid undertook the mission of infiltrating non-Communist relief organizations. At first the tactic proved successful, until the Nazi-Soviet pact in 1939 dealt a severe blow to the *Apparat*.

It was of the utmost urgency that channels of rescue and relief be opened for those who opposed both Fascism and Communism. This was the objective of the founders of the IRC. Throughout the 1930s, the little office in New York became the headquarters for the rescue and resettlement of a constantly growing number of democrats. Quietly and as rapidly as possible representatives of the Committee in European capitals carried out the essential tasks — providing money; setting up escape routes; obtaining necessary documents and visas; organizing relocation assistance; rallying an ever-growing body of public opinion to support the need for rescue.

"SURRENDER ON DEMAND"

In 1936, Hitler began to devour Europe — "course by course," as Churchill put it. The Fuehrer marched into the Rhineland, and another stream of refugees spurted westward. In early 1938, Hitler swallowed Austria in one quick bite. The flow increased, branching through Czechoslovakia. Then Czechoslovakia was eaten, and again the human tide mounted. Refugees found themselves in a nightmarish game, trying to keep one step ahead of the Nazi aggressor: from Germany to Austria to Czechoslovakia. Eventually some were to flee from Czechoslovakia to Cuba — only to be driven from there by another dictator twenty-four years later.

Soon the southwestern end of the continent exploded. The year 1938 saw the footpaths of the Pyrenees come alive with an army of Spaniards fleeing from the victorious Franco. The following year Hitler invaded Poland, and then, in 1940, France fell before the advancing *Wehrmacht*. A world, horrified by the spectacle of Nazis parading on the Champs Elysees, watched Frenchmen become refugees in their own country, along with the anti-Nazis who had sought shelter.

As Hitler made his armistice with Marshal Pétain, allowing the old man to retain some semblance of independence in the "unoccupied zone," the fate of the refugees trapped in Vichy France seemed sealed. Pétain had cast off the last shred of honor by agreeing, in the infamous Article 19 of the armistice, "to surrender upon demand all Germans named by the German Government in France, as well as in French possessions." Before long, the term "German" came to mean any inhabitant of the new "Greater Reich" — Austrians, Poles, anybody coming from German-occupied territory — and then anybody the Nazis wanted.

France, which had been a land of asylum for people from all the Nazi-occupied countries, now became a giant man-trap. The Gestapo calculated that it could proceed in leisurely fashion to track down the political figures who were dedicated to democracy and the artists and intellectuals who by their daily work bore testimony to the independence of the human spirit.

From New York Sheba Strunsky planned maneuvers aimed at saving the people interned by the Vichy government. Sustaining her efforts was Freda Kirchwey, treasurer of the Committee, a brilliant young woman in her thirties who could always spare time from her duties as managing editor of *The Nation* to aid refugees. Together the two combined the Committee's meager finances with a wealth of ingenuity, imaginativeness and daring. Sheba

Strunsky has described the methods the two women used to breach the walls of malevolence and red tape imprisoning persons on the rescue roster. A number of them were interned in the unspeakable Camp Vernet from which they were not permitted to leave. But to obtain the visas already issued for them they had to go to Marseilles. How to resolve the dilemma? Strunsky recalls:

When the situation looked practically hopeless, I had the idea of trying to break the bureaucratic stranglehold. We wrote letters to the Camp Vernet authorities with the name of each refugee promised a visa, saying, "This is to state that 'John Brown' has been granted a visa for the United States and is therefore under the protection of the U.S. government which demands that he be permitted to travel to Marseilles to receive his visa." These letters were signed by Freda Kirchwey, stamped with the New York State incorporation seal of the International Relief Association done in gold leaf. Of course, this was sheer nonsense, but it worked! More than 60 refugees were then released from Vernet, travelled to Marseilles and received their visas.

Among those who had been incarcerated in Vernet was the Hungarian-born novelist Arthur Koestler, a disillusioned former Communist who had fought against the fascists in Spain and been a Franco prisoner under sentence of death. He has described his experiences in the French concentration camp in his widely read *Scum of the Earth*. His works, including *The Yogi and the Commissar*, an analysis of the nature of communism, have become classics in the political literature of the twentieth century.[3] In later years he toured the United States to raise funds for the International Rescue Committee, addressing great crowds in New York's Carnegie Hall and other major centers in Chicago, Los Angeles, San Francisco and Boston.

UNDERGROUND RAILWAY

As the Gestapo prepared its death lists, the leaders of the then Emergency Rescue Committee in New York were drawing up rosters of individuals believed to be in France who were likely to be "wanted" by the Nazis. Alfred H. Barr, Jr., director of the Museum of Modern Art, provided the names of world-famous artists and helped to raise funds to finance the planned escapes. Trade unions, concerned about fellow-unionists abroad, furnished similar lists and money. The U.S. government cooperated by unofficially promising visas for those who could be extricated from the Gestapo's web that was spreading rapidly through unoccupied France.

For the dangerous work of finding the individuals and building the underground railway to take them out, the Committee selected Varian Fry, a young, scholarly looking journalist, former editor of an intellectual magazine called *The Living Age*. It did not take much persuading from the usually persuasive Karl Frank to convince Fry that he was the right person for the job. He had a reading knowledge of half a dozen languages, including French. But his experience included nothing that would seem to qualify him for underground work. One of the associates he acquired in France, an experienced anti-Nazi, said years later: "Fry's innocence was his great advantage. A more sophisticated man would not have dared to undertake the tasks he carried out so successfully."

Fry set up his operation in Marseilles, the principal seaport of "unoccupied France." On the scene, he found as a valuable ally Dr. Frank Bohn, a veteran labor publicist who had been sent by the AFL. Fry arrived with $3,000 in cash and a list of some forty persons. Somehow they were to be located among the mass of refugees and spirited out of France. Choosing who was to be helped was a harrowing task, performed by an advisory committee comprised of nationality representatives — journalist Max Ascoli for the Italians, Catholic philosopher Jacques Maritain for the French, novelist Thomas Mann for the Germans, statesman Jan Masaryk for the Czechs, and so on. The list expanded interminably after Fry's arrival. During the following thirteen months he succeeded in saving some 2,000 men and women, many of them cultural and political leaders, who had been marked for slaughter by the Nazis.[4]

Among them were author Franz Werfel and his wife. Fry found the couple hiding in Marseilles. With the fall of Paris they had fled originally to Lourdes, where Werfel had begun his work, *The Song of Bernadette*. The novel, written in a profound religious spirit, was completed; it has since been read by millions and viewed by countless other millions on film, thanks to his rescue. Equally famous is his novel, *The Forty Days of Musa Dagh*, which salutes the heroic resistance of the Armenians to the genocidal policy of the Turks in 1915 — the twentieth century's rehearsal for the Nazi Holocaust.

The escape route used by the Werfels, organized by Fry and his associates, lay through the Pyrenees, across Spain and Portugal to Lisbon and thence by boat to freedom in America. Accompanying the Werfels on their journey was Heinrich Mann, the novelist-brother of Thomas Mann. At the age of seventy he made the strenuous ascent with his wife to "go over the hill." Avoiding the traveled roads and footpaths, cutting through the underbrush, skirting habitations, and remaining ever alert to possible Vichy patrols, the party crossed the border, uncertain of their reception by Spanish officials. Among the group was young Golo Mann, today a distinguished historian and one of West Germany's leading political writers. Curiously, he was the only one in the group who was questioned by an armed sentry on the Spanish side of the border, even though his papers contained a visa for entry into the United States where he was to meet his father at Princeton.

"So you are the son of Thomas Mann?" said the sentry.

"Yes," he answered, anticipating that he would soon be turned over to Gestapo agents known to be in Spain. "Does that displease you?"

"On the contrary," answered the sentry. "I am honored to make the acquaintance of the son of so great a man." And then, to complete the miracle of human solidarity, he telephoned for a car to take all of them down from the mountaintop.

Many such groups escaped because of a combination of luck and hard, dangerous work. Papers were forged; the prestige of the American visa was brandished before bureaucrats; policemen cooperated by warning Fry of impending arrests; services were purchased from underworld characters more interested in cash than in patriotism. Ruses, like misrepresenting refugees as French soldiers on the way to North African colonies for demobilization, permitted hundreds to slip out of the Nazi net. But the main route was across the mountains into Spain and then on to Lisbon. Gerald S. Jeremias, who was later to work for the joint committee on refugees set up by the AFL and the CIO, recalls how he and his wife Ava endured the physical ordeal, the long climb, the anxious hours, the cold night, the bruises on ankles and legs as the very boulders seemed to resent their escape, the confrontation with the Vichy border police who were obviously reluctant to do their duty to their employers, the arguments that finally proved persuasive.

Fortunately there were French patriots eager to help the anti-Nazi cause. Aristide Maillol, one of the great sculptors of our time, made his studio at Banyuls-sur-Mer a safe-house for refugees waiting for the right moment to cross. At the age of eighty he had personally led his famous model Dina Vierny, whose beauty and serenity he immortalized in stone, along the steep passes so that she might know how to guide the refugees on their way. The route was never discovered, and long after the Rescue Committee's mission was ended it continued to be used by young Frenchmen joining de Gaulle. Maillol died in September 1944, knowing that the Allied forces had landed in his country and freedom was at hand.

Moving refugees into and across Spain required a legerdemain of red tape. American authorities cooperated. President Roosevelt had ordered that visas be issued in special cases. In the race with the Gestapo, travel documents had to be made easily available. U.S. consular officials in Marseilles invented something called an "affidavit in lieu of passport" which facilitated the granting of exit visas. The form, despite its lack of international standing, saved Konrad Heiden, whose book *Der Fuehrer* was the first worldwide exposé of Hitler; by writing it Heiden had written his own death warrant — should the Gestapo have caught him. Fry arranged for Heiden to travel with a series of papers that included a Czech passport identifying him as businessman David Silberman, and a U.S. entry visa stamped on an "affidavit in lieu of passport" with his correct name. Since he had to leave Lisbon by the same name he had used on entering, he presented the passport to the Portuguese on the dock and, a few feet later, switched to the affidavit on boarding the ship.

Among the mass of refugees pouring into the south of France, Fry located artists such as Marc Chagall, Jacques Lipchitz, Max Ernst and André Masson. All of them were high on the most-wanted list of the Gestapo in Paris — and the Museum of Modern Art in New York. The latter won, though not without difficulty from the artistic temperament itself. Many were reluctant to leave. A petulant and vain Chagall, for example, had persuaded himself that he was safe from arrest, being a naturalized French citizen and a world-renowned figure. But when Vichy adopted the anti-Jewish laws, the painter of rural boyhood scenes anxiously asked Varian Fry, "Are there cows in America?" Hearing an affirmative, he consented to being rescued, but was seized by the Vichy police before he could leave. Fry, threatening the authorities with denunciation by the world press and "lifelong disgrace," obtained his release.

Not the least of Fry's difficulties was the unwillingness of many among the refugees to believe the Nazis would really descend to the ultimate depths of inhumanity. The German Social Democratic leaders Rudolph Breitscheid and Rudolph Hilferding argued that their worldwide reputation as political leaders in pre-Nazi Germany would protect them. Repeatedly they deferred their departure despite Fry's anguished pleas. When sympathetic Vichy police got word to Fry that the Gestapo was coming for the two men, they agreed to go. Too late. They died in Nazi hands.

Others left in time. Jacques Lipchitz, for example, immersed in his sculpting in a studio in Toulouse, agreed to take the journey only when friends refused to go without him. Thereafter, until his death in 1973, he continued to create his masterpieces of sculpture in Hastings-on-Hudson, New York, interrupting his work frequently to help later generations of refugees.

BETWEEN TWO WORLDS

Unlike Chagall and Lipchitz, who were Jews, Max Ernst illustrates the plight of the prodemocratic "Aryan." In World War I he had fought in the Kaiser's army. Living in France when the second World War broke out, he proceeded to execute his famous painting, "A Moment of Calm," after which he was interned in 1939 by the French as an enemy alien because "he is under the jurisdiction of the German Reich." Released on the petition of French intellectuals, he enjoyed four months of freedom only to be interned again in a camp at Nîmes. He escaped, was recaptured, escaped again, and then, as he put it, he accepted "an offer of shelter secured in the United States by several friends including Marga Barr [of the Museum of Modern Art in New York], and son Jimmy, expedited through the Emergency Rescue Committee." Ernst settled down to many years of creative work in New York, where his retrospectives draw tremendous audiences.

Among those rescued, many returned promptly to their homelands at the end of the war. One of these was Giuseppe Modigliani, leader of the Italian Social Democrats and brother of the artist Amadeo. Modigliani had been one of Fry's problem-children in Marseilles, unreasonably flaunting both his long white beard and the fur coat presented to him by an Italian local of the International Ladies Garment Workers in New York just before the war.

During this period the Committee helped such distinguished figures as the late Wanda Landowska, generally recognized as the world's greatest harpsichordist; the orchestra leader Eduard Fendler; the Hungarian writer Hans Habe, author of *A Thousand Shall Fall*; Fritz Kahn, the famous medical authority, author of *Man in Structure and Function*; Alfredo Mendizabal, Spain's leading Catholic philosopher; the poet Walter Mehring; Charles Stirling, a young Frenchman, formerly director of the Ingrès Museum at Montauban, ultimately a curator at the Metropolitan Museum in New York; Jacques Hadamard, mathematical physicist frequently referred to as the Einstein of France; Otto Meyerhoff, Nobel Prize-winning biochemist; and Hannah Arendt, political scientist and philosopher.

As a cover for his presence in Marseilles, Fry had organized a *Centre Américain de Secours*, ostensibly a relief agency for the wholly innocent purpose of distributing milk and food to the needy. Word of his real mission soon spread among the refugees, and a steady parade came to the doors of the *Centre*. Heartbreaking, painstaking decisions were required. Applicants had to be screened to ferret out both Gestapo agents seeking to entrap the Committee and Communist agents whose party line called for implementing the Nazi-Soviet pact by sabotaging Britain's lone resistance. Priorities had to be established for the escapees. Prominent refugees were in greater danger than obscure ones and therefore had to be the first ones shipped out.

The work progressed, but there were also disasters — escapes that miscarried, betrayals by Vichy agents, fake documents detected under scrutiny, chartered ships that never left port. Among the victims who did not make it to freedom was Bill Freier, a gifted Austrian cartoonist, who joined the staff of the Committee and used his talents to forge identity cards as well as to draw amusing caricatures of Varian Fry and his associates. Freier was finally captured and deported to Poland where he was killed.

Another fatal loss was the German philosopher and critic, Walter Benjamin, associate of Gershom Scholem and Martin Buber, the leading Jewish thinkers of this century. In recent years, Benjamin's work has enjoyed a renaissance among contemporary intellectuals. Susan Sontag, in quoting him at length, notes that his "Surrealist sensibility is the most profound of anyone's on record." *Kirkus Reviews* has described him as "perhaps the most subtle, intuitive, and creative critic of the age." Gershom Scholem's biographical memoir of his friendship with Benjamin, published in the United States in 1981, describes the events leading up to his death.[5] He had left Germany for France shortly after Hitler's victory. On the outbreak of war, he was interned by the French as a German citizen but later released. When Paris surrendered he fled south. Escaping from Marseilles, he and his companions were arrested by the Spanish police after successfully surviving what one of them called twelve hours of "absolutely horrible ordeal" during which they had to "climb on all fours" much of the way across the Pyrenees. Returned to France and now within the Gestapo's reach, having already contemplated suicide in the belief that the war would destroy civilization, he ended his life in September 1940 at Port Bou. Ironically, his four companions were permitted to resume their journey to freedom once money ("quite a bit of it") had changed hands.

Since students of German literature now regard Benjamin as the most important critic in the period between the two wars, his death at the early age of 48 was a major loss to German letters. No one can calculate, of course, the enormous cost to civilization, culture, science and the arts caused by the depredations of Hitler's Gestapo and by the war he launched. That the damage was reduced by Fry's underground operations in France is evidenced by the number who did survive and who were enabled to join the pantheon of thinkers, writers, artists, musicians, political leaders, executives and workers.

A DEDICATED STAFF

To carry out his mission Fry surrounded himself with a group of trusted aides, including some Americans who had been living in France before the war, or who had volunteered as ambulance drivers for the British and French. Invaluable was the work of a number of the refugees themselves who explored and mapped escape routes, handled details like providing hiking supplies and cash, prepared "visas" and "passports," helped others to escape, and then in the final days also went over the hill.

Working alongside Fry's Emergency Rescue Committee was a Czech youth named Charles Sternberg, known to his associates as Carel, who represented the International Relief Association. Even after Fry had to leave Marseilles, Sternberg stayed on the scene until he too found it necessary to take his departure for safer regions. A central figure in IRC's history, Sternberg does not like to talk about himself. He loses his reticence when issues of principle or practice are under discussion. His speech is crisply to the point. Among diplomats and leaders of relief agencies he is now regarded as one of the most authoritative sources of information and counsel. Compatriots who met him in the chaotic days of flight from the Gestapo recall him as a slight, intense and energetic youth.

He had fled from Czechoslovakia to Paris in 1938; in 1940 he again found it necessary to flee. In an unguarded moment of reminiscence, Sternberg recounted his personal experience: "I had a bicycle and the bicycle broke down somewhere near the river Loire. But I had a head start of about 48 hours. I carried virtually nothing, not even money. The roads were filled with refugees of every nationality. It was actually a beautiful summer. I sometimes slept out in the open. It was a strange combination: it was like

20   *Escape to Freedom*

hiking, and it was also like the end of the world. Let me not dramatize it. It was my assumption that the Germans would take it all, that it was to be a Nazi world instead of the present world."6 But despite — maybe because of — this pessimism Sternberg joined in the human salvage effort that he was to continue for the rest of his life.

Among the people recruited to aid in the perilous mission was a young anti-Nazi with impish eyes whom Fry dubbed "Beamish." German-born, Beamish was in the greatest personal danger for he had fought in the French army against the Nazis. He was assigned the major task — logistics. He roamed the Spanish border probing for openings through which the refugees could be sent out. Easily mistaken for a Frenchman, he became the Committee's spokesman in dealing with the black bourse and made every American dollar yield every possible franc. On behalf of the underground, he maintained contact with Marseilles' underworld, buying services that only a criminal element could deliver — and often did not, in spite of payment. Not until the Vichy police came searching for him at the office one day did Beamish consent to leave by one of the routes he had established for so many others. In the United States he resumed his old interests, doing economic research at the University of California under a Rockefeller Foundation grant that had been waiting for him since 1939. In 1943, he entered the U.S. army and was assigned to work with the Office of Strategic Services.

Today he is known to a worldwide audience of economists as a leading expert on the problems of underdeveloped countries. He is Albert O. Hirschman, Professor of International Economic Relations at Columbia University. His *Strategy of Economic Development* is a basic text in its field, and his book, *Latin-American Issues*, is regarded as the most authoritative analysis of South American problems. That he still retained, at the age of sixty-seven, the youthful humor of the days when he was "Beamish" is reflected by the *New York Times Book Review* commenting on his new book, *Shifting Involvements: Private Interest and Public Action*, published in 1982: "Albert Hirschman must have had fun writing this book.... Mr. Hirschman, one of our most distinguished economists, is no ordinary writer, however, and even his offhand ruminations have always been interesting."

SOURCES OF HELP

In later years, long after the events, historians turned their eyes on the troublesome question of whether the democracies could have done more to help in the work of rescue. How many deaths might have been avoided and how much talent might have been saved for humanity will never be known. Among the undisputed facts are shameful episodes — ships of refugees denied the right to disembark and forced to return to the European snakepit. This story repeats itself in the late 1970s as boatloads of Vietnamese refugees were forced back to sea and hundreds drowned in sight of land, in the very presence of those who pushed them away.

In the Hitler period, nations barred the doors because the refugees were thought to be "only Jews." On the initiative of President Roosevelt, 31 nations met in July 1938 at Evian-les-Bains, a spa on the shores of Lake Geneva, to discuss the plight of the political and religious victims of Nazism who were fleeing from Germany and Austria. The sessions produced nothing to match the size of the problem. The United States stepped up admissions within immigration quotas that had been left unfilled for five years. But the Wagner-Rogers Child Refugee Bill of 1939, which would have admitted 10,000 German-Jewish children, failed to win even White House support. Australia said it would take 15,000 over a period of three years. Some South American countries announced their readiness to accept immigrants. Thus the Dominican Republic's dictator Trujillo offered to take 100,000; by 1947 only some 700 had actually arrived, though some 5,000 visas had been issued and were probably used by people to flee elsewhere.

The announced purpose of the Evian Conference, namely, to achieve an orderly flow of emigration from Nazi territory, was never accomplished. Hitler needed hostages. If the purpose of the Evian meeting was to assuage guilt, however, it was effective; it helped to mask the world's indifference to what was happening.

Nevertheless, individuals — some in high places and some with little authority — demonstrated what could still be done. In her book, *Illustrious Immigrants*, Laura Fermi, wife of the refugee-physicist Enrico Fermi, has paid tribute to the assistance given by Eleanor Roosevelt:

The operations in France would not have been so successful, Fry told me, without the co-operation of the State Department and the aid of Eleanor Roosevelt. After the fall of France, President Roosevelt ordered the State Department to issue visitor's visas to "those of superior intellectual attainment, of indomitable spirit, experienced in vigorous support of the principles of liberal government and who are in danger of persecution or death at the hands of autocracy." The State Department agreed to do this, but it was Eleanor Roosevelt who made sure that the promise was not forgotten. She went daily to prod officials and to speed up the more difficult cases; she obtained visas for some men and women in peril with little to go by but the assurance of emigrés (for instance, of Thomas Mann) that the person was all right. As long as the Emergency Rescue Committee functioned in France, she never tired of her self-imposed task, nor did her efforts slacken.[7]

Mrs. Roosevelt's contribution to the effort frequently brought her into conflict with White House officialdom and even with her husband. In his Pulitzer prize-winning *Eleanor and Franklin*, Joseph P. Lash describes in detail "the running argument" between the President and his wife as Dr. Karl Frank and Joseph Buttinger of the Emergency Rescue Committee armed her with data on the individuals in peril. When Buttinger told her that only forty visas had been issued by September 1940, though 576 names had been approved by a presidential advisory committee on refugees, she prodded with curt memoranda ("FDR—Can't something be done? ER") and with lengthy telephone calls to the Oval Office. In the presence of Frank and Buttinger, after a sharp twenty-minute phone conversation with FDR from her apartment, Mrs. Roosevelt concluded her lengthy political and humanitarian arguments with this statement:

If Washington refuses to immediately supply the necessary visas, the German and Austrian refugee leaders, with the financial support of many Americans, will rent a ship, load it with as many as possible of the endangered refugees in France, cross the Atlantic and sail up and down the eastern coast of the United States, until the American people, furious and ashamed, compel the government through demonstrations to allow these victims of political persecution to enter the United States.[8]

The visas were forthcoming. What Einstein had called "a wall of bureaucratic measures" was being surmounted. Valuable help was provided by Harry Bingham, the vice-consul in Marseilles who was in charge of visas. He participated personally in the successful plan to smuggle Lion Feuchtwanger out of a French concentration camp. The novelist later gave a graphic account in his book, *The Devil in France*, a classic in that new literary genre of the twentieth century that has reached a kind of climax in Solzhenitsyn's *Gulag Archipelago*.

As Fry continued to work on refugee escapes he found himself involved in helping British prisoners of war and Gaullist Frenchmen. On a trip to Spain he made contact with the British ambassador, Sir Samuel Hoare, whose place in history was earned as foreign secretary in 1933 when his "Hoare-Laval plan"—a proposal made jointly with the French foreign minister—would have ended the Italian invasion of Ethiopia by giving Mussolini half of the country; only a public furor defeated the sellout and led to Sir Samuel's resignation. Fry now tried to persuade the putatively wiser diplomat to arrange for a British ship or submarine to rendezvous at night with a group of political refugees somewhere on the French Mediterranean coast. In an article published twenty-five years later by the American Labor Conference on International Affairs, Fry wrote: "As bait, and to help persuade the Ambassador of the idea, I brought with me a map of the French mine fields on the north side of the Mediterranean. Hoare turned down my idea immediately. It was contrary to Admiralty policy, he explained, to detach a unit from the fleet, and it would be embarrassing to him as Ambassador if a British naval vessel were discovered carrying refugees opposed to the [Franco] government to which he was accredited."

But the British diplomat was not all Colonel Blimp; he responded with a counterproposal: "There were, he said, several hundred members of the British Armed Forces interned in an old fort in Marseilles. If I would agree to help them escape, and get over the Pyrenees into Spain, he would give me

$10,000 for their expenses, and would have his military attaché look into the possibility of sending a Spanish fishing vessel to France to take our political refugees to France."[9]

Fry accepted the offer and the money. But the plan was only partially implemented. No fishing vessel ever came, though the Emergency Rescue Committee fulfilled its part of the bargain. Doling out the money, Fry succeeded in making arrangements for the release of the young internees in pairs, substituting for them overaged British merchant seamen who had been stranded in Marseilles. The escapees were then escorted across the Pyrenees. Back home again, the pilots among them participated in the Battle of Britain; the soldiers and navigators helped fill the ranks of sorely needed personnel.

It was inevitable that Fry's activities should become known to the Vichy authorities. His office was raided from time to time and he and his staff interrogated. On the occasion of a visit to Marseilles by Pétain, Fry and his colleagues were picked up in a general dragnet put out for all antifascists; for several days they were interned on a ship until the Marshal had departed. Eventually, the American consulate warned Fry that the Gestapo was bringing pressure on the French government to arrest him. But too much unfinished business remained, and he refused to leave—until one day he was summoned to the prefecture and ordered out of France. Demanding an explanation he was curtly told by the *intendant de police*: "You have protected the Jews and the anti-Nazis too much." For this, he was taken to the Spanish border by a shamefaced police inspector who shook his hand on parting and pleaded: "I hope you will not think ill of France."

With his departure, Europe seemed to be sealed off completely from the rest of the world. But the exits to the West set up by the Emergency Rescue Committee were destined to become entrances into occupied Europe. Agents of the Office of Strategic Services were thus enabled to maintain contact with the *maquis* and other democrats still fighting behind the enemy lines.

In the furnace of the late 1930s and the early 1940s a group of American citizens had forged an instrument that in postwar years was to become a vital expression of the free world's desire to help those who choose freedom. The International Rescue Committee had taken shape. The merger of the International Relief Association and the Emergency Rescue Committee had been negotiated in March 1942 partly as an answer to the problem created by differences among the political refugees themselves. The factionalism threatened future rescue operations. Leaders of various German groups, divided on basic philosophy in some cases or on tactics in others, sought to give priority to their own associates. By uniting the two organizations, Dr. Frank Kingdon, head of the International Relief Association, believed that the difficulties could be overcome at one stroke.

Playing key roles in the negotiations were two politically sophisticated Europeans—the Viennese Joseph Buttinger and the Berliner Karl Frank. As a leading Austrian socialist, Buttinger had maintained close ties with the antifascist underground in his own country, and then, through Paris asssociations, with the German refugee community there. He and his wife, Muriel, an American who combined the practice of psychoanalysis with lifelong concern about refugees, had been active in refugee work during the 1930s. In April 1945, she would return to France to head IRC's postwar operation, while her husband continued to function on two continents in behalf of those unable to go home. Frank had been one of the founders of an anti-Nazi movement within Germany called the *Neu Beginnen* group. His knowledge of underground activities equipped him for leadership in developing plans for the emergency rescue program. Though he had planned originally to return to a liberated Germany, he eventually decided to remain in the United States where he practiced psychoanalysis until his death.

Buttinger had brought with him bitter recollections of how refugees were being interned in France. He said years later:

I am still embarrassed to describe the unbelievably terrible life which we anti-fascists had to lead in the camps of a democratic country which had received us as political exiles, and now treated us exactly like the German fascists in France, namely as "enemy aliens." Since the tents to house us near the town of Meslay were not yet erected at the time of our arrival, we had to sleep a whole week long on the wet grass of a meadow. The tents were too small for the number of the camp's inhabitants, and of too poor quality to protect us against wind, rain and the increasing cold. Most of us had to sleep on hard ground, some without blankets, and all of us were constantly not only hungry but also had not enough water to wash ourselves, clean our teeth, shave or even to drink. A whole week of rain turned the ground of the camp into an ocean of mud, into which our feet sank deep on the way to the food center and to the special open pit which served as our toilet.[10]

In January 1940, he had become an active leader in the International Relief Association, and in midyear, after the collapse of France, he, Frank and the Jewish Labor Committee leadership met with Eleanor Roosevelt to lay out a course of action resulting in the underground activities of the Emergency Rescue Committee.

The imperatives of the crisis led inevitably to unification of the two groups, with Frank Kingdon designated as chairman of the International Rescue and Relief Committee whose name was shortened thereafter to International Rescue Committee. Historian Charles A. Beard became honorary chairman, and the directors included, among others, Elmer Davis, journalist and radio commentator; John Dewey; college presidents Harry Gideonse and William Allan Neilsen; and the widely syndicated columnist Dorothy Thompson.

The Marseilles operation had continued longer than anybody had ever expected — even after the Nazis discarded the fiction of "unoccupied" Vichy France and seized the whole country. Following Fry's expulsion, another 300 refugees were saved. Daniel Bénédite and Dr. Paul Schmierer, who succeeded Fry, were imprisoned several times by the Pétain government. But the office continued to function until July 2, 1942, when it was shut down by a police raid. From 1942 until 1944 Bénédite led a group of *maquis* and in May of that year was captured by the Gestapo. Sentenced to death before a firing squad, he was saved only by the landing of American troops in southern France. In the years that followed, he continued to make his contribution to a democratic France as business manager of the liberal anti-Communist daily *Franc-Tireur*.

The year 1944 was a crucial one. Immediately after the liberation of the French capital, IRC opened its headquarters in Paris. Until that memorable day, Turkey had been a major haven for those who could still make their way eastward. With the help of IRC, several hundred prominent anti-Nazis had reached Istanbul and Ankara in the 1930s. Among them was Ernst Reuter, a German Social Democrat destined to become the mayor of West Berlin and to play a key role in the postwar struggle against both communism and the remnants of Nazism. Shortly after his arrival, he became director of IRC's Ankara office, where he was succeeded by Leon Dennen of New York.

In August 1944, Turkey severed diplomatic relations with Germany. But Reuter and Dennen feared that pro-Nazi police officials in Istanbul were cooperating in a Gestapo plan to deport pro-Allied refugees. The two IRC workers rushed to communicate with the Turkish officials in Ankara who took prompt action. Planeloads of anti-Nazis were literally stopped on the airport apron in Istanbul and saved from almost certain death. Many of them, like Reuter himself, lived to return to Berlin, where their prodemocratic activities ultimately saved the city from total Communist domination.

The story of the work done in Marseilles during the early war years is best summarized in the words of one of the men who lived with it day after day, through every moment of peril. Beamish once said to Fry:

I've always thought that what we did for the refugees in France resembled the obligation of soldiers to bring back their wounded from the battlefield, even at the risk of their own lives. Some may die. Some will be crippled for life. Some will recover and be the better soldiers for having had experience of battle. But one must bring them all back. At least one must try.[11]

In the thirties and the first five years of the forties, bringing back the wounded from the battlefield was the work of an emergency rescue committee. In the decades that followed, it became apparent that the times would require a permanent rescue committee.

III

"An Iron Curtain Has Descended"

It was March 5, 1946. On a college campus in Fulton, Missouri, in cadences that had become familiar to the ears of English-speaking people throughout the world, Winston Churchill said:

From Stettin in the Baltic to Trieste in the Adriatic, an iron curtain has descended across the Continent. Behind that line lie all the capitals of the ancient states of central and eastern Europe. Warsaw, Berlin, Prague, Vienna, Budapest, Belgrade, Bucharest and Sofia. Our difficulties and dangers will not be removed by closing our eyes to them. They will not be removed by mere waiting to see what happens; nor will they be removed by a policy of appeasement.[1]

Millions behind that line were not waiting. They had begun to move. In the chaos that followed the collapse of the Nazi Reich, other millions of Europeans displaced from their homes — prisoners of war, forced laborers, expellees, refugees — refused to go back to their homes behind the Iron Curtain.

FORCED REPATRIATION

In 1945, there was still a belief that the Allies could work out a *modus vivendi* with Stalin. The madness of the Soviet dictator, which his own successors would acknowledge a decade later, made any permanent understanding impossible. But the nations of the West, weary of conflict and eager to return to their normal ways of peace, could not face the reality. Their governments, under popular pressure for quick demobilization, rushed to bring the troops home. In its haste, Britain, with American approval, signed a "surrender on demand" agreement with Stalin, pledging to hand over Russian expatriates, including the Ukrainians who had defected to the Nazis during the war. Years later, Alexander Solzhenitsyn was to voice a bitter, unforgiving condemnation of the Allies:

. . . Or take the well-known story about how the British in Austria, after the War had already ended, handed over some one-and-a-half million people to the Soviet Union, knowing that they would be ruthlessly punished there — people who knew that what awaited them was death, and who begged with tears not to be handed over. There were old men among them, women and children, people of all ages, people who knew that they had to expect death or exile, but the British military command handed them over without mercy. I heard these stories from many people when I was still in the Archipelago, and they always said the same thing: the British betrayed us.[2]

Even non-Soviet citizens were caught in the dragnet. Several dozen of them survived ten years of horror in the labor camps and, after Stalin's death, were permitted to return to the West. The British government gave them some monetary compensation in the effort to assuage its own sense of guilt. More impressive than that token action, however, was the resistance that some of the Allied soldiers offered to their own officers when they were ordered to deliver the victims. Nicholas Bethell, who has documented the terrible story in a book published in 1974, honors those who defied higher authority in the name of the values for which the Allies had fought:

The violent and cruel operations carried out by the British and American soldiers lasted only a few days. But it took them no longer than this to realise that something was indeed badly wrong, that they were being asked to use methods which, as they had been instructed, were the peculiar inhumane hallmark of their Nazi enemies. And once they realised this, they protested. For instance, Alec Malcolm, after one day of his battle against unarmed Cossack women and children, said to his superior officer, Brigadier Musson: "I don't know what's going to happen tomorrow, but I'm not going to do this again." There were the soldiers serving with Major-General H.E.N. Bredin who did not hesitate long before telling their superiors that they could be "counted out" of any more operations; they did this so firmly that they were replaced by recruits from another unit. There were General Murray and Lieutenant John Grieg, who clearly "bent" their orders; they took the liberty of telling the Cossacks they were guarding what was roughly in store for them; the result was that thousands took to the hills and survived.[3]

The policy had various rationalizations, of course. The British, even this early in the postwar period, feared that those of their own troops who had been captured by the Germans and who were now in Russian hands would be held hostage by Stalin. Suspicions of their erstwhile ally were confirmed by the fact that the Soviets were already making a mockery of their pledge to permit free elections in occupied countries. Instead, Europe witnessed the other kind of election — men and women voting with their feet.

THE NEW WAVE

As the Russian Empire expanded westward, establishing hegemony over East and Central European nations, millions of refugees fled to the American and British occupation zones in Germany and Austria. They swelled the ranks of the liberated inmates of the concentration camps and the forced laborers who had originally been kidnapped to Germany to maintain the Nazi war machine.

In addition, there were Jewish refugees who found it psychologically impossible to return to homelands that had been the graveyard of their loved ones. Similarly, Poles, Balts, Ukrainians, Yugoslavs, Hungarians, could not contemplate living under the hammer and sickle in their native countries that had become an abattoir for their aspirations. Victims of Nazism, their ranks included people expelled from their homes in Czechoslovakia, Poland and other Central European nations that had fought against the *Wehrmacht*.

Responding to this emergency, IRC representatives were among the first American volunteers to reach Germany and Austria after the war. "Displaced persons" roamed the highways of Europe, or found themselves confined again in DP camps. Moving them to genuine havens of refuge became the immediate task.

Now the enemies were postwar fatigue, bureaucracy, and even callousness. Ann Gould, one of the young staffers dispatched by Sheba Strunsky to the European theatre to help resettle displaced persons, recalls the psychological obstacles that had to be overcome in dealing with local authorities. The attitudes often ranged from unconcern to hostility. On one occasion in Germany, it had taken days of wrangling to extricate a group of DPs from a wretched camp even though they had been cleared for emigration. Further efforts finally produced a train to transport them. As she watched it pull out of the station, a sudden suspicion dawned on her. Racing after the train in a rattle-trap automobile, she finally caught up with it as it headed into a siding. The indifferent railway personnel, ready to depart for their own beds while leaving their passengers to freeze in unheated cars, found themselves confronted by an angry young American woman. Shrugging their shoulders they refused to take any further action until she threatened to haul them before the nearest "denazification committee" of the Allies for investigation. The train was moved promptly to its destination in town.

A worldwide effort was needed to cope with the great migration. Governmental action was being undertaken through the United Nations Relief and Rehabilitation Agency (UNRRA) and the International Refugee Organization (IRO) to help those who had been swept into displaced persons camps by the war.

An IRO Reparations Fund of $25,000,000 had been set up, financed by the sale of nonmonetary gold captured from the Nazis. The Allied governments designated 90 percent for Jewish victims of the Hitler terror, since they were the overwhelming majority, and 10 percent for the remainder. Because of the nature of its work before and during the war, the International Rescue Committee's case rolls contained the highest proportion of political victims. It therefore became one of the chief instruments for the disbursement of reparations to Austrian and German non-Jews with proven antifascist backgrounds. IRO had assigned $2,500,000 for this purpose; $819,000 was distributed through the International Rescue Committee to more than a thousand victims of Nazi persecution for their rehabilitation in Europe or in the United States.

In the field IRC staff members scoured the camps for individuals long separated from their families. Many of those eligible for resettlement were isolated and bewildered, in need of counseling and interim assistance. Even when no other obstacle barred the way, bureaucratic bungling frittered away months and sometimes years before a new life could begin.

CAPITAL OF THE INTELLECTUALS

Paris, which had always been a home for exiles, became the magnet for many of the sophisticates—politicals who had watched Europe's descent during the 1920s and '30s and who now had grim forebodings about the new medievalism that was taking over in the wake of the Red Army; teachers and students whose yearning for free inquiry could be satisfied only by remaining in foreign lands; unionists who believed that the function of organization was to represent the workers as against the employer, whether an individual, a corporation or a state; writers and artists who had no intention, after their liberation from Hitler, of subjugating their pens and paint brushes to ideology.

Other exiles had preceded them to Paris throughout the nineteenth century. A hundred years before, a prescient Heinrich Heine, writing in Paris, had said, "This much we know, that communism, though it be at present little discussed, and now yearns away its life in forgotten garrets on wretched straw-pallets, is still the gloomy hero to whom a great if transitory part is assigned in the modern tragedy, and which only waits its cue to enter on the stage. We should never lose sight of this actor." And then a few years later in his *Confessions*:

My horror of communism has nothing in common with the fear of the lucky businessman who is afraid for his capital, or with the indignation of prosperous tradesmen who fear that their sharp dealings will be hampered; no, I am rather troubled by the secret anxiety of the artist and scholar, for we see our whole modern civilization, the laborious achievement of so many centuries, the fruit of the noblest efforts of our predecessors, threatened by the victory of communism.[4]

Now it was coming to pass, and again Paris was to be the refuge. More specifically, the refuge, initially under the direction of the Buttingers, was to be an office at 35 Boulevard des Capucines, located midway between France's famed Opéra and the imposing church of the Madeleine built by

Napoleon. The Spartan rooms are still the Paris headquarters of the International Rescue Committee. From their windows one can look out at the
Hotel Scribe and the Café de la Paix of the Grand Hotel down the street.
The building is ancient, and even the walls seem weary. The visitor must
take a deep breath to climb the rickety three-story stairway. The steps and
flooring consist of narrow oak planks well worn by the feet of refugees
through more than four decades.

Hannah Benzion, in her mideighties, recalls for her guests the lines of
exiles extending down three flights, through a courtyard and into the boulevard. Such was the scene on three occasions — after 1948, the year of Red
takeovers in Eastern Europe; 1956, the year of the Hungarians; and 1972,
when Russian Jews who could not identify with Israel began to arrive. She
herself had been born in the Sudetenland, had come to France in 1930 and
married a French citizen. In 1942 her family who had remained in Czechoslovakia were deported by the Nazis, but not until 1945 did she learn that
they had all perished. For almost thirty years, from May 1945 until January
1974, Mme. Benzion was to work for IRC. Starting as receptionist-typist,
she soon found herself involved in every aspect of refugee activity: repatriation for those who wanted to go home, many of them after a few short years
being forced again into exile; providing temporary stipends, housing and
work; finding a place of permanent resettlement.

She describes the menial jobs the refugees were willing to take. Pointing
to a learned tome on her bookshelves, she mentions the author, Étienne
Balasz, a Sinologist who later lectured at leading Western universities,
including Yale. When Mme. Benzion sought to place him and his wife as
valet de chambre and cook respectively, the prospective employer protested, "But I do not need a Sinologist." Her answer was a tart, "Do you need
a surgeon and his wife? I can provide them." The employer was persuaded.
Balasz, eager to make good on the job because he wanted to remain in Paris
where he could have access to Chinese studies, proceeded to prepare himself
with scholarly precision: he visited a wealthy friend to observe just how an
experienced butler performs.

Among others similarly helped were artists whose names eventually
became bywords in the circles of Western culture: Erdoch, the Hungarian
ceramist; Leibovici, the Rumanian painter; the painter Thomas Gleb. At the
time Mme. Benzion was being interviewed for this book in 1978, she had
just received a personal invitation from the *graphiste* Johnny Friedlaender,
the talk of Paris's art world, to attend his three exhibits then running in the
city. In his refugee days IRC had helped him find studio space and placed
his wife as a seamstress to keep the family going.

Life was not simple for an IRC staff member: one day the secondhand
shops would be scoured for a bedstead; the next day the search would be for
a fine piano so that a musician could keep his fingers in readiness for a
concert. "A refugee has all the problems of other people, plus being a

refugee," says Mme. Benzion, "and he remains a refugee for the rest of his life."

Mme. Ruth Fabian, a Frenchwoman who had been IRC's Paris director in the postwar period, recalls vividly the plight of those who came for assistance. Many were thrice persecuted between 1933 and 1942 — fleeing from Hitler into France in 1933 or from Spain in 1937; then flight from occupied Paris to the Vichy zone; and thence to whatever haven. Returning again to Paris after the war, they found a city and a nation emotionally exhausted and physically debilitated. Housing was scarce; a roof for newcomers was a daily challenge. Some of the flats rented by IRC in the late 1940s, particularly in the Chatenay-Malabry section, have continued to be occupied by successive refugee-tenants for more than thirty years.

Money was desperately needed. Back in the States IRC was conducting clothing collections, and CARE packages were being sent to refugee families. Every effort was being made to repatriate those who wanted to go home, but France's state of disorganization multiplied the difficulties. Many did go back to Austria, Czechoslovakia, Rumania. Others had no choice. Particularly ironic was the fate of some German Communists. In the 1930s they had fled from fascism and then returned voluntarily during the Nazi-Soviet pact only to be drafted into the *Wehrmacht*. When Hitler launched his Operation Barbarossa against the Russians, they defected. Now they were uncertain about their political and geographical direction. As for the Spanish Loyalists who had reached France before the war, they still had to stay on along with the host of new refugees. But whatever their nationality, it was to IRC that the homeless were turning for help.

Mme. Fabian interrupts her interview to seek out some of the files that record the activities of the immediate postwar years. She picks up a faded, brown little copybook, the kind schoolchildren use to enter their daily homework assignments. It contains the names of refugees who climbed the stairway at 35 Boulevard des Capucines to receive assistance. Some names stand out, like that of Erich Cohn-Bendit and his wife, parents of two children, one of whom was to become known as "Danny the Red" during the student uprising in May 1968 that almost toppled de Gaulle; Robert Liebknecht, grandson of the socialist leader Wilhelm — still working in Paris as an artist; Erich Podach, who was to become one of the leading authorities on the life and philosophy of Friedrich Nietzsche; Lotte Herz, wife of Richard Lowenthal, one of Europe's leading political analysts; Bruno Cassirer, eventually a prominent publisher; Berthold Jacob, collaborator of Nobel Peace Prize-winner Carl von Ossietzky. Mme. Fabian's eyes glisten as she reads off the names of lesser known individuals, describing what they were and what they ultimately became:

A German who had created an antiwar museum in Berlin before World War II, which offered free entry to soldiers and dogs; after the war he set up his museum on a boat in Paris.

The first two Jewish deputies ever to have served in the German Reichstag.

A man who is now a typewriter-repairman in Paris, once an active figure in the German labor movement.

A refugee who was suspected by his fellow refugees of being a Gestapo agent — no one knows what became of him.

A *bouquiniste* whose bookstall along the Seine is near the Chamber of Deputies.

A businessman who, as a refugee, started out selling the *Herald-Tribune* on the Champs Elysée and is now a major distributor of foreign newspapers in France.

A physician who became a medical adviser on refugee reparations.

A producer of documentary films.

Artists in jewelry and sculpture.

Literary, art and film critics.

A miscellany of people who became historians, teachers, union leaders, handymen, journalists, government officials.

These recollections of what life was like and what it became for European refugees in the years after World War II are inexhaustible. Both Hannah Benzion and Ruth Fabian emphasize the continuity of the refugee problem and IRC's continuing involvement. Mme. Benzion, interviewed in her home, is surrounded by mementoes sent to her by one-time refugees who have never forgotten IRC's contribution to their survival. "The refugees have done much more for me than I have done for them," she says. Her colleague, speaking in the office at 35 Boulevard des Capucines, reiterates her conviction that ultimately "to aid others on the way to freedom is to protect our own freedom."

She is interrupted as the telephone rings, and Margaret Hussman, current director of IRC/Paris answers, crisply picking up the threads of previous conversations with U.S. embassy officials about a Vietnamese refugee who had left New York for Paris to meet a niece newly arrived in France but had failed to assure her right to reenter the States. Where once bread and housing had been the major problems for a Benzion and a Fabian, now the problem of a Hussman, formerly a member of the U.S. Consular Service, is to disentangle immigration regulations so that a helpless Vietnamese woman can gain readmittance to the United States along with a young ward. And meanwhile sustenance has to be provided along with psychological support.

That such support is available was evidenced by the testimony of a young Vietnamese Eurasian from whom a letter had arrived that day. His father, whom he had never known, was a Frenchman who had abandoned the mother and child and never returned to Vietnam. The boy, raised in a Catholic orphanage, had managed to reach Paris, and with Margaret Hussman's help had finally found a permanent haven in New York. He wrote to her:

"Mary is my mother, Jesus is my father, and IRC is my family." Indeed, the problem of the refugee in all eras *is* a family affair.

NEW BATTLES BEGIN

The International Rescue Committee had been set up by men and women whose approach to the refugee problem was not only humanitarian in the Judeo-Christian tradition but also political in the broadest democratic sense. The immediate objective after World War II was a massive effort to repatriate the friends of freedom who wanted to return to their own homes where they could continue to serve freedom and their fellow-countrymen. But many of the bravest spirits of Europe, still seared by the war traumas, needed care before they could reenter the struggle, this time against the spreading totalitarianism of the Soviet Union. In Adelboden, Switzerland, IRC set up a hospitalization program to speed their recovery.

Many who had been fortunate enough to escape the concentration camp, a goodly number of them with the aid of the IRC, were eager to return to Germany, Austria, Italy and Czechoslovakia. Prague was still hanging in the political balance at this time. Though the governments of the West had not yet awakened to Stalin's postwar strategy, the sophisticated political refugees had already learned the truth from their compatriots at home. Eager to resume the fight in their own countries, they sought IRC help to facilitate their repatriation.

Among these was Ernst Reuter, who hurried from Ankara to Berlin. In his native city he was elected mayor, an office he held until his death in 1953 and which he used as a bulwark against the waves of Soviet pressure that would have broken a lesser man and a less resolute constituency. From Sweden came Willy Brandt, who had fought in the German underground and then in the Norwegian army against Hitler, and who was destined to become the Social Democratic chancellor of West Germany in 1969.

Another was Rudolphine Muhr, a fragile Viennese woman whose road back to Austria included a stay at the IRC home in Adelboden. She had been imprisoned by the Nazis after *Anschluss*, had continued her resistance on being released under surveillance, and had outwitted the Gestapo on many occasions to help Allied airmen and prisoners of war escape. Returning to Vienna after the war, she was repeatedly elected to the Austrian Parliament. Because of the courage and political skill of people like Rudolphine Muhr, Austria finally succeeded in ending the Russian occupation, paid off the reparations exacted by the Soviets, and was free in 1956 to become a haven for the valiant Hungarian freedom fighters and later a way station for Russian Jews heading for Israel or other countries.

It was not until the summer of 1946, however, that the outline of the future could be clearly discerned. In central and eastern Europe the Soviets had hoped to win control by virtue of the Red Army presence. But the display of military power was not enough. Opposition to the Communists persisted. In quick succession, the Kremlin cracked down on the democratic parties, transforming provisional governments into pseudo-coalition cabinets and finally into one-party totalitarian regimes.

By March 1947, threats of Communist subversion in Greece and Soviet expansion into Turkey produced a response from the West in the form of the Truman Doctrine which promised assistance to those under attack. In June the Marshall Plan, aimed at providing economic aid and developing a self-help program for the rehabilitation of Europe's economy, was announced. No nations, not even the Communist countries, were to be excluded, but Moscow was adamant in asserting its domination and forbade its satellites to participate.

Stalin was on the move. In February 1948, Communist "action committees" seized Czechoslovakia. For the second time in a decade, the conquest of Prague sounded the knell of Europe's hopes for genuine peace. As the broken body of Jan Masaryk, son of the founder of modern Czechoslovakia, lay below his bathroom window, more voters with their feet began the journey westward. They knew what they were fleeing—a regime that had no scruples. In her book, *The Masaryk Case*, the noted journalist Claire Sterling has reconstructed the final moments of Jan Masaryk's life and the final moments of Czechoslovakia's freedom:

He never doubted that they'd get him and he wouldn't give in: his last act of tribute to his father, or indestructible love of life. He was still resisting when they forced him to the bathroom window, overturning the window seat, tugging at the stubborn sash. He clutched at the wall, the sash, the frame, getting paint under his fingernails, ripping the front of his pajamas, grazing his abdomen, managing somehow *not to fall out.* It isn't so easy to throw a man six feet tall, weighing two hundred pounds, out of a window four feet from the [floor], with an opening only half his height and no wider. Defenestration was a method familiar to them and preferable, too, as a national tradition. But they gave it up, for the moment. Somebody's elbow, or head, struck the medicine chest. The contents tumbled to the floor, to be at once trampled underfoot. They finally got him into the bathtub, where two men alone could more easily pin him down, arms immobilized. They held the pillow over his mouth and nose until he was half-gone, resistance drained away. They hauled him to the window, got his legs up—lighter than his torso—and rested him on the sill to get purchase. Then they pushed him out, with a vigorous shove.

Nobody heard him fall. They left as quietly as they had come, a bit winded. Who would have thought the old boy had so much fight in him?[5]

SECOND ROUND OF EXILE

The horror film of suppression was being unreeled again. In mid-1948, the Communist police in Bulgaria rounded up the leaders of the opposition democratic parties, the Agrarians and the Social Democrats, men and women who fought valiantly in the anti-Nazi underground during the war. Dr. Georgi Petkov, Social Democratic leader who in Parliament led the resistance to the Communists, had been warned repeatedly that a prison cell awaited him. He escaped it only by an accident. He had been traveling on a plane that was hijacked by passengers and forced to land in Istanbul instead of Sofia. In Istanbul he learned that seven of his colleagues on the Party's Central Committee, all members of Parliament, had been arrested. There was no sense in returning. IRC assisted him in Turkey while arranging for his migration to the United States.

In Yugoslavia the same pattern was unfolding. Gligor Tashkovich, leader of the Serbian Agrarian Party, had the unique record of surviving one arrest by the Gestapo, three by the Bulgarian occupation authorities during the war, and one by the Yugoslav Communist regime. At war's end, he was drafted into the Partisan Parliament because of his great prestige, but his term of office lasted only one day. At the very first session he accused the new regime of using dictatorial methods, a charge it hastened to prove by imprisoning him the next day without a trial. He escaped, got to Turkey via Bulgaria and then, with the aid of IRC, emigrated to the United States where he resumed his professional career as an architectural engineer.

During 1949 the last stronghold of opposition to the Communists in Eastern Europe was the Hungarian People's Party, led by Dr. Istvan Barankovics escaped. Arriving in the United States under IRC sponsorship, he then worked underground against the collaborationist regime. The People's Party was one of Europe's many Christian democratic parties usually located somewhere in the center of the political spectrum. In the last half-free elections of Hungary, held in 1947, the People's Party won more votes than the Communists, a fact that did not prevent the Red regime from claiming electoral victory. Despite great pressure, Barankovics and his party refused to join a Communist-dominated "coalition government." In February 1949, a few days before the trial of Cardinal Mindszenty, Barankovics escaped. Arriving in the United States under IRC sponsorship, he continued to work for the liberation of his people.

IRON CURTAIN REFUGEE CAMPAIGN

Mass arrests, tortures, concentration camps again became the pattern in eastern and central Europe. Convinced democrats who had stayed to fight as long as there was hope now had to flee for their lives. By the thousands each month, they poured across the borders into Germany, Austria, Italy, Turkey. In the forefront of the new exodus were those who always become the principal targets of the dictator — political and religious leaders, university professors and schoolteachers, lawyers, physicians, artists, scientists, technicians. In addition there were the plain people of humble origin, often unionists, who were marked for elimination because of their differences with the regime.

Whether of high or low station, they were not being cordially received because of their great numbers. At the end of 1950 the *New York Times* reported that "despite bitter winter weather and the increased vigilance of frontier controls, refugees from behind the Iron Curtain are pouring into Western Europe at a rate of 2,500 a month." A chill had settled over official governmental policies, including those of the International Refugee Organization. As the *Times* reported: "These refugees are not tempted by free maintenance or chances for resettlement under international sponsorship. Since October 15, the IRO, by direction of the Governments constituting its council, has refused aid to newcomers. At present, the Western powers are offering no inducement for victims of Communist tyranny to escape."

The closing years of the 1940s had been a confusing period for public opinion in the United States as well as Europe. Demobilization had come quickly as Americans rushed to get back to normalcy. Still warming themselves in the glow of wartime comradeship, they were reluctant to see issues raised with former allies. In 1948 Henry Wallace's appeasement policies seemed attractive to enough liberals to justify the possible defeat of President Truman for reelection. The nation had little desire to involve itself in new problems like that of the postwar refugees. On the other hand, a number of prominent Americans were convinced that war-weariness could not be permitted to block fulfillment of the nation's moral obligation to those in Eastern Europe who were now resisting Stalin's tyranny.

Gradually, leading figures began to coalesce around the various campaigns of the International Rescue Committee. Included in their ranks were General William Donovan who during the war had organized and led the critically important and highly effective Office of Strategic Services; Henry Luce, the publisher who during the Hungarian uprising brought out a special edition of *Life* magazine, the proceeds going to IRC for refugee assistance; General Lucius D. Clay, who served as military governor in West Germany; business executive Herman W. Steinkraus, president of the U.S. Chamber of Commerce; and Admiral Richard E. Byrd, the polar explorer, who was to serve as honorary chairman of IRC's board of directors until his death in 1957.

It was under Admiral Byrd's leadership that IRC initiated its Iron Curtain Refugee Campaign in 1949. At a gathering assembled to inaugurate the drive, refugee leaders from all the captive countries filled the dais. Admiral Byrd sounded the keynote, declaring that the new refugees "are a symbol of the spirit we would like to mobilize to hold back totalitarian darkness." Thus the Iron Curtain Refugee Campaign began to create a climate of public opinion in which actions like the United States Escapee Program and cooperative policies on the part of receiving countries became possible.

As a result of such activities by IRC and sister organizations in religious and humanitarian circles, the refugees were ultimately given legal status under the aegis of the United Nations High Commissioner for Refugees. Later, the UN proclaimed a World Refugee Year, which ended on June 30, 1960, during the course of which some 15,000 displaced persons were helped to leave the remaining World War II displaced person camps in Austria, Germany, Italy and Greece.

In addition to the function of public education, IRC's Iron Curtain Refugee Campaign tackled the concrete work of providing emergency relief to many thousands of escapees strung along the Iron Curtain from Sweden to Turkey. Most of the men and women who broke out of Communist confinement had done so at the risk of their lives: Poles who seized a military plane and flew to Sweden; a Czech railroad engineer who crashed his loaded passenger train through a border barrier — thirty-two of his passengers, finding themselves on free soil, elected to remain. All were resettled by IRC in Canada. Day after day, the newspapers were filled with accounts of daring escapes, like that of fourteen slave laborers in a Czech uranium mine in whose ranks were a lawyer, an architect, a former machine-shop operator, a food distributor. They had spent three and a half months literally digging their way to the surface and then crossed into West Germany.

As the Communist regimes sought to close the holes in their borders with barbed wire fences, mine fields and even with a literal wall in Berlin, escapes grew more difficult but never ceased. The urge to freedom endures. Not the least of the services rendered by the escapees is that their heroism does not allow the conscience of the world to sleep.

IV

Island Outpost — West Berlin

Political fashion puts a changing value on once widely accepted
terms. In a later atmosphere of détente, the phrase "cold war" has fallen into
disfavor. Indeed, a whole generation of political leaders has come to be
derogated as "cold warriors." The label has been tagged to such men as
Churchill in Britain, and in the United States to Truman, Eisenhower,
Kennedy and Johnson. Presumably Nixon, who initiated the policy of
détente by visiting Moscow and Peking, escaped the designation. It is ironic
that the propaganda parlance of this later period rarely applied the term to
Stalin, the dictator described by his successor Khruschev as a "madman."

Whatever the debates revisionist historians may initiate, one fact is clear:
the cold war, like all other forms of war, produced a wave of refugees. For
them, cold war was not a politician's stratagem or a fool's self-deception,
but harsh reality. The direction from which they moved, often at peril of
execution on the spot, bore witness to their familiarity with the ugly face of
tyranny.

"The center of the cold war is in Europe," wrote a political analyst. "The
center of Europe is Germany. The center of Germany is Berlin." Events in
the city of Berlin during the 1930s had been responsible for the creation of
the International Rescue Committee. Postwar events in Berlin were to
present IRC with a series of recurrent challenges: at the time of the 1948-49
blockade; in 1952-53, when East Germans were escaping into West Berlin
and East Berliners were rioting in the presence of Soviet tanks; in the
summer of 1961, when the prison guards of Communism built a naked wall
across the divided city. In the 1930s, IRC had helped freedom fighters
escape from Berlin; in the decades that followed the war, IRC was called
upon to help preserve the city as a haven to which freedom-seekers could
repair.

Churchill, Roosevelt and Stalin had agreed at Yalta that the German
capital was to be ruled by four-power occupation (France was to be included) even though the city stood isolated inside East Germany. American
and British planes had virtually reduced the city to rubble; then a twelve-

day pounding by Soviet artillery administered the *coup de grace*. The Allies formally decided that the Red Army should have the honor of capturing the city. But despite the Yalta agreement, Stalin did not permit the Americans and the British to enter until two months later. In the interim, he dismantled and carried off four-fifths of what was left of the city's industrial establishment and seized 75 percent of the raw materials and finished goods. Not until July 1945 did the Allied Control Council begin to function. Then the city was divided into four sectors under the authority of a four-power committee—the *Kommandatura*.

THE FIRST ASSAULT: BLOCKADE!

From the start the Russians showed they had no intention of cooperating. Gradually they stepped up their efforts to achieve sole control of the entire city. When the Western powers refused to capitulate, the Russians resorted to a blockade that struck at the whole civilian population. Under the blatant hypocrisy of "technical difficulties," highway traffic into West Berlin was slowed down, then cut off completely. Railway trains headed for Berlin were halted. By the end of June, no supplies—food, fuel or raw materials—could enter through any land or water route.

After almost a year's effort to starve the people into submission, the blockade failed. West Berlin had administered the first setback to Moscow's postwar drive to dominate Europe. Three factors were responsible for the Communist defeat: (1) the skill and courage of American airmen who carried out an unprecedented airlift; (2) the unity of the three Western powers; and (3) the morale of the Berliners, who suffered deprivation, hunger and cold, but would not surrender.

The zonal line that divided East from West began to bristle with barbed wire, concrete barriers, ripped-up paving blocks, Communist sentries with submachine guns. The facilities that provided electricity, water and gas for the whole city ceased to be jointly operated as the Russians deliberately monopolized whatever was located in their sector. With the major power station in Soviet hands, West Berlin had to build a new electrical plant, now called the Ernst Reuter power station. It was an appropriate name. For Ernst Reuter as the *Oberbuergermeister* had become the personification of resistance to Communism just as he had been to Nazism a decade earlier. In a city where political kidnappings and assassinations were taking place, he walked the streets without a bodyguard and infused others with his own courage.

THREAT AT WHITSUNTIDE

On May 4, 1949, the Communists called off the blockade and shifted to tactics of harassment. Finally, in 1950, they planned another major move—a so-called mass "youth demonstration" scheduled to convene in East Berlin.

The Communist press made it clear that the demonstrators would be let loose during Whitsun weekend to invade West Berlin. What blockade could not accomplish, a physical stampede might.

It was a moment of many perils for the free half of the city. Tens of thousands of refugees had been pouring into West Berlin. Ironically, every Soviet effort to conquer the island outpost had only succeeded in stirring more East Germans to seek its shelter. But each wave of refugees compounded the already difficult situation of the free Berliners: supplies were low; housing shortages persisted as the population soared; unemployment was acute. In this sea of troubles, the Communists believed that a show of force would bring surrender.

Response was necessary on two fronts: a political reply had to be forthcoming from Mayor Reuter and his people; and an economic answer had to be given by the free world to the hunger that threatened the citizens of free Berlin.

Reuter moved quickly on the first front — in fact, he beat the Communists to the punch. The zero hour set by the Communists was May 27. Reuter summoned his Berliners to demonstrate on May Day in the *Platz der Republik* in full view of the East Berlin Communists. "We must stop acting like rabbits in the presence of a snake," Reuter told 500,000 cheering fellow-citizens, and their roar of approval could be heard on the other side of the Brandenburg Gate. Pointing toward the East, he said, "They are foolish enough to believe that ideas can be stopped by roadblocks and ditches." Then, explaining the significance of the city's resistance, he said: "Berlin has shattered the myth of Soviet invincibility."

PROJECT BERLIN

Equally fast action was needed on the economic front. The May 27 deadline was only a few weeks off. Help from outside would take time in arriving. The International Rescue Committee initiated its "Project Berlin" — an emergency campaign to flood West Berlin with massive quantities of food as democracy's answer to the Communist plan to inundate the city with young toughs.

Under the leadership of Admiral Richard E. Byrd, General Lucius D. Clay, and former Under Secretary of State Sumner Welles, an appeal was directed to the American people. It recited the alarming evidence that the Soviets contemplated violence on Whitsun weekend — "among other things . . . the fact that they are issuing compulsory insurance for every demonstrator, which would pay $132 in event of death. . . . The Western democracies have taken a firm stand. They have warned that any attempt to seize control of Western Berlin will be forcibly resisted. High Commissioner McCloy has added further that, if there are broken heads, the Communists would have only themselves to blame."[1]

Would there be enough time for economic help to arrive? Fortunately, government surplus food was available to relief agencies prepared to pay the shipping costs. The International Rescue Committee asked the American people to finance the transportation out of their own pockets: "'Project Berlin' — the shipment of this food — will be an unmistakable demonstration of the solidarity of the American people with those in Berlin who are on the front line fighting against totalitarianism."

Americans who had felt frustrated by an inability to play a direct role in the intensifying cold war now saw an opportunity to participate. They responded with sufficient funds to ship 4,224,000 pounds of milk, butter and cheese to the West Berliners. Nine days before the scheduled invasion, the first delivery was made at the Schoeneberg Rathaus, the free City Hall of Berlin. Tens of thousands gathered in front of the building filling every inch of available space. They heard addresses by Mayor Reuter and General Maxwell Taylor, commander of the American forces in Berlin. Throughout the city, posters were put up expressing gratitude for the gift and for the fact that the American people were supporting the Berliners' decision to be free.

THE HEART OF THE MATTER

Why had Berlin become a key target for the Communists? Looked at geographically, West Berlin is only a small candle inside the darkness of Communist-held East Germany and can be snuffed out by military action with one puff. But strategically, Berlin is everything that threatens Communist pretensions and aspirations. Berlin, behind the Iron Curtain, stands as a showcase for democracy.

For the Kremlin, Free Berlin remained the crack in the Communist armor. If the West made a mistake in allowing the Russians to precede them into Berlin at the end of the war, the Russians made a mistake in allowing the West to take up a position, however weak, in isolated Berlin. Totalitarianism feels itself endangered by the existence of even a tiny spot of freedom. For more than two decades following the war, Berlin represented to the Communists a bleeding wound through which the economic strength of the so-called German Democratic Republic was being slowly drained. The city has been a gateway to freedom for at least a million refugees from Communist East Germany. The flight of farmers, skilled workers, teachers, doctors, scientists, was a visible blow to Moscow's satellite state.

Because it lies in the heart of Communist-held territory, West Berlin was the obvious sanctuary, and therefore a port of first call, for German refugees. Despite the most painstaking efforts to apply a tourniquet, the Communists could not stem the flow. In the 1950s, there was hardly a year in which the number of refugees fell below 150,000. In 1950 alone — the year of the Whitsun weekend — the number was just a shade below 200,000.

It was clear that Stalin would try again.

THE SECOND ASSAULT

The refugee rate is Communism's fever chart. After the peaks reached in 1949 and 1950, there was a pause but no end to the tension.[2] Stalin was pre-occupied on other fronts, notably in Korea.

In 1951, the number of refugees coming from East Germany was 165,000; in 1952, it rose to 182,000. They brought with them news that in the East zone the authorities were spreading rumors of a new plan to overrun the city. Fear that escape might become forever impossible caused a surge in the underground pipeline; in 1953 the number rose to 330,000. In the early 1950s, Communists in Central Europe and the Balkans were being executed or jailed in what was to be Stalin's last purge. East Germany was conscripting its young men for service in the Soviet-controlled "police forces." People living in areas bordering on the West zone were being forced to leave their homes and move eastward. Restrictions on travel were being further tightened.

In the summer of 1952, one could see a visible parade of refugees coming into West Berlin at the rate of a thousand a day — white-collar workers who brought with them only the contents of a briefcase, farmers with nothing more than the work clothes on their backs, mothers pushing a pram that held a baby and a small bundle of clothing, students carrying their schoolbooks.

In January 1953, the burden of caring for the influx threatened to overwhelm Free Berlin's economy. Reuter appealed for help. In response, the International Rescue Committee instructed its chairman, Leo Cherne, economist and executive director of the Research Institute of America, to proceed to Berlin where he helped to plan a campaign of support. His report to IRC described what was virtually a scene of impending battle:

Control points have been set up [by the Communists] at 61 streets crossing the border. Another 28 streets are completely shut off. You can see workmen building barricades to seal the Western part of Berlin off from the surrounding countryside. Homes and stores are being evacuated to establish "a zone of death" around Berlin like that which now bars escape along the entire West German border.

Temporary shelters have been improvised.... When I arrived, Berlin had 72 camps. When I left one week later there were 82. One camp had been improvised on three hours' notice to shelter 500 persons; when I was there it held 4,200.

Again it was necessary to appeal directly to the humanitarian and political sensibilities of the American people. In the course of Cherne's discussions with the West Berlin authorities, it was agreed that Mayor Reuter should come to the United States as the spearhead of an IRC campaign to raise funds and provide food. A National Committee of Welcome and Support for Mayor Reuter was organized. More than a thousand business, labor and cultural leaders joined the committee.

During a two-week period, Mayor Reuter addressed huge audiences in New York, Washington, Minneapolis, Houston and San Francisco. He met with President Eisenhower and congressional leaders. In what was destined to be the last year of his life, Reuter had the opportunity to see at first hand the generosity and determination of the American people. In a few short weeks, his tour helped to raise $850,000 in cash; contributions of goods brought the total to more than a million dollars.

An Ernst Reuter Fund was established, to be administered by a joint German-American board of directors that included IRC representatives. Part of the fund went immediately to meet the current emergency in Berlin. Part of it was set aside for future refugees, whose coming was a certainty. In addition, IRC sent in large quantities of government surplus foods, particularly powdered milk and butter. Distribution of the latter attracted widespread attention in Germany, for butter had become a symbol of the economic difference between a free society and the austerity of Communism.

The American response to the plea from West Berlin could hardly have come at a more appropriate moment. For Berlin was about to be rocked by an unprecedented political earthquake—the first overt rising of a people against Communism. It would open the way for similar acts of popular resistance in Poland, Hungary and Czechoslovakia in the years to come.

GIRDING FOR THE LONG HAUL

By now it was clear that assistance to refugees could not be a sporadic effort. What had been thought of as rivulets spurting from various openings was becoming a permanent stream whose flow would not be stopped as long as the world remained divided between dictatorships and democracies. Unhappily, history had entered upon a period in which the number of dictatorships would increase. By 1980, Freedom House's annual assessment of the state of political rights and civil liberties in the world would classify fifty-one nations as "free," fifty-four as "partly free," and fifty-six as "not free." In terms of population, says Raymond D. Gastil, principal author of the study, this means "that roughly 42 percent of the world was considered not free, 37 percent free, and the remaining 21 percent fell somewhere in between. To be sure, hundreds of millions classified as free were just marginally so, and almost as many classified as partly free could, with slight shifts of arbitrary category boundaries, have been considered not free."[3] In such a state of affairs, it was inevitable that those denied freedom would gravitate toward freer countries as surely as plant life reaches toward the sun.

But in the early 1950s it was already obvious that building a permanent organization to aid the refugees was imperative. Public interest would be fickle. Dramatic events would make the front pages, only to be displaced by new sensations. Domestic pressures—economic cycles, political campaigns,

social aberrations such as crime waves and the spread of drug abuse —
would push foreign developments into the background. Nevertheless, as
various ethnic groups in the United States found their kinfolk being victimized by dictators, they would raise their voices. So it would be with Jews,
Germans, Czechs, Hungarians, Poles and various Asian-Americans. The
kaleidoscope of international tragedy would leave an uncertain image on
the nation's consciousness.

As a result, IRC has found itself periodically on the verge of closing its
doors. Its veterans recall, for example, the dark days in 1951 when its chairman, Reinhold Niebuhr, suffered a stroke which, though mild, made it
impossible for him to direct efforts to stave off impending financial disaster.
Richard Salzmann, as executive director, rallied the active spirits to meet
the challenge. Faced with insolvency, each of six members of the board
signed $5,000 bank notes to raise a loan that could do little more than fund
the organization's liquidation. Cherne, newly arrived as chairman of IRC,
turned to the foundations. Lessing Rosenwald, who had been active in seeking the widest possible range of migration for displaced persons in the
aftermath of World War II, was approached. In his home in Pennsylvania,
he and members of his family assembled to hear Cherne's presentation of
the IRC story. That day they authorized a grant of $100,000 from the
Rosenwald Fund. Rosenwald himself undertook to approach the Ford Foundation, which provided an additional $500,000. Again and again through-
out IRC's history, such emergencies would arise, as popular support for
refugee assistance waxed and waned in the United States. This kind of spiral
in the fortunes of voluntary public-service institutions is not unfamiliar, but
it takes a special hardihood to survive more than half a century of such
recurring crises.

V

After Stalin — The Winds of Revolt

On March 5, 1953, a medical bulletin from the Kremlin announced that Joseph Stalin had died of a brain hemorrhage. Three months later, the people of East Berlin built street barricades in a heroic but hopeless effort to regain their freedom. The odds were formidable—stones and Molotov cocktails against Soviet tanks. But, as the *New York Times* commented, "The German people have branded Communism with an iron that will sear so deeply that the Reds will never lose the scar."

THE RISING IN EAST BERLIN

The June 17, 1953, uprising was the first response of the oppressed to the knowledge that the twenty-nine-year reign of the Soviet dictator had come to an end. Others would take his place, but in the hiatus between the two regimes, pent-up feelings could be vented. At least for a while, the monolithic ranks would be in disarray.

It was inevitable that the Red Army's might should prevail over the barefisted East Berliners. Their brothers in West Berlin watched in utter frustration, unable to help. No governmental power in the free world could legally reach a hundred miles into Soviet-occupied territory to aid the embattled East Berliners with arms. The least that could be done was to prepare a welcome for those who would soon be fleeing to West Berlin and West Germany. That year 331,000 refugees arrived.

The new Soviet leadership, of course, was still bent on Communist world domination, but it faced the same urgent necessity that Stalin had confronted after Lenin's death some thirty years before. Khrushchev, on his way to victory in the Kremlin power struggle, first had to broaden his base and therefore initiated the so-called policy of "liberalization." But the essential nature of the totalitarian society remained the same. With the support of the Red Army's Marshal Zhukov, Khrushchev executed Beria, the head of the secret police. Next, with the help of Bulganin, he dislodged Zhukov. As his grip became firmer, he dropped Bulganin, Malenkov and Molotov.

The new atmosphere stirred hopes of moderation among those who had passively accepted the Communist regimes in Eastern Europe. In 1956 underground opposition came boldly to the surface in both Poland and Hungary. It startled the world by demonstrating that men never forget freedom, no matter how cruelly and how long suppressed. During the four years that followed Stalin's death new battles raged and produced a fresh crop of escapees.

THE SOVIET REDEFECTION CAMPAIGN

Khrushchev, more than his predecessor, was aware of the deadly damage being done to Communist morale and propaganda by the living testimony of the millions of refugees who had fled the barbed-wire paradise. He was determined to act — both to plug the leak in Berlin and to undercut the political victory the West was winning with each escapee who reached safety. He began a campaign to persuade expatriates that since the death of Stalin "things are different at home."

Increasingly in 1955, IRC representatives posted at the receiving stations along the Iron Curtain reported that refugees were showing signs of exceptional fear. It became clear that the *Apparat* had been pushed into high gear to bring about "redefections." The Communists were using all available weapons — from persuasion to pressure to force — in an extravagantly financed, carefully planned and centrally directed campaign. Against the background of the first summit meeting between East and West, held in 1955, and Khrushchev's "peaceful coexistence" campaign, the Kremlin had every reason to expect its redefection drive to be successful.

Reading the political winds, IRC organized an emergency commission under the chairmanship of General William J. Donovan. One of the nation's leading lawyers, he had achieved fame in many fields of public service. He had commanded the Fighting 69th in World War I, was wounded in action three times and won the sobriquet "Wild Bill" along with the Congressional Medal of Honor. In World War II, he had directed the Office of Strategic Services and supervised the principal behind-the-enemy-lines effort of the Allies. Donovan believed deeply in IRC's work and served it in many capacities.

In February 1956 he organized and directed the IRC-sponsored Commission on the Soviet Redefection Campaign and personally took to the country the urgent message about the new Communist tactics of terror and blackmail. The Commission investigated the situation all along the edges of the Iron Curtain. Its findings revealed that from January 1955 to February 1956, a total of 1,100 Iron Curtain refugees had redefected, excluding East Germans, Poles from France and Yugoslavs. "With every returning refugee," said the report, "the hope of eventual liberation is undermined for those remaining behind the Iron Curtain, the illusion of invincible Communist power is strengthened, and the resolve needed for escape is weakened."

The Commission's exposure of the methods used by the Communists was in itself a major influence in reinforcing the resolve of the refugees. Awareness that the Soviet approaches were not based on any personal interest in the individual but were part of a mass campaign helped the refugees to understand the political character of the redefection maneuver. Thus they were better able to resist appeals to nostalgia accompanied by threats to relatives left behind, bribes and kidnappings. Describing these techniques, the Commission said:

All this is done with remarkable knowledge by the Reds of the personal histories, backgrounds and present circumstances of those they would victimize. Communist Embassy officials execute this campaign behind diplomatic immunity, and the emergence of the new Soviet embassy in Bonn, for example, represents a potent instrument in this campaign of terror.

With particular effectiveness, the redefectors as well as family members have been used (probably under compulsion) in radio broadcasts directed to individual refugees and camps. A mysterious phone call, an unexpected visit from a Communist agent, an anonymous message — all these are implements skillfully utilized. As a last resort come the threats of reprisal against relatives and friends behind the Iron Curtain, thus creating a moral responsibility which cannot be turned aside. The kidnappings and murders reported in the Berlin and Munich areas, although carefully camouflaged, are indelible reminders that the iron hand is still beneath the velvet glove.[1]

That these methods did not produce a greater number of redefections was remarkable. But the propaganda value of even a small percentage of returnees was important for the Communists. Among the members of refugee communities in every free country, the redefection campaign generated suspicions and insecurity. Even in the United States, refugees who thought their whereabouts had been well concealed were shocked by a sudden phone call or a visit from a Communist agent.

FOR QUICK RESETTLEMENT

Among the recommendations made by the commission was a proposal "that the processing and resettlement of refugees be expedited to avoid the collapse of morale that inevitably results from long periods of waiting."[2] Whatever effectiveness the Communist campaign achieved was due to the sense of stagnation in refugee camps, failure to get suitable work, a lack of counseling during periods of readjustment. The ultimate answer to the Communist counterblow could be only an acceleration of aid to the refugees.

This was to be a recurring problem in the history of IRC. It had already been encountered in the displaced persons camps after World War II. The mills of bureaucracy grind slowly, especially when the bona fides of refugees must be established and the circumstances themselves make credentials inaccessible and investigation laborious. Accelerating the processing of refugees through the intricacies of immigration regulations would become a major aspect of IRC's work, eventually reaching a climax in the years following the Indochina wars when refugees from Vietnam, Laos and Cambodia moldered in the detention camps of Thailand, Malaysia and the Philippines. The know-how acquired in the successful effort to counter the Russians' pressure on refugees was to prove invaluable in later years.

This was a critical period of learning for the International Rescue Committee. The patterns of the long haul were being set by the thrusts and counterthrusts of what came to be called the Cold War. The Kremlin's domination of Eastern Europe, with no effort to demonstrate the consent of the governed in any kind of plebiscite as mandated by the Yalta agreement, was now in place. Aspirations for freedom in East Germany, Hungary, later in Czechoslovakia and Poland, could be ruthlessly crushed. For organizations like IRC, though these were active times, resources were severely limited. Expenditures outran revenue, as the Committee sought to do what was needed, rather than confine itself to what could be prudently handled.

At the helm in this period was a young Lutheran minister, Richard R. Salzmann, serving as executive director. A student of Reinhold Niebuhr, a writer on existential theology and the changing values of society, a keen social and economic analyst, Salzmann kept IRC abreast of the changing scene. He is credited with developing and refining the technique of utilizing commissions, like that headed by General Donovan, to meet particular emergencies. This instrument would be used again in the Indochina crisis to reach the conscience of the world and to influence the policies of nations that were threatening to turn their backs on the boat and land people of Southeast Asia. In the succeeding years, Salzmann has remained an active member of the IRC leadership, making available his wealth of experience with refugee problems.

In expressing thanks to the IRC's Commission on the Soviet Redefection Campaign, President Eisenhower called for an intensification of governmental and private efforts "to insure the frustration of this Communist design. Support of the principle of asylum and assistance for the refugees are fundamental principles of American foreign policy. I share your determination to make sure that these principles are effectively carried out."

One of the major objectives of Khrushchev's redefection campaign was to staunch the flow of blood pouring out of the economic arteries of East Germany — the best of its manpower. Whatever propaganda victory he might win by displaying a few thousand returnees, he could not conceal the economic defeat involved in losing the elite of East Germany's working class, middle class and professional elements. From 1955 until 1958, another

997,773 persons succeeded in crossing the barriers and reaching the West. And Berlin, which Khrushchev called "the bone in my throat," remained the principal avenue of escape.

PRESSURE RISES IN BERLIN

On November 27, 1958, in formal notes to the three Western powers, Soviet Russia demanded that Berlin "become a reunified city within the framework of the state in whose territory it is situated." At this writing, almost twenty-five years later, the West still persists in its refusal to surrender on demand the more than two million free citizens of West Berlin. Several times Khrushchev set a deadline for the surrender, but on each occasion the firmness of the Allies and the Free Berliners forced him to retreat from his demands.

With his economic wounds still open, however, Khrushchev found it necessary repeatedly to tighten the tourniquet. In East Berlin, his puppet Ulbricht complained that the economy was being bled white by American agents who were "seducing" German workers and professionals into flight. In 1959, Khrushchev took a new tack, proclaiming another détente and agreeing to withdraw his time limit for a Berlin "settlement." That year, the number of East Germans fleeing to the West dropped to 144,000, the lowest it had ever been in the decade of the fifties. But the truth about Communism reasserted itself despite the siren-call of "peaceful coexistence." In 1960 the number of escapees began to soar again, reaching 199,000. In the first six months of 1961, the total came to 103,000.

Again the tourniquet had to be tightened. But each twist only caused the flow to spurt faster. Desperate for manpower, the East German Communists in Berlin stepped up restrictions on movement between the two parts of the city. On July 7, 1961, they barred the 52,000 *Grenzgaenger*, the East Berliners who worked in West Berlin, from going to their jobs, ordering them to seek employment in East Germany.

Far from reducing the exodus, the restrictions increased it. By August, the number of refugees arriving in West Berlin was 2,000 a day; then it rose to well over 3,000 a day. On the streets leading to the Marienfelde reception center, one could see files of men, women and children, carrying unobtrusive luggage like portfolios and overnight bags, containing the minimal possessions they could not leave behind. Many had walked miles across the East German countryside, run risks to get into East Berlin, and then braved the hazards of crossing the line. One of the dramatic cases in IRC's files for 1961 was that of a mother and daughter who successfully made their way by train from Manchuria, across the Soviet empire to East Berlin, and then were spirited to freedom in West Berlin.

THE WALL OF SHAME

For the Communists, the last remaining turn of the tourniquet became essential, even if the result was to be amputation. On August 13, 1961, the Wall of Shame was erected. Not since the Middle Ages have architects been ordered to enclose a city with stone and brick and mortar. Then it was intended to keep out the invader; in the twentieth century, in East Berlin, the purpose was to lock in a citizenry yearning to break out.

Thereafter the flow abated, but it was never wholly stopped. Elderly women jumped to the West from windows in the East zone and were caught in life nets held by West Berliners. Youths swam canals and rivers. Workers tunneled under the wall. Truck drivers barreled through the stanchions. One member of the Communist *Volkspolizei*, doing sentry duty at the barriers, suddenly dropped his gun and jumped over the barbed wire. Shoot-to-kill orders were issued to the border police, and bullets whistled around the ears of those who tried to climb the wall or swim to freedom. At least fifty known deaths were reported in the following year.

Elsewhere along the grimly guarded Iron Curtain, refugees from other Soviet-dominated lands also penetrated the ring of concrete and barbed wire. Alone, by pairs or in groups, they too found their way to Western asylum. Poles, Czechs, Balts, Yugoslavs, men and women of every East European origin, chose freedom — and acted on their choice.

Meanwhile IRC was able to carry out tasks that West European governments had left undone. Mental health programs for refugees were operating in IRC's German and Austrian centers. Where necessary, vocational training was being provided in Germany, Austria and Belgium. Students who had fled were helped with scholarships so they might ultimately enter careers similar to those they had planned at home. In Trieste, Nuremberg, Vienna, and Paris, clothing depots were set up. With funds of its own and with contributions from the United States Escapee Program and the United Nations High Commissioner for Refugees, IRC concentrated on the problems of helping exiles to achieve integration in their new environment — providing housing, vocational tools, allotments of cash or clothing to help on the way to self-sufficiency.

VI

Heroism in Hungary

In the fall of 1956, a message in terse cable-ese went from Vienna to the office of IRC-New York. It read:

THEY MUST HAVE ASSURANCES FREE WORLD SUPPORT AT THIS DECISIVE MOMENT WHICH MAY WELL BE TURNING POINT WORLD HISTORY. BEST WE CAN DO TO DEMONSTRATE OUR SYMPATHY, SOLIDARITY AND TOTAL IDENTIFICATION WITH HUNGARIAN LIBERATION FORCES IS TO RUSH AT ONCE MASSIVE QUANTITIES RELIEF SUPPLIES.

...WE ARE PREPARING, TOO, FOR TRAGIC POSSIBILITY SOVIET RECAPTURE CONTROL, WHEN COUNTLESS ESCAPEES WILL FLOOD INTO AUSTRIA AND THUS MUST BE READY WITH RESOURCES.

The cable was signed by Leo Cherne and Angier Biddle Duke, chairman and president of IRC respectively. Six days before — on October 23, 1956 — workers, students and intellectuals in Budapest had publicly proclaimed their decision to be free by staging a peaceful demonstration. They had been fired upon by the Communist secret police and had responded with open revolt. The counterrevolutionary Red Army had intervened, but after three days of bloody fighting the Soviet troops had been withdrawn from Budapest.

Within hours of the first word from beleaguered Budapest, the IRC instructed its chairman and president to proceed to Vienna, some thirty miles from the Hungarian border, to make a close-range study of the relief requirements. Cherne had been on the firing line in Berlin and had worked with Mayor Ernst Reuter and Willy Brandt, the future chancellor of West Germany.

Cherne's whole career had prepared him for what was to become the major preoccupation of his life — the rescue of those seeking freedom. As a lawyer and economist, he had achieved a national reputation and participated in planning for the industrial mobilization of the United States in the prewar years. As executive director of the Research Institute of America, he headed an organization of analysts whose studies of legal, social and economic developments gave guidance to molders of public policy, business executives, union spokesmen and other leaders in American society. In 1946, he had been summoned to Tokyo to serve as adviser to General MacArthur on the reconstruction of the Japanese economy. His service in behalf of freedom has been officially acknowledged by Western governments: France awarded him the National Order of the Legion of Honor, and the Federal Republic of Germany decorated him with the Commander's Cross of the Order of Merit.

At the same time, he was winning distinction as a sculptor. His bust of Albert Schweitzer, whom he visited in Lambaréné in 1954, stands in the Smithsonian Institution, and his head of Abraham Lincoln dominates the Cabinet Room in the White House. His bronzes include portraits of Winston Churchill, Sigmund Freud, John F. Kennedy, Lyndon Johnson, William Donovan, Ralph Bunche, Eleanor Roosevelt, and the Russian poet and novelist Boris Pasternak.

Early in his career, Cherne had come to be recognized as a fighter for freedom, not only on the international scene, but in domestic issues involving freedom. He was the very first to debate Senator Joseph McCarthy before a national audience; in 1947, the two faced each other before the microphone of "America's Town Meeting of the Air." They jousted again in 1952 when McCarthy was at the peak of his influence—a debate that was deemed so effective in exposing the senator that *Life* magazine published the transcript in its entirety. The following year the International Rescue Committee, overwhelmed by the enormous burden of refugees pouring out of Eastern Europe, looked for new sources of support. It asked Cherne to take on the responsibility of serving as chairman of the board. From that year the central focus of his life became what Beamish had called "the obligation of soldiers to bring back their wounded from the battlefield, even at the risk of their own lives."

Now, in 1956, Cherne and his colleague Angier Biddle Duke were in Vienna on the eve of what was to be the largest emergency operation in point of numbers yet undertaken by the International Rescue Committee. Duke brought to the task a background that contrasted sharply with Cherne's and that complemented it with additional resources.

His had been a career in the U.S. diplomatic service. He had served in the American embassies in Buenos Aires and Madrid, and in 1952 President Truman had appointed him ambassador to El Salvador. Later he was to be chief of protocol in the State Department and would be President Johnson's ambassador to Spain and then to Denmark. Seven governments, including Britain, France, Sweden and Greece, have decorated him in recognition of his international contributions. From 1954 to 1960 he held the office of president of IRC, and thereafter headed or participated in many of the commissions IRC has sent to develop refugee programs in given emergencies.

During the Bangladesh crisis he was to become the chief architect of IRC's enormous relief effort in West Bengal. His presence on the scene in Vienna during the Hungarian uprising meant that a seasoned diplomat was available to maintain lines of communication and speed the delivery of supplies to those in need.

A HISTORICAL LANDMARK

Within hours after the first news had come out of Budapest, IRC leaders sensed that the world had reached a landmark in the history of freedom. Cherne remembers an impassioned call from Bill Fitelson who, with an election campaign under way in the United States, urged that an effort be made to have both candidates, Dwight Eisenhower and Adlai Stevenson, issue a joint statement of solidarity with the Hungarians. To demonstrate further that a unified American people supported the aspirations for freedom being expressed in the streets of Budapest, Fitelson proposed that at noon of a given day all traffic come to a halt in America, and that the church bells be rung. Unfortunately, both political parties shied away from any action that might have an unpredictable effect on their campaign strategy, and Cherne's telephone calls to their headquarters proved unavailing.

But IRC was prepared to act on its own. It dispatched its two top officers, Cherne and Duke, to the Austro-Hungarian border with orders to establish a base in Vienna. They carried with them as a first installment of American aid, procured by John Richardson who had offered personally to buy the supplies, some $200,000 worth of antibiotics contributed by Charles Pfizer Company. More medical supplies for the wounded and sick would follow.

In Vienna, U.S. embassy officials sought to discourage American citizens from illegally crossing the border into Communist territory. But the arrival of the Pfizer pharmaceuticals led to the inevitable decision: they must be delivered to the freedom-fighters, whatever the difficulties. Five days after the outbreak, Cherne and Marcel Faust, director of IRC-Vienna, loaded the latter's 1946 Chevrolet with the supplies and headed across the frontier. Duke remained in Austria to keep open the lines of communication. Though the Russians still controlled large parts of the country, the capital itself was accessible and seemed the logical center for IRC's relief operation. The two men arrived in a city whose geography was unfamiliar but in which maps would have been useless in any case because pitch darkness prevailed. Periodically, the IRC car was halted by armed men whose lack of uniforms attested that they were part of the popular forces. Suspicions were quickly allayed by Cherne's and Faust's eloquence in English and German, and by the material evidence of the medical supplies that filled the rear seats.

After hours of fearfully groping their way through empty streets, they reached their destination, the Hotel Duna, only to learn that there were no rooms available. They were sent on to the Astoria, where they found quarters that were open to the night air because the building had been damaged by shelling. But there was little inclination to sleep; the lobby was a scene of activity as reporters exchanged bits of news by candlelight. Among them was the noted European journalist François Bondy who, years later, on the twentieth anniversary of the uprising, recalled the setting into which Cherne and Faust walked:

There had been no room for us in the Hotel Duna (formerly the Bristol) where most of the foreign correspondents gathered. Instead we had put up at the Astoria which had been half destroyed in the first round of fighting (in October) that had led to the temporary Soviet withdrawal. An icy wind blew through the lobby and halls, and the usually so elegant hotel-manager shivered in a sheep-skin coat. A small altar (with a red cloth and four candles) commemorated the reception-clerk who had been killed. In the town centre the telephone wires were down and the rusting wrecks of tanks had bitter slogans written on them in red letters: *"This is Soviet culture."* The Russians had carried away their own casualties, but dead bodies of AVO secret policemen were still hanging and rotting. Barricades had been built of overturned tramcars. At night there was no lighting in the streets, and nothing was open — unless open means accessible through smashed windows. (Yet nothing was stolen: there was no looting.)[1]

On his return to the United States, Cherne set forth his observations in a guest editorial written for the *Saturday Review*. He describes the revolutionary zeal of the people, especially the young, but notes the enormous human cost: "The revolution is also terrible and terrifying. As you drive at night through shattered streets over glass and rubble, tangling your car in overhead electric cables lying in the streets in distorted shapes everywhere, you suddenly know with nauseating shock that under your wheels is something which had been alive just yesterday."[2]

Within three hours following Cardinal Jozsef Mindszenty's liberation from his eight years of Communist imprisonment, Cherne, the first American to reach Budapest during the uprising, was on hand to greet him. The life of this Hungarian cleric epitomizes the political conflagrations of the twentieth century. In World War II, when the German troops moved into the country, Mindszenty was serving his God and his church as bishop of Veszprem, about a hundred miles from Budapest. His opposition to the Nazis resulted in his being imprisoned by Hitler's puppet government. In 1946, because of his outstanding service to his people, he was designated Archbishop of Esztergom, and in 1946 he was elevated to the high office of cardinal. In the next two years he found himself embroiled in battle with the Communist state which had determined to nationalize all church schools. In 1948 he was arrested on trumped-up charges of illegal money transactions and treason against the state. In advance he warned his followers that he would be forced to confess guilt, as he did subsequently in a show-trial staged by the authorities.

One of the first acts of the Hungarian rebels in 1956 was to free him. After the Soviet recapture of Budapest, the Cardinal was sheltered in the U.S. embassy and remained within its walls for fifteen years. In 1971, with the Russians maneuvering for détente, he was given safe-conduct out of the country to live in Vienna. There he remained as cardinal in absentia for Hungary, but in 1974 he was stripped of the red hat as Pope Paul VI sought to improve church-state relations in Hungary.

The churchman and the IRC chairman were to meet again almost twenty years after their original encounter in Budapest. Mindszenty had finally come to visit the country that had given him asylum in its embassy. In a Holiday Inn in the town of Elizabeth, N.J., where he had gone to speak, the former cardinal recalled vividly the occasion when he had received the antibiotics, and once again thanked IRC and the American people.

In 1956 Mindszenty was already sixty-four years of age, gaunt and ashen-faced but nevertheless a figure of strength. To him, the chairman of the International Rescue Committee delivered the supply of medicines that was desperately needed for wounded freedom-fighters. Scant days later — on Sunday morning, November 4 — the Red Army returned and struck en masse against the people of Budapest. The withdrawal had been only a stratagem for regrouping and bringing up stronger forces. The Hungarians fought back courageously, holding off the Soviet troops long enough to permit thousands to escape across the temporarily opened border into Austria. To receive them, the relief operation that Cherne and Duke had anticipated in their cable to New York became a matter of urgency.

As Duke worked feverishly in Vienna to set up the necessary machinery, Cherne rushed back to New York to initiate a campaign for funds. Immediately on his arrival he appeared for a few minutes on Ed Sullivan's national television program to tell the story of Hungary's glory and need. Virtually by return mail, the American people responded: viewers sent in $357,000. Within sixty days IRC raised $2,500,000 for the freedom-fighters.

Meanwhile, at headquarters in New York, executive director Richard Salzmann, with the aid of Abe Becker, a veteran activist in IRC programs, and David Martin, author of important works on the politics of Eastern Europe, were busy organizing a huge mass meeting. But by the time the audience assembled in Madison Square Garden, Russian tanks had ended the uprising. The frustration produced a tumultuous, almost riotous gathering that frequently seemed on the verge of violence. But though it could not save freedom in Hungary it succeeded in emphasizing the need to rescue those who could still make their escape.

FLOOD-TIDE IN AUSTRIA

The Soviet recapture of Budapest accelerated the mass flight of Hungarians. Facilities in Austria were swamped. To work out an international program of aid and resettlement IRC asked its honorary chairman, General

Donovan, and William J. vanden Heuvel, who later assumed IRC's presidency, to go to the border area. They reached Vienna on November 18, and found 25,000 Hungarians already there. Ten days later, more than 100,000 were on Austrian soil. Before the Soviets could repair the rip in the Iron Curtain, at least 185,000 slipped through.

IRC workers, during the past four decades, have noted that no two waves of refugees are alike. Even in the grimness of their plight, the refugees stand out as unique individuals, though as groups they carry with them the characteristics of their distinctive cultures. Indeed, it is this infinite variety in human nature that totalitarianism seeks to crush.

One of the striking features of the Hungarian wave was the high percentage of young people. As IRC staff noted: "Of over 100,000 refugees in Austria at that time, it appeared that at least 60,000 were young men under 30 years of age. They did not leave because they feared death in the streets of Budapest. In our talks with the countless refugees, the primary factor given to explain their flight was the deportation by the Soviets of Hungarian men to Siberia."[3] Also notable was the number of very young children, many unaccompanied by their parents, some carrying written pleas pinned to their clothing that foster parents be found — human packages addressed "to whom it may concern."

Americans were notably among those concerned. Joseph Buttinger and Claiborne Pell (later U.S. senator from Rhode Island), stayed in Vienna for many months to direct the IRC work. They reported: "For political reasons, no government dared to take action at the borders or inside Hungary to help these brave men and women. But all Europe was at the borders. People of all nationalities stood there to help the refugees across the last perilous miles. For America, IRC was there, along with CARE, the Red Cross, the great American religious agencies and others. In the international political paralysis of those days, this was the only way that America could act, express its feelings and be heard on the banks of the Danube."

The scenes at the Austro-Hungarian border will remain forever vivid in the minds of those who participated. The report of the IRC Commission, for example, says:

On Thanksgiving night we stood on the border of Hungary again. A bonfire had been built both for warmth and as a beacon. A small hut was used by a single Red Cross nurse to hand out hot tea and chocolate bars. The IRC had brought a supply of warm clothes. We had ordered a special truck, which was available to carry the refugees the last nine kilometers to shelter. The refugee flow had considerably decreased this day. The Soviet patrols had been on the border and the sound of shooting was unceasing. We were told that hundreds of refugees were lying in the marshes waiting for dawn to avoid Soviet patrols. A young Hungarian Freedom Fighter decided to go to the border and to tell those hiding in the marshes when it would be safe to come across. We shall never forget the cold gaunt figures of these fleeing hundreds as they finally reached the bonfire in sanctuary.[4]

Cherne's observations at the border, described in his *Saturday Review* editorial, include scenes like the following:

Your life has been changed by an image that will never disappear — three students crossing the canal with gunfire at their backs: the first reaches your side with a triumphant smile; the second stumbles in the cold water with painful cramps, laboriously pulls himself out while tears flow from his eyes and he falls before you on free ground; the third struggles in the water and fails to escape as the cold numbs the muscles and stiffens his body before he can reach midstream.[5]

Particularly moving was the nine-year-old child who crossed the border alone, his name and age pinned to his shabby coat, along with the note: "Please take care of our child. We remain behind to fight to the last. God bless you."

AMERICAN VOLUNTEERS

America can be proud of the number of its citizens who flocked to the Hungarian border to help exhausted refugees over the last mile to freedom. The volunteers were desperately needed as the staff of the various relief agencies found themselves overwhelmed. IRC-Vienna had gone from an eight- to a sixteen-hour day. Personnel from Geneva, Paris and Munich were ordered into Austria. The frustrations of inadequate facilities had to be overcome by adding desks, typewriters, telephone lines, vehicles to shuttle back and forth to the border.

Typical of the volunteers who appeared on the scene were Paul Heber, a Hungarian-born American psychologist, and Alex France, a Fulbright scholar in Paris. On their first trip to the border, as Heber recalls, they saw "scores of people struggling across icy waters on flimsy straw rafts. One look and Alex knew what was needed — a rubber boat." And that item was added to the list of extraordinary purchases made by IRC, ranging from handkerchiefs to instruments for scraping the mud off one's shoes. As many as 300 persons a night were carried to freedom in that boat; four such boats transported 3,000 Hungarians into Austria. Heber and France worked to the point of exhaustion, the latter finally requiring hospitalization. Heber joined the IRC staff and was responsible for the extraordinary success of the IRC Children's Home at Hainbach in Austria.

In New York, too, volunteers were offering their services to help in every possible way — from carrying mail sacks to collecting funds and medicines. A Wall Street lawyer and executive named John Richardson, Jr., put down his copy of the *New York Times* in which he had been reading an editorial about IRC's work, entitled "Freedom's Defenders." He left his office and went to Charles Pfizer and Co. to buy $15,000 of terramycin for the Hungarians. When the company learned the purpose of his proposed purchase, it refused payment and instead made available the more than $200,000 of antibiotics that Cherne and Duke took with them. Richardson went to the IRC office in New York, and like scores of others proceeded unassumingly to help with clerical tasks like opening the envelopes that were flooding in.

John Richardson is among those whose lives were changed by the Hungarian revolution. He had served in a parachute field artillery unit in Europe during the war, and returned to take his law degree at Harvard where he had earlier received his bachelor's degree. Until 1955 he was an associate in the celebrated law firm of Sullivan and Cromwell.

Now he began a new career of public service — treasurer and then president of IRC; president of the Free Europe Committee; and for seven years Assistant Secretary of State for Educational and Cultural Affairs. His wide-ranging interest in the issues of freedom has involved him in such organizations as the Foreign Policy Association, the Council on Foreign Relations, the National Association for the Advancement of Colored People, and in movements for integrated housing. He has served also as president of Freedom House, an organization that monitors the state of freedom in the United States and abroad. His initiative in humanitarian causes is illustrated by his relations with Communist Poland. In 1957, he learned of shortages of pharmaceuticals in that country. He personally organized a private effort that raised several million dollars worth of drugs from American firms as contributions to hospitals throughout Poland. Soon thereafter he became an original sponsor and board member of the American Research Hospital for Children in Cracow.

Another volunteer whose fate was altered by the Hungarian revolution was a young woman with an already established reputation as a journalist and news photographer. Dickey Chapelle had taken her camera and typewriter to the Hungarian frontier to help tell the story of IRC's work. Seized by a Communist patrol at the very border, she was sent to Budapest where she was held in an isolation cell for almost two months. Finally released during the period when the regime sought to quiet outraged world opinion, she was able to resume her career as journalist and photographer until it was ended in Indochina where she fell victim to a Viet Cong booby trap.

A PATTERN OF COOPERATION

During the frantic days of fall and winter, 1956, American and European relief organizations threw all their resources into helping the nearly 200,000 Hungarian refugees. The pattern of cooperation was magnificent, a model of that "people-to-people" relationship through which the solidarity of the free world can express itself most eloquently. In line with its past tradition, it was agreed that IRC, along with the Austrian Student Coordinating Committee, would concentrate on aiding students and professionals. The Austrian press advised all refugees in these categories to register with IRC.

A special IRC project involved the University of Sopron, located not far from the Austrian border, with one of the oldest schools of mining and forestry in Europe. Its 450 students and their professors had been a center of anti-Communist sentiment. In the last days, they crossed *en masse* into Austria. With the cooperation of the Austrian government, IRC set up a virtual university-in-exile near Salzburg until resettlement could be arranged. In addition, hostels were organized to accommodate 600 students, and 300 more were supported in private Viennese homes. Within a month after their flight from Hungary, another 300 students were on their way to America, many of them with scholarships. For others, scholarships were arranged in European countries.

In the United States, from 1957 to 1959, IRC handled a caseload of 3,377 refugees, of whom 2,466 were Hungarians. Of this number, 1,162 were professionals or students for the professions — engineers, technicians, physicians, artists, entertainers, scientists, lawyers, teachers, writers, journalists, clergymen, and so forth. For these, language was a serious barrier to the resumption of a normal life. The teaching of English was therefore an essential service. IRC/New York set up a language center, using intensive study methods developed at Columbia University. At its peak the center, which was open to all Hungarian refugees regardless of agency sponsorship, had a registration of almost a thousand.

The Committee's international ties were invaluable during this period. IRC-Canada, which had achieved a remarkable record of resettlement on behalf of European refugees, set up a special committee under the direction of leading academicians to prepare Hungarian students for Canadian universities. Earlier, when it was urgent to remove refugees from dangerous border areas, IRC-Canada had sent two Land Rovers capable of transporting twenty-five persons, for which the Knights of Malta in Austria provided the crews.

Obviously, the economy of Austria could not permanently cope with the huge refugee population it had generously received in November 1956 and the months that followed. To facilitate resettlement, IRC stepped up its activities in half a dozen countries. Sheba Strunsky Goodman and A. E. Jolis, IRC board members resident in France, raised funds and paved the way for the arrival of many. The Paris office found itself concerned principally with occupational rehabilitation. Mme. Hannah Benzion, who had directed IRC-Paris for many years since the armistice in 1945, recalls the frenetic activities of those days: "It really is rescue when you give a seamstress a sewing machine so that she can resume her trade; or when you buy a violin for an accomplished musician so that he can earn a living in his profession; or if you buy a typewriter for a Hungarian secretary for whom there will be no dearth of work in Paris."

THE MULTIPLYING NEEDS

Activities were going forward in IRC centers in England, Belgium, West Germany and Sweden. Ironically, IRC representatives also worked in

Yugoslavia — a country that has sent its own stream of anti-Communist refugees to IRC, both before and since the Hungarian revolution.

For staff on the scene in Europe, the most heartbreaking problem was the plight of the children and teenagers who constituted a large proportion of the refugees. Immediate attention was given to their requirements, especially in matters of health. The IRC children's home in Switzerland, which had housed youngsters from Greece, Germany and all the Iron Curtain nationalities, prepared to receive the Hungarians. Alida De Jaeger, director of IRC-Geneva, described the arrival of the first group in these words:

I wish you could have seen with your own eyes the immense relief and happiness they showed on their arrival — Adelboden was its worst, dark and cold, a snow storm raging. For hours, despite their fatigue after 24 hours' train journey, they did not leave off inspecting the home from top to bottom, repeating two of the few words they knew in German, "Sehr Schoen." What shook me most was that two of the big boys — not children any more, but grown-ups who had participated in the fighting — had tears running down their faces when they asked, "Who is offering this to us?" All of them are now undergoing a thorough medical checkup by our doctor. The real problem, however, is psychological and pedagogical rather than physical. After five months of inactivity in the camps of Austria even the eleven-year-olds have become chain smokers. . . .

Protecting the physical and mental health of refugees, especially refugee children, had long been an area of concern for IRC. After years of experience in this field, its professional staff at Adelboden reported that three to four months in the rest home usually proved sufficient to restore a rundown child to robust health.

In Austria, IRC's program aimed especially at combating the dreadful effects of waiting and idleness — the scourge of refugees, particularly those who have just come through a period of conflict and the tensions of escape. Small libraries were set up in refugee camps and later expanded into a mobile library. To prepare for resettlement, IRC printed 20,000 copies of a Hungarian-English phrase book.

Together with the Rockefeller and Ford Foundations and the Committee for Cultural Freedom, IRC helped to establish the seventy-member symphony orchestra, Hungarica Philharmonia, in Baden outside Vienna. The Committee took over and supported for years the Hungarian Handicraft Shop, a dressmaking and sewing enterprise that gave employment to more than forty Hungarian refugee women. Some eighty teenagers were received by IRC-Brussels. With the aid of Paul-Henri Spaak, Belgium's foreign minister and later Secretary-General of NATO, the youngsters were enrolled in government trade schools to assure that they would become self-supporting.

SAVING THE LEADERS

At the same time that IRC, along with many other agencies, was advancing this vast humanitarian program, the political implications of the Hungarian tragedy could not be overlooked. IRC brought several major leaders of the revolution to the United States.

One of them, Mayor Joseph Kovago of Budapest, was enabled to give first-hand testimony before the United Nations. An engineer by profession, he had been a key figure in the Hungarian anti-Nazi underground, barely escaping execution by the Gestapo only because of the timely liberation of Budapest. In 1945, he was elected mayor of Budapest but was forced out of office in 1947 by Communist pressure. Because he advocated Hungarian ties with the West, the Communists sentenced him in 1950 to life imprisonment, but he was released in September 1956 in time to be elected president of the revolutionary National Committee of Budapest during the first heady days of the uprising. When the Soviet armor finally proved insuperable, he made his escape. In a national tour under IRC auspices, he visited many cities in the United States as the guest of their mayors, and addressed the National Conference of Mayors in Washington.

Another of the Hungarian leaders brought to the United States under IRC sponsorship was Paul Jonas, president of the famed Petofi Circle which is universally credited with sparking the revolution. During World War II, as a student at the University of Budapest, he was imprisoned for anti-Nazi activities. The defeat of Hitler brought his release, and he resumed his studies, taking a doctorate in economics. In 1945, he became president of the National Union of Hungarian Students, and in that post resisted Communist efforts to take over the student movement. Arrested towards the end of 1947, he was jailed for five years without a trial. In 1954, at the age of thirty-one, Jonas helped launch the Petofi Circle, whose daring discussions of literature, education and economics soon attracted huge audiences of both workers and intellectuals.

In June 1956, no topic was more avidly discussed than the Poznan demonstrations in Poland which had produced some "liberalization" and forced a change in the leadership of the Communist Party. It had taken an uprising of 50,000 Polish workers and students to effect that result. The Hungarians were not reluctant to adopt the same course. Jonas, as a leader of the Petofi Circle, fought actively in the revolt and escaped at the last moment when it was clear that he was risking death if he stayed. Brought to the United States through IRC, he resumed his scholarly career and became a member of the economics department at Brooklyn College, City University of New York, and later at the University of New Mexico.

Jonas's life illustrates the problems of one type of refugee. A sensitive man, he never recovered from his nostalgia for home. In an article published in *Harper's* magazine in 1977, twenty years after his arrival in the United States, the Hungarian scholar gave expression to the irreparable hurt that some exiles are destined to carry with them for the rest of their lives. No matter how comfortable their circumstances in the new environs, the ineradicable associations of childhood still rise to consciousness. There are times when the new culture in which they live must strike them as unacceptable. They would not surrender for a moment the freedom they have gained, but they are conscious of the price they have paid — the broken ties with a past that gave them their identity. As intellectuals, they retain their function of social criticism and apply it to their new country. Not all or even most of Jonas's fellow-Hungarian refugees would agree with his assessment, but his reflections on life in America are worth pondering:

Now? Life is not bad. The teaching load at the University of Mexico is six hours a week, the salary is more or less adequate for nine months of teaching and moderate publishing, the surroundings are pleasant, and there is a dramatic view of the Sandia mountains. . . .

My friends are living similar, comfortable lives, confirming the proposition of some sociologists who suggest that the 1956 Hungarian refugees have arrived at positions normally not reached till the second or third generation.

We have the expected freedom and material rewards, but are we really happy in this joyless society haunted by the Puritan ethic and wholly inexpert in the art of loving, living and laughing? Do we have real friends with whom we can sit down for a conversation about personal things, music, literature, politics, legends? Are we still able, after the second bottle of wine, to cry with laughter and laugh with tears? Doesn't the lack of strong and emotional relationships drive us, along with our American acquaintances, into the arms of predatory psychiatrists? In the impersonal atmosphere of common eating places that remind us of filling stations, don't we think about the taste of smoked meat, the skin of bacon cut in small pieces and served with chopped golden onions, fried and sprinkled with paprika?[6]

Such a tormented confessional from a refugee may not make comfortable reading for Americans, but the nation is all the richer for the presence of such critics. Their writing, as it must, carries the existential scar left by the rupture with their own culture. As Carel Sternberg has said, "The refugee condition, once experienced, does not wash off." Professor Jonas's words are a reminder that the refugee suffers not only material deprivation but a deep psychological wound that is never truly healed. This too is part of the punishment that exile imposes on its victims. It is another count in the indictment that history brings against the totalitarians who drive a wedge into their own people.

AFTERMATH

Though Hungary eventually passed out of the headlines, the survival of its refugees remained a principal concern for the next five years. The IRC Children's Home at Hainbach in Austria, continued to serve Hungarian children; as late as 1961, a majority of its residents continued to be Hungarian, alongside a growing minority of Yugoslavs, Poles and Rumanians.

Long after the fighting, IRC workers were still wrestling with the problems of relocating the refugees and integrating them into a new environment.

Some idea of the burden can be gathered from the fact that it took a team of workers, including four IRC staff members, ten months to empty Yugoslavia of the 19,000 Hungarian refugees who had fled there after the revolution.

At the same time, IRC was concerned about the "forgotten refugees" — those who were being overlooked because the spotlight had been so dramatically fixed on Hungary. The simultaneous Suez crisis, which had complicated the West's political problem in Hungary, also produced a jet of refugees. Thousands of persons, mostly Jews, had to flee or were expelled from Egypt. They were forbidden to take money or household goods with them; most of them arrived with little more than their clothing and a few personal effects. A goodly number, speaking French, chose France as their destination.

Humanitarian considerations made it inevitable that the Hungarians, still bleeding from Russian-inflicted wounds, should be given priority in the world's eyes. Even within this priority, further priorities had to be established. Like other organizations swamped by the sheer numbers, IRC had to go through the painful task of deciding who was to be helped first. Rough classifications were established: those who had registered first; those with close relatives in the United States; professionals and students; those who were active in the revolution. As the Vienna office reported at that time, it had become impossible to service all applicants. "Sadly," Marcel Faust wrote from Vienna, "we must turn away every third applicant."

All of the voluntary agencies on the scene were experiencing the same problem. Yet in retrospect, one statistical fact stands out to emphasize the monumental contribution made by Americans through religious groups, welfare agencies and the IRC: in a period of eight months, more than 34,000 Hungarians were processed for immigration and transported to the United States. From December 1956 through September 1958, IRC alone disbursed $2,180,000 in support of its special programs for Hungarian refugees, and shipped $463,000 worth of material aid — medicines, food, beds, clothing — to the refugees. By the end of a year, the West as a whole had absorbed 170,000 Hungarians.

Unfortunately, these statistics need a sobering footnote. America had been generous. But the generosity was born of frustration and guilt at standing by helplessly while the Hungarians were fighting. The man in the street gave coins and dollar bills; unions appropriated sums from their treasuries; executives sent checks; corporations donated money, medicines and foods. In a very important way, the character of refugee aid had been changed by the Hungarian Revolution. Once the preoccupation of a handful, it had now become the concern of many. Something new had been brought into the awareness of the average American.

VII

Homeless in Europe

It was almost a decade and a half since the celebration of V-E Day had sent dancing millions into the streets of the great cities of Europe and America. A weariness of the memory had now set in; few people wanted to be reminded of those grim events. But the human residue left in the displaced persons camps of Europe insistently warned that the effects of World War II were not yet spent.

Some 40,000 Europeans still lived in barracks, unable for a variety of reasons to return to their birthplace. Another 100,000, it was estimated, were surviving on pot-luck as "out-of-camp refugees." In the changing semantics of the social workers, these 140,000 were first referred to as "hard-core refugees." Then, as a linguistic cushion against the harsh reality, they became "difficult to resettle" cases, until even that was considered too odious and the term was altered to "static refugees."

Before the world had resolved the plight of these " stateless persons" — still another euphemism that came into vogue — a new strain of the genus refugee began to filter into Europe. In 1957 the Hungarians had been absorbed and resettled by a conscience-stricken world that had originally stood by, wringing its hands helplessly, while the Russian tanks clanked through the streets of Budapest. But now the subterranean volcanic pressures in Europe were opening new vents.

YEAR OF THE REFUGEE

The General Assembly of the United Nations, whose composition has since changed dramatically, adopted a resolution designating the year beginning June 1959 as World Refugee Year. The proposal was sponsored by the United States and nine other nations, and was adopted by a vote of 56 in favor, 8 against, with 9 abstentions and 8 delegates absent. The nations voting against the resolution were those responsible for the problem.

It had now become apparent that the postwar period was producing another major wave of migration. West Germany took in 3,700,000 East Germans in the years from 1945 to 1961, when the Berlin Wall went up. This was hardly surprising, and it did not even strike world consciousness as a movement of refugees. For the most part it was viewed as an internal migration; the Bonn government was expected to take care of its own. When Russia defeated Finland in March 1940, some 415,000 Karelians were transferred to Finland proper as their territory was incorporated into the Soviet Union. On that occasion, too, there had been no assumption of obligation by the rest of the world. Only when refugees were asking to be sheltered by countries of different nationality did it become clear that a permanent problem had been created for the last half of the twentieth century: political upheavals would henceforth generate a constant flow of aliens that would tax the resources of receiving countries.

A CITIZENS COMMISSION

By January 1959, Europe had absorbed almost a million displaced persons; the United States, some 460,000. That meant that Europe had taken about 48 percent, the United States about 24 percent, and other regions of the globe about 28 percent. Almost as if by prescience, the world community decided that it had better clean up the "residual refugees" of World War II so that it might be ready for the new waves.

To prepare for the developing contingencies, the International Rescue Committee resorted to a technique it was to use with increasing frequency in later years, notably in the Bangladesh and Indochinese crises. It set up a commission of public-spirited citizens to study the problems and speak to the conscience of the world.

In 1957, under the chairmanship of Harold I. Zellerbach, president of the Crown-Zellerbach Corporation, and Ambassador Angier Biddle Duke, president of IRC, the task was undertaken. The members of the group included Eugenie Anderson, former U.S. ambassador to Denmark; Irving Brown, European representative of the AFL-CIO; Mrs. David Levy, of the New York State Youth Commission; Eugene Lyons, senior editor of *Reader's Digest*; and Bishop James A. Pike of the Protestant Episcopal Church. Serving as Executive Director of the Commission was David Martin, author and expert on Eastern Europe. The immediate purpose was to focus public attention on the need to heal, once and for all, the wounds still suffered by World War II's displaced persons. One of the results was the designation of 1959 as World Refugee Year. Perhaps more important, the Commission prepared Americans for the realization that refugee assistance was to become a permanent responsibility of free nations in a divided world.

Obviously, more than UN rhetoric was needed. The report of the Zellerbach Commission highlighted the urgency of the United States Escapee Program which, from 1952 until 1958, had operated on a budget of some $6 million.[1] It had helped at least 150,000 refugees, separate and apart from the efforts on behalf of the Hungarians. USEP, as the program came to be known, was a precursor of other responses that America, a nation of refugees, would give to those in need. In line with President Eisenhower's concept of "people to people relations," it had channeled funds through America's voluntary agencies, the VOLAGS. Direct government aid, of course, was being sent through the formal structure of the United Nations High Commissioner for Refugees and through the Intergovernmental Committee for European Migration, whose tags reading ICEM have been clipped to the clothes of refugees from Asia as well as Europe. A large proportion of the funding required by both organizations has come from the U.S. government. Up until the World Refugee Year, the United States had contributed 37 percent of the UNHCR's $17.5 million budget. Even little Lichtenstein had contributed $3,601. The only Communist nation that made any contribution was China — $5,000.

Among the recommendations of the Zellerbach Commission was a proposal for the convening of a world conference to develop a program for closing the books on the displaced persons problem by emptying the camps of the "hard-core" and the out-of-camp "statics." Many of them had already suffered a dozen years of rootlessness and helplessness. The conference took place in Geneva in November 1958. President Duke of the IRC used words that were figurative then; twenty years later, the words were to take on a frightful quality of literal truth:

We have, in effect, thrown life-belts to the drowning, but left them in the sea. We now have to pull them to land. We must put an end to the flow of unproductive millions that have gone into camp upkeep, small subsidies, parcels, etc. — without helping the refugee to reestablish himself. The refugee must be given constructive aid that will enable him to become self-supporting and self-respecting, instead of being compelled to exist on alms.[2]

This observation continues to reverberate whenever the economics of refugee assistance is considered. No ledger can compute the waste of human resources left to rot in the miasma of camp life. The constricted living quarters, the constant invasion of privacy, the absence of sanitary facilities, the stultifying idleness, the degradation of dependency, the sense of worthlessness that comes with a denial of the chance to work productively — all these are part of the price we exact from those who have already been victimized by a society that compelled them to break out.

But there is also a paradox in the dollar-and-cents entries that sum up an aberrant economics of aid: it is cheaper to resettle a refugee than to maintain him in a camp. The Zellerbach Commission, like its successors in other refugee crises, pointed this out, analyzing, for example, the costs involved in caring for a Yugoslav refugee couple with five children who had been in various camps since the end of World War II and who wound up in Camp

Capua, Italy. All five children, aged one to ten, had been born in refugee camps and had never known any other life. Since at that time the average cost of supporting a refugee in camp was $300 to $400 a year, and this family represented a total of some fifty refugee years lived in camps, the cost of maintaining it in a nonproductive existence had already exceeded $15,000. Said the Commission, "Had a small portion of this amount been invested in this family as a rehabilitation grant ten or eleven years ago, the chances are that they would now be satisfactorily integrated in some Western country, making a modest productive contribution to the society in which they lived rather than having to exist on charity." Again and again, the uneconomic approach, aimed at easing the conscience rather than solving the problem, has been repeated.

"A EUROPE OF THE HEART"

There were indeed some heroically successful efforts made by individuals and groups. In 1958, the Nobel Peace Prize was awarded to a Dominican priest, Father Georges Henri Pire, for his service to the "hard-core" European refugees. Launching a crusade for *un Europe du coeur*, he set up an organization called Aid to Displaced Persons that sponsored the "adoption" of some 15,000 families. Many of the "difficult cases" proved to be elderly people. A study of one camp with 20,000 foreign refugees located in Germany, conducted by the Academy for Public Health in Hamburg, found that 40 percent of the "difficult cases" consisted of people over sixty. Father Pire undertook to set up homes for such persons. In addition, he built special villages in Belgium, Germany and Austria to rescue large families particularly, and to save the children from a life without a future. His European villages, whose inhabitants numbered a maximum of 120 — or about thirty families — were staffed with counselors whose function was to direct the adults toward a life of normalcy and the children toward patterns of healthy growth.

Visiting such a European village in the suburbs of the picturesque old Austrian town Bregenz on the eastern shore of Lake Constance, the Commission brought back to the American people the human reality behind the impersonal refugee statistics:

This was a Saturday — and if one approaches the villages when school is not in session, the first thing one becomes aware of is the shouting and laughter of children at play in the large field that forms part of the settlement. That the children are happy is obvious even from a distance; that they are wholesome by any standards becomes apparent as soon as one comes within camera range. To anyone who has seen the wretchedness stamped on the faces of the children in refugee camps, the transformation that has come over these children in Bregenz would by itself be justification for the project.

For the older folks, however, the memory of past suffering persisted. An interview with two elderly Russian sisters and the daughter of one of them, aged twenty-three, told a typical story: they are dispossessed by the Russian Revolution as "members of the bourgeoisie"; they lose father and brother; a child dies during the infamous famine deliberately created by Stalin in 1934. In 1938, the husbands of both sisters disappear into the hands of the secret police and are then sent to Siberia, never to be heard from again. For fourteen years the three survivors live in a little corner of a railroad barracks, together with other Russians and Ukrainians. The next years are spent in barracks at Lembach, Austria, with sleepless nights constantly haunted by the terrifying memories of the past twenty years. Now, at long last living in a small duplex, with the amenities of a kitchen, a bathroom and two bedrooms — all their own — and with the twenty-three-year-old daughter working in a factory in Bregenz, they still weep when they talk of the years in which they thought themselves forgotten by God and the world. "But now," they tell Commission members, "we can believe again that God exists."

There is also the former teacher of classical languages, a Czech married to a Polish office worker he met in the camps in 1950, where they remain until after four children have been born to them. Speaking little German, he has no prospect of pursuing his profession in Austria and therefore, under the guidance of one of Father Pire's counselors, he agrees to take work in a chemical factory, knowing that at least his family will have the freedom denied to them in their native land and that he will be able to provide them with the necessities.

These instances illustrated what could be done with the so-called "hardcore" or "difficult cases," to use the labels of the times. But despite the efforts of men like Father Pire, there were still many who had not been resettled either *sur place* or in new communities. The IRC Commission warned that the longer the delay in helping people to sink real roots and renew their lives, the worse the problem would become. A survey of the Bothfeld Camp in Germany underscored the dread impact of camp life on the children. The proportion of "backward" children was far above that of the general population; one out of four was found to be attending classes for the slow. Time stands still for those who wait, but the process of deterioration does not.

TITO'S VICTIMS

The sponsors of the World Refugee Year hoped that stepped-up resettlement activity in 1959 would wipe the slate clean, but even as they were lobbying for votes in the corridors of the UN building in New York and in the ministries of foreign affairs, it was apparent that there could be no mopping up, or even a catching up. The voluntary agencies found themselves under pressure from new directions. For example, Yugoslavia, which in 1956-57 had received Hungarians fleeing from the Khrushchev-installed regime, was now filling the pipeline. Refugees were heading into neighboring Greece, Italy and Austria in surprisingly large numbers. Escape was possible primarily because of the favorable geography and a less-than-Stalinist efficiency in Tito's proletarian state.

Yugoslavia held a unique position. It had broken with Stalin on the heels of the postwar restoration of the Communist International, rechristened the Cominform, with its headquarters set up in Belgrade as a sop to internationalism. Locating it in Moscow would have been confirmation of what the French socialist Léon Blum said of international communism — that it was simply "a Russian Nationalist Party." By 1949 the rift between Stalin and Tito was so wide that the Yugoslav Communist Party was expelled from the Cominform, which later, in 1956, gave up the ghost as another sop to Tito, this time because Khrushchev was seeking reconciliation.

Though ideological issues are never lacking in internecine radical politics, the conflict had begun when Soviet Russia vetoed Tito's aspirations to head a Balkan federation. Moscow's answer to that proposal had been to groom a potential Yugoslav opposition. Tito lost no time in applying the ultimate political weapon of communism: he arrested his rivals and thus achieved stability, both domestically and externally. He seized the opportunity to get the best of both possible worlds. Raising the banner of communism and maintaining his one-party state, he used his opposition to Stalin as a basis for winning financial aid from the United States. Adam B. Ulam, the authority on Eastern European affairs, reminds us: "As early as 1921-22, Lenin had had the insight that socialism in one country could succeed, even without purges, mass resettlements, and a lowering of the standard of living — if the capitalists would help. Now, what he had not dared to dream about Russia in 1921 — that the capitalists would help without exacting concessions in return — was coming true in Yugoslavia."[3]

Nevertheless, the inherent nature of the monolithic state still required repression. Though American foreign aid strengthened the regime, men like Milovan Djilas, who had been a devoted Communist and second in command, began to question the premises of a government that denied to its people free speech, free press and a free choice of officials. As his philosophy evolved from totalitarian communism to a democratic socialism based on a multiparty system sustained by a genuine bill of individual rights, his stubborn patriotism led him to reject exile in favor of imprisonment.

For a while the regime basked in the sunshine of ideological success. Khrushchev's secret speech to the 1956 Congress of the Soviet Communist Party had lifted the veil on the true face of Stalinism, and Tito could boast that he had been the first of the de-Stalinizers. Khrushchev and Bulganin invited themselves to Belgrade, and bear hugs between the leaders were duly photographed. But the days of the Gulag, both Russian and Yugoslav, were by no means over. When the logical outcome of de-Stalinization became apparent in the uprisings in East Germany, Poland and Hungary, it was clear to the Communist theoreticians that the slightest breeze of freedom in a totalitarian state is enough to threaten a whirlwind.

The barometer readings in such matters are calibrated in refugee statistics. In 1957 alone some 26,000 Yugoslavs crossed the frontiers into neighboring Greece, Italy and Austria. Almost 80 percent of them were youths under twenty-five, mostly students, peasants and workers intent on gaining a better life in democratic societies. Like their counterparts in other migrations, they faced not only the hazards of the journey but the possibility that they might be returned to their own country where they would face a fury even more violent than the fate that impelled them to escape originally. It is estimated that in the late 1950s, as many as 60 percent of those who crossed into Austria were handed back to Tito's border police.

"REFUGEE" OR "ECONOMIC MIGRANT"?

The reason given for this callous treatment was to be heard repeatedly in many of the refugee movements that would shake the earth in the 1960s, '70s and '80s, and that are yet to occur in the decades ahead. 'These are not 'political refugees' fleeing from governmental oppression," so goes the argument, "these are 'economic migrants' and therefore not entitled to asylum."

The distinction may seem neat enough in the minds of those who write pettifogging legislation or regulations. But is there really a psychological scalpel fine enough to dissect the complex of pressures that lead people to tear up roots and strike out into the unknown? Can we measure to what extent the Pilgrims sought freedom of worship in the New World and to what extent they were escaping the economic restrictions imposed on them by English society? The realities have long been recognized in the history of American immigration. *A Manual for Emigrants to America*, by one Calvin Cotton, published in London in 1832, said expressly:

For some (for many probably) there are sufficient inducements, well-founded, to emigrate to America. . . . The motives depend upon the various considerations of station, rank, amount of wealth; the kind of business, trade or profession which anyone is pursuing, and his comparative prospects of success in either country; his family connections, difficulties of removal, etc. His religion also, his partialities for one form of government rather than another . . . will all naturally come into the reckoning.

Max Lerner, in his book, *America as a Civilization*, has summarized the variety of impulses that populated the New World: "The people who came to our shores felt intensely about the American experience because for each of them America was the wall broken down, door broken open. Some, like the Negroes, came against their will and in chains. But as for the rest, whether they came for land or economic opportunity or freedom, *they came because of the past denials in their lives.*"[4] The contemporary newcomers also flee deprivation. In escaping from Communist or right-wing dictatorships, they seek to secure what they perceive to be their human heritage, the basic freedoms that include the right to live and work in an open society.

In surveying the refugee scene, IRC's Zellerbach Commission found it necessary to bring the issue into the open by asking directly: "What is a refugee?" The United Nations had defined the term in 1951 in its statute creating the Office of the UN High Commissioner for Refugees:

... any person who, as a result of events occurring before 1 January 1951 and owing to *well-founded fear of being persecuted for reasons of race, religion, nationality or political opinion*, is outside the country of his nationality and is unable or, owing to such fear or for reasons other than personal convenience, is unwilling to avail himself of the protection of that country; or who, not having a nationality and being outside the country of his former habitual residence, is unable or, owing to such fear or for reasons other than personal convenience, is unwilling to return to it. (Emphasis added.)[5]

At the same time it had declared paradoxically that the work of the UNHCR was to be "of an entirely non-political character; it shall be humanitarian and social. . . ."[6]

Obviously, in declaring that a given individual has fled his country because of a "well-founded fear of being persecuted for reasons of race, religion, nationality or political opinion," the UNHCR is making a political judgment on the nature of the regime. A definition that might have avoided the issue is the one used by Elfan Rees in his book, *We Strangers and Afraid*: a refugee is "anyone who has been uprooted from his home, has crossed a frontier — artificial or traditional — and looks for protection and sustenance to a government or authority other than his former one." This bypasses entirely the question of his specific reasons for leaving his former country of residence. The UN formulation, on the other hand, requires that the refugee's decision be primarily a political one.

The Zellerbach Commission's examination of the distinction between a refugee and an economic migrant was destined to become increasingly important. In the early 1980s it became an overt issue in the case of the Haitians who began their own boatlift to escape both the tyranny and the poverty of the Duvalier regime. A more subtle variant of the problem arose when the U.S. Immigration and Naturalization Service was called upon to decide the status of Russian-Jewish refugees who reached Israel, were granted Israeli citizenship and then left shortly thereafter for other countries. Had they lost their status as refugees, and were they no longer entitled to the right of asylum in potential receiving countries? Were such persons also to be denied the services of the UNHCR and ICEM, the intergovernmental agency that provides transportation? The distinction could have been critical also for ethnic Chinese, who were forced out of their homes in Vietnam after being deprived of their property and ordered to move to the "new economic zones." There they were expected to begin a life as virtual serfs in the jungle, even though their families had lived and worked for generations in Vietnam.

IRC's early work helped to address some of the ambiguities. In the IRC Commission's 1959 report, the authors dealt directly with the plight of the Yugoslavs who were being shipped back as "economic migrants." Said the Commission:

There are certain facts about the present exodus from Yugoslavia which are difficult to reconcile with the "economic migrants" thesis. Such migrations traditionally have involved adults of mature age and family groups primarily. The migrants have left their countries in the expectation that, when they arrived in the country to which they were moving, there was prospect of immediate employment. And they have taken with them in small trunks and suitcases their few worldly possessions — and worldly possessions can be as precious to the poor man as they are to the rich.

None of these criteria are met by the Yugoslav refugees of today. They have fled despite the knowledge that no jobs were waiting for them in Austria and Italy; that they stood at least a small chance of imprisonment if caught by the frontier police; and that they would have to wait for six months at least, and more probably a year or more before moving on to another country. They have left with only the shirts on their backs, because an escapee, unlike a migrant, cannot take a suitcase with him. In many cases they have risked their lives to escape by stealing small boats to cross the Adriatic or by swimming across the bay at Trieste. At the best, the act of escape was a physical ordeal. The Yugoslav refugees who have entered Austria have had to make their way through a difficult mountain frontier. In some areas the frontier can be crossed without too much difficulty. But there are other parts of the frontier where the escapees have had to spend several days moving over mountains that range up to 10,000 feet. That they were able to make this journey, in many cases bringing small children with them, is a tribute to their physical vigor and strength of character — but more than this, it supports the belief that they were impelled by motivations somewhat stronger than simple economic discontent.[7]

Also evidence of the fact that such persons seeking refugee status are propelled by motives greater than economic security is the obvious correlation between events and the increased flow. As governmental policies become more stringent in the Communist countries, each tightening of the screw extrudes an increasing number of escapees. In many cases, the individuals are professionals, well aware that they will not be eligible to practice in the country of destination, or highly skilled personnel who know they will have to make a fresh start, probably in a different line of work. The prospects of higher, or even equal, income are so unlikely that they cannot justify the risks of crossing mine fields, crawling under electrified barbed wire, evading watch towers, swimming rivers, or slipping through forests and mountain passes.

In any case it is impossible to draw a line between the political and economic, especially in a totalitarian state that recognizes no such distinction. Milovan Djilas, who has been in and out of Yugoslav jails ever since he broke with Communism, has emphasized this fact in his book, *The New Class*, a major work of social analysis for the twentieth century. He wrote: "The totalitarian tyranny and control of the new class, which came into being during the revolution, has become the yoke from under which the blood and sweat of all members of society flow. . . . The limitation of freedom of thought is not only an attack on specific political and social rights but an attack on the human being as such."[8]

A Yugoslav escapee gives his reason for entering Austria: "The Communists are trying to force us to abandon the ways of our fathers; we think that the ways of our fathers were good ways, and we don't want to abandon them."[9] Is he not fleeing from what he perceives to be political persecution? To establish his refugee status, a young Yugoslav in Trieste is asked whether he has been personally persecuted. He replies:

Your question proves to me that the West understands very little of the real nature of the Communist system. If by persecution you mean a term of imprisonment, then I must confess that I have not been persecuted. But there are a thousand little pressures in the everyday life of every person which, taken together, make life unbearable. I have not been arrested, but one night at midnight the UDBA [secret police] called at my apartment house and took away the man who lived above me. On another night they drew up across the road and carried away someone from that house. If a person is articulate and if he is known as a non-supporter of the regime, then he must live in constant fear of a possible visit by the UDBA. . . . Finally there is the impossible economic situation and the fact that the State is the only employer to whom one can turn. In reply to your question, I cannot say that in Yugoslavia I was singled out for individual persecution. But like the majority of the people in Yugoslavia, I have suffered oppression. It is from this that I am a refugee, and it is because of this that I do not wish to return.[10]

But what of those who are forcibly repatriated? Are they not immediately the targets of official attention and punitive action? Are they not likely on their return to experience the "well-founded fear" that qualifies the refugee under the UN's definition? At the very least, their original flight was a declaration of opinion on the worth of the economic system imposed by Communism. It was Lenin, after all, who stated that the people vote with their feet, and escaping is therefore a political pronouncement.

These arguments were addressed not only to countries of first asylum but to the group in the United States who preferred to remain silent about the policy of returning escapees in order to facilitate American wooing of Marshal Tito. In a joint statement to the U.S. Congress, William J. vanden Heuvel, then president of IRC, and Bishop Edward E. Swanstrom, executive director of the National Catholic Welfare Conference, said, "Although they [the Yugoslav refugees] may not be able to articulate the reason which makes them come, it is invariably a desire to escape the police state, its totalitarian control as well as its economic deprivation. A man's yearning for freedom and human dignity is quite compatible with his hope for economic betterment."

CONFLICTING VIEWS

The attention received by the Zellerbach Commission contributed to the convening of the Geneva Conference of 1958 under the auspices of ICEM. There two schools of thought seemed to emerge. On the one hand, some of the nations felt that an all-out attack on "the residual refugee problem" would dispose of the issue. Once the UNHCR's Camp Clearance Program had been carried out, normalcy would return to Europe and the last vestiges of dislocation created by World War II would be erased.

IRC's spokesman, Angier Biddle Duke, addressing the meeting, expressed concern that simply liquidating the camps would only make the plight of the refugees less visible. Failure to resettle the even larger number of out-of-camp refugees would multiply the suffering. Moreover, before the World War II backlog of refugees had been resettled, a new wave from the Communist countries was in full flow.

Unfortunately, as the Commission noted, people were becoming "tired of hearing of the same problem year after year." Only a few weeks before, a member of the British delegation to the UN, in a speech supporting the resolution for the World Refugee Year, had indicated that her government was interested primarily in ringing down the final curtain on the drama. "We would be less than honest," said Patricia Hornsby-Smith, M.P., "if we did not make it plain that we regard this not just as a means of providing support to *bring about a gradual tapering off of international assistance to these refugees*—who, if they have not left their country of first asylum at the end of this final two-year period, in one direction or another, should become the responsibility of the host countries." (Emphasis added)[11]

One consequence of such a policy, it was feared, would be to encourage countries of first asylum to slam the gates in the faces of future escapees. This was of particular concern to those on the borders of the refugee-creating countries. Even while this point of view was being advanced, the press was reporting daring escapes from countries like Bulgaria, Albania and Yugoslavia into Greece, which could hardly afford to accept permanent responsibility for the influx. Some thirty or forty, every month, were crossing the rugged mountain frontiers. Among the dramatic incidents was the escape of a group of sixty Albanian shepherd families who made the crossing with a thousand sheep and goats and a hundred head of cattle. Ingenious methods were resorted to. In May 1958, the Ivanov family broke out of Yugoslavia by creating a unique escape vehicle: they lined the inside of a 1927 Chrysler with concrete slabs, mounted a heavy, angled steel plate on the bumpers, and contrived a home-made periscope. Crouching on the floor, they plunged headlong through the frontier barriers, while the border guards gaped at the seemingly driverless car.

AVOIDING THE ROT OF IDLENESS

Awaiting them and others like them was life in primitive Greek facilities at Camp Lavrion or Camp Styros where the atmosphere was one of rigorous military discipline. The U.S. Escapee Program had assumed responsibility for providing medical care, some personal amenities, heating, bedding, language and vocational training, immigration documentation costs and other resettlement expenses. In many such situations, United States government agencies such as USEP found it desirable to remain "nonoperational"; they could accomplish their objectives more efficiently and at less cost by contracting out the tasks to the voluntary agencies. Thus, in Greece, where many of the refugees were of the Orthodox faith, the World Council of Churches was the leader among the VOLAGS, administering a completely nonsectarian program without discrimination against members of other faiths, including many Moslem escapees.

Generally the host country is reluctant to permit refugees who are "in transit" to take employment, especially — as was the case in Greece — if native unemployment is already a problem. A policy of enforced inactivity awaits the refugees who thus begin their life in a free society as jobless persons dependent on charity. A prolonged period of such sterility inevitably erodes morale. Some delays are unavoidable since interrogations and examination of bona fides are necessary. But when the lapse becomes protracted, extending from months into years, despair deepens into bitterness.

This pattern was being repeated throughout Europe. Sweden had become the country of first asylum for Poles escaping across the Baltic Sea. In the 1960s France was busy bringing home Algerian repatriates. Rumania, Hungary, Czechoslovakia and Yugoslavia, now firmly fixed in the Soviet satellite system, were continuing to disgorge their more intrepid spirits. Spain was accepting Cuban refugees — from 1960 to 1962, some 10,000 — and the International Rescue Committee was helping to send a substantial number of them on their way to permanent resettlement in the United States, Canada, Australia and occasionally in Latin America. At the same time, IRC was sponsoring 1,788 Indonesian refugees who had first gone to the Netherlands and who were admitted to the United States under special legislation.

At this time too Jews were leaving Egypt in great numbers and heading for France. At the initiative of the American Council for Judaism's Philanthropic Fund, directed by Anna Matson for many years under the presidency of Charles Tanenbaum, IRC had undertaken a substantial relief program on their behalf. Almost a thousand, each year, were helped to sink roots in France. The figure peaked in 1962 when some 1,500 refugees of the Jewish faith were given financial assistance in France alone, with most of the resources being provided to IRC by the Philanthropic Fund. By that time the program had been extended into many areas of Jewish refugee needs, covering families from behind the Iron Curtain and, in increasing numbers, from Algeria and the other Mahgreb countries.

Europe was under siege again; from Yugoslavia alone, 10,000 were coming in every year. And the greater the number of arrivals, the larger the delays in resettlement and the more serious the attendant economic and emotional problems. Austria, West Germany, Italy and Belgium respected the obligation to admit them, but needed help in coping. IRC was on the scene to address both the physical and psychological needs. A Youth Guidance Clinic, set up in Vienna during the Hungarian crisis to provide treatment for minor children, continued to operate. In Germany an IRC mental health project offered psychiatric services to refugee university students. With joint funding from other organizations like CARE and the UNHCR, youngsters were placed in meaningful apprenticeship programs. Special university scholarships were made available in Italy, Belgium and Austria with the help of the Rockefeller Foundation; a similar program for Cuban medical students in Spain was financed jointly with the Milbank Memorial Fund.

In the early 1960s IRC's Geneva headquarters under Garrett G. Ackerson, Jr., became the focal point of operations in Austria, Italy, Germany, Sweden, France, Belgium and Spain. Though U.S.-based, the International Rescue Committee had become a truly international organization both in services performed and support received. IRC people around the globe have worked closely with foreign VOLAGS. Non-American sources providing support for IRC's campaigns included individual philanthropists; foundations like the Witting Trust in Great Britain; private national groups like the Norwegian Refugee Council; West German trade unions like the Metal Workers; the British organization Lifeline; and the World University Service.

FROM EVERY DIRECTION

There was no predicting what new political development would send people hurtling into exile. Unexpectedly a handful of students from Afro-Asian countries under Soviet influence might show up in West Berlin and the Federal Republic. Disillusioned by the conditions they found in the Soviet Union or the satellite countries, they could not return to their homelands. In such cases IRC's contribution would be financial assistance, often through other organizations, for example, in the case of the students, through the *Bundesstudentring*. A collapse of empire and the emergence of Arab independence brought Jews from North Africa to Paris in considerable numbers.

Again in conjunction with the Philanthropic Fund, IRC found itself addressing the needs of 612 Jews from Algeria, 252 from Morocco, 606 expellees
from Egypt, 1,575 from Tunisia. Sometimes the flow from North Africa
outnumbered the Iron Curtain refugees seeking IRC assistance. The North
African Jews arrived in France with few possessions — only what they could
carry themselves. Their departure was, in many cases, clandestine. Pretending to be tourists, they had even purchased round-trip tickets. With assistance from the Philanthropic Fund they were given housing, furniture, care
and maintenance allocations as well as emergency grants.

These refugees, of course, were only the backwash of a cyclone that had
struck the Middle East. The recurrent wars since the UN's partition of Palestine in 1948 have precipitated new waves of refugees, exceeded in numbers
only by the population exchanges that took place between the Hindus and
Moslems in the partition of India in 1947, the Bangladesh crisis in 1971, and
the Soviet invasion of Afghanistan in December 1979. Following the Six-
Day War in 1967, IRC sent representatives to both Israel and the Arab
countries to determine whether it could provide humanitarian assistance.
Ellas Laursen, the director of IRC/Germany, reported from Jordan:

Since the war ended, a continued flow of refugees has crossed the Jordan where a
dozen desert camps have been readied for them. Surrounded by sand, they lack
water, sanitary facilities, clinics, everything. In one of the camps I visited, holding
9,000 people, the only concrete help the refugees were receiving was from a team of
four British women of the Save the Children group. They live with the refugees
under the most awful conditions. When I sat down in their tent, I asked if there was
anything I could do to help. "Yes," said the leader of the group, "stop that wind and
sand blowing!"... I have been in refugee work for 22 years in different parts of Europe and in very difficult circumstances. Yet this particular problem here does not
leave me in peace.

The Mideast events left nobody in peace. In what has remained a stubborn irreconcilable conflict between the Arabs and the Jews, made more
complex by the politics of oil and the southward expansionism of the Soviet
Union, there has been little room for assistance from outside, nongovernmental agencies like IRC. Following the birth of the state of Israel with
United Nations approval, the UN General Assembly in December 1949
created a special agency for Palestinian refugees — the United Nations Relief
and Works Agency for Palestine Refugees (UNRWA) which has supervised
the camps. Since the October 1973 war, a major hurdle in peace negotiations has been the future of the Palestinians, especially those in the occupied
West Bank. The contending parties cite their own concern with refugee
populations, the Arabs asserting the claims of a million Palestinians who
fled from the Israelis, while the latter speak for more than a million Jewish
refugees from Europe, North Africa and Arab lands who came to rest in
Israel. As the methods of war, terrorist infiltration and incursions across

boundaries became the prevailing operating procedures in the Middle East, nongovernmental agencies found it impossible to function in what had become armed camps.

But the spillover of refugees from the Middle East into Europe was amenable to assistance by the VOLAGS—the denominational groups and the secular organizations such as the International Red Cross, the International Social Service, the YMCA and the International Rescue Committee. Relief in the Middle East camps has been provided principally by UNRWA, with the largest portion of the funding coming from the United States. Thus, UNRWA announced that for the year 1980, some $91,000,000 had been pledged by forty-one nations, with the U.S. contributing more than half — $52,000,000. Second in line was West Germany with $6,000,000. The largest contribution from the Arabs was Saudi Arabia's $1,200,000. Iraq, also a leading oil producer, pledged $121,600. It should be added that the American contribution included a grant of $9,500,000 contingent on whether a matching grant would be forthcoming from the members of OPEC, the Organization of Petroleum Exporting Countries.[12]

Private agencies have been kept off the scene as the Palestinian camps have become centers of guerrilla activities and bases for what its partisans call the "Palestinian revolution." In 1967, while IRC's director of operations in Germany was visiting the Jordanian camps, its president William J. vanden Heuvel, later the United States deputy ambassador to the UN in the Carter administration, was visiting Israel. He concluded his report with these words:

When I was a young boy, we sang a hymn about "The New Jerusalem." In some of the most exciting and overwhelming moments of my life, I have been in the "New Jerusalem" where supposed enemies have embraced and historic barriers have melted in the face of human needs. We are close enough to the desert so that it may all be a mirage, but this cradle of man's dreams is still spawning them. Who knows, the dreams and the hopes of this day may well find reality among men of goodwill — and thousands of parents and children who have lived their lives in the despair and darkness of refugee camps may yet inherit the earth.

The dreams and hopes so eloquently described still await fulfillment.

Less noticed than the much publicized Arab-Israeli conflict was the plight of the Kurds. Descendants of the ancient Medes, they had waged a historic struggle for self-determination in recent decades against both the Shah and Ayatollah Khomeini in Iran. In the Machiavellian politics of the Middle East, the Shah had armed Iraqi Kurds and the U.S. had provided financial support in the amount of $16 million. In 1975 the Shah came to terms with his neighbor. About 200,000 Kurds found it necessary to flee across the mountains into Iran. Some 40,000 were forcibly returned to Iraq. Like 300,000 other Kurdish villagers, they were compelled to leave the mountain regions of the north for the arid deserts of southern Iraq. The elderly and the young died by the hundreds. News of their fate led thousands to remain in Iran under conditions of utmost deprivation.

Their leader, Mustafa al-Barzani, wrote Secretary of State Henry Kissinger: "Our hearts bleed to see that an immediate byproduct of their agreement [Iran and Iraq] is the destruction of our defenseless people.... We feel, Your Excellency, that the United States has a moral and political responsibility towards our people who have committed themselves to your country's policy." But in a choice between the Shah and the claims of Barzani's *Pesh Merga* — "those who face death" — Washington's decision was to abandon the Kurds.

To meliorate the obvious cruelty, the United States announced that it would admit 400 Kurdish refugees. IRC promptly accepted responsibility for eighty of them. They began to arrive in 1976, and among them was Barzani himself who died three years later in Virginia. In succeeding years, as handfuls were admitted, IRC continued to address itself to their needs. The problem was particularly difficult: the newly arrived Kurds had no affinity to other groups who could help them adjust and their occupational skills were hardly appropriate to American society. But they are a hardy people. Their ancestors had driven off the best troops of Xenophon and had battled the toughest warriors of European history — the Parthians, the Romans, the Mongols and the Christian crusaders. Today, in Iran, they exchange fire with Khomeini's soldiers and they remain a significant force in the Middle East. A vigorous, colorful mountain people, the 14 million Kurds who regard themselves as one nation now live under five flags — Iran, Iraq, Syria, Turkey and the Soviet Union. They will continue to demand autonomy, both from within the countries of their domicile and from their places of exile.

NEW ERUPTIONS — CZECHOSLOVAKIA

Sometimes, inexplicably, a sudden wave of defections brought "tourists" from the Baltic and Balkan states knocking at the doors of IRC offices in Vienna, Rome, Paris, Berlin, Geneva, Madrid. In 1964 IRC estimated that at least 40,000 new refugees had entered or passed through Western Europe in search of first asylum. An increasing percentage were showing a preference for remaining in Europe rather than moving on to the Western hemisphere or Australia. This was particularly true of artists. Among such persons assisted by IRC was a singer who became first soprano at the Trier Opera in Germany, and a Russian dancer who joined the Vienna *Volkoper*. One Russian musician went on to become a cellist with the New York Philharmonic.

It was now twenty years after the close of World War II, but there was still a residue. Back in 1958, the Zellerbach Commission had said of Camp Valka in Langwasser, Germany: "Nobody defends it; nobody wants it;

everybody agrees that it is an abomination. But Valka still stands." In 1964 IRC staff revisited the camp. They found the name had been changed, the stone barracks were no longer an official camp, but 678 people were still being housed there. By the end of 1965, all of the Langwasser families had been relocated by IRC's branch registered under German law as the International Rescue Committee, *eingetragener Verein*, with General Lucius D. Clay as honorary chairman and Senator Otto Bach, president of the Berlin Chamber of Deputies, as chairman.

But even when it seemed that the old slate was at last beginning to be wiped clean, a new score was being chalked up. On August 21, 1968, the Soviet Union and others among its satellites in the Warsaw Pact nations invaded Czechoslovakia to put an end to the "Prague spring" and plunge the country into a Muscovite winter. Some 50,000 Czechs and Slovaks fled to the West, ultimately finding themselves in Austria, France, Italy, Belgium, the Netherlands, the Scandinavian countries and the United States.

Of all the countries in Eastern Europe that had fallen under Soviet control in the late forties, Czechoslovakia was the most Westernized. Its national heroes, Thomas Masaryk and Edward Benes, had hoped to model their nation after the multiparty liberal democracies of Britain and the United States. Masaryk's son Jan, who with Benes was seeking to rebuild the country after the cruel years of the Nazi occupation, had been assassinated, and those responsible for his death were in turn devoured by the revolution. (As Albert Camus said, "Every revolutionary becomes an executioner or a victim.") This prologue to the 1968 Soviet assault on the liberalizing leadership of the Czech Communist Party has been described by the Russian dissident Roy A. Medvedev, who insists that he is still a Marxist-Leninist despite his cutting analysis of Stalinism in the book, *Let History Judge*. How adventurism, totalitarianism and the lust for personal power have combined with anti-Semitism and Stalinist paranoia is illustrated by the massive purge that brought death to the founders of the Czech Communist movement, including Rudolf Slansky, general secretary of the party. Medvedev writes:

The Slansky trial is worth considering in detail. We have a thorough knowledge of its mechanics, which, we may assume, were essentially similar in the other trials. The principal source is Eugen Loebl, Party member since 1931 and Deputy Minister of Foreign Trade at the time of his arrest in November, 1949. Loebl survived to win complete rehabilitation in 1963, and in 1968 published an account of his experiences. He describes the treatment that got him to the point where he would sign anything. He was forbidden to sit down during interrogation and even in his cell. He was wakened thirty or forty times a night, kept on hunger rations, and given an injection of some narcotic that weakened his will to resist. (Other prisoners were worked over by such methods as the torture of a wife in her husband's presence.) The depositions Loebl was forced to sign changed with the passage of time. First he was an agent of Tito, then of international Zionism and Israel, and finally of Slansky's underground committee. He had to memorize each of these depositions in turn, and go through rehearsals. When he cooperated, he received good food and even medical care. The whole business was directed by agents of the Soviet security organs. Loebl knew nothing about Slansky's affairs, but fear prompted him to testify that Slansky was trying to restore capitalism.[13]

Most of the defendants were shot, but Loebl received a life sentence. Later he was released and lived to tell the story. Antonin Novotny emerged as the party leader. In 1953, because of economic discontent, popular riots broke out, as they did in East Berlin and later in Poland. But the iron grip of the party could not be broken. In 1957 Novotny became president, and a mild liberalization was permitted, during which the Czechs' creative spirit seemed to find fresh release. In sharp contrast to the sodden art being produced generally in the Soviet sphere, the Prague theatre and film industry began to strike a fresh experimental note. The mood carried over into political affairs. When Alexander Dubcek succeeded Novotny in January 1968, a heady breeze began to blow as a new leadership attempted to introduce a "communism with a human face." In the course of the next few months, censorship was eased; the Slovaks gained political autonomy under a new constitution; there was even talk of eventual democratic elections.

Moscow did not wait long. The Kremlin issued its Brezhnev doctrine which says in effect, "Once a Communist country, always a Communist country." The Russians made it plain that no nation in the Soviet orbit would be allowed to soften the tenets of Communist dictatorship—and punctuated this position with a rumble of tanks and a barrage of artillery. Dubcek and his comrades were forcibly removed to Moscow, mass arrests began, and the voting feet were once more in motion.[14]

Again Europe was dotted with camps, filled to overflowing. The year 1968 had gotten off to a dismal start for people in Poland, Rumania and Hungary, as evidenced by the increased outflow. In March there had been student disorders at some of the Polish universities, inspired perhaps by the action of students in the West who were free to attack their "establishments." The Polish press, radio and television had responded by launching an "anti-Zionist" campaign aimed at driving out of the country the few thousand Polish Jews who had survived Hitler's extermination camps. Their plight was intensified in later years when the Polish government decided to use anti-Semitism as a weapon against the rebellious union movement, Solidarity, which ultimately was to be subjected to martial law. On March 8, 1981, Warsaw witnessed a government-organized demonstration that sought to label Solidarity as the product of a "Zionist" plot. By way of response, the organization deliberately flaunted its support of equal rights for Jews in meetings and in its publication *Solidarnosc*, since suppressed. For example, the issue of October 2, 1981, reported in its lead story:

The Chairman of the session asked all delegates to rise and then he announced, "With us now, in this hall, is Marek Edelman, one of the leaders of the Uprising of the Warsaw Ghetto. Today he is a delegate from Lodz." A tremendous applause followed. This time, the applause was dedicated to the heroes of the Warsaw Ghetto.[15]

The simultaneous confluence of refugees from Czechoslovakia and Poland, Cubans pouring into Spain, Jews from North Africa fleeing to France, Greeks escaping from the hardening military dictatorship of the colonels, confronted IRC in all the major capitals of Europe with awesome responsibility for individuals left adrift by the political developments in their homelands. Several thousand Czechs who had been permitted by the Dubcek government to holiday abroad were touring Austria on August 21, 1968 — the day the Soviet Union attacked. Additional thousands managed to cross the border and join them. Some 20,000 never went back, preferring resettlement in Switzerland, Canada and Australia. By the end of the year, with Dubcek and his comrades released from imprisonment in Moscow, some felt they could return. But by the spring of 1969, a deteriorating political and economic situation drove additional thousands over the border.

Again IRC mustered its resources to meet a European crisis. Unlike the situation in Hungary twelve years before, in this case the Russians did not vacillate. Their tanks moved in immediately to end the "Prague spring." A look at the geographical and political map suggested that the new refugees would have nowhere else to go but Germany and Austria. William J. Casey, then serving as president of IRC, and Leo Cherne headed for the scene. The former went to Bonn and the latter to Vienna. On learning that West Germany did not anticipate a heavy influx, Casey joined Cherne in Austria which, as events soon proved, was to become the major destination for those fleeing.

The two agreed that something might be learned by making a straightforward effort to enter Czechoslovakia, whose border was scarcely an hour's drive from Vienna. They rented a chauffeur-driven car, and, to their own surprise, succeeded in talking their way in. But scarcely a mile from Bratislava, within sight of its houses, they were suddenly surrounded by Soviet tanks, armored vehicles, motorcycles, and foot soldiers armed with machine guns. None of the Russians spoke English, which may or may not have been helpful. Cherne says that in such circumstances the soldiers are likely to be more nervous than those they stop. Not quite certain of their own responsibilities, they are afraid they may be blamed later for some misstep.

As Cherne tried to pierce the language barrier with no success, he kept asking for the officer in command. Meanwhile, his colleague, Bill Casey, sat silently in the car, reading an Allen Drury novel, until Cherne turned on him with the question, "How can you just sit there reading?" To which Casey answered, "Can you think of anything more useful I can do right now?"

Finally, a superior officer did appear, and the two succeeded in persuading him that they were simply curious tourists who had heard that something was happening and wanted to see for themselves. They were allowed to return to Vienna.

But even though the adventure had been aborted, it was not uninstructive. It helped to point up a contrast between the Czech experience and the Hungarian events: in the intervening years, there had been a dulling of conscience in the West. When Cherne had traveled the road to Budapest, there were others also on the way. The highway then was crowded with young people from the democratic countries who came at their own expense in vehicles of every description — cars, trucks, station wagons, bicycles. But the road to Bratislava had been virtually empty. Though history may repeat itself, enthusiasm does not.

Almost immediately IRC found itself responsible for 14,000 individuals. As in other such crises, the largest proportion consisted of students and intellectuals, those who had made themselves particular targets of the regime. Writers who commanded a second language were helped to find employment in publishing houses or to obtain book contracts; teachers were put in touch with academic institutions; students were given scholarships. Formats that had proved effective with the Hungarian refugees were revived — for example, the Innsbruck Social and Cultural Center which IRC had been helping to maintain ever since it was set up to serve World War II DPs and then Hungarian refugees who had fled to the Tyrol in 1956.

In this period, West Germany began to attract refugees, primarily because, unlike other countries, it granted work permits to the newcomers with little reluctance in view of a continuing labor shortage. Of some 6,000 refugees who sought asylum in Germany in 1968, about 60 percent were Czech, and most of them managed to fit into the economy. A statistical study of the 573 refugees aided by IRC's German agency, the *Deutsche Internazionale Fluechtlingshilfe*, gives some sense of the variety and composition of the refugee movements from the neighboring East European Communist countries: 54 percent of the Czechs and Slovaks were professionals and white collar workers, as against 23 percent of the Poles and 15 percent of the Yugoslavs. On the other hand, 63 percent of the Poles, 24 percent of the Hungarians and 23 percent of the Czechs and Slovaks were manual workers.

But no individual segment of refugees could be taken as typical. Their composition varied with the method of escape. IRC/Sweden, for example, found a group of escapees who had arrived on Polish excursion boats and simply walked down the gangplank to freedom. Following the August 21 *Schrecklichkeit* in Prague, no day passed in 1968 without some Czechoslovaks asking the Swedish government for permission to stay. Among them were seventy physicians for whom the Swedish National Medical Board set up special language classes. By year's end, forty-five of them were working in hospitals all over the country.

As new crises arose, the events in Czechoslovakia receded from public attention. The Soviets resumed their posture as the defenders of national independence, and even Western journalists tended to forget the shackles that had been riveted more tightly on the Czechoslovaks in 1968. But the passion for freedom continued to burn in Prague and the other major centers of Czech culture. It flared up vigorously four years after the disaster of 1968, inspired this time by the Helsinki agreement of 1975 under which the Communist nations had joined in a verbal commitment to respect the "fundamental freedoms, including the freedom of thought, conscience, religion, or belief." In January 1977, a group of 700 courageous Czechs put their signatures to Charter 77, a document demanding that the government respect the language of its own constitution and the Helsinki agreement. In quick succession, the authors issued a series of statements documenting their charge that human rights were being violated.

The government's response ranged from organizing counterstatements to imprisoning the human rights activists. Individuals were subjected to repeated police interrogations, fired from their jobs, expelled from their homes, placed under house arrest, or jailed without charges. Jan Patocka, one of the three leading figures in the promulgation of Charter 77, a respected sixty-nine year old philosopher, was subjected to two days of relentless questioning before being released in a state of complete exhaustion; he died a few days later of a cerebral hemorrhage. Vaclav Havel, the country's leading playwright, advocate of pluralism and opponent of totalitarianism, was held for four months without a trial. The London *Times* in May 1978 published a Charter document revealing that 20-30,000 human rights advocates had been jailed for an average of three months under the harshest of conditions, with wardens frequently assaulting prisoners. Among those arrested in 1978 for "incitement" were three youngsters who supported the human rights movement; the charges against them included possession of tapes made by a banned pop group in Prague. The repression made it difficult for dissidents to escape in great numbers, but in the year 1978 IRC found itself helping forty-three Charter members who had succeeded in reaching Vienna.

GREEK DICTATORSHIP

In the scramble of refugees for safety, it sometimes appears as if they must compete with each other for the attention of the world. The Russian invasion of Czechoslovakia naturally commanded the headlines, but it pushed into the background the less dramatic though equally poignant plight of other groups. While it is true that Soviet aggression has produced migrations on a vast scale, the rightist dictatorships have done their share in spawning exile populations.

In 1967, a military junta in Greece had overthrown civilian government. For six years it held power, during which democratic leaders were imprisoned and many fled. Again France became the lodestar, in great part because, for many of the intellectuals among the refugees, French has been a second language. IRC has remained sensitive to the needs of the neglected — whether they were Kurds from the remote mountain fastnesses of Iran and Iraq, Hmongs from the hills of Laos, Haitians fleeing the *Tontons Macoutes,* or Watutsis hiding from the Bahutus. The Greek exiles, as the president of the *Mouvement Franco-Hellénique* noted, were in a "truly tragic situation," ignored by a world whose attention was focused elsewhere. "It is only thanks to the International Rescue Committee," he said, "that it was possible to respond to some desperate appeals. The IRC is the only organization which has provided substantial financial assistance to numerous Greek democrats who have taken refuge in France."

The problem of the Greek refugees persisted into 1974. In January the *Mouvement Franco-Hellénique* noted the continuing state of affairs: "Not only do the Greek refugees need the help of the International Rescue Committee as much as in the past, but if feasible an increase in the relief funds for Greek refugees should be contemplated. Economic conditions in France have deteriorated so much that people in need of relief cannot possibly live on the same amounts as a year ago."

It was another example of the interdependence of the world. The war in the Middle East had produced economic repercussions that led to worldwide recession, compounding all the preexisting problems. European willingness to integrate newcomers into the society faltered, and resettlement became more difficult. IRC found itself, for example, wrestling with the problem of 216 Asian and African students who had defected from East European universities. They were helped to find asylum in West Germany.

RUSSIAN EMIGRATION

It was a hard year for refugees in general, for 1974 was the year in which hundred of thousands were fleeing their countries. Leo Cherne, IRC's chairman, recalled the enormity of the challenge that faced the organization in 1974 and 1975:

At no time have so many refugees come to our country so suddenly: 130,000 in the brief period of ten weeks. We are reminded of the exodus of 675,000 Cuban refugees to the United States; we forget that this massive emigration was spread over 15 years. We are reminded of the influx of Hungarian refugees after their revolution was crushed in 1956; we forget that only 35,000 came here, spaced over a six-month period.

Cherne was referring to the flight of the Vietnamese. But at the same time that the effort was being made to cope with that tidal wave, another movement of refugees, also from Communism, was in full swing. For a variety of reasons the Kremlin had been forced to let some people go in an unprecedented migration. Mounting internal pressure — the new boldness of dissidents; the stubbornness of Jews intent on maintaining their group identity; deepening economic problems — had combined with the pressure of world opinion. Russia's need for some kind of détente, and American imposition of a human rights price on desperately sought trade relations, began to pry open the sluice gates.

In 1968, only 231 Jews had been permitted to leave. In 1973, however, the number reached 32,049. The following year it slipped to 20,632, and in 1975 fell even further, about 50 percent lower than in 1974. During 1976 the number of departures was about a thousand a month. Then it began to inch up. In 1977 it reached 16,737, and in 1978 it shot up to 28,874. By the middle of 1979, there was hope that the number for the year would reach 50,000 — a record-breaking total thought to be aimed at winning American approval of the SALT II agreement and the loosening of the trade restrictions in the Jackson Amendment that preconditioned "favored nation" status on liberalization of emigration. But by year's end the actual total was in the neighborhood of 30,000 — a reflection of the chill that had set in as the USSR prepared to take advantage of the Iranian upheaval, a crisis that paved the way for an invasion of Afghanistan.

In the first half of 1981, only 6,628 were permitted to leave, and the numbers continued to dwindle as tensions between the United States and the Soviet Union mounted, following the crackdown in Poland against the Solidarity movement. The statistics on Jewish emigration furnish a mathematical mercury reading on the temperature of Russo-American relations.

Other nationalities, trapped inside the Soviet Union, have sought to emulate Jewish efforts to emigrate. In November 1981, a group of Germans, a handful of the 1,700,000 descendants of German settlers who have maintained their ethnic identity, actually demonstrated in Red Square with banners reading: "We want to go home." Within three minutes they were hurled into police vans by plainclothesmen and security agents. During the decade of the 1970s, some 85,000 Russo-Germans had been permitted to leave, but at the time of the demonstration it was said that 100,000 unprocessed applications by Germans for leave to go to West Germany were on file with the authorities.

By and large, however, emigration was taken under consideration only when the individual could claim some kind of Jewish origin. The Kremlin had decided, as its Polish satellite had done in the late 1960s, that Jews were the most undesirable among the nationalities that looked outward. But departure, even in the most favorable of times, was never easy. The emigrés had to surrender virtually all their possessions, taking with them only the equivalent of $100. Before exit visas were granted the applicants had to wait months or years, during which they were denied the right to work. Jews interviewed after their arrival in the West have indicated that they were subjected to personal indignities and physical abuse by the border officials.

In the first years of the emigration, most of the refugees went on to Israel after stopping over in Vienna. For these there was ready assistance from Jewish agencies. But by 1977 a new trend appeared: a majority were seeking settlement elsewhere, and a number of those who had gone to Israel were leaving after a brief period in which they found Israeli life too difficult.

Many who obtained exit visas with the stated purpose of going to Israel indicated on arrival in Vienna that they really intended to seek resettlement in the United States, Canada or Australia. Immigrants waiting for permission to enter the United States often needed maintenance and counseling on legal procedure. They included prominent dissidents — writers, artists, musicians and scientists — who had been persecuted because they were human rights advocates or because they had applied for emigration. Some of them carried with them bitter memories of discrimination against their children, for example, rejection for admission to universities, simply because they were Jewish.

From Geneva, Garret G. Ackerson, Jr., a full-time IRC volunteer leader who serves as vice-president for Europe, coordinated the activities of the staff in Rome, Vienna, Paris and Munich as they attempted to handle the new wave. Ackerson had prepared for his role in refugee work by accumulating a long record of achievement in the American foreign service during which he had been posted to Pretoria, Lima, Copenhagen, Bogota, Havana, Warsaw and Buenos Aires. In the wake of the Hungarian uprising he had been U.S. consul general in Budapest, serving from 1957 to 1960. On joining IRC, Ackerson found himself involved in virtually every major refugee crisis, no matter how distant from Geneva. If IRC representatives in Calcutta needed medical supplies, Ackerson would be knocking on the doors of European pharmaceutical houses; if the IRC surgery in Nairobi called for a piece of lab equipment, Swiss manufacturers were certain to hear of it.

Under his direction, IRC staff had become a major repository of knowledge about American and European immigration regulations. Applicants for admission to the United States who had reached Vienna were required at this time to go to Rome for processing by the European office of the Immigration and Naturalization Service. (The Refugee Act of 1980 has since enlarged the number of INS offices around the world to fifteen so that authorization is now within easier reach.) While waiting in Italy for permission to enter the United States or other Western countries, a substantial number of the Russians who had lived briefly in Israel were being put up in the seaside town of Ostia where, during most of the year, summertime apartments are vacant.

A visit to Mihail X, one of the Russian Jewish refugees housed in Ostia, then being cared for by IRC with help from the Philanthropic Fund, revealed a tidy apartment in a building occupied by fellow-refugees. All would soon be moving out temporarily as the resort season was about to begin. But there was new hope among the tenants. A hospitable Italy was allowing them to work at odd jobs so that they could earn a few lire by doing errands or delivering packages. American immigration authorities, who had been debating whether these people had lost refugee status by first going to Israel, had become more amenable and was authorizing on "humanitarian" grounds the admission of those with close relatives in the United States.

Mihail tells his story in fluent Yiddish: He was born in the town of Zetl, originally a part of Poland that the Russians had seized in 1939 and that has remained a part of the Soviet Union. In 1941 the Germans attacked the village and he fled. His parents and siblings, however, were trapped and perished in the Holocaust. From 1941 to 1946 he served in the Russian army where, he recounts, he was put in the front battle lines because he was a Jew. After the war he moved to Moscow, but in March 1973 he received an exit visa. He had no real desire to go to Israel but had to state such an intention in order to leave Russia. A year later his wife was able to join him.

All told, he spent three years working in a kibbutz and then decided to leave. He gives two reasons: coming from a cold country, he could not acclimatize himself to the hot weather of the Middle East; but more important, he felt that his wife, whose mother had been a gentile, was not fully accepted by the Israelis. He reached Rome in February 1976, hoping to enter the United States, but was told that in the eyes of the immigration authorities he had lost his refugee status.

Originally, Jewish organizations, favoring what the Israelis call the "ingathering of the people," were reluctant to assist those who had left Israel or had refused to go there. But as the U.S. immigration service tightened the eligibility requirements, some of the Jewish groups liberalized their approach. The Hebrew Immigrant Aid Society (HIAS), which had played a primary role in the Jewish migration from Czarist Russia before World War I, and the American Jewish Joint Distribution Committee, along with IRC, provided assistance.

By the summer of 1978 there were only about fifty emigrants from Israel living in Ostia, along with a larger number who had come to Italy directly from Vienna. Toward evening, the visitor could meet most of them as they congregated at the Ostia post office — as many as 400. Physical evidence reveals a tug-of-war in process: on the walls of the post office are hand-lettered signs in Russian, one inviting the Jews to a meeting under the auspices of the Israeli government, another urging them to attend a prayer meeting organized by Baptist missionaries. The conversation invariably turns to grievances past and present. "For five years," says one Russian in Yiddish, "we have lived like *Tzigainer*, but we are not sorry we escaped from Russia." Another, with the approving nods of those around him, adds, "You must go to the Soviet Union to see how bad it is there — only then can you see how it really is."

THE EXIT PROCESS

The reasons for giving up one's homeland and venturing into the troubled uncharted waters of refugee life are varied. Laraine Lippe, an IRC case worker functioning in Rome under Dr. Radovan Korach, once a Yugoslav refugee himself, and his wife, Violet, an Englishwoman whose father had served in Britain's consular service, has assembled a cross-section of reasons given by Jewish refugees for their departure.[16]

S., age 48: "I left the USSR because I wanted to be able to grow up *finally*. People in the USSR remain children. . . . They don't learn to think."

V., age 26: "We envied our distant relatives who had emigrated from Russia at the beginning of the twentieth century. Part of my interest in America is the result of being a Jew. . . . I read, when I could, Sholom Aleichem's writings about Russian Jews going to America and their lives there. We tried to figure out what made their lives so happy there, while our lives were so unhappy. . . . Perhaps it was just a case of poor relatives thinking about their rich relatives."

N., age 41: "My decision to leave was of a religious nature. It was not possible to live in the USSR having an open heart to the spiritual level of life. Most people live only on the material plane and do not imagine that there is anything else to life. . . . Their interests are narrow. Communism takes care of the material needs of the people only, but what about their spiritual needs?"

V., age 40: "I did not leave the USSR for political reasons. I was never imprisoned; I lived rather well in the USSR. I had good work in my field, good pay as an engineer (200-300 rubles a month), my own apartment. In fact, when my boss found out that I intended to leave, he asked me, startled, 'But what else do you want? — You have everything!' Yes, I had everything, but I did not leave for material reasons. The USSR is a very big, but also very unhappy, country. I felt trapped there; but there was no place to go. I only live once. I want to know other cultures, the whole world, other psychologies, art, technology."

B., age 30: "I left the USSR for every possible reason there is: material, moral, cultural — everything."

Lippe concludes that even those who did not suffer direct persecution themselves lived in a state of perpetual inner turmoil. Theirs was "a flight from constant fear," with personal overtones dictated by economic, political, professional, personal, religious and psychological pressures. The more intense the fear, the more likely it was that the pressures were left unarticulated or even completely repressed.

The very process of leaving was fraught with peril. Soviet law allows applications for exit visas and travel permits, but a fee of 500 rubles is required, more than twice the monthly earnings of a well-paid worker. The average Russian engineer earns about 120 rubles, the average doctor 100. Another penalty that must be paid by the applicant is the renunciation of his Soviet citizenship, followed by loss of employment during the waiting period before his departure is finally authorized — a matter of months and even years. But other hurdles must be overcome, as Lippe indicates on the basis of observing more than 1,500 families during a four-year period of IRC work:

In order to make an application to leave the Soviet Union, a person must have received an invitation (*vyzov*, in Russian, which means literally "a call") from a real, or invented, relative or friend in Israel. There are some who receive the necessary *vyzov* directly from the U.S. as they have relatives who have promised to aid their support there. Most, however, must rely on the Israeli *vyzov* to leave the USSR. Some families may be sent as many as 15 *vyzovs* before *one* reaches them, and can then be used as the basis for an application. During the early years the procedure was even more complicated than it is now. An education tax had to be paid to the Soviet government for any advanced degrees obtained. This often involved some 1,300 rubles per diploma, an enormous amount of money. If a family had more than one member holding a higher degree, they could not even begin to think of leaving unless they had a great deal of money, or else borrowed the necessary sum from various known money lenders in their particular city, with the agreement that the debt would be repaid to another specified person already living in Israel.

In addition to the financial hurdles, a potential emigrant had to obtain a *characteristika* from his or her employer, i.e., a reference attesting to the good work and character of the applicant. An employer could easily block a worker's emigration by refusing to grant the document. Also required was a Statement of Permission to leave the USSR signed by the parents of the applicant. This was necessary even if the applicant were 55 years old, and himself a grandparent! This requirement is still enforced, since during these last three or four years I have interviewed several men whose wives had to be left behind as they could not receive parental approval. In two such cases, the wives later rejoined their husbands: one woman's elderly mother who had refused the permission died, while the second woman persisted until she found a town where the Statement of Permission was not asked for, and reapplied from there.[17]

Applicants for exit visas find themselves the victims of ostracism as "anti-Soviet persons." The *otkazniks*, those turned down, are virtually excluded from the society. Their protracted unemployment may lead to charges of "parasitism" under laws like the decree adopted in 1961 by the Presidium of the Supreme Soviet of the Russian Republic which reads: "Able-bodied citizens of full legal age (18) who do not want to fulfill the most important constitutional duty — to work honestly in accordance with their abilities — and evade socially useful labor, leading parasitic lives, are subject to eviction to localities especially set aside for that purpose for a term of two to five years. Their property acquired not by labor is subject to confiscation. They must be made to work at the place of their new domicile."[18]

One instance that was given notoriety in the West was the case of the distinguished physical chemist, Dr. Veniamin G. Levich, who applied in

1972 for permission to emigrate to Israel with his family. In 1975 his sons were permitted to depart, and he was informed orally that he would be allowed to join them in a few months. In 1977 he was still in Moscow, no longer a professor at the university, barred from his laboratory, his lecture hall and classroom, and shunned by his former associates. Emigration officials claimed that his past research had made him privy to state secrets and therefore he could not be permitted to leave. Describing his predicament, Dr. Levich told the *New York Times*: "As a Jew, I felt a strong sense of identity with the people who fought the Six-Day War. . . . But beyond my original reasons for wanting to leave, it has now become a question of professional life and death. I may be the property of the State, but if I am never again permitted to work, what use am I to anyone?"[19] Eventually, in 1978, after worldwide protests on his behalf, Dr. Levich was permitted to leave and was welcomed as a visiting professor by the City College of New York.

The Russians who made their way to Rome from Vienna found three VOLAGS waiting to help: the Hebrew Immigrant Aid Society (HIAS), which concentrated on counseling Jews on immigration requirements and helping them process the inevitable paperwork; the American Joint Distribution Committee, which addressed financial needs and distributed aid; and the International Rescue Committee, functioning as a completely secular organization, which cared for "mixed" families who did not really consider themselves Jewish or who had pretended to be Jewish in order to get a *vyzov* from fictitious relatives in Israel. IRC/Rome has processed many such. One complicated situation involved a gentile couple who had divorced each other in Russia in order to marry Jewish spouses and thus qualify for emigration. On their arrival in Rome, IRC faced the problem of reassorting the couples with appropriate divorces and remarriages.

The most absurd instance of a gentile permitted to leave as a Jew was the case of Andrei Amalrik, the historian, who arrived in Vienna with an entry permit for Israel. It was imposed on him by the authorities even though he was not Jewish and his wife, who accompanied him, is a Muslim Tartar. They hoped to settle in the Netherlands, but Amalrik was fated to die in an auto accident on the way to a "Helsinki watch" meeting in Madrid organized by Freedom House.

In general, those of non-Jewish faith who reached Vienna found voluntary agencies awaiting them: for the Russian Orthodox, the Tolstoy Foundation; for Baptists, Evangelicals or other Protestants, the World Council of Churches. Persons of Jewish birth were first met in Vienna by representatives of the Jewish Agency where efforts were made to persuade them to engage in *aliyah*, immigration to Israel. By the end of the 1970s, a majority were seeking other destinations. The reasons they gave were lack of identification with Judaism or things Jewish; a comfortable familiarity with English in contrast to a complete ignorance of Hebrew; the absence of economic opportunity and the constant menace of war in Israel.

"WATCHMAN, WHAT OF THE NIGHT?"

The year 1979 started out with some promise for Jews in the Soviet Union who were intent on leaving. The creaky door did seem to be opening wider, as the aging Kremlin leaders grew more weary under the pressure of economic difficulties at home. In reality, the foreign policy of the country was pushing more aggressively for expansion in Africa and Asia. Kalashnikov rifles were being brandished in an increasing number of places, and Moscow's Cuban mercenaries were swaggering through the bush from Ethiopia in the northeast to Angola in the southwest. In Southeast Asia, the Soviet surrogates in Hanoi sent their war-hardened troops against the Khmer Rouge, cementing the three dominoes — Vietnam, Laos and Cambodia — and threatening a fourth, Thailand, which had become a major haven for refugees from Communism. And soon the Kremlin's conflict with Red China was exacerbated by Peking's foray into Vietnam.

With so much turbulence abroad, the secret police at home stepped up their activity against the human rights activists who had been emboldened by the luminous provisions of the Helsinki agreement to which Moscow had assented. At midyear, Major-General Pyotr Grigorenko, a Red Army hero of World War II, now a spokesman for the human rights he believed he had defended in the war against the Nazis, reported to the outside world on the fate suffered by his fellow-members of the "Helsinki Group." In July and August 1979, in the Ukraine alone the toll was as follows:

Six members sentenced to long prison terms, one of them exiled to the West on being released.

Two members of a family, father and son, arrested by the Ivano-Frankivsk KGB.

Ukrainian writer Oles Berdnyk, already held for five months by the Kiev KGB, fighting back with a hunger strike.

An engineer, serving as a correspondent for the Helsinki group, sentenced to three years in a "strict regime camp."

A philologist, four months after his arrest, still awaiting what passes for a trial in the Soviet Union.

A well-known composer and a prominent Ukrainian writer "tortured to death behind KGB walls," according to the statement of General Grigorenko, writing inside the Soviet Union.

Two artists "killed under suspicious circumstances."

And added Grigorenko: "The Government reveals its colonial character even more brutally in the Crimea. The Crimean Tatars, who have returned to their homeland, are being evicted from their own homes. Their houses are being razed. They are sent into exile, and mass arrests and imprisonments are taking place. They are unable to find work of any kind, and the threat of starvation is very real. Some, having lost all hope, commit suicide. Thus, in order to protect his family, Musa Mamut immolated himself by fire. Three other Crimean Tatars, the breadwinners of their families, committed suicide."

For his courage in describing such appalling facts, General Grigorenko was to pay a heavy price. He himself fell victim to the new technique of persecution invented by Stalin's successors: incarceration in a psychiatric institution. To its everlasting shame, official Russian psychiatry, without a murmur of protest, allowed its practitioners to diagnose political dissenters as suffering from "paranoid delusional (*bredevoi*) development of the personality." Such was the judgment on General Grigorenko by physicians who gave as their reasons "that he was active, gave loud voice to his opinions, was abusive, insulted the voluntary police, calling them fascists and Black-Hundreders, that he drew a crowd around him, to which he spoke about himself, shouting that he would fight for democracy and truth." For this he spent some five years in Soviet mental hospitals, surrounded by criminally insane and violently psychotic patients. Allowed to leave Russia on a temporary exit visa, he was denied readmission despite his insistence on returning.[20]

The international psychiatric fraternity at first maintained its own mental iron curtain around the behavior of its Soviet colleagues. In 1971, the annual congress of the World Psychiatric Association refused to act on the data that Vladimir Bukovsky had assembled and that had resulted in his imprisonment for "anti-Soviet propaganda." But in 1977, the blatant behavior of the Soviets led to a straightforward denunciation by the WPA.[21] In 1982, the American Psychiatric Association considered withdrawing the status of "Distinguished Fellow" from Andrei Vladimirovich Snezhnevsky, the dean of Soviet psychiatrists, who had discovered a new mental ailment, "sluggish schizophrenia," whose major symptom was disagreement with Soviet policies. A mere handful of Soviet psychiatrists dared to condemn the prostitution of their profession to political ends. Dr. Semyon Gluzman was imprisoned for refusing to endorse such a diagnosis.

Only a few of the brave men and women who comprise the Helsinki Watch in the Soviet Union are able finally to come out of the darkness; most of them are forced to stay on and resist. For those among them who are religious, there is special comfort in Isaiah's words: "Go, set a watchman, let him declare what he seeth." The biblical dialogue continues: "Watchman, what of the night?" and the answer: "The morning cometh. . . ."

OF DISSIDENCE AND CAVIAR

Perhaps the most amazing phenomenon of the twentieth century is that the enormous power of the totalitarian state has not been able to suppress the aspiration for freedom that wells up in the human soul. It was logical to expect that Soviet literature, which had produced a Dostoyevski, a Tolstoy, a Turgenev, a Chekhov, would not lie fallow forever even though the sickle of Communism was constantly poised to cut off the first stalks of dissent and intellectual pioneering.

Totalitarians maintain their power over the people by standing astride the network of communications — the press, the electronic media, the lecture hall, and the postal channels. Nevertheless, *samizdat* literature — in manuscript, carbon copy or mimeograph — finds a ready, if limited, audience in the Soviet Union. Even without access to the state publishing houses and the official journals, literary reputations surface. But there is retaliation. Alexander Solzhenitsyn, Nobel prize-winner for literature in 1970, was forcibly expatriated and deprived of his citizenship. Andrei Sakharov, the nuclear physicist who received the Nobel Peace Prize in 1975 for his human rights activity, has been a frequent prey of the KGB: in 1978 his home was ransacked and documents, including a manuscript on "The Human Rights Movement in the U.S.S.R. and Eastern Europe — Its Goals, Meaning, and Difficulties," were seized. Thereafter, he was exiled to Gorky and cut off from foreign contacts with colleagues and friends. Despite their isolation, he and his wife successfully staged a hunger strike in 1981 to compel the authorities to grant a visa to their daughter-in-law who was thus enabled to join her husband in the United States.

Others identified with the monitoring of human rights in the Soviet Union were jailed: a sampling of the names now well known in the West includes Orlov, Scharansky, Ginzburg, Bukovsky, Daniel, and Sinyavsky. Absurd pretexts were used to justify arrests: Feliks Serebrov was sentenced for carrying an expired work-pass (the very existence of such documents is a commentary on the ignominious condition of the working class in the Soviet Union). The painter Oscar Rabin was dealt the same fate as Valentin Turchin, the scientist, except that the latter was released from prison and permitted to emigrate. In 1980 Aleksandr Podrabinek, a young paramedic who was among the first to publicize the government's policy of confining dissidents in mental institutions, was sentenced to five years of "internal exile" for slandering the regime. But his efforts led to international condemnation of Soviet Russia's conversion of psychiatry into a form of torture.

The ferment of dissidence generated by the intellectuals soon began to spread among the workers. Stirrings of genuine unionism became visible. An unemployed miner named Vladimir Klebanov urged workers to form genuine unions outside the government-controlled company unions. The regime reacted by imprisoning him in an insane asylum, and his two associates in the movement, Vladimir Svirsky and Mark Morozov, were placed under arrest.

This spate of activity, however, had its effect on world opinion. Intellectuals in many countries pulled back from cultural exchange programs with the Soviet Union on the ground that their Russian colleagues were being abused. In the presence of this groundswell, some prominent figures were permitted to leave — physicists such as Veniamin Levich and Sergei Polikanov, and the dissident philosopher Alexander Zinoviev. But for the lesser known freedom fighters, the odds in most cases are insuperable. Yet they carry on. Their *raison d'être* has been well summarized by one of their number, a young Pole named Adam Michnik, a leader of KOR, a group that inspired and later merged with Solidarity. He had been in and out of prison ten times before the imposition of martial law in December 1981. "Every act of courage," he says, "saves some measure of freedom, dignity and truth. It helps to rescue some values without which no nation can exist."

A goodly number of the dissidents who did succeed in getting out turned to France, the classic home for literary and artistic exiles. There IRC/Paris has taken some of them in tow. Among the more prominent arrivals was Dr. Mikhail Shtern who was made the target of a particularly vicious slander campaign by the Soviet government when he indicated his desire to emigrate. Though the official press charged him with extorting money from his patients, most of them spoke up courageously in praise of the care and concern he had given them. Another case that attracted international attention was that of the distinguished mathematician, Leonid Plyushch, who, like so many others during three and half decades, climbed the long flight of creaky stairs at 35 Boulevard des Capucines. Before he received his exit visa, he had been punished for three years by incarceration in a Soviet mental institution. On his arrival in the West, he gave a firsthand account of the "horror of the madhouse where political prisoners were mixed with criminally insane murderers and rapists and harassed by Soviet doctors." In the year of his release, 1976, another prominent refugee, Russia's foremost sculptor, Ernest Neizvestny, was among those assisted by IRC. That year more than a thousand of the Russians who reached Western Europe — Vienna, Rome, Paris, Munich and Brussels — made their way to IRC's open doors.

Such Russian escapes were long and painful. By contrast, some East Europeans found a route that was relatively simple — defection. Thus the *New York Times* reported the case of a twenty-eight-year-old Hungarian Ph.D. whom it described as "a familiar figure in literary and intellectual circles in Budapest." In New York for a brief visit, he decided that he liked the freedom of his new surroundings. The *Times* writes:

Mr. Follinus told no one of his plan to defect. That morning he simply walked out of the hotel, took a taxi to the International Rescue Committee and asked for help. The committee put him in a hotel, gave him money, steered him through the channels at the Immigration and Naturalization Service, where he was given refugee status, and helped him to obtain a Social Security card.[22]

This steady brain-drain is characteristic of a trend in all totalitarian regimes. Original minds cannot permanently acquiesce in the rigidities of dictatorial discipline. Whether they are writers, scientists, musicians, painters, ballet dancers, self-fulfillment requires a freer air to breathe.

Throughout the world, countries that offer asylum reap a golden human harvest that enriches their culture and economy.

It was with some amusement and considerable pleasure that the IRC staff read in *Time* magazine of September 7, 1978, about a Russian refugee named Serge Doroshov whom IRC had assisted to resettle on the faculty of the University of California at Davis. In the United States only one year, Doroshov, "who had helped develop the advanced Soviet aqua-cultural, or fish-farming programs," had "discovered a way to speed up the sturgeon's maturity cycle from 15 to 20 years to four to six years. At Davis, internationally renowned for its research into food and wine, officials expect to receive federal money for a $500,000 pilot hatchery." *Time's* correspondent, who rated Doroshov's caviar as 8 on a scale of 1 to 10, licked his chops over the result — especially since he noted that the price would be about half that of the imported caviar.

MAKING THE TRANSITION

For many of the Russian refugees, adjustment to the freedom of the Western world has been difficult. Tasks that are ordinarily considered matters of personal initiative in non-Communist countries seem threatening to those who grew up in a totalitarian society. Thus IRC staff members report that helplessness seems to overcome many such refugees. Dr. Marcel Faust, who directs IRC's Vienna office, recounts a typical conversation:

"You will have to go to the consulate at Innsbruck if that is what you want," says the case worker.

"But where will I get permission to go to Innsbruck?" asks the Russian refugee.

"You do not need permission. You simply buy a ticket at the railroad station."

"But how will the ticket agent know that I am permitted to go to Innsbruck?"

"He will ask no questions."

"But what documents will he want me to show him? In Innsbruck, how will I get into the consulate?"

And so on.

Such hangovers from the Soviet past dog every step of the way to ultimate resettlement — the acquisition of lodgings, tracking down scattered belongings, registering for English classes, applying at consulates. Even after a permanent home has been provided, the individual may suffer severe culture trauma when he discovers that the government will not automatically assign him to an apartment (or a room within an apartment) and to a job. The uncertainties of a free economy, even though he receives assistance from voluntary agencies like IRC and the various religious groups, present a constant challenge, at least during the first years.

On the other hand, there are those who react to their liberation from the stifling atmosphere of totalitarian society with an explosive burst of self-assertiveness, even aggression. Simon Markish, son of Peretz Markish who was among the group of noted Yiddish writers executed by Stalin in the anti-Semitic frenzy of 1952, has tried to explain the state of mind of some refugees. His words describe the attitudes of Jewish emigrés of whom he is one, but they are often true of others. Subjected to a series of indignities by government bureaucrats when they apply for emigration — months of waiting, loss of job, threats of imprisonment — these refugees come to feel that they are entitled to special consideration once they make it to the outside. It is well for those who grant asylum to recognize the reality that Markish describes:

But even if everything has gone smoothly the emigré has had to overcome his terror of the all-powerful state and authorities, a feeling which is incomprehensible to anyone in a free society. And overcoming that terror is a feat in itself. Every emigré, moreover, has to tolerate all manner of humiliation and loss to the very last, at the various customs checkpoints — and not only in the USSR; if he goes by train, he is openly robbed by the Poles and the Czechs — and his sufferings acquire the nature of virtues in his mind. He is a hero and a martyr, and therefore has a legitimate claim to retribution.

Judging as he does by Soviet standards, he is not capable of understanding that his retribution begins from the moment he steps off the train or the plane in Vienna. Everything that comes his way he accepts as his just dessert. This is not only because he is a hero and a martyr, but because everything has already been paid for by the American Jews. And Israel has nothing to do with it, he owes nothing to Israel. Hence the fierce aggressiveness of some emigrés in their very first moments on Israeli soil, in the immigration hall at the airport.[23]

For many, there is additional pressure awaiting them as they confront the immigration authorities of Western countries like the United States. Some will be admitted as "conditional entrants," so certified by the Attorney General because they have fled Communist countries in fear of racial, religious or political persecution. After arrival they are subject to investigation for a period of two years, and if no negative information has been uncovered they may then remain permanently. Five years after their conditional admission they are eligible for citizenship.

Entry into the United States may also be effected on the basis of a procedure known as the Parole Program, administered by the Attorney General. This provides for quicker admission — sometimes a matter of weeks or just a couple of months, unlike conditional entry which may take as long as two years. Thus, in December 1977, the United States authorized the admission of some 5,000 Soviet refugees in order to alleviate the pressure created by the exhaustion of the available conditional entry visas.

To be sure, other countries, like Canada, Australia and New Zealand, also beckon, especially to professionals. Doctors and dentists who are admitted into the United States are required to pass the examinations of the Educational Council for Foreign Medical Graduates before they may practice—a difficult undertaking for many of the Russians, whose training in their native country was comparatively superficial or narrowly limited. In Australia, however, they are permitted to practice for four years after their arrival before they are subjected to examination. This is due to a shortage of skilled personnel in the country, a fact that has reversed a long-standing policy of limiting refugee admissions.

Particularly difficult is the situation of the "handicapped" refugee. The term covers not only the individual suffering from physical, mental or emotional difficulties, but hardship cases involving advanced age, an excessively large family, obsolescent skills and even a criminal record. To meet those contingencies, the United Nations High Commissioner for Refugees has devised a special humanitarian program called the "Ten-or-More" Plan. Participating countries are asked to take ten or more such cases a year; some, like Norway, insist on a modification under which they take a hard-core case only once every three years. Because the refugee's file is submitted to only one country at a time, and is then passed along from country to country until there is an acceptance, many years may go by before resettlement. Laraine Lippe describes two such cases in the files of IRC/Rome, both of them single men who had already moldered for three years in Italy:

They were both victims of persecution by the Soviet regime for their dissident activities. As a result of this torture, they have been maimed, each in his own way, and cannot function normally. One man is a chronic alcoholic, and has been in an Italian psychiatric hospital for over one year just so that he may be taken care of adequately. The other, an intensely high-strung young man of 31, was jailed from the age of 17 until 27 for having distributed anti-Soviet propaganda. Having been confined to prison camp during the years when one ordinarily receives professional training of some kind, he has never had the chance to acquire a trade (though he taught himself English during his prison years, and speaks it quite competently). He speaks constantly, many times without thinking, and since his three years in Rome have only embittered him, he offends those he meets, lashing out at the ills of Western life and of its people.

The irony of the situation is that the longer no solution can be found for either of these two men, the more accentuated and ingrained their handicaps will become, thus making it that much more difficult to resolve their cases in the future. We only hope that one of the countries approached will eventually offer them a new home.[24]

In the presence of such psychic wounds, it may be well to recall again the words of Albert Hirschman describing his underground days as Beamish in IRC's Marseilles office during Hitler's occupation of France: "I've always thought that what we did for the refugees . . . resembled the obligation of soldiers to bring back their wounded from the battlefield, even at the risk of their own lives. Some may die. Some will be crippled for life. Some will recover and be the better soldiers for having had experience of battle. But one must bring them all back. At least one must try."

VIII

Hurricane in the Caribbean and Latin America

Tyrants breed tyrants. Fulgencio Batista fell in Cuba, and his place was taken by Fidel Castro.

During the first days of 1959 the "July 26 movement" inherited the reins of government in Havana, and Castro proclaimed that free elections would soon be held. But on May 1, 1961, he announced that Cuba was a "socialist country" and there would be no need for elections.

The mask had dropped. On December 2, 1961, he declared that "I absolutely believe in Marxism." To the consternation even of Kremlin apologists, he gloated that he had always held Communist views but had concealed them lest he lose popular support during the fight for power.

Since his achievement of mastery over Cuba, Castro has forced his countrymen to submit to the foreign policy of the Soviet Union. He has converted his island into a military base for potential Russian aggression against the United States and Latin America. In the 1970s he took on the role of international swashbuckler, sending Cuban soldiers to serve as shock troops for the leftists in the fratricidal civil wars of Africa. A revolutionary soldier of fortune, his depredations have carried him over the continent — from Ethiopia in the north to Angola in the southwest — thus generating new flows of refugees into countries like Zaire and Kenya. By 1978 some 25,000 of his soldiers and "civilian advisors" were operating in areas from Mozambique to the Horn.

Twenty years after seizing power he still found hundreds of thousands of his subjects unabashedly straining against the prison gates he had erected. In one of the weirdest episodes of refugee history he concocted a witches' brew of escape and expulsion, much like that of his comrades in Vietnam, only his was offered to the world with smirks and bombast.

At the very outset of his regime, he seized church schools, expelled priests from Cuba, purged the universities of independent minds, and subordinated the trade unions to government control. He jailed some 50,000 Cubans for "political crimes" and executed more than 1,000 people, including 22 American citizens. By the beginning of 1963, some 255,000 refugees had fled, all but 35,000 of them receiving asylum in the United States. Another 200,000 Cubans were in possession of visa waivers and were desperately waiting for some method of transportation. In short, about half a million Cubans had decided to make their break for freedom. Eventually Cuba would lose a million of its people — more than 10 percent of its estimated 9 million. Many who had looked to Castro as their savior from Batista fled in disillusionment from the new tyranny. They had learned that Castro's revolution was nothing less than a fraud on freedom.

It took only six months for Castro to reveal that he had no respect for constitutional government. On July 17, 1959, Dr. Manuel Urrutia Lleo, first president of Cuba after Batista's overthrow, was removed by Castro for publicly expressing opposition to Communism. That event alone was enough to signal the direction of the new regime. It was therefore no surprise in 1962, three years after Castro's conquest of power, when the world learned that Russian troops were digging in on the island and that missile launchers were being built.

THE FIRST WAVE

The disillusionment of Cubans who had fought with Castro against the Batista dictatorship came very quickly, as IRC was among the first to discover. The ouster of Dr. Urrutia from the presidency and his house arrest in July left no doubt that IRC's services would be needed on this new battlefront. But even before that, one month after Castro's triumphant entry into Havana, two IRC leaders independently went to Havana to see for themselves what was going on. One was Bill Fitelson, who had been among the original founders of IRC in the early Hitler days. A lifelong student of revolutions, Fitelson was not content to study Castro from a distance. Within a few days of his arrival in Cuba, Fitelson met some of Castro's close lieutenants who had already made the break with what was fast becoming a totalitarian movement. Although fearful of imprisonment or execution, they nevertheless spoke frankly of their concerns.

By chance Fitelson ran into his old friend and associate Leo Cherne who had also come to explore the situation. The information they shared made it clear to them that IRC would face a challenge right on the nation's doorstep that would last for several decades.

The turmoil in Cuba had accelerated the ferment of resistance to both rightist and leftist dictatorships in the Caribbean. In September 1959, IRC's Board of Directors formally offered its aid to democratic refugees from Castro's Cuba, Trujillo's Dominican Republic and Duvalier's Haiti. Since then, refugees from the Trujillo terror who were aided by IRC have been able to return to their land — a result yet to be achieved in the other two countries. Several IRC-aided Dominicans played important roles in the democratic governments established in 1962 and thereafter.

The Caribbean Refugee Program was IRC's answer to the greatest burden it had yet encountered. Not even the Hungarian uprising of 1956, which produced 180,000 refugees, could match the magnitude of the task now presented and that would be exceeded only by the Bangladesh, Southeast Asian and Afghan crises. For the United States, this was a new experience. Never before in American history had this country been the point of original asylum for such large numbers of political exiles. Because this was the first tidal flood of refugees created by a Communist government in the Western hemisphere, America could not afford to fail. All Latin America was watching.

Only ninety miles from Castro's island-tyranny, Florida was the logical first port of call. That state has since borne the brunt. The refugees came by all routes and through a variety of ruses:

A Cuban airline pilot stowed away on a commercial plane. IRC helped him with clothes, expense money, and finally a job. Working and saving he was able to buy plane tickets for his family to join him.

A distillery worker, refusing to serve in the "Revolutionary Militia," decided with seven other men and two women to escape the imprisoned island. In a small outboard motorboat, they navigated for Key West, but sixteen miles from their destination they ran out of gas. Caught in a gale, they were blown out to sea, losing sight of land. Next day, their food and water gave out. On the third day, after abandoning hope of rescue, they were sighted by a merchant ship that radioed the Coast Guard to bring them in.

Not all of the voyagers were so fortunate. On March 2, 1963, eighteen refugees set out from the southern coast of Cuba in the direction of Jamaica. Eighteen days later the boat drifted onto Grand Cayman Island. Seventeen of the passengers were dead — among them six women and five children.

The hulks of small boats, now rotting on shore in Key West, were only the predecessors of another, more numerous, weaponless armada that would cross the South China Seas some fifteen years later. The sequel would be a "freedom flotilla" out of Mariel Harbor.

The files of IRC case workers are replete with the stories of average men and women who risked their lives rather than remain under Castro's tyranny. Many of them had fought alongside Castro against the Batista dictatorship, only to find themselves betrayed into the hands of the Communists. Nevertheless, retaining their love of freedom, they refused to yield to disillusionment and cynicism.

Through the 1960s, two major outlets for Cuban escapees were Mexico and Spain, the only countries that maintained air service with Havana. Spain was liberal in granting visas to Cuban nationals and therefore, despite its own tyranny, became a way-station to freedom. As late as 1968, IRC's Cuban caseload in Madrid was more than 5,000. In addition, some 7,000 new arrivals were given initial support by IRC with funds from the UNHCR.

Emigration counseling and processing became major activities, with some 2,500 leaving Spain under IRC auspices.

Of particular concern to IRC were the unaccompanied Cuban boys, most of them under age fifteen, who were sent to Spain by their parents. The impetus for their flight was the fact that conscription in Cuba takes fifteen to twenty-seven-year olds, and they are therefore forbidden by the Castro government to leave the country. Most Cuban emigrés who were permitted into Spain were expected ultimately to rejoin relatives who had already made their way to the United States. For others, however, the detour via Spain was more perilous than a ride in a plane cabin. In 1969, IRC president William J. vanden Heuvel described "one man's compulsive hunger for freedom that led him to conquer almost impossible odds." Vanden Heuvel wrote:

Statistics tell us that the world refugee population amounts to 17,226,915 people. But the story of one person can say more about the meaning of being a refugee than any number of astronomical statistics.

On June 4, 1969, such a story was widely reported in the nation's press. Two young Cubans hid in a wheel compartment of a jet airliner going from Havana to Spain. The temperature during the nine-hour flight was 40 degrees below zero, and oxygen was almost non-existent in the tiny, unpressurized and unheated wheel pod. Doctors say that ordinarily a man can retain consciousness for about three minutes under such conditions, and live for only a short while thereafter.

When the plane approached Madrid, one of the Cuban youths fell into the sea and vanished. The other one dropped from the wheel casing when the plane landed — unconscious but alive. In a few hours he regained consciousness and eventually recovered from his ordeal — a case which doctors termed "an unparalleled and unexplainable miracle." When asked why he had taken such an incredible risk, the new refugee replied, "I was looking for a better world and a new future." He asked repeatedly and tearfully whether he would be sent back to Cuba.

Not long thereafter, this seventeen-year-old Cuban, Armando Socarras Ramirez, was in the United States, sponsored by the IRC.

Many of the Cubans first reached Mexico, then crossed into the United States to make their way to Miami where friends and relatives had preceded them. Ignorant of American law, they lived in terror of deportation to Cuba, until steps could be taken to legalize their status as political refugees.

AMERICAN HOSPITALITY

In Florida, America learned at firsthand the kind of problem that European cities like Vienna had experienced when the refugees poured in. The pressure on Miami was compounded when Castro applied Hitler's technique of using would-be refugees as a source of income. People were permitted to leave legally, provided they agreed to turn over all their property to the regime. At the gangplank of ships and planes, refugees with exit visas were stripped of wristwatches and wedding rings before being allowed to board. Arriving in Florida with no possessions but the clothes on their backs, with no money, no place to stay and no jobs, their only hope for making a new start in life was the hospitality of the American people.

Governmental action was based on the premise that voluntary agencies would do the basic resettlement job. In the Miami area, federal policy provided for direct refugee relief payments up to $100 monthly per family. The local school system was reimbursed for the additional pupil load, and a small sum was provided for those who sought to move out of Miami.

America's volunteer organizations once again filled the gap. As a nonsectarian agency, IRC joined hands with the religious groups in providing immediate relief, followed by more permanent aid: finding jobs, reuniting families, speeding resettlement and integration in other localities. Some idea of the achievement can be gathered from these figures: as of April 1963 the government had officially listed 162,210 Cubans in Miami; of these, 35,623 were registered with IRC. Of the 58,000 refugees moved to other parts of the United States, 13,000 were resettled by IRC.

In a twenty-two-month period, the record shows that IRC/New York alone carried a caseload of more than 20,000. In addition, it operated the only clothing center for Cuban refugees in the area, which in the same period provided apparel without charge to more than 30,000 men, women and children. It addressed itself directly to one of the most disturbing aspects of flight — separation from one's family. As IRC pointed out:

People, exposed to the danger of police repression, frequently must leave alone. Yet once they reach safety, reunion with their families becomes their foremost aim. Often it was not the heads of families who preceded their wives and children into exile. Thousands of Cuban families sent their children to the United States because they did not want to expose them to Communist indoctrination in Cuban schools. And sometimes the variety of escape opportunities took one family member, who may have sought asylum in a foreign embassy in Havana, to South America, while another availed himself of a Jamaican or Spanish visa, and a third made use of a U.S. tourist permit.

Under such circumstances, family reunification must always be a major objective.

WHO ARE THEY?

"What kind of people do they think we are?" Winston Churchill once said during the war against the Nazis. What kind of people were these who were ready to break all ties with the world they had known and, amidst the greatest uncertainties, undertake to rebuild their lives from the ground up?

The Communists had a ready answer: the idle rich. In actual fact, however, this wave of refugees came from every stratum of Cuban society. A random sampling of 750 IRC cases revealed this distribution:

Professionals	15.6%
Proprietors, businessmen, executives, administrators	12.4
Small store owners	6.8
White collar and sales personnel	27.0
Skilled & unskilled workers, including agricultural workers	35.0
Farmers	2.0
Others	1.2

An independent study by Stanford University produced similar results.

Influenced as it was by its initial experience with refugees from Hitlerism, IRC has continued to maintain its special interest in refugee-professionals. In the Cuban exodus, it was in a position to render a major service to doctors. With special foundation grants it helped them qualify for practice in the United States and find employment in American hospitals.

Like most refugees, the Cubans believed their exile would be short-lived. The unsuccessful invasion of the Bay of Pigs in 1961, however, had a sobering effect in many ways — on the refugees and on the American people. It meant that the chain of Cuban events was by no means complete. The following year Khrushchev matched President Kennedy's misadventure by undertaking his own ill-fated enterprise and attempted to make Cuba a potential launching pad for Soviet missiles. The memory of those events still creates shudders among those who lived through the crisis.

In later days, there was to be some satisfaction in the negotiation of an exchange of Cuban prisoners for U.S. medical and other supplies, and the subsequent expatriation to the United States of a number of political prisoners. IRC had played a part, along with General Lucius Clay, in working out the ransom program on the basis of "commodities for people." A photograph taken at the time shows Senator Jacob Javits, New York Mayor Robert Wagner, and Leo Cherne standing atop a Cuban-bound tractor.

Even while Castro was mouthing the slogans of détente in the latter 1970s he took no chances. Twenty years after his ascension to power, he still could not allow the slightest measure of free expression. Herbert L. Matthews, who has written sympathetically of the Communist regime in Cuba, nevertheless concedes that "the worst that can be said of the revolutionary regime . . . is that the practice of holding political offenders in prison and rehabilitation labor camps goes on, year after year. Even Franco in Spain — and when he was in power — Papadopoulos in Greece . . . gave amnesties to political prisoners. Fidel Castro has not given one in sixteen years."[1]

In the late 1970s, however, even before the centrifugal outburst of 1980, Castro decided to let some of his captives go. He released 3,900 "counter-revolutionaries" and gave them visas to leave with their families. But in May 1977, as President Carter and former Venezuelan President Romulo Betancourt reported in separate statements, Cuba still held between 15,000 and 20,000 political prisoners.

Among them were people like Huber Matos, a schoolteacher who had held the highest officer rank in Castro's rebel army. He had led the successful assault on Santiago, Cuba's second largest city, and Castro had rewarded him with appointment as military governor of Camaguey province. In the months that followed Batista's overthrow, Matos watched with horror the growing power of the Communists. He expressed his concern directly to Castro but his protestations were futile. Resigning his post, he wrote a restrained and dignified letter to Castro in which he said: "I do not wish to become an obstacle to the Revolution, and I believe that, having to choose between accommodating myself or getting out of the way in order not to cause any damage, it is honorable and revolutionary that I go."[2] He went — to the Cabaña Fortress prison. Two days after his letter was sent, on October 21, 1959, he was arrested and charged with treason. Castro himself took charge of the trial as public prosecutor, concluding the ritual proceedings with a seven-hour denunciation that was broadcast over the radio. Matos was condemned to twenty years' imprisonment, a sentence he completed in 1979 after suffering the atrophy of one shoulder and the paralysis of his left arm during his incarceration.

The kind of country that Cuban refugees flee from is made amply clear in a letter to the London *Times* that Matos was able to smuggle out of his dungeon in his nineteenth year of imprisonment:

No arbitrariness or vileness of Castro and his system can surprise me. I am more than used to suffering, to my own flesh and spirit, mistreatments and vexations in these forgotten and tortuous paths of offence to the human race that are called Castro's jails, but there is something I cannot understand. Why isn't this denounced, loud and clear, day after day in the streets of Caracas, in the universities of Mexico, in the pulpits of churches in Scotland, on French television, in the Canadian press, in the United Nations?[3]

Some voices were raised, those of the International Rescue Committee and of Amnesty International. American intellectuals became concerned. Irving Howe, literary critic and social analyst, a member of IRC's Board of Directors, wrote: "No pleas from human rights groups, no whispered embarrassments from foreign friends who regard Castroism as different from other Communist dictatorships, nothing has thus far been able to soften the heart of the ruler in Havana. The sick and broken Huber Matos must serve the full 20 years — such, apparently, is the dispensation of the new society."[4]

As Matos's sentence neared its end, rumor had it that he would never be released. Public opinion throughout the world began to be heard. Journalists, clergymen, legislators and labor organizations, especially teachers' groups who felt an affinity with a fellow-teacher, called upon Castro to release his prisoner. Soviet dissident Vladimir Bukovsky, who had been among those traded by the Russians for Chilean prisoners — a cynical transaction deemed profitable by the two dictatorships — addressed an appeal to Castro in Matos's behalf within forty-eight hours of his own release from Vladimir Prison. Matos's wife and his children who had grown up without a father rallied support for his release. In December 1976, young Huber Matos, Jr., traveling through Latin America to plead his father's cause, was the target of an assassination attempt in Costa Rica. His car was struck six times by bullets and two shots wounded him, one in the shoulder and the other just between the liver and the heart.

At first, Castro remained adamant in the face of world opinion. Ben Bradlee, executive editor of the *Washington Post*, spent seven and a half hours with the Cuban leader to raise the issue of human rights. He came away with this conclusion: "These suggestions outrage Castro, and if one single message came ringing loud and clear through these conversations with Castro, it was this: 'Don't talk to Castro about human rights.'" Nevertheless, even the stone walls of Communist obstinacy can be breached by practical political considerations. With Russia seeking to shore up the shaky structure of détente, Castro finally decided to seek some accommodation with his North American neighbor. He was met with a statement by Secretary of State Cyrus Vance that Matos's "release . . . would help the process of normalization of relations with Cuba" and that the "release of these political prisoners as a gesture of goodwill and as a humanitarian act would be one indication that Cuba is seriously interested in starting a dialogue with the United States."[5]

Matos was released, and his first act was to call for the freeing of those who remained behind in the prison cells. Organizations like Amnesty International, Freedom House, the Inter-American Commission on Human Rights, the Inter-American Association for Democracy and Freedom, as well as the IRC, publicized the grim facts. In 1977 IRC said: "Estimates of the number of prisoners vary from 5,000 to more than 50,000. The 5,000 figure has been given by Castro himself and by other Cuban officials. It is obviously understated. No dictatorial government has ever given a correct account of its opponents in prison. Yet even this figure in proportion to Cuba's population is higher than the number of political convicts in the Soviet Union in relation to Russia's population." The statement went on to describe the variety of prisoners: "There are separate camps for draft evaders, military personnel, Jehovah's Witnesses, homosexuals, and a 'special plan' for peasants, dissatisfied *campesinos* who have run afoul of Cuba's policies in the agrarian sector." The Organization of American States, in a 1976 report, described the treatment visited on women prisoners:

Las tapiadas. This name is given to female political prisoners in Cuba incarcerated in cells where they are isolated for violations of the iron discipline of the prison. In these cells, there is no light and almost no water. The prisoners are kept naked in a very confined space. Their food is served to them at different times of day, so that they lose all notion of time. They do not receive visits or letters. They remain there, in a state of confusion, for weeks at a time.[6]

No matter how effectively they monopolize the means of communication, totalitarian states cannot conceal this behavior from their own people. Indeed, they need the dissemination of news about the regime's brutality as a major bulwark of power. One result is quiescence among the population; another is the encouragement of flight.

Such was the "new" Cuban society from which men, women and children were escaping, often at peril of their lives. Newspaper readers continued to find items in the back pages of their dailies like this Associated Press dispatch dated August 1, 1978:

A Cuban handyman pulled from the sea near the Florida Keys said he used pingpong paddles as oars and fought off sharks and dodged Cuban Navy patrols during the seven-day journey to freedom on two inner tubes.

The ordeal of Ramon Estevez Cordova, 27, ended when he was rescued Sunday by the crew of a pleasure boat about five miles off the coast of Key Largo. He said he has been trying to reach New York, where he thought his sister lived.

Mr. Cordova said he had launched his makeshift craft—two inner tubes bound together and covered with burlap—on July 23 after having planned his trip for a year. He said Cuban Navy boats and helicopters searched for him the first day but could not see him because of high waves. However, he said, sharks and hunger were his worst problems. . . .

Coast Guard officials at Key West said they received a radio call from a German cargo ship about a man aboard a raft Saturday night, but a search of the area turned up nothing. Mr. Cordova later told officials that he refused to be picked up by the ship because he feared it was a Russian vessel.

Such episodes required that IRC stand ready to meet the needs of those who did succeed in making it to land. Waiting to receive them was an IRC staff headed by Roberto Fernandez, a Cuban refugee himself, whose work of rescue has taken him on perilous but necessary journeys. It is estimated that more than 10 percent of the island's population has now found shelter in the United States, a fulfillment of the pledge made by President Johnson in 1965: "I declare to the people of Cuba that those who seek refuge here will find it. The dedication of America to our traditions as an asylum for the oppressed will be upheld."[7]

A MASS BREAK-OUT

That pledge was put to its severest test in the spring of 1980. A series of Castroite mistakes, from which he attempted cleverly to recover, lifted the mask so that the world could see clearly that Fidel had not succeeded in tamping down the sparks of freedom still seeking to catch fire after twenty years of Communist rule. A veritable tidal wave of humanity, reaching a total of more than 125,000 refugees, swept out of Cuba, generated by a subterranean eruption that had long been heating.

The first of these mistakes was Castro's decision to allow previous emigrés to come back to visit relatives on the island. The reason for this change in policy was not a sudden conversion to bourgeois respect for the family but the need for foreign exchange that the tourists could bring — an estimated $10 million a year. But the *"gusanos"* or "worms," as they had been called, now rechristened "butterflies," brought with them also accounts of what life was like on the free mainland of North America. Penniless when they fled, they were now able to demonstrate that in the United States the newcomer could still work his way up. They bore personal witness not only to their own success but to the fact that they had been able to make a contribution to the country that had welcomed them. Of this generation of refugees, the Miami *Herald* had written:

The United States, and particularly South Florida, have gotten a significant boost from the Cuban refugees. During the early, violent upheavals of the Castro revolution, most Cubans of talent and accomplishment fled Cuba to avoid a very real persecution. Their skills brought a new dimension to life [in Miami]. They filled in many cracks in the economy and offered new vitality. Now, they are part of us, brothers in the community, and their contribution should be honored.[8]

This mutuality of reward was the message the Cuban-Americans carried back to those who lived in the repressive austerity of Castro's dictatorship. No dynamic, protracted oratory, no slogans displayed in garish posters and billboards, no tendentious broadcasts, could conceal the contrast. Even the most fanatical Communist had to recognize the personal cost he paid to the regime, even if he thought the price was necessary: the mandatory attendance at rallies and the day-long speeches by Fidel; the halter on his own tongue; the cruelties visited on those who dared to think their own thoughts; the "volunteering" to cut sugar cane; the long queues waiting for monotonously packaged staples; the perennial meat shortage; the military service of sons in the far-off jungles of Africa, and word-of-mouth news of the casualties; the loss of privacy even in one's home, to which the Committee for the Defense of the Revolution, the block committee, could gain access with no warrant; the denial of choice — for example, the student interested in literature and philosophy ordered to study accounting. There were achievements to which the regime could point, such as better health care, paid for, however, by an exorbitant tax on personal freedom. The mere appearance of the tourists from "imperialist North America" and the gifts they brought to relatives were a powerful rebuttal to much of the propaganda emanating from the press, radio and television. The resulting contacts were bound to excite a desire for escape.

Castro's second mistake was to increase the severity of government pressure in the hope that naked force could contain faltering work performance, declining productivity, deteriorating transportation, inadequacies in the public health system, and mounting waste. The economy had been paying for the extravagance of military adventures in foreign lands. The country's political influence, to be sure, was growing: in Grenada, Nicaragua, San Salvador, Guatemala, Angola, Ethiopia.

But even though he had just presided over a conference of ninety-two "unaligned" nations in Havana, Castro had found his old admirers increasingly suspicious of his role as an agent of the USSR. In October 1979 his brother Raul had delivered a lengthy radio address admitting serious domestic failures. In December, Fidel himself was forced to acknowledge the hard economic facts to his puppet National Assembly as a prelude to what he hoped would be a campaign of rededication. Recognizing that Communist policies in Cuba, as in China, had failed to achieve production goals, he said: "We do not intend to do traumatic things; we do not intend to unleash a Cultural Revolution here." The resulting shakeup nevertheless produced a new wave of arrests, estimated in the thousands, and initiated widespread changes in administrative personnel. But these tactics could not provide an answer to unemployment, inefficiency, lack of incentive, shortages and unfavorable balances of trade. An increasing minority of Cubans were now ready to face the realities and rush for the exit once the latch was loosened.

Castro's third mistake was his decision in April 1980 to punish the Peruvian government because it persisted in upholding the distinctive Latin-American doctrine of asylum, which provides for safe-conduct out of the country once a fugitive has reached sanctuary in a foreign embassy. A more than tacit agreement on this policy has existed throughout the Caribbean and South America, a product of the many political upheavals, coups and revolutions. Several of the countries have formalized their understanding in a Latin-American Convention of Asylum. Even military juntas with little regard for human rights have honored the tradition and granted *salvos conductos*, or safe-conduct passes, to those who gained sanctuary in foreign embassies. Other nations, though respecting the invulnerability of diplomatic premises (with the notorious exception of Iran), have not always authorized free departure. Thus, Cardinal Mindszenty spent fifteen years living in the American embassy in Budapest; as this is written, seven Russian Pentecostalists have been living in the basement of the United States embassy in Moscow since June 1978.

Because the Peruvian embassy refused to surrender a handful of Cubans who had crashed their way in, Castro ordered the withdrawal of the policemen usually stationed at the gates. In the light of the Iranian occupation of the U.S. embassy in Teheran, this step seemed to imply a threat of mob action. Instead, 10,000 Cubans used the opportunity to fill every available inch of space in the unguarded embassy grounds. From all over the island, the discontented headed for Havana in the hope that they would be able to climb the walls to freedom. No sanitation was available, and the sedate mission soon became a "foul mass of excrement and mud," as one journalist described it. Improvised shelters sprang up on the lawns and under the trees as the days crawled on in a stalemate between the governments.

Those seeking entry had to fight their way through lines of Communists shrieking vile epithets — *escoria*, meaning scum, seemed to be the favorite. With almost obsessive repetition, the thousands inside the embassy were denigrated as homosexuals. Some onlookers paused to jeer and then jumped the wall to join the defectors. A taxi driver taking journalists to the scene denounced the would-be refugees; the next day they recognized him inside.

One woman described her family's first unsuccessful attempt to reach the sweltering Peruvian sanctuary. Her brother, who had made his way to the United States years before, had returned to rescue them in a preview of what was later to become the freedom flotilla; he had been captured, killed and his body returned to his native village as an object lesson to all. Drawn to Havana by the new developments, she was stopped at the embassy gates, beaten over the head with electrical cables, a truncheon other victims have described as popular among Cuban Communists. Children were subjected to the same treatment as the police looked on indifferently.

World opinion was not slow to recognize the significance of these events. The *Washington Post* said editorially: "The incident at the Peruvian embassy in Havana is as close as Cuba ever gets to a free election. For nothing but the hope of leaving — a hope that, if frustrated, would leave them vulnerable to the state's vengeance — these people were ready to abandon their whole stake in their homeland and take a chance in a foreign land. The incident casts a rare, revealing light on the 20-year record of Communist Cuba, so often portrayed by sympathetic visitors as a proud and plucky little country that plays David to the imperialist Goliath and provides working mothers with good day care to boot." Peru, Costa Rica, Ecuador, Spain, Canada and Belgium declared that their doors would be open to some of these courageous Cubans.

THE FREEDOM FLOTILLA

The United States, which had been admitting a steady stream of Cubans all along, announced that it would take 3,500 of the embassy squatters whose total now numbered about 11,000. Before this new upsurge of rebels, in the first eight months of 1979, IRC alone had registered for resettlement in the United States a total of 1,546 Cubans out of 2,768 arrivals in Spain.

After the long years of worldwide protest against Castro's refusal to amnesty political prisoners, some headway had finally been made. IRC had been in the forefront of the pressure. In the fall of 1978, intent on reopening commercial relations with non-Communist countries and particularly the United States, Castro had begun to release a limited number of politicals. The first group consisted of women who were permitted to leave for Venezuela. In November 1978 the U.S. Attorney General announced an agreement with Castro that would bring 3,500 political prisoners and their families to the United States at a monthly rate of 400. But action had been very slow during the early months of 1979. Few were actually being admitted. In concert with other organizations, IRC urged the government to expedite the flow. By the end of the year about a third of the eligibles had been resettled, many of them through the IRC office in Miami. During the first quarter of 1980, another 800 arrived with their families.

Now the drama of the Peruvian embassy, headlined around the world, made Castro turn to measures he had not considered before. He decided to treat homeopathically the disease that he himself had caused. Shrewdly he reasoned: If you can't recork it in the bottle, pour out all the contents. His political sleight-of-hand would divert attention from his defeat at the embassy. By declaring that anybody who wanted to leave was free to do so if boats came from the United States for them, the onus would be on the Americans.

Cuban exiles were assured officially that they could arrive by sea and take their relatives, a promise that turned out to be a shameful lie. The strategy worked precisely because it seemed unlikely that any formal government, even a Communist one, would expose itself so nakedly. And it worked also because America's policy response was at first nonexistent, then contradictory, and finally too improvised to be efficient. Nevertheless, however one calculates the costs in human tragedy, it is clear that on balance Castro lost. More than 125,000 Cubans did make their way to freedom in the United States. Hugh Thomas, author of *The Spanish Civil War* and *The Cuban Revolution*, summed up what must be the ultimate verdict of history: "The recent flight of refugees from Cuba must be the most vivid condemnation of a Communist system since the Hungarian revolt in 1956."[9]

More than one kind of heartbreak was suffered in the process. Families were deliberately sundered, much as the Pol Pot regime had done in Cambodia. At first Castro approved an airlift to Costa Rica, but called it off after 600 Cubans had been flown to San Jose. A shrewder device, he decided, was to promise relatives in the United States that they could make the crossing from Florida to a designated port where they would be allowed to pick up relatives. Motorboats, sailboats, pleasure craft of all kinds, shrimpers, scows, headed for Mariel, twenty miles from the capital in an evacuation that resurrected memories of Dunkirk. At one time there were 1,300 boats in the harbor waiting for the relatives whose names had been provided to the authorities. Cuban corvettes of Soviet manufacture policed the scene, their guns poised ominously.

Back in Havana hundreds of people lining up at the Swiss embassy, which handles American affairs, after being told that freedom was within their grasp were beaten by *porras*, thugs armed with chains and iron rods. The houses of Cubans who had indicated they wanted to leave were surrounded by members of the local Committee for the Defense of the Revolution, chanting abuse, cutting off water and utilities, smashing the windows with a shower of refuse, hanging the inhabitants in effigy, plunging them into darkness and terror.

At anchor, the rescue boats waited for days and weeks, denied permission to depart and forced to buy provisions at extortionate rates. Then came the final turn of the screw: instructions from the government that the boats could not leave with the families they had come for. At most they could take one or two relatives but would have to fill up to the gunwales with strangers from the Peruvian embassy in some cases, unidentified *escoria* in others. Many of the Cuban-Americans who had come to Mariel, trusting in Castro's word, had made great sacrifices to reunite their families, selling their cars, mortgaging their homes, emptying their bank accounts to pay for the charter. Now they had to participate in heart-rending debate over which family member would go on to freedom and which would remain under Castro.

It will be many years before the full details of this saga of the sea can be compiled: the dismemberment of families in Mariel Harbor; the Coast Guard rescues necessitated sometimes by bad weather and sometimes by the ineptness of landlubbers who ran risks to rescue loved ones in unseaworthy craft; brushes with the law as U.S. immigration policy oscillated between the approving and the punitive. A seamy side of the story that will not be forgotten is the commercialization that intruded—the price of a thousand dollars per passenger demanded and received by some entrepreneurs, one of them the captain of a large fishing boat who reportedly collected $75,000. But the inspiring aspect of those days was the host of volunteers who made the run from Miami to Mariel out of a deeply felt desire to help fellow human beings achieve a new life. One of these was Anthony Drexel Duke, a member of IRC's Board of Directors, who gave this firsthand account to the organization:

Feeling strongly that this build-up of would-be anti-Communist refugees constituted a significant crack in the armor of Communism's prime Western hemisphere show-case, my son John Duke and I sailed on April 23rd on his 38-foot sailboat from Miami to Cuba, via Key West. In checking out of the country we were informed that in accordance with new U.S. policy going into effect that day at 11 A.M. we would be fined $1,000 a head for each returning illegal immigrant, that is, each person coming back with us not in possession of a valid visa, and that the boat would be impounded.

My judgment was that the trip was worth taking from an informative standpoint and to assist refugees from Communist tyranny. Our experience proved out. Two Cuban-Americans came as passengers, hoping and trusting with heartbreaking sincerity to return with 25 family members. This was not to be.

We sailed on a 15-knot breeze across the straits all night, seeing the lights of many large and small boats blinking off in the distance all along the way. The following afternoon we entered Mariel harbor about 25 nautical miles west of Havana. There, immigration and military officials came aboard a few hours later and told us that we could take on 30 to 40 refugees from the Peruvian embassy, and 2 or 3 family members. They told us to anchor out in the harbor amid approximately eight or nine hundred other vessels of varying descriptions, and to await further instructions.

On the third day at anchor, Duke reports, an 80-mile-per-hour squall hit the harbor, sinking many small boats and driving others onto the rocks. Four people were killed and many others injured. His own hull suffered damage when a ninety-foot shrimper was blown across his anchor line. After seven days of "lies and deceptions by Cuban officials," the Dukes decided that there was little hope and urged their passengers to agree to a departure. But the circumstances were far from promising. "One boat tried to leave without refugees," according to Duke. "On that particular day no official Cuban policy dictated Yes or No; yet she had her bow blown off by a Cuban gunboat. Her crew were picked up and put on other vessels in our fleet." With hundreds of additional boats coming in, the Cubans were allowing only five or six to leave. Rumors spread to the effect that Castro was planning to keep the boats as hostages to compel the U.S. to surrender Guantanamo.

Duke himself attempted to radio the State Department directly to urge clarification of U.S. policy, to send a hospital ship plainly marked with a red cross, and to urge people to stop coming in view of the fact that Castro was not allowing the retrieval of family members as he had promised. Once the hoax had become clear to relatives who had made the trip, they were being harassed in various ways — compelled to linger on in Mariel until food and money had run out, capriciously denied permission to depart, and finally forced to take out strangers, leaving behind the people for whom they had come.

Most devastating was the experience of Cuban-Americans who had informed parents, spouses, siblings, cousins, that they were coming to bring them to the United States, only to find their hopes brutally crushed. Some, in violation of Cuban law, went ashore and disappeared — never to return to their boats. Those who sailed home empty-handed feared that they had multiplied the dangers confronted by relatives whose names had been submitted to the Havana authorities. No wonder that so many "crossed the line," as the flotilla people called it, and made the desperate effort to effect individual rescues. Duke says: "Our passenger, Carlos, who lives in Miami, made a last contact with his mother, who was not permitted to return to her job or home once she announced her intention to leave with us. Her end is unknown." Carlos had to be restrained physically by his shipmates, literally tied up, to prevent him from "crossing the line."

Once again it was demonstrated that the Communists were amenable to the payment of ransom, as was Hitler in Germany when the wealthy were able to buy their way out. East Germans have been literally purchased by the Bonn government. In Vietnam, the boat people report, a formal system of payment, especially by the ethnic Chinese, created a veritable mart in human merchandise. One man, Duke says, paid $80,000 to Cuban Communists to come away with twenty-six relatives. Duke himself finally departed, but with none of the people his passengers had expected. "It is quite apparent," he noted, " that very few family members are coming out. Castro is carrying out his hoax by emptying his jails as well as sending people who just plain wish to leave. There are unknown quantities behind this whole drama." And then he proceeded to ask questions that will not be answered until that day in the future when free inquiry is again permitted in Cuba:

"What is happening to countless family members who thought they were going to leave on this boat lift, but couldn't?"

"What has happened to those Cuban-Americans who couldn't resist 'crossing the line' to see their families?"

"How many people have drowned in the straits coming and going?"

Nevertheless, no matter how much Castro peppered the departing hundred thousand with those he wanted to expel, the facts demonstrate how widespread is the desire of Cubans to escape the Communist paradise of the Caribbean. Among those brought in by Duke were workers and middle-class people — a tailor, a hospital dietitian, a sailor, an instructor in the military. Some had been political prisoners who still bore the scars of their imprisonment and who related incidents of brutal treatment.

THE MIXED RECEPTION

The American media did not hesitate to reveal the flaws in U.S. policy. Throughout there was indecision, the ambivalence of wanting to help Castro's victims coupled with fear of the "undesirables" who had been forced on the rescue fleet. Moreover, not having any firm lead from Washington, public opinion, already distressed by the economic recession, was reluctant to accept the newcomers. News treatment, as is almost inevitable in such situations, stressed the sensational. A thousand refugees quietly studying English are less newsworthy than a handful of teenagers rioting in a camp where bureaucratic and often justifiable delays are holding up their departure.

Yet the overall record, despite administrative blunders, stands up well when one considers that there had been no time for preparation in handling this unprecedented influx. In most cases of mass migration, screening is possible. Even in the first wave of Cuban arrivals in the 1960s, the airlift was accomplished after some measure of individual inspection. In most situations, checking has been possible in the country of first asylum. Castro had deliberately made this impossible. With characteristic cruelty he had sought to label all of the departing Cubans as criminals and homosexuals. The tactic was effective because he had seen to it that these "undesirables" were made part of a "tie-in sale" of the human commodities in which he deals.

Nevertheless, the most objective data available show that on balance — in a situation that Castro had tried to unbalance for propaganda purposes — the evacuation had been another plus for the free world. At the first Dunkirk, too, there had been serious losses, but the rescue of Britain's 300,000 troops was a *sine qua non* for the eventual victory against fascism. If the United States had written off the Cubans clamoring for escape, it would have damaged the very idea of asylum that Castro had placed under siege by his stance at the Peruvian embassy. While there was disappointment at the ineptitude with which the challenge was met in the United States, both on the policy and the administrative levels, the statistics are impressive. At least 120,000 Cubans did break out of the prison walls. On their arrival, most of them in Key West, less than 50 percent went into refugee camps; the others found relatives waiting for them on the dock and were cleared within a day or so of their arrival. By September 1980, three months after the boatlift had ended except for a continuing trickle, some 20,000 — about 15 percent — were still in the four refugee camps. By November it was down to 6,900.

To effectuate prompt resettlement, the government had assigned a given caseload to the various voluntary agencies on the basis of choices made by the refugees themselves. Some had preferred the assistance of the religious groups — specifically the Catholics, Lutherans and Protestants generally. IRC, as the leading secular organization, received a caseload of about 15 percent. Considering that the very nature of the situation required improvisation, both the government and the VOLAGS had a remarkable degree of success. Each individual had to be identified, investigated and cleared by health authorities, immigration, the FBI and, in some cases, the CIA. For a goodly number the procedures took as long as six weeks; for those whose credentials were suspicious, it would take longer. Before a refugee could depart from the camp, a sponsor had to be found.

Often the prime reason for delay was difficulty in locating a relative whose address was unknown to the refugee or whose whereabouts were identified merely by the name of a city. Elizabeth Landreth, an IRC vice-president who had worked with Cubans in the previous migrations, went to Eglin Air Force Base in Florida as a volunteer. There, among other tasks, she functioned as a one-woman Missing Persons Bureau. Her major resource was the police departments in various cities and local communities. The cooperation and ingenuity were extraordinary. "Cops are the best," she said. "They know where to look. Elmhurst, Rego Park — I know 'em all by now. A man in the Stamford Police Department made just one call and found the woman I needed — it turned out the girl I was helping was a long-lost niece this woman had been trying to find."

Such efforts were supplemented by other IRC volunteers. Mrs. Andrew Goodman, a board member, and Sophie Gimbel rallied financial support. Dolores Smithies Leviant alone raised $150,000 in Miami and New York. A major role in the process was played by leaders of the American-Cuban community, many of them former refugees who had integrated themselves into an effective ethnic group within the national culture. In a one-night "telemarathon," they raised $2 million for the newcomers, to be distributed by IRC which allocated the proceeds among all the agencies. The Spanish press and radio throughout the country broadcast names and brought relatives together after the lapse of years. Eager to get out of the camps, some Cubans found it possible to "rent a cousin."

IRC, like the other agencies, concentrated on establishing contact with relatives and sponsors. A statistical report by Barbara Nagorski, coordinator of IRC's Cuban campaign, dated August 11, 1980, suggests the degree of success with which the voluntary agencies were meeting the challenge. The partial figures indicate that out of a total caseload of 7,488 at four of the refugee centers — Eglin, Chaffee, Indiantown Gap and McCoy — IRC had found sponsors for 5,390, of whom 4,368 had already departed for resettlement or to Miami where they were to await departure for their ultimate homes. Indicative also are the data that show where they went. Miami, of course, was first, followed closely by New Jersey, then California, next New York, and finally a sprinkling going to Puerto Rico and Massachusetts.

Acceptance of refugees in large numbers inevitably puts a strain on local resources. Miami was complaining as Cubans began to pile up in the Orange Bowl where temporary facilities had been installed. Many of these refugees had been cleared but sponsors had failed to appear. The fumbling administrative machinery in Washington found it difficult to implement the ideal that President Johnson expressed in 1965 on signing the new immigration act ending the national origins quota system: "All who seek refuge here will find it." The federal government had stated that 75 percent of the welfare funds laid out by the states on behalf of the refugees would be reimbursed, but in a period of budget-cutting the funds were not forthcoming. Nor were promised food stamps. Social services formerly available were now under constraints. Cuban-Americans who had gone to great expense to bring in family members, or who had taken in strangers on the assumption that help would be provided, now had to shoulder the economic burden by themselves.

The voluntary agencies like IRC, which were entitled under the regulations to partial reimbursement, found that assistance was drying up.

President Carter's Coordinator for Refugee Affairs, Victor Palmieri, notified the VOLAGS in June 1980 that there would be a per capita grant of $300 for refugees resettled after June 19, and for those released before June 19 a subsidy for "employment counseling and referral services" computed on the basis of $100 per refugee. The actual costs were much higher, but even these amounts were not forthcoming as the State Department could find no budgeting source. Instructing IRC's local offices to proceed nonetheless with Cuban assistance, Charles Sternberg wrote: "I know from long experience that such plans are chancey and long in materializing. So we must tighten our belts before we loosen them."

To compound the difficulties, episodes of rioting involving frustrated youths in centers like Fort Indiantown Gap in Pennsylvania, or by provocateurs and the misfits of Communist society that Castro had planted, aroused great public concern. By June 1980 about 700 of the more than 125,000 refugees had been identified as possible criminals subject to deportation, if there were any place to which they could be sent. But the tension created by this small minority was bound to reflect on the overwhelming majority of bona fide refugees, even though only a relative handful were committing violent acts. At Indiantown Gap a riot had resulted in injuries to sixteen Americans and forty-two refugees. Five of the Cubans were seized and charged with responsibility. People living near the base began to talk of arming themselves with shotguns against the possibility that the refugees might break out. Despite heavy pressure from the excitable, the town board of supervisors finally voted down proposals for organizing a vigilante force. Instead, Pennsylvania Guardsmen were deployed near the base.

In general, according to IRC staff in the various sites around the country, U.S. personnel stationed in the refugee centers had displayed great consideration in dealing with their charges. The Red Cross had provided many volunteers who were intelligent and sensitive. English classes were opened quickly to help the Cubans prepare for a new life. Movies and other entertainment sought to alleviate the boredom of waiting. Food was good and crowding was avoided, though the living quarters consisted of the kind of wooden barracks used by American soldiers. Every effort was made to show that people cared. Yet there were flaws, some of which could have been avoided by better organization. For instance, communication between the authorities and the refugees sometimes failed, and the complexities of the paperwork and the processing machinery were often left unexplained.

Castro had done his utmost to confuse American public opinion. Controlling who was free to leave and who was doomed to stay, he had deliberately sent out a high proportion of blacks, thinking to play on a putative American racism. Actually, in the United States there was little concern with, certainly no public discussion of, the ethnic mix of the newcomers. Ironically, there was no suggestion that the high percentage of blacks among those expelled as "undesirables" bespoke a Castroite racism. What was noteworthy was the contrast with prior waves of Cuban refugees. The educational level was much lower; though a result of Castro's selectivity, it did little to confirm the reports of Cuban successes in education. It was clear that Castro had made a determined effort to prevent the flight of professionals. There were fewer teachers and engineers than in previous emigrations from the island. One physician who did get aboard at Mariel had pretended to be a worker; he carried his medical diploma in his shoe. Some of the refugees reported that there had been a large number of professionals among those in the Peruvian embassy. According to these sources, such individuals had been told that they had safe-conduct to go home and then leave for Mariel, but many were not heard from again. A high proportion of those who did make it proved to be skilled or semiskilled workers.

The political reactions in the United States were not uniform. With a national election approaching, both the administration and its adversaries kept a careful eye on the gyrations of public opinion. President Carter, after vacillating between an open-arms policy and cautious restraint, finally dropped anchor on the activities of the freedom flotilla. He warned of strict enforcement of penalties for bringing in further refugees and even ordered the impounding of boats after a fixed date. Some 270 commercial fishing vessels were actually seized, causing financial losses to their owners; 430 private boats were also impounded. Court action made it possible for the administration to relent, in line with its own basic sympathies. The result was also made easier by the fact that President Carter's Republican opponent, Ronald Reagan, had unqualifiedly supported the admission of the Cubans. To resolve quickly the status of the new arrivals, the President ordered that they be classified as "asylum-seekers" rather than refugees. The distinction, as IRC hastened to point out, was a significant one: it meant that the Cubans would be entitled under federal regulations only to food stamps, and not to welfare allotments.

It would be a long time before all the ripples of the boatlift ran their course on the American scene. As late as November 1981, the country was startled to learn that two Episcopal priests in New Orleans, who had hired a World War II submarine chaser rechristened "God's Mercy," and who had brought in 402 Cubans, were convicted of violating the Trading With the Enemy Act; it was charged that their activities had been motivated by profit. A nation troubled by economic recession and high rates of lawlessness in the inner cities could not view with equanimity the inevitable difficulties involved in absorbing an alien population.

Public opinion remained perplexed. Though the "undesirables" and potential troublemakers among the refugees could not have numbered as much as 5 percent of the total, fear of unemployment and crime were reflected in the opinion polls. Gallup reported that 62 percent believed the government "should not allow Cuban refugees to live in the U.S." and only 38 percent favored their admission. The figures in Dade County, Florida, which includes the Miami area, were even worse. According to a *Miami Herald* survey, 73 percent of the non-Latin whites believed that the new-comers would be "bad for Dade or more bad than good." Yet the polls also showed that a majority of non-Latin whites, 57 percent, believed that the impact of Cuban immigration over the last twenty years had been "good for Dade County or more good than bad" while a minority, 33 percent, took the contrary view. The attitudes of blacks tended to be more negative; only 50 percent expressed approval of the past record while 47 percent were dis-approving. Of course the Latins registered an overwhelmingly affirmative view, with 94 percent supporting the past record and favoring the new immigration.[10]

Particularly troubled was the City of Miami. The state of Florida on the whole found itself burdened with a new population that could not yet be self-supporting. When national budgetary policy in the Reagan administra-tion turned against federal aid for welfare and entitlement programs, Florida found itself overwhelmed. During the latter part of the Carter administration, at least one White House adviser, sociologist Amitai Etzioni, later university professor at George Washington University and director of its Center for Policy Research, had urged unsuccessfully that the federal government leave the refugee problem to the states, to the VOLAGS and to the larger agencies like the Red Cross, the United Way, the YMCA, and so on. Later, in line with its political philosophy, the Reagan adminis-tration did move in that direction.

In the meantime, public opinion in communities like Miami was being sharply aroused by rising crime statistics that put the city at the head of the nation's crime roster. Those concerned with refugee resettlement pointed out that Miami's problem could not be attributed wholly to the refugee population, though the historical fact is that overcrowded immigrant com-munities have had a high incidence of crime during the period of accultura-tion. Miami, however, has been bedeviled particularly by its location as a major port of entry for the drug trade from South America, a factor un-related to the refugee problem.

Perhaps most important in arousing public fears was the impression created by the printed and electronic media. Dr. Etzioni, summarizing his experience as a "Senior Adviser" to the White House during the Carter administration, concludes, despite the rejection of his basic recommenda-tion, that the handling of the Cuban refugee challenge was quite successful. Simultaneously the government and the VOLAGS had to provide assistance for the Indochinese, the Cubans and some 12,000 Haitians who were arriv-ing at the same time. He also notes that the VOLAGS did a remarkable job in arranging for sponsors and in moving the refugees into permanent settings. He writes:

Ironically, the failures of the voluntary resettlement process, rather than its successes, made the headlines. For instance, a *New York Times* headline, dated December 18,

1980, read: "Many Cubans Remain Hard to Place in U.S." The story reported that about 8,000 of the 125,000 Cuban refugees were still in camps and in prison. It also noted that many of the "resettled" refugees had problems with their initial sponsors. But the reporter's assertion that many were "at loose ends on the street" was not substantiated. Indeed, most who had "first sponsorship" problems were subsequently resettled elsewhere, either through second sponsors, or by making it on their own.

Other newspapers showed the same kind of misplaced emphasis. A *Washington Post* headline, dated February 10, 1981, read: "Resettling of Cuban Refugees Is Proceeding at a Slow Pace." The story concerned one Luis Valladares who was "finally" on his way to a sponsoring family, "joining the 120,000 Cubans who have been resettled in the last several months." Another 4,750 therefore remained unsettled. Slow? Well, maybe — but what is the right pace for settling 125,000 refugees, especially when the ones remaining in camps were especially hard to place because of criminal backgrounds, handicaps, and the like? . . .

In the case at hand, the press emphasized the situation of the few Cubans remaining in the camps rather than the vast majority who were resettled, making it seem as though most were *not* taken care of for long periods of time.[11]

With public opinion being addressed in this fashion, and with the awareness that Castro had indeed included undesirable elements in his Mariel manipulation, it was no surprise that legislation surfaced in June 1980 seeking to put a tight lid on the number of refugees to be admitted annually. Parliamentary maneuvering and compromise, marked by valiant efforts on the part of Senator John C. Danforth, blocked a move that might have ended America's reputation as a haven for the oppressed. But the vote was close: 51-43.

Yet even in the areas carrying the heaviest part of the load, powerful voices spoke up. Clergymen reminded local communities of their moral obligations. Business leaders like David A. Wollard, president of the Southeast First National Bank of Miami, spoke of the immediate problems created for Florida by the influx of Cubans, especially in view of already overburdened educational facilities and a housing shortage. "But," as he told his fellow-citizens, "in ten, fifteen or twenty years, we shall see that the net result of this new migration will have been beneficial." Economists were quick to point out the value of the new human resources, particularly for local businesses like the garment industry and for the agricultural sector of the area. Professor Myra Wilkins of Florida International University in Miami, an expert on the local economy, came to this conclusion: "Frankly, I believe we shall have only a brief period of economic indigestion. The Cubans will be absorbed quickly and well and their economic contribution will be very positive almost immediately."[12]

Even as these comments were being made, the resettlement of the Cubans was moving ahead, though not always smoothly. On June 18, 1980, President Carter wrote to Leo Cherne: "The Coordinator for Refugee Affairs at the State Department informs me that your organization is providing critical aid in the processing and resettlement of Cuban exiles. In this effort, as in others, you set a standard of humanitarian concern and action that governments might emulate."

THE HAITIAN BYPRODUCT

One unexpected result of the Cuban upheaval was the fact that it forced the United States to face up squarely to the problem of Haitian refugees whose claims to humanitarian treatment had been ignored over the years. Because the victims of the Duvaliers, *père et fils*, were mostly dismissed as "economic" migrants rather than refugees fleeing political persecution, government authorities tended to regard them as illegal entrants into the country. With the spotlight on the Cubans, humanitarian agencies and church groups were in a position to challenge the double standard that was being applied as between Haitians and Cubans.

Throughout the years, IRC had been concerned about the victims of the dictatorial Duvalier regime. In the early 1960s, relatively few Haitians could make their escape. The brutal special police, the *Tontons Macoutes*, seemed to be everywhere. Attempting to cross a two-mile wide militarized zone along the Dominican border was virtually suicide.

In the late 1960s, however, a growing number began to escape by sea, some of them reaching the Bahamas. A group of about a hundred wound up in Nassau's Fox Hill prison. Participating in an international effort to effectuate their release, IRC helped to arrange asylum in the United States, Canada, France and Belgium. Forty-nine of them were admitted to the United States under the auspices of IRC which paid their fares, gave them clothing and housing, and funded them until they found employment. In 1970, a group of 116 Haitian sailors who had staged a shelling of Port-au-Prince in an effort to end the dictatorship, escaped to Guantanamo, from there to Puerto Rico, and finally to Miami where IRC conducted a ten-day legal fight to block extradition and to assure their right to stay permanently.

Much assistance was provided to colonies of refugees like the estimated 30,000 Haitians in the Dominican Republic and the Bahamas. In the 1970s, several hundred began to make their way to the United States each year. IRC provided guidance through the mazes of immigration law and also provided the necessities until they could become self-supporting. Not atypical was the case of the young Haitian schoolteacher whose father and brothers were in jail back home, who was himself a leader of the Haitian democratic movement in exile, and who was now facing deportation from the U.S. IRC pressed his case before the Board of Immigration only to hear the authorities rule that "it would appear that his services as a teacher would be highly desirable in Haiti in view of the illiteracy which he has quoted as existing there." Not every effort can be successful, and this cynical judgment could not be reversed.

It was essential that Americans learn what was going on in Haiti. Jean-Claude Duvalier was trying to present a benign picture as compared with the blatant brutality of "Papa Doc" but the American press was beginning to penetrate the mask. In 1976 the *Wall Street Journal*, in a lengthy and detailed article, wrote: "Haiti's notorious Tontons Macoutes, the president's personal henchmen, are less obtrusive, but they are still there, wearing wide-brimmed hats and knit jump suits, riding around in jeep-loads, revolvers stuffed in their hip pockets." Nevertheless, Haitians were still being denied refugee status in the United States and were forced to return to the island. Outraged, a group of congressmen in 1977 sent a letter to the chairman of the Subcommittee on Immigration saying: "Recent evidence indicates that the Haitian refugees who have returned to Haiti are subject to reprisals, the Haitian government's denials notwithstanding. Credible sources, both in and out of Haiti, continue to indicate that political repression and the continued violation of human rights are a fact of life in Haiti."

IRC continued to serve as the principal agency to receive those who did manage to escape. In 1977 a leaky boat brought sixty-one to Florida after thirty days at sea. Another arrived with seventeen. A third, with more than a hundred, reached the Guantanamo Naval Base. They were a mere trickle compared to the Cuban and Indochinese torrent, and they constituted the "poorest of the poor," as IRC described them, with the fewest friends. IRC staff wrestled with the problems of keeping them alive while deportation and adjustment-of-status issues were being disentangled.

As compared with the more than half a million Cubans who came after Castro's victory, the Haitians had been virtually invisible. The lack of publicity hurt them seriously. They had come in small groups, but in June 1978 there was a sudden spurt in their numbers; that month 600 arrived, and in the months that followed hundreds more began to land their rafts and leaky tubs on Florida beaches. Some of them paid smugglers as much as $500 a head, and never reached land. Particularly horrifying was the episode in August 1979 when, in the early hours of the morning, Florida police at Lantana Beach saw passengers being thrown into rough seas. Five children and a young mother drowned, and ten persons were rescued by the police. Two of the smugglers were prosecuted and convicted of manslaughter.

By 1980 the government figured that there were at least 30,000 Haitian refugees in the United States. Most of them had no legal status and were in constant danger of deportation. A Haitian Refugee Center had sprung up in Miami to assure that due process by American standards would be observed. American black spokespersons, like Representative Shirley Chisholm, charged that racism underlay the distinction between "political" and "economic" refugees and that skin color was being used to disqualify the Haitians who survived the sea crossing. A law suit was brought against the immigration authorities on the ground that constitutional rights — access to counsel, equal protection of the laws, fairly conducted hearings, assistance on the same basis as given to other refugees, the right to remain in the United States — had been denied. Evidence presented to the court showed that 179 refugees had been sent back to the torture chambers of "Baby Doc" Duvalier, and that another 450 had "voluntarily" returned after being threatened with life imprisonment by immigration officials. Federal District Judge James L. King issued a temporary restraining order preventing further deportations. A year later, after full hearings, he ordered an end to the discriminatory treatment. In the interim, the Refugee Act of 1980 had clarified the definition of refugee to include any person who had "a well founded fear" of persecution if he were repatriated. Both logic and empirical evidence confirmed that such fear on the part of Haitians was neither pretended nor paranoiac. The Court's decision, according to official estimates, meant that some 15,000 Haitians had now been removed from under the threat of deportation, and that another 15,000 who had not yet been involved in any immigration proceedings could breathe free again.

In 1980 the government's policy took a sharp turn. Cubans and Haitians were promised equal protection. All were immediately given a six-month parole to remain in the country. President Carter announced that he was sending legislation to Congress authorizing the permanent admission of the 130,000 Cubans and Haitians recently arrived. In addition they were declared to be equally eligible, if otherwise qualified, for such benefits as Medicaid, the Aid to Dependent Children program, and "emergency assistance under the rules of the states in which they are residing and with normal Federal/state matching." Because much of the resettlement burden still remained with agencies like IRC, the policy statement continued: "Per capita grants will be provided to private resettlement agencies for all persons leaving processing centers after June 19, 1980, and for Cuban/Haitian entrants being relocated out of the south Florida area after that date. In addition, funds will be provided to the resettlement agencies to provide employment counseling and referral services to all Cuban and Haitian entrants already released from camps or resettled directly into the Miami area."[13]

But, as IRC's Charles Sternberg noted, the funds had not yet been appropriated by Congress, nor were they available in other programs. At the very least, the administration estimated, a total of $385 million would be needed just for the fiscal year 1980. But even though these problems existed administratively, those who had fought for equal treatment on behalf of the Haitians had achieved some measure of success.

By 1982, however, the plight of the Haitians had deepened. Recession had struck in the United States, and like the pattern in the past, the first impulse was to slam shut the gates. Seen as competitors for scarce jobs, the Haitians were being told to go elsewhere. The federal government had been following a policy of providing assistance for 36 months in states that contribute aid to the unemployed. Refugees in states that had no such programs were told in May 1982 that their monthly federal subsistence checks of $119 were to be cut off if they had been in the country 18 months or longer. This meant that some 32,000 Cubans and Haitians were to be denied assistance. In a communication to those affected, Florida officially informed them in which states federal aid was still forthcoming — Hawaii, Kansas, Massachusetts, Michigan, Minnesota, New Jersey, New York, Ohio, Rhode Island and Wyoming. This tacit invitation to move elsewhere may have had some economic justification, but for the refugees it meant in many instances breaking family ties and other personal associations.

Ultimately, the issue of whether refugees like the recent Haitian arrivals are political or economic migrants will have to be resolved by the Supreme Court. At this writing, the lower courts are hearing arguments that the detained Haitians who enter without visas or other documentation are the victims of discrimination at the hands of the Immigration and Naturalization Service. The position taken by the Reagan administration is that it is necessary to protect the borders against an illegal tide. Moreover, so the argument runs, to admit those who arrive on the beaches would be discriminatory against Haitians who have applied for admission through the regular channels and who have been patiently waiting their turn.

In the formulation of the nation's policy, all three branches of government will have to participate. The courts have been confronted with allegations of inhuman treatment in overcrowded detention centers. Press accounts described as "miserable" the Haitian detention facilities in Fort Allen, Puerto Rico; Lake Placid, N.Y.; Otisville, N.Y.; Brooklyn, N.Y.; Morgantown, W.Va.; Lexington, Ky.; and Big Springs, N.Y. To such charges, the position of the administration is set forth in the words of Attorney General William French Smith, speaking to a press conference in Miami in April 1982: "There's not a single Haitian who can't walk out the door and go home. They can leave voluntarily any time they want to. All they have to do is go home."[14]

A letter to President Reagan, signed by thirty-eight Haitian women held at Fort Allen, put the situation in another light: "We did not flee our country in search of food and drink, like they say. You know this as well as we do, and yet you treat us like animals, like old rags forgotten in some corner. Do you think that in acting that way you dissuade us from our purpose? Do you think that you are thus morally destroying us? You are wrong."

And then a final plea addressed to the American tradition of asylum: "This is a cry of despair, a final call to your nobleness, to your good judgment, to your title as a great power. We would be honored by a satisfactory answer from you, an answer to these luckless refugees who ask only for the charity of liberty."

So far the policy of protecting our borders against unauthorized intrusions by fleeing Haitians has led to a systematic procedure for intercepting boats heading out across the Windward Passage between Haiti and Cuba, and pointed toward Florida. The 378-foot cutter, the *Hamilton*, accompanied by a search plane and two helicopters, was assigned to such duty. On board, in addition to the regular crew, were two immigration officials, a physician and two interpreters speaking Haitian Creole who could make the passengers of interdicted vessels understand that they were not welcome and were to be denied "the charity of liberty."

CHILE

Immediately after taking power in Cuba, Castro turned to the fomenting of Communist revolt throughout Central and South America. The old-fashioned Latin-American dictatorships offered fertile soil. Throughout their history South American countries have been swept by violent political upheavals, each of which has generated a flow of exiles. But not until Castro's coming had there been mass migrations in Latin America to match that of the Jews out of Europe, or the population exchanges during the creation of states like India, Pakistan and Israel, or the march southward of North Vietnamese after the Geneva treaty, or the millions of East Pakistanis running for shelter in West Bengal during the birthpangs of Bangladesh, or the outpouring of Indochinese from the sieves of Vietnam, Laos and Cambodia. Those who lose power or fail to capture it in coups count on the revolutions of the wheel of fortune in Latin America to bring them back again. Generally these exiles stay close to the scene by taking refuge in the nearest haven that will accept them. Indeed, mutual need has led to a virtual policy among the countries of taking in each other's exiles.

Raymond D. Gastil's annual survey of freedom prepared for Freedom House offers little reassurance about the trend in Latin-American politics. Listed among the nations that are "not free" are the major population centers of the continent. As of 1980, military juntas ruled the 119 million people in Brazil, the 27 million in Argentina, and the 11 million in Chile. Listed as "partly free" were countries like Peru, with a population of 17 million, Ecuador with some 8 million, Guatemala with somewhat less than 7 million, El Salvador with 4.5 million, and Sandinista Nicaragua with 2.5 million.[15]

From these and smaller countries in Central America, lone individuals, usually defeated political figures, have had to make their escape. Generally they have been supported in exile by their own underground movements. But occasionally a major upheaval, followed by a series of executions or mass imprisonments, has created a period of terror in which a substantial group has found it necessary to flee.

Such was the case in Chile, which for some forty years had enjoyed democracy. Crisis, characterized by runaway inflation and violent labor struggles, had led to the electoral victory of the Marxist Salvador Allende Gossens, head of the Popular Unity Party. In a free election, he received a plurality of the votes, the democratic parties having refused to coalesce. Allende's nationalization of private industries failed to stem inflation. Shortages of consumer goods stirred rebellion and a wave of strikes swept the country. The Chilean army, which traditionally had kept hands off civilian affairs, now made demands on Allende for representation in the cabinet. His appointment of some military officers, however, did not appease his adversaries. With the backing of American interests and, as later evidence demonstrated, with the intervention of the U.S. Central Intelligence Agency, Allende's government was overthrown by a military coup in September 1973. Allende himself was assassinated, though his successors asserted that the death was a suicide. The new regime, headed by Augusto Pinochet Ugarte, began a systematic repression of every possible source of independent action. The technology of dictatorship was brought into play —censorship of the press, denial of the right of assembly, crippling of the labor unions, jailing of the opposition, torture, and disappearances.

At the beginning of 1974 IRC dispatched Cecil Lyon, one of its most seasoned volunteer activists, to ascertain what was happening behind the censorship. Lyon had retired from the U.S. State Department after a long and distinguished career to join IRC. He had been the American ambassador to Ceylon and to Chile, which he was now to revisit with a view to launching a program of assistance for the new refugees. Behind his courtly diplomatic air, a sharp, analytical mind cuts through to the heart of the issue and proceeds to develop practical solutions.

His inquiries revealed a high degree of ambivalence among Chileans. A prominent leader of the left-of-center Christian Democratic Party, suffering from the ban placed on all political activity, described the situation to Lyon in these terms: "We have lived the last few years in a madhouse and we are still living in a madhouse. You can't conceive how bad it was. It was worse than anything you've heard or read about it. The country was being led into ruin, broken to bits. If all presidents had their own arms, bombs and tanks and private armies the world system couldn't work. The military had no choice but to take over. But we are now paying for the last three years. We're under a very severe dictatorship." Criticism of the Allende government and its extra-legal methods of control was heard everywhere. Though there was widespread satisfaction over its demise and even an afterglow of optimism, especially because consumer goods had begun to reappear in the shops, many already discerned the dangers always inherent in dictatorship. Thus Lyon reported:

One Chilean with whom I talked, however, who was not suffering from the present euphoria of most of his countrymen that all's well in Chile, was Cardinal Rene Silva (whom I had known sixteen years ago as Bishop of Valparaiso). He said that the Allende regime was a complete fraud and was thrown out primarily by the middle class. He also said that although Chile was predominantly a middle class country (a change which had struck me immediately on my return to Santiago), the Junta was surrounding itself with and working with the upper class. Many of the middle class and laborers are out of work, and all are having a very hard time living in a period of rising prices. The military were being too severe, the Cardinal thought, throwing people out of jobs, imprisoning many, torturing, etc. As a result, he said, many people of the middle and lower classes had become disillusioned with the Junta and were turning against it.[16]

Lyon also noted "that as a result of the military's determination to root Communism out of the country, probably never before in Chile's history have so many middle class people been investigated or taken into custody by the *Carabineros* and the police."

His report included a series of facts that were of prime importance to IRC's executive committee when it met to consider its course of action. As of November 1973, inquiries by the International Committee of the Red Cross led to the conclusion that there were 7,500 politicals in 55 prisons throughout the country. At least 10,000 people, probably more, had been dismissed from their jobs. Though the military government had ordered a universal wage increase to five times the prevailing rates in January 1973, the inflationary noose continued to tighten on the workers. In the capital, Santiago, a waiter told Lyon, "Before we had money but couldn't get anything; now we can get anything we want but we have no money." Visiting the *poblaciones* or workers' housing, Lyon found soldiers and jeeps in ostentatious array and two tanks commanding sidestreets. A midnight curfew was in effect and occasional shooting could be heard in the suburbs.

Already flight was beginning. About 15,000 Chileans were in the Argentine, some of whom had arrived as tourists and stayed as refugees; others had rushed to cross the border illegally. The local representative of the UN High Commissioner for Refugees told Lyon that 1,200 to 1,400 persons had taken refuge in foreign embassies in Santiago, 700 of them in the Argentine embassy. Most of them had been expatriated without any difficulty to Sweden, France, Austria, Switzerland, Holland and Belgium. None had gone to the United States, he said, "since to do so would be considered sort of treason." But U.S. embassy personnel reported otherwise—that about a hundred applications had indeed been received.

On the basis of the available data, Lyon concluded that the political composition of the refugees was as follows: terrorists, about 4 to 5 percent; Communist supporters of Allende, about 10 to 15 percent; the remainder, democratic socialists and liberals of various shades. Initially the UNHCR attempted to send the refugees to countries that matched their political coloration—for example, Communists to Cuba. For some unexplained reason, Castro was slow to admit them. As of the time of his visit, Lyon noted ironically, East Germany had accepted twenty-two refugees; anti-Communist West Germany had taken twenty-four.

While pursuing efforts to bring about the admission of Chileans into the United States, IRC began a program of aid to those who had reached neighboring countries. In the fall of 1974 John Lester Lewine, a noted writer and teacher of Spanish, was sent into the area. At Mendoza, where the refugees were crossing over from Chile into the Argentine, and in Buenos Aires, he noted that about 12,000 had arrived. In Peru, where a rotating population of about a thousand refugees was the norm, he reviewed IRC's health program already in action. He recommended extension of a nutrition program to supplement the $85-per-month allocation that UNHCR was giving each refugee. In addition, the Board of Directors of IRC felt that the United States, which had allocated $1,400,000 to aid Chilean refugees, had a responsibility to those Chileans who asked for haven here.

Relations between the Pinochet junta and Washington had grown increasingly strained, though U.S. companies were returning to Chile. In 1976, the American people had been shocked by the assassination in Washington of a former Chilean diplomat, Orlando Letelier. FBI investigators soon determined that the killers were under the direction of the Chilean secret police. Based on the testimony of an American who admitted his complicity and turned state's evidence, three men were convicted. Requests for the extradition of Chilean military officers, including a general who had initiated the plot, were received with indifference by the Chilean government and were finally rejected by its Supreme Court. Both countries recalled their ambassadors in the traditional diplomatic gesture of disapproval.

While this drama was unfolding, however, the Ford administration moved at a snail's pace in admitting Chilean refugees. Official policy was to welcome them provided they were not found to be "ineligible under the provisions of the Immigration and Nationality Act because of membership in the Communist party or in a leftist revolutionary movement or other terrorist groups, or who have criminal records." In June 1975, the U.S. Attorney General announced that he would authorize the admission of 400 Chilean families, and IRC was to be one of the resettlement agencies. Because the United States still had relations with Chile, a unique decision was made by the junta: those in prison would be released under an "exile decree" if they could present evidence of acceptance by another country. By October, however, little had happened in Washington other than that the State Department reported it had received "biographic information on 46 detainees and 120 dependents. These biographies are passed to voluntary agencies which will use them in placement in the United States. The detainees come from a wide variety of occupations: 19 are skilled workers; 7 come from business; 4 are students; others were formerly employed in the media, in teaching, agriculture and the military."

Senator Edward Kennedy, as chairman, called a meeting of the Senate Subcommittee on Refugees and opened with the following remarks:

Foot-dragging and excuses have characterized our government's approach to the Chilean refugee problem. We have heard a litany of promises, but have seen very little action. For two years, letters from the Department of State, in response to my inquiries over our government's policy, and the testimony of Department officials before this Subcommittee, have given assurances of an intent to provide generous parole for refugees from Chile. Those assurances were not fulfilled. Press releases were issued announcing a willingness to receive Chilean refugees. But that willingness has been contradicted by the lack of positive action.

And then only when we were engaged in requesting those same international organizations and agencies for help in resettling Vietnamese, the red-tape barriers suddenly were broken and a Chilean parole program was formally established in early June.[17]

But it was not until December 1975, more than two years after the overthrow of Allende's government, that the first Chilean refugees began to arrive in the United States. In 1976 about a thousand were admitted, with IRC sponsoring 276 of them. All had been political prisoners. In 1977, the focus shifted to the resettlement of Chileans who had found temporary refuge in Argentina, only to find themselves in a second detention as the military dictatorship in Buenos Aires oscillated between arbitrary violence and measured relaxation, depending on the state of internal terrorism at the time. The United States agreed to take 200 Chilean refugee families from Argentina, but their rate of departure was slow. IRC assumed responsibility for one-fifth of the number. Though the American administration announced in April 1978 that it would accept an additional 500, Argentina released only two persons, both of whom were sponsored for admission to the United States by IRC.

Resettlement of the Chileans occasioned many difficulties. Unlike the Cubans, they had no pre-existing colony of fellow-nationals who could help in overcoming the language barriers, arranging housing, and finding jobs, especially in the current period of economic recession. IRC therefore had to serve as the surrogate in providing the essentials and in speeding ultimate integration into American life. Valuable aid was forthcoming from teachers, doctors and dentists who contributed their professional skills, and from trade union officials who helped to find jobs, collected clothing and placed the newcomers in industrial training programs. Many of the refugees faced the added problem of recovering from the trauma of torture.

The Chilean group was resettled for the most part in New York, Colorado, Texas, Washington, D.C., and California. Local groups greeted them warmly. In San Jose, the Sacred Heart Church offered its assistance immediately. In Colorado, among the organizations that cooperated was the local Amnesty International, which resettled eight families; thirteen other families received the hearty support of Christian and Jewish congregations and persons with humanitarian interests. Medical care was a major need of the Chileans. Funds provided for surgery included, for example, the correction of a baby's congenital heart defect. Most of the adults and children needed dental care.

These had made good their escape. But as the UNHCR reported in June 1976, many had been abducted, tortured and murdered.

A TRUST FUND FOR DEMOCRACY

Cubans, Haitians and Chileans are the Western hemisphere's principal contribution to the world's ocean of refugees. Europe, Asia and Africa have provided their quota, and for generations the United States has received them. But not without qualms. Whenever the nation has been asked to accept a new tide of refugees from the old world or from its own Spanish-speaking neighbors or from the esoteric cultures of the Far East, objections have been raised: Will we be putting additional burdens on our economy? Will our own customs frustrate the aliens? Will the poverty of the refugees translate into criminal activities? Will not our own social stability be undermined? Every wave of immigration has raised such questions. But the historical answer has been consistent: the net result has been the enrichment of our pluralist society. The newcomers have proved to be a resource for democracy — a human trust fund whose value appreciates with the passage of time.

Concerning the Cubans, for example, *Business Week* wrote in 1973: "Since Cubans began fleeing to the U.S. from Castro they have made faster progress in their adopted country than has any other group of immigrants in this century. Almost overnight, they have emerged from the deprived refugee state and moved into the middle class." Their success has strengthened the local economies of which they are a part.

And yet Castro's castaways were not really different from those who preceded them in the great migrations of the eighteenth, nineteenth and twentieth centuries. America had been built by men and women fleeing political, religious or economic oppression. Many accepted the status of immigrants —permanent settlers in a new land. Some, especially the "politicals" who fled from the Nazis, the Stalinists, or the Latin-American dictators of the right and the left, were determined to go home some day. For most of them —indeed for most of the refugees now on the march in Asia and Africa— there is a similar dream. They are confident that some day their native land will witness a rebirth of freedom, and that they will be reclaimed as its citizens.

But that may be a long time coming. Whole generations of exiles have died and left a legacy of children who have become permanent citizens of a pluralistic American society. As the fortunes of politics have permitted, others have been able to return to their native lands, bringing with them a democratic doctrine confirmed by their American experience — a respect for diversity, not as something to be tolerated, but as a value that enriches a people. In the intermingling of populations effected by political upheaval, all too many find they cannot return, and sink into depression and pessimism.

IX

Birth Pains of a Nation — Bangladesh

On March 25, 1971, in the city of Dacca, then in East Pakistan, Dr. Das had finished seeing his patients and was settling down for an evening with his wife and parents. After some nine years of married life, Mrs. Das at long last was pregnant, and the couple were looking forward to happy days. For the past few years they had lived in England where Dr. Das had taken advanced medical degrees and enjoyed a successful gynecological practice. But his parents had written to him, arguing that they had few years left, and had urged him to return to his native city. So, four months earlier, he had sold his house in London, his car and his practice, transferred his bank account to Dacca, and returned to East Pakistan.

The quiet of the evening was broken first by sporadic shots, then by continuous gunfire, and finally by heavy shelling. Dr. Das turned on the radio. There was music but no news. He went to the roof of his house and could see sharp bursts of light. He could hear shouting in the streets. Returning to his living room, he listened to an authoritative voice on the radio: "All doctors must report to the hospital at Dacca Medical School." A dutiful citizen, he set out on his professional mission, but en route he encountered a colleague. "You must not go to the hospital," he was told. "They are shooting the doctors on the spot."

He rushed home, gathered up his family, told them to take only objects of value that were small and could be concealed on their person (the universal strategy of the refugee) and prepared for the 200-mile journey to the Indian border. They traveled on foot and purchased ferry rides on the rivers, making their way slowly. Recognized as Hindus, they were harrassed and robbed by Moslem villagers until all they had left was the clothing on their backs.

Their highway to safety led them through the jungle, and it was there that Mrs. Das's time came. Being an obstetrician, Dr. Das recognized that his wife needed a Cesarean section, but he did not dare to enter any of the villages for this was a Moslem area. During eight days Mrs. Das suffered labor pains until her husband could bring himself to make the only possible decision. Persuading his wife that the baby was already dead, he killed his own child in the mother's womb so that his wife might live.

The family reached West Bengal. There Dr. Das joined the staff of the International Rescue Committee's Child and Maternity Center, an emergency field hospital pitched in the fields of a village called Barasat where some 50,000 refugees were housed, a mere fraction of the estimated 10 million men, women and children who had made their escape.

FIRST WORD IN THE WEST

News of the full horror was slow in reaching the West. An East Pakistani lawyer named Chaudhuri, who happened to be visiting in London at the time, rushed to New York. There he met with Leo Cherne and Charles Sternberg of IRC and Leonard Sussman, executive director of Freedom House.[1] He told of the massacres on the campuses of the country's two leading universities, Dacca and Chittagong, and the massive flight of the people. Within days, Cherne obtained a $1.5 million commitment from Maurice Williams, head of the U.S. Agency for International Development, to provide sustenance for the refugees.

There had been some newspaper reporting about the political situation in Pakistan that had led to the conflict. Elections had been held in the geographically divided country, its two wings separated by a thousand miles of Indian territory. The Awami League, which advocated full autonomy for East Pakistan, had won an overwhelming victory, made possible by the fact that West Pakistan, the governing center, had the smaller population. Yahya Khan, the dictator who had miscalculated the results, answered the electorate by ordering the army into action. Hundreds of thousands are said to have died in the first onslaughts.

The flight of the refugees undoubtedly constituted the largest of the many mass migrations that have occurred in human history. As they poured across the border into the Indian states of West Bengal, Assam, Tripura and Meghalaya, they brought with them stories of massive terror. At the offices of the International Rescue Committee in New York, word was received that the first targets had been the intellectuals and the professionals, the people on whom the viability of a modern nation depends—doctors, nurses, pharmacists (or compounders, as they are called on the Indian subcontinent), writers and journalists, university professors and teachers. As Leo Cherne pointed out, "Especially in underdeveloped countries, if you want to destroy any independent vitality, that is where to strike. All totalitarian countries know this."

Inquiry brought the bloody details. All who had been on the campus of the University of Dacca on March 25 — professors and students — were sum-marily shot. An American educator who visited the university two weeks after the event described to the author the ineradicable evidence of the mas-sacre — caked blood on the stairwells in solid streams. The vice-chancellor of the University of Chittagong, whose campus had also been attacked that same night, recounted a tale of similar executions. In the first nationwide attack it is estimated that some 200,000 persons were killed.

MISSION TO INDIA

To assess what kind of program would be needed, a special mission was dispatched to West Bengal. It was headed by Ambassador Angier Biddle Duke, the former IRC president who had played a major role in the Hunga-rian crisis. He was accompanied by Mrs. Lawrence Copley Thaw, one of the organization's most active Board members; the IRC counsel Morton I. Hamburg; Thomas W. Phipps, the writer; and Dr. Daniel L. Weiner of the Einstein Medical School, an authority on tropical diseases who had served in the Far East.

They discovered that the refugees had already set up a skeleton govern-ment in exile, giving high priority to a "Bangladesh Red Cross" that was registering all medical personnel who had succeeded in reaching Calcutta and its environs. Their number was estimated to be about 1,500. The first recommendation of the IRC mission was to provide stipends for the refugee physicians, nurses and paramedicals, the purpose being two-fold: to keep them alive as against the day when they would be needed on their return to their own country, and to put them to work in the refugee camps and thus serve the needs of their fellow-refugees. As Leo Cherne recalls: "The mission came up with a remarkably creative response to the situation. Why, they asked themselves, dole out a stipend of rupees to keep a person alive and non-functioning when for the same money you can employ him in the camps, using his professional capability to assist his own people?"

By American standards the monthly stipends seemed absurd, ranging from a hundred to five hundred rupees, or roughly $13.50 to $67, depend-ing on professional status. Amounts were deliberately fixed to conform to the rates being paid by the Indian government to its own nationals for sim-ilar services.

It was anticipated that the practical problems ahead would involve three elements: (1) locating the physicians; (2) providing supplies and equipment since most doctors had fled without taking as much as a stethoscope with them; and (3) arranging for transportation to their stations. The mission reported that discussions had been held with Minister of Transportation Ghosh, and that he had approved the hiring of vehicles brought out of East Pakistan by some refugees that normally would not have been permitted to operate in India.

THE MEDICAL PROGRAM

What ultimately proved to be the major problem, however, was the one considered most manageable—equipment and supplies. Despite the fact that large amounts of medical material were being sent from abroad by agencies like UNICEF, foreign governments and the U.S. aid program, shortages persisted. On many occasions it was necessary to seek out black-market sources, for delay in getting supplies and medications meant death to people already under the care of IRC-sponsored physicians.

Transportation remained a continuing problem. Public carriers could not be trusted because of the incalculable delays and because, all too often, cargoes simply disappeared. Because of the primitive conditions in the countryside where the camps were located, IRC staff would have to make the deliveries themselves by jeep, or the doctors would come into Calcutta and take back supplies by train and rickshaw. In the monsoon season, the roads to and within the camps became a sea of mud that even the four-wheel drive of the jeep often failed to overcome. On some occasions, a return to a facility would reveal that a whole camp, numbering thousands, had been moved to another location to escape the high water.

The medical program, of course, had top priority. Many of the refugees brought with them a long history of malnutrition, a condition that was now intensified by weeks of starvation en route. New arrivals told IRC representatives that they had not eaten for as much as four days; many reported a toll of death suffered by their families along the way. Any delay in establishing new clinics and treatment centers was unthinkable. In fact, even as the mission was reporting its recommendations in New York, the plans were already being implemented. One member of the mission, Mrs. Thaw, had remained behind for several weeks to organize the work of some fifty physicians who were already available.

SAVING THE TEACHERS

Because the initial target of the genocidal attack had been the professional and cultural leaders of East Pakistan, virtually the entire educational system of the nation had vanished—murdered, gone underground or in India. It was estimated that some 10,000 school teachers were in the refugee camps. To keep them alive and productive, the IRC mission had already set in motion a plan to fund a series of makeshift classrooms so that the children might have a few hours of elementary education each day. Indian officials reported later that they had found the morale of refugees to be higher in those camps where the children were spending some time in those improvised classes. The very presence of a school, however rudimentary, was a promise for the future.

In conjunction with a newly formed Refugee Teachers Association and the Calcutta University Assistance Committee, some 3,800 teachers had been registered, including 94 university professors and 339 undergraduate college instructors. IRC's plan was to pay the primary and secondary school teachers $25 a month and college level faculty $40, again to match the prevailing rates in India. The proposed monthly budget for a camp school, intended to serve about 600 children, came to less than $500, as follows:

10 primary and secondary level teachers	$250
3 higher level teachers	120
2 non-teaching staff	40
Teaching materials	50
Contingency fund	20
Total	$480

These figures were basically adhered to throughout the program, though sudden emergencies could mean higher expenditures. Thus, a visiting IRC staff member was informed by the teachers at the Kalyani camp that they had 400 additional children waiting for admission and that tarpaulins were available; all that was lacking was a supply of bamboo poles, at a cost of 1,300 rupees, or $13. The new school was authorized, and funded, on the spot.

The mission had returned from India at a time when the American public was not yet awake to the enormity of the tragedy being enacted in the northeast portion of the Indian subcontinent. Duke and his associates had noted that "the response of the people of the United States has fallen short by far of the traditional response our country has been capable of in similar emergencies — none of which in recent times has been of similar scope in suffering and disruptive impact. It is our firm conviction that this lack of response is largely due to a lack of information and specific indications as to how help can be channeled into a meaningful program." IRC decided that among its tasks would be the enlightenment of the American public.

Simultaneously, the work in India went forward without delay. The government in New Delhi from the start had welcomed the refugees with open arms despite its own economic difficulties, which were hardly a secret to the Western world. Four months after the human flood began, a top official, with no show of emotion, told IRC personnel that more than half of the administrative resources allocated for the development of West Bengal was being consumed by refugee needs.

The most massive push of the refugees was toward Calcutta, both because of the lure of a big city and because of kinship ties. The two Bengals had once been a united region, but long before independence Britain had partitioned the area into West Bengal, now an Indian state, and East Bengal, which later became East Pakistan and then Bangladesh. The purpose was to reduce the friction between Hindus and Moslems who dominated the two sections respectively.

But the old religious hatreds have repeatedly come to the surface. In 1947, with the ending of the British Raj and the creation of the two nations on the subcontinent, a vast exchange of populations took place. Some 6 million Hindus and Sikhs left West Pakistan, while 6.5 million Moslems left predominantly Hindu India; from East Pakistan 4 million Hindus headed for India, and a million Moslems trekked east. The hegira was bloody. The ensuing massacres overshadowed the communal riots of 1926, 1930 and 1946. How many refugees were killed in the population exchange is still unknown, but Gunnar Myrdal, in his three-volume study, *Asian Drama*, reports that the estimates of the dead range from 200,000 to almost a million.[2]

CALCUTTA — IN THE EYE OF THE STORM

The city of Calcutta bore the major economic impact following independence, and remained permanently a city of refugees where successive familial generations live and die in the streets. In 1971, a second tidal wave of humanity struck. The long tradition of commerce and industry, now in eclipse to be sure, still glimmered like a bright light that lingers on the retina even after the source has been extinguished. The shared Bengali language, the common culture and even more important the presence of relatives in a society where family ties impose an obligation of hospitality, made Calcutta the lodestar. Significantly, the vast majority of the refugees were Hindus, though the leadership in exile, and those who ultimately went home to govern, were Moslems. It is said that at least a third of the refugees in West Bengal did not seek shelter in the government camps but took up residence with friends or relatives; many of these chose not to return after the crisis.

Adding to the burdens of the city was a virtual state of anarchy — crippling *bandhs* or strikes, paralyzing sit-ins in government offices, police clashes with the Maoist Naxalites, large-scale crime, student disruptions, and daily assassinations. A coalition of Communist groups had won political control of West Bengal only to be removed by action from New Delhi. Even before the flood-tide of refugees, West Bengalis were already in despair. As cities go, Calcutta is young. America's Pilgrims had already landed at Plymouth Rock when Job Charnock, an enterprising Englishman, founded a settlement on marshland, barely twenty feet above sea level. Today, this outpost has a population of more than 9 million, but unlike other cities of great size, it is virtually all slum, broken up by pockets of affluence. The filth and disease seem ineradicable. The three-month summer monsoon drenches but fails to cleanse the streets and alleys.

During the height of the refugee crisis, the Calcutta *Statesman*, the leading English-language newspaper in the city, wrote daily dirges on[3]

the disintegration of Bengal's sixth capital. A browning at the edges; a more lush growth of jungle; brick and mortar powdering under the sun; streets swollen into monsoon rivers: these, for those who care to gaze into the darkling crystal of the future, may signify that the "very small spot of rising ground" on which Job Charnock placed his settlement is no longer able to contain the fierce passions that have since been generated. As school holidays are indefinitely extended, examinations repeatedly postponed, factories remain closed and streets are either swelling with riot or shrouded in the silence of hartals [general strikes]. . . .

This was the city which became the base of operations for one of the major undertakings of the International Rescue Committee.

CRISIS IN BENGAL

To get the program into actual operation, the mission had left behind Mrs. Lawrence Copley Thaw, a prominent New Yorker described by the *New York Times* as a "petite Park Avenue socialite." She has been for many years one of the most active volunteers in the IRC. Her slight build and soft-spoken manner conceal a dynamo of energy and organizing ability. For six weeks, she did the ground-breaking work of assembling the necessary Indian personnel, getting out into the steaming refugee camps, establishing contact with government officials, persuading camp commandants to assign space for IRC facilities, supervising the pitching of tents or the raising of tarpaulins on bamboo poles to provide the simple structures that served as clinics in some cases or as schools in others. Tough Indian army officers, assigned to refugee duty, were delighted to take orders from the American lady and speed the necessary work.

At the camp in Barasat, an outpatient dispensary was set up, which became a prototype for others throughout West Bengal. In addition, the commandant urged IRC to set up a maternity center and a hospital for children suffering from malnutrition and the resultant diseases. He made available a huge cowshed capable of holding a hundred patients. Its corrugated tin roof and concrete floor provided its staff a luxury not enjoyed by the less fortunate physicians elsewhere who worked in tents, ankle-deep in mud. For the open sides of the cowshed, tarpaulins were provided that could keep out the rain or could be raised to give relief from the humid heat. Along the center of the floor was a trough once used by the cattle; now it was occupied night and day by mothers who accompanied their ailing young ones.

As the commandant watched the activities of the medical staff, he hastened to provide blankets, gave the hospital a block ration card for staff, patients and their families, constructed cinder paths through the ever-present mud, and even strung wires to the building to replace the kerosene lamps with electric bulbs.

A hundred cots had been made to order in Calcutta. The day the first twenty-six were delivered, even before the hospital was opened, each cot was occupied. Within ten minutes the physicians were fighting in vain to

save a baby dying of malnutrition. In the neighboring cots, the other children lay staring as if they had no chance to survive. But two weeks later
many of them were sitting up or even playing on the floor with toys provided by the staff.

The challenge Mrs. Thaw faced in initiating the IRC program is virtually
indescribable. Her reports to the New York office presented a series of what
seemed like insurmountable hurdles. Emergency shelter was at a premium.
There were not enough tents, and India had literally run out of tarpaulin.
At Salt Lake, a suburb of Calcutta, people were living in cement sewer pipes
intended for what was to have been a large-scale housing development.
Water was being provided by "tube-wells" sunk to a depth of only about six
feet—a condition that made cholera a constant threat. In camps that contained thousands of people, sanitary facilities were nonexistent; a field
would be set aside for that purpose, with the result that one could know
that he was arriving at a camp by the stench that reached for miles.

The refugee diet consisted primarily of rice provided by the authorities,
but since it had to be cooked, fuel became a major problem. In many cases it
was provided by the camp, but as the landscape became denuded of wood,
refugees were reported to be stripping the bark from fruit trees, leading to
violent conflict with the local population. Some powdered milk was available, but the most critical shortage was in powdered milk-glucose supplements for the infants. Distended stomachs, nutritional edema, skin infections,
gastrointestinal disturbances with vomiting and diarrhea, and chronic
coughing symptomatic of respiratory diseases, were encountered everywhere. Even against the background of India's prevalent poverty, the refugees were recognizable by their hollow cheeks, revealing low caloric intake,
and by their inadequate clothing.

The Duke mission had initiated the relief program by retaining two
Indian nationals who knew their way through the mazes of local bureaucracy and who were familiar with the patterns of government operations.
Tapos Shaha, a sharp-eyed Calcutta journalist, plunged into the work of
locating and assigning medical staff, keeping them supplied and meeting
their personal needs. A dynamic young man, Tarun Mitra, took leave from
his permanent position with the American Institute for Indian Studies in
Calcutta to set up a network of schools and to implement a program of
stipends for journalists, poets, lawyers, college professors, and so on.

When Mrs. Thaw handed over the reins to her successors, Professor
Aaron Levenstein of Baruch College, City University of New York, and his
wife Margery, the apparatus was in high gear. As the Levensteins wrote to
Ambassador Duke on their return to the United States, the mission and
Mrs. Thaw had "created a firm roadbed, and all we had to do was roll on
the tracks. The program laid out and first set in motion by IRC early in July
met all the conceivable criteria for IRC work: it was simple and direct; it
allowed for rapid action and produced immediate benefits; it went to the
heart of some major needs; and it fit in with the long tradition of IRC itself."

No ledger can contain a full accounting of the individual tragedies suffered by the millions of refugees. Heartbreaking were the countless episodes
of separated families, the curse that befalls most refugee populations. The
pathetic efforts to reestablish contact can be illustrated by a letter passed
from hand to hand in the desperate hope that it might ultimately reach the
addressee, somewhere among the wandering millions. It never did. It finally
came to rest in the files of the International Rescue Committee, along with
the English translation by the calligraphist Rabindra Nath Basak. It reads:

Father, where you are today we do not know. My elder brother, the elder sisters,
maternal uncle, all of them have been killed by the Pak army. Whatever little savings
we had, it is all finished. Mother has become insane; the whole day she laughs or
cries. Where you have left us, those people have turned us out. We are now sitting
on the road and spending our time in starvation. Father, you come back. Probably
we will not live any more.

Greetings, Your daughter Bevi

THE HEALTH CHALLENGE

By the end of the summer of 1971, five months after the East Pakistanis
had begun their migration, IRC had placed 218 medical personnel in 28
locations. The Barasat dispensary alone, which kept detailed records, recorded as many as 500 patients in a single day. As the number of refugees
mounted, IRC installations were found to be treating 250,000 patients a
month.

As in many of the other crises in the history of refugees, IRC was not
alone. Various voluntary agencies staked out different areas of special concern; cooperative councils increased efficiency by avoiding duplication and
by sharing resources and supplies. IRC representatives worked closely with
such groups as the Catholic Relief Services, the Save the Children Federation, the International Red Cross, the Lutheran World Relief, and the
British-based Oxfam. In October 1971, IRC and Oxfam-Canada joined
forces to bring Dr. Pierce Gardner and Dr. Jon E. Rohde to Calcutta. ("IRC
has a fantastic reputation here," wrote Dr. Rohde on his arrival.) In conjunction with Harold Grimes of IRC's New York staff, who had taken over
in West Bengal, they surveyed the situation in the camps and reviewed the
medical activities. Their purpose was to develop a specific health care
program that would be based on "rigorous statistical epidemiologic studies
of the medical problems."

One immediate result was the preparation in layman's language of a
memorandum on the new rehydration treatment of cholera and the appropriate schedules of fluid replacement, a dramatically effective answer to the
frequent epidemics that struck not only the camps but the entire subconti-

nent. Translated into Bengali, it was widely distributed, and was read frequently over the Indian radio. The initial printing addressed to personnel in the IRC and Oxfam camp facilities was paid for by IRC.

Doctors Rohde and Gardner prepared a twenty-four-page manual for medical staff in the camps entitled *Guidelines to the Common Medical Problems Among Bangladesh Refugees.*[4] It provided a total approach to the patient, including the taking of medical history, examination procedures, and a detailed method of handling each of the common conditions found in the camps, e.g., gastroenteritis, respiratory ailments, skin diseases, malnutrition, female problems related to anemia and pregnancy, and so on. To reinforce the impact, the material was issued under the imprint of the Indian government's health agency.

In addition, Dr. Gardner undertook what was probably the first scientific study ever made of the physical condition of a refugee population. Because Barasat was the largest IRC facility functioning on a twenty-four-hour basis with a staff of forty-seven doctors, nurses and aides, the whole camp was chosen for study. To obtain a random sampling, Dr. Gardner took all families whose ration card numbers ended with 2 or 7 and arranged for them to be interviewed. Whether patients or not, they were located and studied. To standardize the medical assessment, each patient's individual history was taken by a Bengali doctor, with Dr. Gardner reviewing a third of the reports. Weight and height were measured with scale and stadometer; tuberculin tests were administered to all under fifteen years of age. Those found to be suffering from severe malnutrition were hospitalized immediately (about 5 percent); those with moderate malnutrition were started on special food programs; and those showing evidence of Vitamin A deficiency (fully 25 percent) were treated on the spot with 300,000 units of Vitamin A injections. Skin problems were widespread, with many dangerous infections due to scabies. Most alarming was the prevalence of tuberculosis.

Part of the study included interviews during a four-day interval with 94 families (453 people) randomly selected. Dr. Gardner and his colleagues reported these findings in Britain's leading medical journal, *The Lancet*: "Of the 94 families interviewed, 23 reported the death of one or more immediate household members since March 25, 1971, when civil war erupted. Seventeen of the 25 deaths were reported to be due to diarrheal diseases, with war trauma or measles responsible for 6 other deaths. The young and the elderly were at highest risk. Only 1 death due to natural causes was recorded between age 7 and age 50."[5]

Staffed by internationally known physicians, IRC was able to join in research and treatment work at nutrition therapy centers organized by the All-India Institute of Medical Science. The findings have since proved to be of great help in other refugee situations, and indeed to children in underdeveloped countries. Groups of youngsters were fed special formulas of easily digested, highly nutritious foods. Slowly over the weeks, they recovered. The swollen bellies receded and edematous legs became normal; the bony chests and matchstick limbs filled out. Refugee physicians who had been kept alive by being remunerated for their work eventually returned to their native land with new knowledge on how to treat the severest forms of malnutrition. It is estimated that one aspect of the program implemented by the IRC medical personnel provided massive doses of Vitamin A to a quarter of a million undernourished children threatened by permanent damage such as blindness, and to 50,000 pregnant and lactating women.

In virtually all refugee situations, malnutrition is a major problem, most serious because of its long-range consequences. Alan Berg, senior nutrition adviser to the World Bank, has said that "severely malnourished children have brains smaller than average size and have been found to have 15-20 percent fewer brain cells than well-nourished children." Children born of mothers suffering from malnutrition are born with abnormally low weight, and of these, it has been discovered, the deficit in brain cells comes to 40 percent.

Initially, medical supplies had been a major difficulty, but as support was rallied around the world the situation improved. The flow of medications from the government to the IRC centers improved; those that required further rations looked to IRC/Calcutta which, in addition to local purchasing, was being assisted by American pharmaceutical houses such as Sterling Drug Company. Most impressive as a source of needed vitamins, basic antibiotics like penicillin and tetracycline, and injectibles for strep, was the "godown" or warehouse of Oxfam which shared its resources unstintingly with the other voluntary agencies.

THE GOVERNMENT DILEMMA

In general the Indian government, staggering under the incredible burden of caring for the refugee millions, faced psychological as well as economic problems. Unknown to the world, the administration in New Delhi had concluded that the ultimate solution would have to be a military defeat of the Pakistani army and the establishment of a new country, Bangladesh, to which the refugees could be speedily repatriated.

Most of the camps, for obvious reasons, were situated along the border which in many places was easily crossed by young refugees. They returned to their own land during the night as members of the *Mukhti Bahini*, or freedom fighters, to harass Yahya Khan's troops. In response, the Pakistanis periodically lobbed shells into the areas they considered guerilla bases. A number of the IRC medical facilities housed patients who had sustained wounds. At Bongaon, for example, an outpost on the Jessore highway — a strip of unpaved road on which cars could pass each other only if one of them pulled up on the shoulder — fully half the patients at a given moment were recovering from military injuries.

Knowing that the country was on the eve of a declaration of war, the Indian government was concerned about the presence of foreign personnel —doctors, nurses, relief workers. Early in July, with the declaration of war more than four months ahead, New Delhi ordered all foreigners to leave the camps, though administrative personnel of the agencies could visit daily for supervisory purposes from bases in Calcutta. British, Dutch and German teams of doctors and nurses were asked to leave the country, creating a serious vacuum in many camps. Fortunately, the gap was filled, in great part, by an extraordinary woman, Mother Teresa.

She had come to Calcutta some three decades before from her native Albania to set up a hospital for the destitute and dying in that city of daily death. "Let them know in their last moments," she said, "that somebody did care about them." Each morning her trucks would rove the streets and pick up the unfortunates, including lepers in the last stages of the disease, and bring them in for a moment of respite before the end. When East Pakistan exploded, sending large masses of humanity into West Bengal, she directed her compassion and her organizing genius to the task of providing assistance. When she learned that foreign physicians and nurses were about to leave, she volunteered to take over the facilities and see that new personnel was found.

IRC, of course, was not affected by the government's order because all of its medical personnel in the camps consisted of doctors, nurses, compounders and aides who were refugees themselves. As Mother Teresa encountered manpower needs, she turned to IRC, which at that point seemed to have a monopoly of refugee medical personnel. Her frequent telephone requests to the author for assistance in staffing her facilities invariably began with the words, "Professor, it is time to do something beautiful for God." After such a plea, she never was left empty-handed. (Malcolm Muggeridge, former editor of Britain's famous magazine *Punch*, has written her biography in a moving book called appropriately *Something Beautiful for God*.) It was fitting that the world should recognize her contribution to humanity and that she be awarded the Nobel Prize for Peace in 1979.

TO SAVE A CULTURE

Though IRC's medical program obviously demanded top priority, a second task had to be assumed—the preservation of the intellectual base of what was to become the new nation Bangladesh. Professors, teachers, writers, journalists, as the primary targets of the terror, needed special assistance.

The easiest group to provide for were the elementary school teachers. They could be put to work promptly in combating one of the worst aspects of refugee life, the corrosive effects of total idleness. As one looked out at the thousands of refugees squatting Asian style side by side, whole families doing nothing but waiting in resignation, the awful silence was like a tangible shroud. But the mere presence of a school, however spare in its facilities, was enough to transform a mass of individuals, each isolated in his own sorrow, into a community where men and women cooperated to assure that their children would have a future.

By the end of the summer IRC had set up thirty-one schools. Each had a staff of fourteen that included a health instructor responsible for teaching adults as well as the children the basic principles of hygiene. A large area covered with a tarp or plastic sheet mounted on bamboo poles was enough of a structure. Representing different grades, groups of children, slates and chalk in hand, squatted on palm-leaf mats. At the suggestion of the teachers made to Mary Pillsbury Lord, president of IRC, when she came to inspect the Kalyani school, footballs (what Americans call soccer balls) were made available. As the handsome, white-haired woman, already in her seventies, kicked and tossed the ball with the youngsters, the parents burst into smiles —perhaps for the first time since they had left their homes months before— and cheered in a mixture of English and Bengali: "International Rescue Committee Zindabad!" (Long live the International Rescue Committee!)

Mrs. Lord and her husband, Oswald, in a long career of humanitarian service, had visited virtually every refugee population since the end of World War II. In the camps of West Bengal, as in so many other hinterlands of the world, Mrs. Lord could be seen in heart-warming communication with the children across the language barrier. How she did it in Kalyani and elsewhere has been reported by Oswald Lord in his witty book, *Exit Backward, Bowing*, describing their travels on many continents. On one such occasion, he tells how three Yale graduates in a remote corner of the globe "were surprised to hear the chant, 'Boola, Boola.' Around the corner came Mary at the head of a parade of about seventy-five children, leading them like a cheerleader. After that we taught the children in the villages to shout 'Boola, Boola' in unison. Any Harvard or Princeton men going up the river are in for a surprise." Until her death, even during her terminal illness, Mrs. Lord remained deeply involved in shaping IRC priorities. In Bangladesh today, there are young people, now adults, who recall playing soccer and chanting the Yale cheer with an American lady.

By December, when the Indo-Pakistani war finally broke into the open, the number of schools had grown to fifty-one, stretching along the border regions from Calcutta in the south to Tripura in the northeast. Thus was the nucleus of an educational system preserved for the nation that was to arise from the ashes of the conflagration.

A more difficult problem was to develop a constructive program for the university professors and other intellectuals. Working with Dr. A. R. Malik, who had been vice-chancellor of the University of Chittagong and was eventually to become Bangladesh's ambassador to the important post of New Delhi, IRC considered the request of the refugee educators that a Bangladesh "University in Exile" be set up in Calcutta. Professor Aaron Levenstein, then co-director of the program in India, pointed out several

objections: IRC policy was based on avoiding capital expenditures — for
space, desks, chairs, and so on — preferring to put the maximum amount of
money directly into the hands of the refugees. Besides, it would be difficult
to obtain a student body with so many young men fighting in the *Mukhti
Bahini*. Instead of spending funds to rent a building for classrooms, IRC
proposed that a "Research Faculty in Exile" be set up. (The clinching argument was the statement: "As professors we have always known that the
ideal university would be one with no students to get in the way of the
faculty.")

A research program was laid out employing some 150 university and
senior college teachers. Most of the projects dealt with the kinds of problems the refugees would face in rehabilitating the social structure on their
ultimate return, for example, health measures, food distribution, the restoration of a police authority. Lawyers and law professors explored the problem of correcting the confusion occasioned by the Pakistani government's
expropriation of refugee property. A group of scholars concerned about the
lack of scientific textbooks in Bengali worked on a project entitled "Science
Education in Bangladesh." Authors, poets and journalists developed a folk-
lore project that collected the legends, tales, poems and songs circulating in
the camps.

BANGLADESH IS BORN

Mercifully the war between India and Pakistan was of short duration.
The humiliating defeat of Yahya Khan's troops opened the way for the refugees' return. Theoretically, the work of IRC on the subcontinent should
now have come to an end, since the organization functions primarily to aid
those in flight and is not usually involved in simple relief situations. But the
officers of the new Bangladesh government who had worked with IRC in
West Bengal urged continued assistance until some kind of normalcy —
whatever that might mean in this underdeveloped area — could be restored.

The plea could not be denied. The people who live in the northeast of the
subcontinent have been subjected repeatedly to the ravages of both man
and nature. The 90 million population of Bangladesh is the densest anywhere in the world (1,600 per square mile), and the congestion has generated both disease and violence. Nature refuses to be outdone by man in acts
of cruelty: in November 1970, only a few months before the assaults of the
Pakistani army, a cyclone and tidal wave roaring in from the Bay of Bengal
drowned some 300,000 people. Indeed, the unconcern and incompetence of
the regime in the capital, Islamabad, located in West Pakistan, had itself
been a factor in the political upheaval that led to the crisis.

Even after the return home, Bangladesh was to experience one disaster
after another. Sheik Mujibur Rahman, who had been the acknowledged
leader during the days of the emergency though imprisoned in West Pakistan, was released to take over the reins of government in Dacca. Four years

later his administration was ended by assassins. One of his successors, Ziaur Rahman, met the same fate in 1981. Today the 90 million Bangladeshis constitute the world's densest population, whose straitened circumstances require the importation of food. Shortly after the establishment of sovereignty, a smallpox epidemic claimed 7,000 lives, a harbinger of similar calamities. The human costs of an inadequate economy are compounded by corruption and internecine warfare in high places. Never had a new nation been cradled in less promising circumstances.

The first task of the Bangladesh government was to resettle the refugees and rebuild the country. The physical destruction could not even be tallied. No newcomers to power had ever faced problems of such magnitude: feeding the millions of uprooted who had made their way back, providing shelter for the orphaned children, healing the wounds of the war casualties, helping the widowed and raped women to reorder their lives. In December, as the war was drawing to a close, IRC officials Leo Cherne, Charles Sternberg and Lee Thaw who had been in at the birth of the program, hurried to Calcutta to reassess the situation. On the spot, they decided to recommend to the Board of Directors that IRC undertake major responsibilities as a refugee resettlement agency on behalf of the Bangladeshis. In January 1972 an IRC mission conferred with the President and Prime Minister of the newly ensconced government to formulate a relief and rehabilitation program. The health care network built up in the Indian camps was moved to Bangladesh, with many of the refugee professionals continuing to serve. By June the following operations were in full swing:

Some 70 IRC medical clinics were located across the country, staffed by 250 doctors, nurses, pharmacists and paramedics. Professional personnel had also been provided for established hospitals, manned, as was the Jessore IRC hospital, by veterans from the Barasat camp. Funds were raised to provide personnel for the Children's Hospital and the Sher-e-Bangla Orthopedic Hospital in Dacca and to train prosthetic specialists, physiotherapists and rehabilitation workers. In cooperation with the world's leading center for such studies, the Cholera Research Laboratory in Dacca, IRC sponsored two-week training programs to bring physicians up to date on the treatment of cholera and related diarrheal diseases, the major killer of children in this part of the globe.

In helping Bangladesh recreate a medical system for the people, IRC was constantly confronted with new and unexpected challenges. The country's hospitals lacked intravenous fluids essential to a new cholera treatment. Instead of merely satisfying the immediate need by importing a supply from abroad, a manufacturing facility that would serve as a continuing source was established. The Director of Bangladesh Health Services hailed the achievement in these words: "The installation of the I.V. Fluid Plant at the Institute of Public Health is a milestone in the history of production of life-saving medicines in Bangladesh. Without the active support and assistance from the International Rescue Committee, it would not have been possible to install this plant. This humanitarian service of the International Rescue Committee is a shining example from which millions of people in Bangladesh will derive benefit."

Youth presented special problems and needs. Many of the young refugees who had served as freedom fighters in the *Mukhti Bahini* found it difficult to pick up the threads of normalcy. Most college students could not resume their studies without financial help and, in many cases, psychological help in the form of some assurance that they would be able to complete their studies and find an appropriate place in the society. After consultation with key Bangladesh officials, IRC agreed to establish a stipend program for 12,000 university and college students. The only criterion was need. Screening was handled by a committee made up of distinguished faculty and student members, working with the vice-chancellors of the nation's six universities and the principals of the colleges.

A number of cooperative ventures were started, the most ambitious being a fishermen's cooperative in the Mymensingh area. Fishing had been the third largest industry of the country and was the major source of protein, but the war had seriously damaged the nation's fleet. IRC's project, aimed as always at ultimate self-sufficiency, was designed to rehabilitate 1,800 fishermen, grouped into twenty-five cooperatives, each with seventy-odd members.

Most heartbreaking was the plight of the large number of women who had been raped by soldiers during the occupation. Considered forever dishonored, they were no longer acceptable to their families. Even Mujibur Rahman's effort to designate them "heroines of the nation" failed to erase the culturally dictated brand. Equally desperate was the plight of war widows left with no family to turn to. IRC's answer was to establish centers where the women could be taught new skills so that they might become self-supporting. If necessary equipment, like sewing machines, was not immediately available, IRC undertook to obtain it.

Meanwhile, the shrunken state of Pakistan suffered internal upheavals as the old regime of Yahya Khan gave way to new leaders like Zulfikar Ali Bhutto, whose career would end in a hangman's noose when he in turn would be overthrown by a military dictator, General Zia-al-Huq. In the transition period that followed the birth of Bangladesh, East Pakistanis trapped in the West needed help in returning to their homes. In New York, for example, a telephone call to IRC's office told of three Bangladeshi seamen being held prisoner on the *M. V. Kaptai*, a Pakistani freighter tied up at a Moore-McCormack pier in Brooklyn. Charles Sternberg and Alton Kastner, IRC's deputy director, dropped everything and rushed to the dock. There they confronted the ship's agent, an American who denied that anybody was being held against his will. He climbed into his car and started the motor to escape the insistent IRC officials. Sternberg, grim-faced, planted his short, sturdy body in front of the vehicle. At his side stood Kastner's long, lean figure, equally obdurate. The car inched forward toward them, but they refused to move. Eventually they won agreement that the ship's owners, who happened to be German, would be notified. Then the two men climbed the gangplank and calmly told the ship's captain, Z. A. Zuberi, that they would not leave without the prisoners. Meanwhile, telephone calls were going out to the Immigration and Naturalization Service, and to the media. On this bitter winter day in March, with the cold wind blowing in from the bay, the IRC representatives kept vigil from 3 P.M. to midnight — until finally they walked off the pier with the three Bangladeshis, one of whom needed medical care as a result of a beating. A few days later the sailors were flown home at IRC expense.

The rescue was repeated on other Pakistani ships as they came into New York harbor. Harold Grimes, the New York staff member who had served for a time as IRC director in Calcutta during the refugee crisis, took over responsibility for East Pakistani sailors. He was successful in rescuing seventeen of them for repatriation to their new country Bangladesh where wives and children awaited them.

AFTER THE WAR

In the years that followed the war, history continued to be cruel to Bangladesh. In its first years, the new nation developed its own problem of "internal refugees" — the so-called Biharis, Moslems from the Indian state of Bihar who had migrated to East Pakistan in the exchange of populations but who had never been integrated into the society. During the crisis, they had become identified with the regime of Yahya Khan, and were now being punished by neglect, abuse and even violence. Because IRC enjoyed the confidence of the Bangladesh officials, it was permitted to intercede and set up a special health care program that reached an estimated 200,000 of the half million Biharis who were ultimately expatriated to West Pakistan.

The dire economic conditions of Bangladesh have contributed to its inability to build the democratic society of which the leaders talked in Calcutta. Religious differences between the majority Moslems and the minority Hindus still separate the groups behind walls of mutual distrust. Conflict among the political elite, allegations of corruption among office-holders, self-interested economic decisions that block growth, the violence of men who vie for dictatorial power, have made it impossible to counteract the general impression that Bangladesh is the world's worst "basket case." Even relations with India, once hailed as the country's benefactor, have deteriorated. Dacca berates New Delhi as an exploiter, charging that India skyrockets its prices on goods that Bangladesh must import from her neighbor. Controversy rages over the use of irrigation waters from the Brahmaputra, one of the branches of the Ganges that originates in India. New Delhi charges that frontier tribesmen in rebellion against the Indian government use Bangladesh as a sanctuary for their hit-and-run tactics, and also complains that Hindus, persecuted in Moslem Bangladesh, are once again crossing the borders.

Despite the dreams of the exiles and the aspirations nurtured in the refugee camps and in the Calcutta meeting places, utopia did not come with independence. Cynicism may find in political outcomes a rationalization for apathy or resignation, an excuse for turning away from the imperatives of the Golden Rule even while one enjoys the benefits of democracy. But a wiser doctrine holds that those who flinch from doing what they can will, in the end, forfeit what others have previously earned for them.

At the height of the Bangladesh crisis, an article in the *Saturday Review* entitled "Friend to the Displaced" wrote of the activities and philosophy of IRC: "The world's catastrophes, both natural and man-made, continue to make the work of the IRC a ray of hope to millions of human beings." It concluded by quoting a letter from Levenstein in Calcutta: "There are moments of despair when we realize that we are trying to empty an ocean of sorrow with an eye-dropper. Marge and I have had to say to each other time and again the words of the Talmud: 'It is not required of thee to complete the task, but neither art thou free to desist therefrom.... He who saves one life, it is as if he has saved the whole world.'"[6]

Photo Section

1. Marc Chagall and Varian Fry, who directed the rescue of the famous artist from Nazi-occupied France, reunited in 1958. (See p. 17.) *(Photo courtesy of IRC.)*

3. Charles (Carel) Sternberg, executive director of the IRC, who began his career in refugee work in Marseilles during the Hitler days, receives young Russian refugees in his New York office. (See pp. 19-20.) *(Photo courtesy of IRC.)*

2. Mayor Ernst Reuter, of West Berlin, who led the free city during the days when Stalin attempted, by blockade, to drive out the Western allies. Reuter himself had been a staff member of IRC stationed in Turkey, where he provided assistance to anti-Nazi Germans. (See pp. 39-40.) *(Photo courtesy of IRC.)*

4. One of the thousands of families who made their escape from totalitarianism with the assistance of IRC. (*Photo courtesy of IRC.*)

5. A Cuban family, after many years of separation, is reunited by IRC. (See pp. 101 *et seq.*) (*Photo courtesy of IRC.*)

6. Former Ambassador Angier Biddle Duke, IRC president, and Board member Mrs. Lawrence Copley Thaw, confer with Mother Teresa of Calcutta on plans for assistance to the millions of refugees who fled from East Pakistan. (See p. 143.) (*Photo courtesy of IRC.*)

7. IRC President Mary P. Lord and the author, with medical personnel at an IRC field hospital in Barasat, West Bengal, during the Bangladesh crisis in 1971. (See p. 144.) (*Photo courtesy of IRC.*)

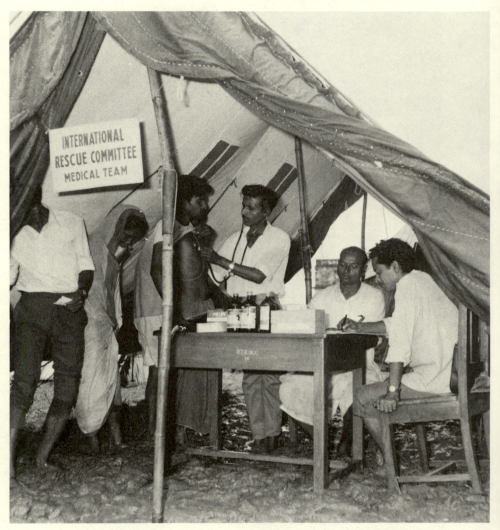

8. An IRC outpatient facility staffed by refugee doctors at work in rural West Bengal during the monsoon season. Note the doctor standing barefoot and ankle-deep in mud. (See p. 135.) (*Photo courtesy of IRC.*)

9. Angolan refugees, still suffering from malnutrition, shortly after reaching safety in Zaire where IRC provided food and medical care for thousands. (See pp. 165-67.) (*Photo courtesy of IRC.*)

10. A Ugandan mother and her child, who fled Idi Amin's terror, arrive at the entrance to the IRC clinic in Nairobi. (See p. 170.) (*Photo courtesy of IRC.*)

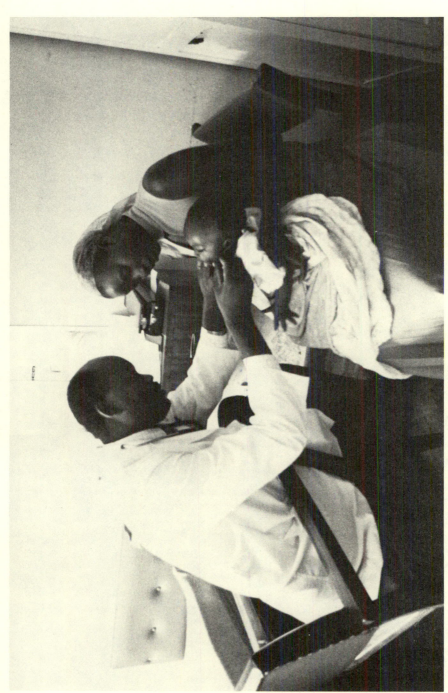

11. An IRC staff physician, himself a Ugandan refugee, examines a child in the Nairobi clinic. (See p. 178.) (*Photo courtesy of IRC.*)

12. Ugandan refugees in Nairobi participating in IRC's furniture-making course. (See p. 181.) (*Photo courtesy of IRC.*)

13. Hong Kong police seize "freedom swimmers" seeking to escape from Mao Zedong's China. (See p. 198.) (*Photo courtesy of South China Morning Post, Ltd.*)

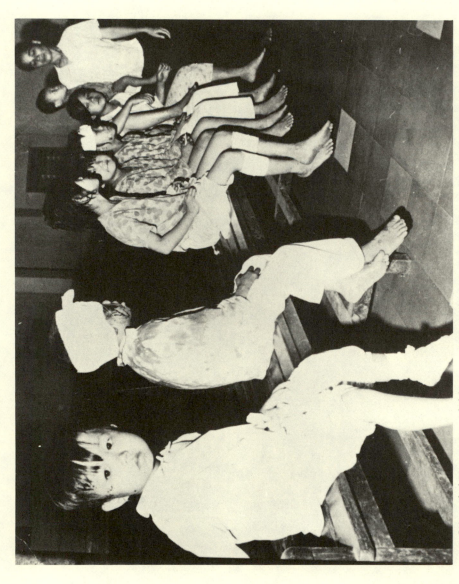

14. Wounded Vietnamese children await treatment at an IRC facility in Vietnam. (See p. 217.) (*Photo courtesy of IRC.*)

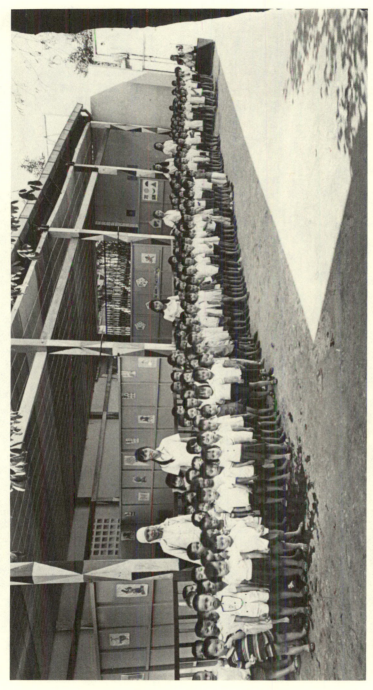

15. While the war rages around them, Vietnamese children receive care at an IRC day center. (See p. 218.) (*Photo courtesy of IRC.*)

16. Photo distributed by the UN High Commissioner for Refugees, illustrating the conditions in which the Vietnamese boat people crossed the open sea to reach Indonesia. (See Chapter XIV.) (*Photo courtesy of UN High Commissioner for Refugees.*)

17. The beachfront sight that greeted the Citizens Commission on Indochinese Refugees at Pulau-Bidong. (See pp. 230-32.) (*Photo courtesy of IRC.*)

18. Vietnamese boat people who made it successfully to the Laem Singh refugee camp in Thailand, seeking resettlement in the United States. (See p. 259.) (*Photo courtesy of IRC.*)

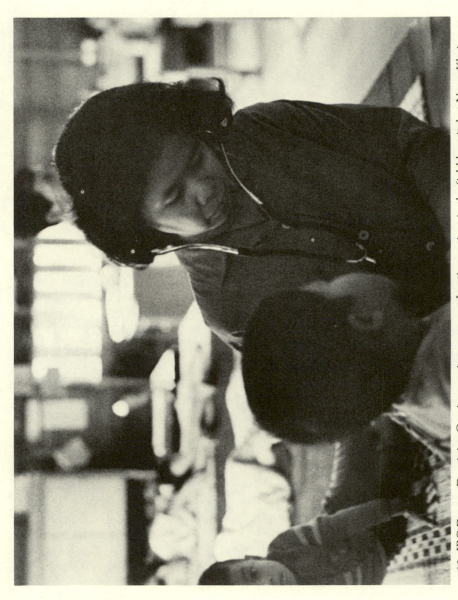

19. IRC Doctor Dominica Garcia examines a young Laotian patient in the field hospital at Nong Khai, Thailand. (See pp. 244-47.) (*Photo courtesy of IRC.*)

20. Bayard Rustin, civil rights leader and IRC Board member, and IRC Chairman Leo Cherne, on a tour of refugee camps in Thailand, in preparation for their report as members of the Citizens Commission on Indochinese Refugees. (See pp. 266-67.) (*Photo courtesy of IRC.*)

21. Vice-President Liv Ullmann on the Thai-Cambodian border during the March for Survival. (See her statement on pp. 278-79.) (*Photo courtesy of Wide World Photos, Inc.*)

22. Some of the Afghan refugees, estimated to number more than two million, who fled from the Soviet army into Pakistan, and who are being served by IRC. (See p. 294.) (*Photo courtesy of IRC.*)

X

Twilight of Empire in Africa

There is a stillness in the African plains unlike the quiet of other regions. In the afternoon hours, the traveler comes on a pride of lions huddled together in secure sleep under the hot sun. Overhead the vultures wheel, waiting for the lions to wake, anticipating a kill before long. A languor covers the sweep of high grass and scrub as the animal world seems content with its destiny. Slowly, activity begins. The lions wake and rise to their feet. Now the wildebeest, the topis and the gazelles that grazed nearby in complete unconcern a moment ago break into a frenzy of flight, hooves pounding beneath them as they look for refuge.

This daily scenario in the contest for survival is a fitting allegory for the story of Africa, both before and after colonialism. While Western imperialism still gripped the continent, African nationalists who opposed the European empires were frequently forced to flee. They were relatively few, a mere handful, until the white man's empire entered its twilight. Then, as underground movements began to win mass support, repression and violence turned a trickle into a stream and finally a torrent.

Independence made it possible for many to return to their homes. But another segment of the people, often in even greater numbers, were now thrust into exile by civil war. Native dictators took control. With the shift in ethnic power, nonblack minorities, like the "Asians," many of them descendants of immigrants from India who had come in the nineteenth century, became the targets of expropriation and deportation.

Winston Churchill, an old Africa hand himself who had spent some of his youthful years as a journalist in South and East Africa, once said that he had not become the king's first minister to preside over the liquidation of the British empire. But the man who had defeated Hitler could not defeat historical inevitability. From the seat in Parliament that he occupied until one year before his death in 1965, he observed the night fall on what Britains once boasted was so global an empire that the sun always shone on its flag.

TRANSITION

The methodical British, once they recognized that the end of empire was at hand, proceeded to arrange a systematic transfer of power. They had trained a native civil service; their universities had educated men and women who were destined for leadership in independent societies; and they had established rudimentary legislatures and Anglo-Saxon jurisprudence. In what had been British East Africa, the decolonization of the 1960s was smoother than in such neighboring areas as the Belgian Congo.

By 1961, a majority of the faces in the chamber of Kenya's Legislative Council, a physical replica of the House of Commons in London, were black. In that year, Jomo Kenyatta, the formidable leader of the Mau Mau, was released from jail to negotiate independence. In 1963 he assumed the presidency of the newly created republic, an office he held until his death in 1978 at the age of eighty-four.

Uganda was given its independence in 1962, to begin a course that was peaceful at first but was finally marked by an unmeasurable record of brutality, even for the brutal twentieth century. Whether Uganda under the indescribable Amin or Cambodia under the unspeakable Pol Pot deserves the badge of lowest infamy cannot be answered until future researchers complete a census of the dead and tortured in both countries.

Tanganyika was the third of the colonies that had been a part of the British creation called the East African Union. It enjoyed a calm transition in 1962. Under Julius Nyerere, it too become a one-party state, and, like Kenyatta, its president could boast a broad base of mass support. In 1964, the merger with Zanzibar produced a new name on the map of Africa — Tanzania.

To the south, Rhodesia and South Africa, intent on maintaining white domination, had seceded from the postwar commonwealth that replaced the empire. Eventually, Rhodesia became Zimbabwe, bowing to the new winds blowing around the world, and sought to compromise by writing a new constitution and installing, in 1979, a black-led government under Abel Muzorewa. A final settlement negotiated by the British resulted in the electoral victory of Robert Mugabe, the guerrilla leader thought to be pro-Communist, but who began his administration with gestures of reconciliation and moderation, only to end his coalition once he had cemented power.

Westward, in the heartland of the continent, chaos had been unleashed. In 1960 the Belgians simply threw up their hands and abandoned the Congo, whose population had literally been decimated during the years of white rule. Little had been done to pave the way for self-government. It was said that at the time of independence there were less than a dozen native college graduates in the land and not a single Congolese accountant available to handle the books of the new nation Zaire. Events had moved fast. On January 13, 1959, King Baudouin broadcast a promise that Belgium would "lead the Congolese peoples, without petty recriminations but also without undue haste, to independence in peace and prosperity."[1] A year later the government set June 30, 1960, as the date on which the Belgian flag would be lowered for the last time in Leopoldville. Even a writer friendly to Belgium argued that "haste can no more be curbed than recriminations can be avoided, and that in the matter of birth, whether of a nation or a child, the shorter the labor, the better for the mother — if not always the child."[2] In matters colonial, the first consideration is always the parent.

The result was civil strife in Zaire, marked by massacres of white settlers, political assassinations of native leaders, separatist movements, tribal warfare and foreign interventions, all contributing to an instability which the new country has not been able to overcome. Even so, Zaire was destined to become a haven for refugees from Angola, while the latter, in turn, became a base for secessionist tribesmen seeking to detach the copper- and uranium-rich province of Shaba, formerly Katanga, from the rest of the country.

The French had followed another course. At first, they resisted the demands for independence. Before the nation had had time to heal the wounds left by World War II — the defeat, the Nazi occupation and the lingering sores of the Pétain collaboration — it decided to bear the costly burden in lives and treasure of the Indochinese and Algerian wars. The initial surrender was in the Far East; Algeria was an even more prolonged anguish. De Gaulle had finally ended the dilemma as only a strong man could, bidding the North African colony farewell rather than suffer continued bloodletting. The liquidation of the French empire in an effort to retain at least economic and cultural ties, both in Asia and Africa, was possible precisely because of de Gaulle's conviction that France was still destined for leadership and glory. Ultimately, however, the price for these long overdue political changes was paid not by social entities, abstractions like national sovereignties, but by individual human beings.

ANGOLA — FIRST WAVE

African refugees at first drew little attention from the world press. But by 1962 the International Rescue Committee could already discern the clouds on the horizon. Its annual report for that year begins with the statement:

1962 was a year of vast movements on all continents. For the first time, however, Africa was the major scene of displacements. More than one million people were on the move, in flight from oppressive regimes or in the wake of national revolutions. By the end of the year, the number of Angolan refugees in the Congo exceeded 200,000. About 130,000 refugees from Rwanda were forced to seek sanctuary in neighboring countries, roughly one-half of them in the Kivu province of the Congo, the other half in Burundi, Tanganyika and Uganda. Close to 800,000 Algerian repatriates entered France, among them 110,000 Jews, four-fifths of Algeria's Jewish population.

Angola, Rwanda, Burundi—these remote places might well have been located on another planet, so far as most Americans were concerned. In the shrinking world exotic names would eventually reach the front page head-lines, and their conflicts would pit the Congress of the United States against the President, as in the case of Angola in 1975 when the two branches of government split on an American response to Soviet involvement and Cuban armed intervention in the civil war.

The story goes back to the days when Portugal was making the last stand for imperialism in Africa and attempting desperately to hold on to Angola, with its population of some 6 million. Portuguese navigators had first explored it in the fifteenth century, long before anybody was aware of its treasures—diamonds, copper, oil, iron and manganese. In the early days, the major raw material sought by the Portuguese was slaves, manpower for the colonists in Brazil. By the twentieth century half a million whites lived in Angola, or Portuguese West Africa as it was better known.

In 1961, however, a native revolt broke out and was put down by the Portuguese army. Hundreds of thousands fled to escape the fury of the mili-tary, seeking shelter in neighboring countries. To the west lies the Atlantic Ocean; to the south, Namibia held by South Africa; to the east, Zambia; and to the north, Zaire. The latter became the principal destination of the refugees. During 1962 the number of Angolans who escaped from the Por-tuguese rose to 280,000. They huddled in a score of isolated refugee settle-ments along the Zaire border, desperate for food and medical care. In response to their need, the International Rescue Committee launched the first of its many African programs.

American sister agencies of the IRC addressed themselves to the problem of food. An IRC observer had noted that virtually every refugee was suffer-ing from some malady, the most common being malaria, worm and parasite infections, scabies and bronchial infections. Exposure to the elements has always been a deadly enemy of refugees on the move. Frequently, rescue teams encounter men, women and even children wounded by rifle fire, mine bursts or shell fragments. Nature, not content with the hardships man imposes on his brothers, multiplies the number of broken bones, hernias, tumors and goiters that call for treatment.

IRC answered the challenge by recruiting a French-speaking surgeon, himself a refugee from Haiti who had reached New York. With the assist-ance of a grant from the New Land Foundation, Dr. Marcus A. Woolley was dispatched to Leopoldville (now Kinshasa) to work with the *Service d'Assistance aux Refugiés Angolais,* known by the acronym SARA. Among his duties was the task of administering the more than $65,000 worth of medical supplies shipped in by IRC as a result of contributions from the

American pharmaceutical industry. In addition to doing all of the surgery carried out at the SARA clinic, he performed many operations at the border camps which he visited frequently by Land Rover. His services and the vehicle had been funded by the Africa Services Institute and by a $15,000 grant from the Norman Foundation. Much of his time was devoted to teaching first aid and preventive care to the refugees, and in training and upgrading the skills of Angolan nurses and medical technicians so that better surgical, anesthesia and general health practices could be made available in dispensaries and facilities in the outlying areas. The enormity of the challenge was reflected by the fact that during 1963 only three other doctors were in the field to serve the needs of 280,000 refugees scattered over large areas and in almost inaccessible jungle stations. It was estimated that the available medicines were not enough to treat more than a fifth of those in need.

This gift from the Norman Foundation, curiously, brought repercussions in later years. During the early 1970s, when the Central Intelligence Agency was under heavy scrutiny, it was revealed that a number of foundations had served as conduits for the secret transmission of CIA funds. The Norman Foundation was said to have been one of them. Its records showed clearly, however, that its contribution to IRC's medical service in Angola came solely from its own resources. It should have been obvious in any case that the CIA could not possibly have had any interest in providing medical care for Angolan refugees fleeing from Portuguese colonialism. Nevertheless, thirteen years later, when IRC was assisting Angolans escaping from the Communists, a *New York Times* reporter wrote a story asserting that the organization and its chairman Leo Cherne had been linked to the CIA's "covert financing activities." When the facts were called to the attention of the editor, a news story appeared under the headline, "Cherne Unit Not Tied to CIA Fund."

The tale developed a life of its own. In 1980 it surfaced again in an article dealing with rumored Presidential appointments to the Board of International Broadcasting. This account referred to IRC as having "reportedly received $15,000 in CIA money in the mid-1960s." The reporter immediately wrote to Cherne, saying, "I can't tell you how sorry I am about the erroneous reference in my story today about that $15,000 payment," and the following day the *Times* published a "correction."

The sequel was not without its rewarding aspect in Congress. The two senators from New York, Democrat Daniel Patrick Moynihan and Republican Jacob Javits, took the floor for more than an hour to laud the International Rescue Committee and its chairman. Moynihan described IRC's refugee work and said of Cherne: "He is a man of implacable attachment to the principles of freedom, beyond party and partisanship." Describing Cherne's efforts on behalf of those who fight totalitarianism, Moynihan said, "He has been anathematized for that by the victimizers, and his intentions have been impugned. He has suffered all that persons with high public purpose endure in any age and perhaps singularly so in an open society. But he has never been the least bit deterred in his purposes."

At the time of the Norman grant funding of Dr. Woolley's activities, there were many threats to IRC's ability to continue functioning in Africa. The mounting turmoil in Zaire, to which the refugees were fleeing, meant that IRC representatives could work only at great personal peril from both insurgent and government troops. The ranks of the escapees were growing constantly. As if by some principle of capillarity, the greater the number who cross a border, the greater the flow becomes.

Fortunately, American concern about Africa increased. Together with the Catholic Relief Services and the Church World Service, IRC was able to win more support for the refugees. In 1964 the amount of supplies sent to the Leopoldville clinic and the border substations — drugs, medicines, beds, surgical equipment, high-protein food — came to $179,000, exceeding the combined total for the previous two years.

But discouraging events were to follow. Dr. Woolley's eighteen-month period of service came to an end, and he returned to the United States. His replacement, a Haitian physician who specialized in obstetrics and malariology, found it impossible to remain after the United Nations forces were withdrawn in midyear and security deteriorated. Fortunately, by that time the SARA clinic had been expanded, and the more difficult cases were now being transferred to the Leopoldville hospitals. Local personnel had been trained. For example, a grant from IRC made it possible for an Angolan male nurse to take courses at Louvanium University so that he might assist in anesthesia.

SAFARI OF THE WRETCHED

As 1964 drew to a close, IRC found itself in a widening African whirlwind comparable to the "red devils," as the natives call the tornados that sweep up the red soil of Africa in swirling cones of destruction. The number of refugees now rushing across the indeterminate borders of African nations had reached a million. All of the potential forces for tyranny had converged: the prejudices of traditional colonialism; the adoption of racist policies by some African governments; authoritarian leadership that had triumphed in internecine feuds; the release of ancient tribal animosities; rivalries among the new sovereign states seeking to rectify the artificial boundaries left by imperialism; religious differences. Reviewing this situation, IRC's Board of Directors concluded that "Africa was becoming one of the most critical locales of refugee need" and authorized its staff to make "serious studies of the areas on the African continent where IRC's future assistance would be appropriate and possible."

By the end of 1965 an adequate native staff was available to assume full responsibility for the Medical Clinic for Angolans in Leopoldville. Two African doctors from the Leopoldville General Hospital took over. IRC thought it could turn its attention elsewhere.

A new project was started in Francistown, Bechuanaland (now Botswana), for refugees coming from the southern part of the continent. The landlocked nation exists with anomalous borders. The major escape hatch for refugees fleeing from white governments was a hundred-yard-wide frontier with Zambia in the north, between Southwest Africa's narrow Caprivi strip and Rhodesia. Located in this area, Francistown was being used primarily as an in-transit center to independent black countries in the north. Activities included providing food, shelter and recreational services; a major effort involved educating young refugees so that they might qualify for admission to secondary schools and universities in Zambia and Tanzania.

The numbers escaping from Rhodesia and South Africa at this time were not large, some 200. Because of turnover, there were usually about seventy refugees being cared for in Francistown. A British group, the Joint Committee on the High Commission Territories, attempted to set up a transit center called the White House, but just as the construction reached its final stages it was destroyed by dynamite. IRC agreed to share the cost of reconstruction. On its completion, the center housed and fed fifty refugees at any given time. There were even facilities in the White House for special classes in eleven secondary school subjects, and the government granted formal permission "to conduct academic testing of refugees." Some forty graduates of "Bush College," as an African newspaper dubbed it, ultimately applied for admission to the American-African Institute's Nkumbi International College in Zambia.

BLACK vs. BLACK

The first generation of refugees in Africa consisted of natives forced to flee by white regimes. Through the 1970s, other black anticolonialists still continued to spill over the borders of the last white-ruled countries on the continent, South Africa, Zimbabwe-Rhodesia and Namibia.

New generations of refugees, however, were due to take their turn on the road to exile. IRC would have to return to Zaire, as blacks fled from their fellow-countrymen in Angola who had won control with the aid of Russian arms and Cuban mercenaries. But this still lay in the future. Meanwhile, in 1967, post-colonial Africa reached a turning point — the beginning of the Biafra horror. More than any other event, the war in Nigeria made the world conscious of the refugee problem in a continent now darkened by civil and tribal strife.

Of all the peoples of Nigeria, the Ibos, living in various parts of this Texas-sized country, had been for a long time the most successful commercially. Now they found themselves threatened by the political power of the more numerous Hausa tribe. Failing to curb the growing authority of the central government, the Ibos began to withdraw to their own tribal lands in the eastern part of the country, a flight that was considerably accelerated in September 1966 when wholesale massacres occurred in the north. In 1967, they proclaimed the birth of Biafra as an independent nation.

The result was full-fledged war. For three years the battle raged, and famine, war's sibling, took the lives of countless Biafrans. It was the first of the post-World War II crises in which television would bring to American living rooms the spectacle of emaciated children with swollen bellies and skeletons limned against parched skin. Governments and voluntary agencies led by the International Red Cross beat against the walls of bureaucracy and political complexity in the effort to save as many lives as possible.

IRC joined with other organizations in the concerted drive to assemble food, medications and equipment for the Biafrans. At IRC's initiative, implemented in conjunction with the Biafra Relief Service Foundation, a "Biafra Christmas Ship" was loaded with a cargo of 3,000 tons of high-protein food, antibiotics, drugs and vitamins specifically requested by Biafran health services. At the last moment, when it was about to weigh anchor, a dock strike threatened to defeat the enterprise. The longshoremen, however, apprised by IRC of the urgent mission on which the vessel was bound, offered their full cooperation, and the ship sailed on New Year's Day of 1969 from Newport News for Sao Tomé in the Bight of Biafra.

At first the Biafran troops seemed headed for victory, at one point even threatening Lagos, the capital of Nigeria. But their initial success in holding the oil fields could not overcome the economic disadvantage of being a food-importing region. Famine, and the superior arms of the central government, including airpower, determined the outcome. Surrender came in 1970, but not until an estimated million civilians had died of malnutrition.

The spotlight stayed on Biafra through those years and in the immediate period that followed when a humane Nigerian leader, General Yakubu Gowon, initiated a Lincolnesque policy of reconciliation rather than retribution. A multinational effort was launched to achieve reconstruction. As part of its contribution, IRC located five Nigerian doctors working as residents in American hospitals and arranged for them to get formal leave so that they might return to their country and apply the skills they had acquired in the United States. One doctor assumed charge of the Convalescent Center at Port Harcourt, a major industrial center and deep-water port in the southeast. Two were assigned to the hospital in Niger, and two were attached to mobile hospitals that brought patients out of the bush, especially children suffering from Africa's horrible nutritional disease *kwashiorkor*, readily identifiable by edema, swollen belly and changes in skin pigmentation.

The magnitude of the Biafran crisis made the focus on West Africa almost inevitable, to the neglect of the rising number of refugees in more obscure places. In other parts of Africa, bruising domestic conflicts were driving ever larger numbers of Angolans, Rwandese, Sudanese, Congolese, Guineans and Mozambiquans into the forests that crossed the nearest borders. Now the techniques that IRC had developed in the camps of the Angolans in Zaire proved useful in the new territories where the refugees had temporarily come to rest.

In Tanzania, a number of Mozambiquan students and Rwandese had clustered together in the area of Rulenge, whose hospital was having difficulty providing appropriate care. IRC learned that the 123-bed facility operated by the White Fathers had just completed a special tuberculosis building — the disease was endemic to the region, as it still is in much of the underdeveloped world — but had been unable to staff it. Funds were raised to pay for a physician and X-ray technician so that the building could be put into operation promptly. In 1968, IRC sent a Haitian refugee doctor to the Rulenge hospital which was now serving a population of about 65,000. His wife, a qualified laboratory technician, doubled as an assistant in surgery. They reported that more than 50 percent of the outpatients treated at the hospital were refugees suffering from respiratory diseases, including tuberculosis, illnesses of the digestive tract, malaria and open wounds. In 1969, the hospital increased its activities by adding a prenatal clinic, a child welfare center and a dispensary. The scope of its staff was widened to include field visits to the refugee camps and to coordinate a campaign of vaccination and public health.

Uganda, under the rule of Milton Obote, attracted refugees from Rwanda, the Sudan and Zaire in impressive numbers. What had been a haven would ultimately become a point of departure, but in the late 1960s, Kampala was receiving several hundred thousand. Official figures for 1967 report the presence of 70,000 Rwandese, most of them aristocratic Watutsis who in recent years had become the targets of Hutu tribesmen; 55,000 Sudanese, many of whom had fled because they were discriminated against as non-Arabs; and 35,000 from Zaire, again victims of tribal warfare. The immediate impulse for taking flight varied. Among the Sudanese, for example, the principal factor was the denial of educational opportunity for their children; in some instances, teachers led whole classes of pupils across the border into Uganda.

The mounting figures led IRC to recognize that it would soon be facing a major responsibility in Africa. The year was 1967, four years before Amin would overthrow Obote and turn Uganda into a snakepit of madness and violence, a decade before the Horn of Africa would become the battleground of Somalis and Ethiopians, and Haile Selassie's kingdom would be replaced by a Communist dictatorship. The IRC leadership reported in sober terms: "Refugee problems in Africa will undoubtedly multiply and intensify as the result of complex tribal, religious, racial, national and political conflicts. Biafra is an extreme example, but it would be unrealistic not to expect more crises in this developing continent where so many new nations are groping for identity and survival. IRC's commitment to the refugee cause, therefore, will require a deepening of its involvement in Africa."

BLACK AGAINST ASIAN

Some two years went by before a new African crisis caught the eye of the Western world. It was precipitated by Idi Amin's racist campaign against the Ugandan "Asians," or more precisely the descendants of Indians brought in by the British at the turn of the century to build the Kenya-Uganda Railway. Many had gone home, but a large number stayed to earn a major place for themselves in the economy of British East Africa. Some started truck farms and raised the vegetables eaten in the port cities of Kenya; others grew sugar and coffee. The railway needed clerical help, and the economy needed skilled craftsmen. Increasingly, the Indian resident worked his way into the ranks of the middle class, as a *dukawala*, or small shopkeeper. A British bureaucrat's report in 1929, snobbish in tone but significant in content, concluded: "There can be no doubt that in the past the Indian community has played a useful, and in fact an indispensable part in the development of these territories. Apart from the construction of the Kenya-Uganda Railway, the services of Indian artisans and mechanics have been widely used by the public at large on works for which European agency would have been too costly and which the native is not yet fitted to perform. The Indian trader has been a potent factor in the process of civilising the African."[3]

It is now forgotten that Mahatma Gandhi first came to public attention as a lawyer in South Africa defending his fellow-countrymen against British discrimination. It was there, in 1907, that he first developed and applied his technique of nonviolent resistance, which became the model for Martin Luther King in the United States. In 1914, he proved the efficacy of nonviolence by compelling the British regime in South Africa to grant the Indians some degree of protection against discrimination. His campaign thus paved the way for his fellow-immigrants to make economic and social progress, transforming them into a middle class.

In 1972, Idi Amin was turning back the clock. Reduced to chaos by unrestrained looting, Uganda's economy was in shards. The Asians were available for ethnic scapegoating, a self-taught technique that Amin did not have to learn from his model Adolf Hitler. By despoiling the relatively wealthy, he continued to buy the loyalty of his Nubian guards whom he released, jackal-like, to feed on the Indian community. The details have faded from the memory of the West, but they warrant retelling. Henry Kyemba, who was a cabinet minister for five years in Amin's government but who finally fled in horror and guilt, gives this account in his book, *State of Blood:*

On August 4 [1972], Amin appeared at the barracks at Tororo, near the Kenyan border, and announced to the troops that he had had a dream the previous night in which God instructed him to order the 50,000 Asians out of Uganda within ninety days. This he proceeded to do.

The Asian community was an ideal target. Asians almost totally controlled Uganda's trade, factories, plantations and industries. They were the managers, the bureaucrats, the accountants, the technicians, the doctors, the engineers, the lawyers. They formed an affluent middle class, a distinctive element in the population, with their own language, behavior patterns, names and occupations. On the whole they were not popular with the Africans. They have been described as the Jews of East Africa. They were, in other words, ideal targets.

By the 1970's, 30,000 of Uganda's Asians had British passports, but the other 20,000 were legally Ugandans. At the time of Amin's original announcement, nobody thought that he intended to expel both Ugandan Asians and British Asians. But it soon became clear that he did not intend to make a distinction between passports. He wanted the Asians' property to hand over to his troops. It was a brutal and thoroughly racist decision, and one that was to deal the Ugandan economy a terrible blow.[4]

Asian businesses were simply despoiled and ceased to be viable enterprises. Retail establishments were looted and shut down. Dairy farms collapsed as stock was slaughtered for quick profit by the expropriators; milk, cheese and eggs disappeared from Ugandan tables. The Nakasero Soap Works, a major producer, was reduced to idleness under the new "management." Kyemba concludes: "Amin was amazed at what was happening. He never realized that businesses needed educated people to keep them running."[5]

As for the former owners and managers, the Asians, they were simply stripped of their possessions, their bank accounts were sequestered, and they were ordered to leave the country with no more than a personal allowance of a hundred dollars. Never before did any government publicly proclaim a policy of private looting with so destructive an effect on its own economy. Just before the deadline of November 8, 1972, an airlift flew out several thousand Indians and landed them in transit centers set up in Austria, Belgium, Italy, Malta and Spain. Many who held British passports went to London. The United States agreed to take some 2,000, and IRC assumed responsibility for settling one-sixth of these. Subsequently, in 1974, the State Department approved the admission of an additional quota of Ugandans — parents, children, and even unmarried sons and daughters over the age of twenty-one.

This kind of resettlement was not a new experience for IRC. With the assistance of Indian societies and student groups, homes were found for the Ugandan Asians in a dozen metropolitan centers across the country. As is the case with most refugee groups, no matter what their origin, they represented a good cross-section of their culture. An analysis of the group aided by IRC shows that 45 percent were Hindus, 23 percent Ismaeli Moslems, 22 percent adherents of other Moslem sects, 5 percent Catholics and 5 percent Sikhs. In Uganda, their economic activities were diverse: 16 percent had been employers; 50 percent, employees; 5 percent, unpaid workers in a family business; and 29 percent, self-employed. In the United States, after a period of adjustment, they made places for themselves with little difficulty and became self-supporting. But it is doubtful that any of them will ever outgrow the scars left by the brutal racism of Idi Amin.

With the Asians out of the way, Amin settled down to an anarchic brutalization of his own people. At least the Indians had been able to depart, but the Ugandans remained to suffer—until in 1979 Tanzanian troops and native guerrillas drove Idi Amin to seek refuge in Libya.

PORTUGUESE WITHDRAWAL

In the early seventies the coastline of Africa had become, and has since remained, a key highway for the Western world. With the Suez canal closed as a result of the 1967 Six-Day War in the Middle East, oil for the autos and furnaces of Europe, Asia and America was being carried through the Persian Gulf, down the Horn, along the littoral of the Indian Ocean, round the Cape of Good Hope, then north past the strategic areas discovered by the Portuguese mariners under Henry the Navigator, Prince of Portugal. The lust for geographical hegemony has been the engine that moves populations. "The first major result of Henry's labors," write Will and Ariel Durant, "was the inauguration of the African slave trade" in the Western world; the Moslems had already set the pattern.[6] A contemporary account by a Portuguese captain, describing a slaving expedition in 1444, tells a story that has remained familiar throughout the history of refugee flight:

Our men, crying out, "Sant' Iago! San Jorge! Portugal!" fell upon them, killing or capturing all they could. There you might have seen mothers catch up their children, husbands their wives, each one escaping as best he could. Some plunged into the sea; others thought to hide themselves in the corners of their hovels; others hid their children under the shrubs . . . where our men found them. And at last our Lord God, Who gives to all a due reward, gave to our men that day a victory over their enemies; and in recompense for all their toil in His service they took 165 men, women, and children, not counting the slain.[7]

Again and again these coasts were bloodied by would-be conquerors, intent on wealth or, more important in the twentieth century, power. Last among the imperial nations, Portugal clung to its African territories. The fascist dictatorship initiated in 1932 by Salazar and led by him until his stroke in 1968 was crumbling. The high cost of holding on to Angola,

Mozambique, Guinea, the Cape Verde Islands, was four years of compulsory military service for the individual and 40 percent of the nation's annual budget. In 1972, the regime attempted to stave off the inevitable by allowing limited autonomy in the colonies. But it was too late. Three years later, reality was recognized and independence was granted.

Under the leadership of Frelimo, the Mozambique Liberation Front, the territory that lies on the Indian Ocean just north of South Africa, slipped into the Marxist camp. Across the continent, on the Atlantic coast, the transition from European colony to Communist ally was more difficult. A three-sided conflict broke out. The National Union for the Total Liberation of Angola (UNITA), which was supported by the country's largest single ethnic group, seemed certain to win if free elections were held. A smaller group, the National Front for the Liberation of Angola (FNLA), also bid for power. But the Popular Movement for the Liberation of Angola (MPLA) was destined to defeat both because it had the support of the Soviet Union in the form of military supplies and overt intervention with Cuban troops.

GEOPOLITICS

The situation that precipitated the second major wave of refugees into the already swollen camps of Zaire was described by two members of the Board of Directors of the International Rescue Committee in 1977. Bayard Rustin, civil rights leader, former aide to Martin Luther King and later president of the A. Philip Randolph Institute, and Carl Gershman, executive director of Social Democrats, U.S.A. and a noted political analyst, summarized the facts in an article in *Commentary*:

Angola, in July 1976, became the first African nation formally to join Comecon, the economic arm of the Warsaw Pact nations. This was part payment for the military arms that Moscow sent to the MPLA. In the second half of 1974, $6 million worth of weapons went to the MPLA through Dar es Salaam, the capital of Tanzania and its major port. During 1975, the Kremlin's military shipments rose to $200 million. According to U.S. officials, by February 1976, the year of MPLA's victory, the Russians had shipped in some $300 million of war materiel in an eleven-month period. The weaponry included 600 tanks, 500 trucks, twelve MIG-21 fighters, and more than a hundred 122 mm. rocket launchers, not to mention lighter equipment.

To counteract this aid, but intent on avoiding an African Vietnam, the United States had authorized some token arms — $300,000 worth of weapons to the FNLA, regarded generally as less effective than UNITA. As the combat situation deteriorated, Washington attempted to provide $30 million in covert aid for UNITA and FNLA, but publication of the fact and congressional opposition interdicted the effort. The leaders of Zambia and Zaire, fearing the presence of a Soviet satellite at their doorstep, turned in desperation to South Africa, despite the political implications of such an intervention. In the end, the South Africans, after seizing some territory, withdrew, leaving the area to be retaken by Cuban troops.

Rustin and Gershman describe the worldwide significance of these events:

That the Soviet Union appreciates the importance of the sea lanes around Africa is indicated by the countries where it has chosen to concentrate its efforts. With the exception of Uganda, these countries – Somalia, Tanzania, Mozambique, Angola, Congo-Brazzaville, the Congo, Equatorial Guinea, Sierra Leone, Guinea, and Guinea-Bissau – are situated along the eastern and western coastline of Africa. Each of these countries now plays host to "the Gurkhas of the Russian empire" (to use Daniel P. Moynihan's apt description of the ubiquitous Cubans). Even the considerable Soviet interest in Uganda is tied to Moscow's coastal designs, in that Amin's brutal dictatorship poses a potential threat to neighboring Kenya, the only country along the eastern littoral of Africa where American vessels are still welcome. (American ships have by-passed South Africa since a boycott was imposed fourteen years ago.) The Soviet Union's extraordinary involvement on both sides of the conflict between Ethiopia and Somalia could (if it does not backfire) strengthen Moscow's position in the Indian Ocean and give it command of the entrance to the Red Sea.[8]

Non-Communist African leaders have recognized their plight. President Kenneth Kaunda of Zambia has described the Soviet Union (and Cuba) as "a plundering tiger with its deadly cubs now coming in through the back door."[9] President Houphouet-Boigny of the Ivory Coast has denounced the Cubans in these words: "In less than two years, they have killed thousands of Angolans – our African brothers, murdered in cold blood. More victims fell in this short period than in the fifteen years of guerrilla war against Portuguese colonialism. Yet the West rarely notes this gruesome reality."[10]

Also little noted in the Western media was the prolonged agony of those forced into exile, especially the people from Cabinda, an enclave that had been cut off from Portuguese West Africa in 1885 to provide the Congo with an outlet to the sea. For a time the Cabindans hoped to achieve their own independence but they have not been able to shake off the grip of the new Angola.

It was in this region that the Cubans were most active in the service of the MPLA. In December 1976, IRC representatives in Zaire found some 30,000 Cabindans, including thousands of children. Many were dying of extreme malnutrition, malaria, tuberculosis and intestinal diseases. A local pastor lamented that the simplest wooden coffins were an unaffordable luxury; he had even run out of blankets in which to bury the dead.

INITIAL HURDLES

On receiving this first report from Zaire, IRC/New York promptly cabled that it was authorizing $50,000 for the next few months. A representative was stationed in Kinshasa to supervise the emergency distribution of food, medicines, vaccines and blankets. An "outreach program" was initiated to penetrate the remote settlements.

Among the initial problems, as in most refugee crises, was "the delicate political situation." The host government is bound to be concerned about the domestic problems that result from an influx of foreigners. What will be the economic costs of harboring the newcomers? How will they be received by the local population? Are the strangers genuine refugees or infiltrators sent in for subversive purposes? As for the representatives of the relief agencies, is their activity a cloak for foreign intervention?

In addition, the host government must consider its relations with the country of origin. The presence of a large refugee population invites raids across the border, with the possible danger to its own nationals. Will the area become a base for a resistance movement, and then a target for retaliation? Nationalist groups, especially those with messianic expectations, are expansionist. Thus Antonio Agostinho Neto, the MPLA leader, openly warned Zambia and Tanzania that Angola-style "socialism" was to be a model for all Africa.[11]

Most delicate is the political position of the United Nations High Commissioner for Refugees—a far-flung agency that is more than the single person referred to by the title. Successor to the International Refugee Organization of World War II days, its mission is to give official status to refugees; to monitor camps or supervise the conditions under which the refugees are being maintained; to keep contact with the host government; to grant initial funds for rudimentary housing, food and clothing; and to coordinate with the activities of voluntary agencies like the Catholic Relief Services, the World Church Service, CARE, the Lutheran World Service, Caritas, the Save the Children Federation, HIAS and the International Rescue Committee. Funding of the UN agency depends on the contributions of member nations, with the United States carrying the largest share. For its many services, the UNHCR was awarded the Nobel Peace Prize in 1954.

Since it is an arm of the United Nations, its activities are subject to the constraints and prevailing pressures of the world organization and those who control it in a given period. Even though the nations responsible for the refugee flow may be able to wield major influence in the General Assembly and the Security Council, the UNHCR has played a remarkably successful humanitarian role. Its officials prudently offer no comment on this subject, knowing that their freedom to act depends on an important political consideration: such countries remain silent lest they put the spotlight on the flight of their own citizens.

Sometimes problems appear, as they must in any large organization, because of the personalities of individual representatives. Though chosen with a view to providing appropriate representation to the member countries, they are expected to serve not as national spokesmen but as international civil servants. Still it would be asking the impossible to expect them to put aside completely the policies of their own countries. Thus, in the case of the Cabindan refugees sitting in the villages and camps along the border with Angola, observers felt that the local UNHCR man was reluctant to move, knowing that his own country was supporting the MPLA. In such situations, UNHCR headquarters may have to walk softly because it carries no big stick and can do little to change the attitude of the local official. Sometimes transfer to a more desirable post is the only remedy.

IRC's Zaire program had been set up by Louis A. Wiesner, former director of the Office of Refugee Affairs of the U.S. State Department, who on retiring from the foreign service joined IRC as its worldwide administrator of medical programs. Always calm and judicious, he finds the right words to win the support of government officials in the host country and is especially mindful of the sensitivities of new nations. Together with Nicholas Erjavec, who remained on the scene after Wiesner returned to his own base in IRC/Washington, he laid out the basic steps to be taken. The two men tried to anticipate the problems of transport and distribution and developed a concept of "outreach" — methods of providing mobile services to the far-flung settlements in the rain forests.

The obstacles were many and frequently could not be planned for at all. Periodic raids by MPLA troops hit suddenly at the refugee camps. Some observers believed that the Angolan Marxists, though now ensconced in power and with nothing to fear from the hapless escapees, were nevertheless intent on effecting their repatriation. Others believed that the strategy was to deter potential refugees by warning that they would be pursued relentlessly even after crossing the border. In January 1977, a church newsletter circulated among Catholic missionaries in Africa reported:

In the beginning, the refugees settled not far from the Cabindan border, but they were often attacked by the MPLA soldiers who destroyed their villages and killed the people. Now the refugees live therefore in small areas, at a distance of 30 or more kilometers from the border. Some of them have been moved already for a third time, which means that they cannot profit of the crops of the fields they had laid out. According to witnesses, the situation is worse than in Bengal (Pakistan-India) in 1971. The misery is greatest in the centre of Ntembe, where 4,000 refugees stay in 288 shelters; they have very little clothing, no blankets, no food, no medicines. Their fate is even worse than that of the Angolan refugees in the region of Songololo, as quite a few of these latter can return to northern Angola, whilst the Cabindans hoping for their independence cannot return home.

Caritas-Zaire has launched an appeal for clothing, medicines and food. It seems that the UNHCR (United Nations High Commissariat for Refugees) has not lent any assistance to these poor people in Rayombe. Mr. Nicholas Erjavec of the International Rescue Committee says the only aid received came from the CCZ (Church of Christ in Zaire), Dorothy Thomas, an American lady dentist at Mikonzi Hospital, and from local Catholics. The team of the International Rescue Committee hopes to come to some kind of coordination in the relief work.[12]

"MANY GRAVES IN THE FOREST"

Despite the extreme poverty of the area, the local population, as tribal kinfolk of the refugees, did not hesitate to accord them a friendly reception. Though the refugee census had mounted to 50,000 by the end of 1976, the Zairois in the area north of Tshela down to Moanda on the Atlantic often made room for the newcomers in their own homes. Many had arrived before as guerrillas fighting the Portuguese; now they had fled again, this time from the new regime installed by Soviet arms and Cuban manpower. The refugees went to work with their Zairois kinsmen, tilling the fields and gathering palm-oil nuts in rain forests.

In October and November of 1976, MPLA-Cuban attacks increased, resulting in the death not only of Cabindans but several Zairois soldiers. The government therefore decided to move the refugees farther into the interior and assigned land for semipermanent resettlement. The effect was to separate the Cabindans from Zairois relatives and friends, though they were given some hope of self-support. IRC shipments began to include agricultural necessities such as machetes and seed. But an unkind nature, joining forces with malevolent man, sent heavy rains to wash away much of the plantings and then drought to wither the stalks.

By the end of 1977, Zaire was giving shelter to more than half a million refugees, including Rwandese who had fled from the Hutus in a vicious tribal war. There were also 11,000 Burundese who had escaped from a conflict in which 100,000 Hutus died—more than 3 percent of the total population. Such were the official figures of the UNHCR. Most of the newcomers, however, were Angolans. Some 60,000 of these were concentrated in the area of Bas-Zaire. Returning from an outreach trip, Erjavec reported to IRC/New York:

Nganda Memba is a refugee center with a little over 50 brick houses built in 1960 by the "old refugees" from the Portuguese era. In addition, there are eighteen satellite villages which consist of hastily built shelters of palm leaves and bamboo. Conditions are the same as in the other villages—undernourished children, poor living conditions. The village chiefs and the Zairois officials confirmed there are 9,725 refugees in the area and about 20-25 are coming out of the forest every week. Ten percent of the newcomers die. Apparently they remain in the forest as long as they can, and then they come out. They need clothing in addition to food. I wished I had *five* truckloads, not just one. . . . There are many graves in the forest.

Under the conditions prevailing in Bas-Zaire, to deliver even one truckload was an achievement. The original problem had been getting the truck. Fortunately, the Mormon missionaries had one and were willing to lease it.

Eventually a Land Rover, addressed to "Oxfam pour l'International Rescue Committee" arrived in Zaire and was admitted *duty free*, a triumph of administrative skill. Erjavec could also boast of the occasion when it took him only twenty hours to drive from Kinshasa to the border areas, with only ten hours spent waiting for the ferry to be repaired. On other trips it had taken as much as ten days to cross the river at this point. Here the traveler can discharge some of his tension by visiting the bronze marker that commemorates Stanley's arrival during his quest for Livingstone.

Most agonizing were the moments in the hospitals, especially those crowded with children. Three or four infants to a cot, their arms no rounder than an adult's thumb. Mothers sleeping on the floor beside the beds or outside the ward, vainly trying to suckle their babies with empty breasts. The macabre silence of a ward with a hundred children too weak even to cry.

In the Kuimba Catholic Hospital, Dr. Badoux had collected more than a hundred Cabindan infants he found starving in the area, stricken with *kwashiorkor*. He had enough high-protein concentrate for his little patients; what he needed was at least partially skilled personnel to administer treatment. Asked how much it would cost to fund the needed staff for this "Cabindan ward," he called his chief nurse, Sister Josephine Wijns, and sought her opinion.

"A hundred zaires," she answered.

"Per week?"

"No, per month," she said.

On behalf of IRC, Erjavec handed over 500 zaires on the spot to cover the next five months. Since the average stay for a child was one month, it does not take much mathematical skill to understand the situation: one zaire to save one child. Oh, yes — a zaire is 80 cents.

The primary objective in 1977, when IRC's program started in Zaire, was to bring in food, nutritional supplements and emergency medications. In that first year, more than 100,000 pounds of rice, beans, salt, fish, powdered milk and canned food were distributed, in addition to blankets and soap. Medical personnel were difficult to find. Before year's end, however, IRC was able to obtain staffing from *Médecins Sans Frontières*, a French group of physicians with whom IRC was already working in Thailand. In addition to maintaining dispensaries, the medical program included an extensive vaccination drive.

The challenge in Zaire did not abate in the following years. In some respects, conditions deteriorated. In April 1978, a correspondent from the London *Sunday Telegraph* worked his way into northern Angola. He reported a large-scale "pacification" operation by the MPLA government during which "tanks and armored cars with helicopter support attacked sleeping villages." His conclusion: "MIG jets are bombing forests with napalm to force out fleeing refugees and a total of one million are believed dead."

XI

Escape to Kenya

"Go to the Ngong Road, near the Ngong Hills Hotel," they told him.
"There you will find the surgery of the International Rescue Committee. They will help you."

Nikodemus Kassujja Mujwala, aged twenty-seven, former "Pilot Officer Cadet" in the Air Force of Uganda, with a record of helicopter and airplane training in Israel and the Soviet Union, pulled himsef up on his one leg, slipped the improvised crutch under his left armpit and headed for what turned out to be a one-story building, fairly large, a converted residence owned by the Quakers but leased to IRC as a clinic for refugees.

Kassujja needed help. On September 23, 1977, together with six others, he had made his escape from the notorious Nakasero prison. Three days before, he and three of his comrades had been brought before Idi Amin to be photographed with him—the picture appeared in the Kampala newspaper—as part of the ritual of punishment and as a lesson for all potential rebels. Amin told the prisoners they would be executed "with the self-same bazookas you intended to use against me." And he added: ". . . so that I see what your bodily pieces will be like."

During his arrest, Kassujja had been wounded and his leg had to be amputated. Before the stitches could be removed he was thrown into a cell and received no further treatment. There he and his companions knew that certain death awaited them unless they could perform a feat no one yet had accomplished—escape from Nakasero. In the presence of Amin, they had confessed that their intention was to assassinate him and overthrow the government. Kassujja had even dared to say to Amin: "If it had not been for a traitor in our ranks, you would be dead now."

The full story has been told in the African magazine *Drum* by Major Patrick Kumumwe, the leader of the aborted conspiracy of June 1977, and a fellow-prisoner.[1] He notes that Kassujja's spirits still soared even though he knew he would never fly a plane again. Intent on breaking out to freedom, he searched the cell for every piece of rubbish left behind by previous prisoners. A small piece of metal turned up. Kassujja honed it to a sharp point on the concrete floor. Before long he had shaped a key that opened the handcuffs on each of the captives. Kumumwe writes: "We passed the secret on to those we felt we could trust in the Luwum group that were to face the firing squad."

The latter reference is to the associates of the murdered Archbishop Janani Luwum, head of the Anglican Church of Uganda. His offense had been twofold: he had dared to protest publicly against the crimes of the regime; and he belonged to the Acholi tribe, a major target of Amin's genocidal intent. (Amin's explanation for the ineptness of his troops during the Israeli rescue of the hostages at Entebbe was "that the Acholi and Langi officers were in contact with the Israelis.") Summoned to a public confrontation with Amin, the Archbishop was excoriated as a conspirator who was storing arms for an uprising. He was handed over to the infamous "State Research Bureau," Amin's euphemism for his Gestapo. A few hours later the Uganda radio announced that the Archbishop, with others accompanying him, had died in an "automobile accident." No one was deceived.

Previous efforts at deception or reassurance had been all too eagerly accepted by the world. It was recalled that in the previous year Bishop Festo Kivengere, of the diocese of Kigezi, had told a New York audience that Christians were not being persecuted in Uganda, even though Amin had become a fervent Moslem to curry favor with the oil-rich Arabs, especially Libya and Iraq. A few months later the bishop, discovering that he himself had become a marked man, fled for his life. Describing these events in an essay on "The Modern Martyrs," the theologian Martin Marty noted that Rabbi Marc Tanenbaum of the American Jewish Committee had "criticized the Christian missionaries for having said little about persecution until it touched prominent leaders. Tanenbaum showed particular interest because of Amin's flagrant anti-Semitism."[2]

Following up on the assassination of Luwum, Amin used the Archbishop's alleged conspiracy as the occasion to arrest others, including many who had no connection whatsoever with the churchman. Some of these were incarcerated in the same cell as Kassujja and his group, quarters they had dubbed "Grave Number One where people are buried alive." For the Luwum group the nickname was all too real; they were soon called out to face a firing squad, leaving Kassujja and his friends to await a similar fate.

Under cover of dark and at various times during the day, the prisoners worked on the bars of a ventilator that they hoped would open up to freedom. Objects found in the debris of the cell served as tools. Most valuable were the frames of two discarded Russian-made movie projectors that could be used as crowbars. At first the prisoners could merely slip their hands through the opening, but persistent effort made it larger. Every hour that could be allotted to the work was precious as the men raced against the executioner's clock. To keep the guards away, Kassujja devised a strategy.

Major Kumumwe writes that "it made our guards fed up, and a little scared, if we continually pestered them for cigarettes. Kassujja, who could not help with the manual labour as he only had one leg, begged continuously for cigarettes, an exercise that always sent the exasperated guards away in double quick time."

In all, the prisoners spent three months in Nakasero, during which time they came to know the repertoire of torture that Amin's lieutenants had devised: "fists, rhino-hide whips, thick electric cables, torches in the eyes, metal canes, knives, hammers, fire between the toes, lighted cigarettes, empty bottles of soda on elbows, knees, strangling ropes; all these were tried on us."

Despite the pain, Kassujja set out to keep up the morale of the group by displaying his own good spirits. Banter served as a shield against the frustrations that might have impaired their solidarity. Kassujja's companions even teased him that, with one leg, he would not be able to keep up with the others in an escape. His answer was to execute acrobatic leaps with just the one limb. When his friends worried that a one-legged man would be easily identified by pursuers, he pretended to be various animals — a chimpanzee waddling through the underbrush, a dog crawling on all fours — and thus disguised would elude Amin's agents. His performances led his associates later to describe him as "a very courageous and talented person."

IN THE HANDS OF IRC

This "courageous and talented person" arrived at the structure on Ngong Road. Behind him were the memories of Nakasero, the escape through the ventilator, the leap over the wall, the race through the dark streets, the plodding through the forest, the easy crossing into Kenya and arrival in Nairobi. He hobbled onto the porch and faced the door on which a metal plaque read:

Joint Refugee Services of Kenya
Surgery
Sponsored by the International Rescue Committee

The facility had been established only a short time before. In the summer of 1977, Leo Cherne had arrived in Nairobi to determine what could be done to help the thousands of Africans who were converging on Kenya from every direction — South Africans, Namibians, Rhodesians, Mozambiquans, Ugandans, Rwandese, Burundese, Sudanese, Ethiopians, Somalis — and eventually even a few Vietnamese boat people picked up by a Greek vessel that had put into Mombasa from the South China Seas.

Already in existence was an organization called the Joint Refugee Services of Kenya (JRSK), which included, along with three representatives of the Kenya government, groups like the African Evangelistic Enterprise, the Kenya Catholic Secretariat, the Friends World Committee for Consultation,

Food for the Hungry, the All-Africa Conference of Churches, and the National Christian Council of Kenya. Providing the bulk of funding was the United Nations High Commissioner for Refugees, represented on the governing council and in all JRSK committees.

Cherne met with Kinga Wamwendia, the executive secretary, who reported an explosive increase in refugee population. The International Commission of Jurists had recently issued a 170-page report on Uganda, citing the statistics of horror: between 80,000 and 90,000 persons, and possibly more than 100,000, had been killed in 1974 and 1975 alone. The Commission found that there was "a total breakdown of the rule of law in Uganda, and all basic freedoms are in abeyance." A frightened people responded in the only way it can when no other weapon is available: flight.

In his report to IRC headquarters, Cherne said: "A most conservative estimate of the number of Ugandan refugees who have fled since the death of the Archbishop in February and the beginning of what seems clearly to be an effort to liquidate the educated community of Uganda is 10,000." No one really knew in detail. Not until 1979, when Amin scrambled to safety in Libya (and thence to Saudi Arabia) before he could be captured by the triumphant Tanzanian army and the returning Ugandans, would the world begin to perceive the full tragedy enacted in this green land of matchless beauty that has dazzled visitors since Livingstone first explored it. In May, when Amin's rout was complete, a *New York Times* editorial pronounced an appropriate obituary on what its correspondent John Darnton called "the institutionalized brutality of a state gone insane." As the *Times* wrote:

Maybe 100,000 persons were murdered in eight years, maybe 300,000, out of 12 million. Mostly they disappeared, one at a time, to be shot or starved, bludgeoned with car axles, sledgehammers and machetes, or thrown to crocodiles. When Tanzanians liberated the Kampala prisons two weeks ago, they found the underground cells packed with corpses; only a few skeletal figures had survived by drinking their own urine and eating the flesh of the dead.

Not only politics but private greed motivated the atrocities. The horror from which the refugees had fled was made vivid by the testimony of survivors. A doctor is quoted: "There were a lot of what might be called personal killings. If I was in the same trade as you, I would have you killed. Or if I wanted your car, or we shared a girl friend, or we were up for the same Government post, someone makes an allegation against you of some sort and you just disappear." One needs no further argument for the imperative of government ruled by law.

THE IRC CLINIC

Before leaving Nairobi, Cherne signed a formal undertaking with JRSK's Kinga Wamwendia under which IRC agreed to pay $10,000 to cover the services of four Ugandan refugee doctors over the next six months. If the pilot operation proved successful, "this program may be expanded so as to make the services of refugee doctors available to meet the medical needs of other refugee nationality groups escaping repressive regimes and seeking asylum in Kenya." He promised also that IRC would explore the desirability of setting up an administrative capability in Nairobi and would apply for representation in JRSK.

A few months later, Cecil B. Lyon, veteran of many IRC campaigns, arrived to follow up. By now it was clear that a continuing presence with full-time staff would be necessary to handle a major segment of JRSK's work. The organization had been set up for the purpose of coordinating activities among the voluntary agencies and avoiding duplication. Thus the Catholic Secretariat assumed responsibility for administering a program under which refugee children would be paid for in the *harambee* school system of the Kenya government. (*Harambee* is a Swahili term popularized by President Jomo Kenyatta and attached to many activities; it means, "Let's pull together!") IRC agreed to run the medical clinic, or surgery, to use the Britishism still prevalent in Kenya.

Dr. Gail Gerhart, a Ph.D. whose specialty is African studies and whose books and articles have established her reputation as a scholar in the field, took command. Assisting her was Douglas Arbuckle, a young graduate of the Peace Corps who had worked in Ethiopia. Their medical staff included two full-time doctors, both Ugandans; two part-time doctors, one a psychiatrist and the other a gynecologist; two full-time nurses and a part-time nurse; two full-time receptionists; one general assistant, referred to as "traffic manager"; and one driver. Virtually all of the staff, except for the two Americans, were refugees. Handling the office machinery were two women — Miriam Lukwago, a clinical psychologist with a master's degree earned in Norway, originally from Uganda, who had not been able to find work in her own profession; and Rita Nynawumwami, a statuesque member of the royal family of Rwanda who had escaped death because she happened to be studying abroad.

The clinic was opened in September 1977. As of June 1978, the records showed that there had been 7,200 patient visits, with 2,700 refugees registered as patients. Through the waiting room and the treatment rooms of the surgery passed a typical cross-section of the refugees who had succeeded in reaching Nairobi. In descending order of percentages, they were Ugandans first, then Ethiopians, Rwandese, Mozambiquans, and South Africans (including Rhodesians and Southwest Africans or Namibians).

The medical staff, working eight hours a day, five days a week, plus Saturday mornings, functioned as general practitioners for outpatients. At the time of the author's visit to the facility, laboratory work was being sent out, but there was high hope that the Swiss government would donate a full laboratory to be installed on the premises and that IRC would be able to employ a refugee technician.

It was to this group of energetic and dedicated people that Nikodemus Kassujja had come. But it was apparent that his condition required more than outpatient service. In such cases, IRC policy was to pay for hospitalization in a local Catholic institution at the regular rates, instead of making a referral to the terribly overcrowded, free public facility, the Kenyatta Hospital; admission there, even for essential surgery, sometimes was delayed as long as a year. IRC policy was not without its problems: government officials received complaints that refugees were getting better and faster treatment than local citizens.

Kassujja's very survival was proof that he was not the kind of man to accept his fate. On his own he appealed to various church groups and other organizations for help. The Lions Club of Nairobi donated a sum of eighty dollars to fit him with an artificial leg, but it proved cumbersome and inadequate. Convinced that with a better prosthetic device he would be qualified to fly again, he went about negotiating with a company that imports aluminum limbs. The cost, he discovered, would be almost a thousand dollars. Finally, he decided that the best solution would be to go to Israel where he had had some of his pilot training. With the clinic still medicating him for the pain resulting from the untreated amputation, he pleaded, "Help me to go Israel!"

A campaign led by IRC personnel among his admirers in the Nairobi area raised special funds for this purpose. Dr. Arych Oded, the Israeli representative in Kenya, paved the way. A special appeal went to B'nai B'rith in New York. El Al, which had a special youth rate between Nairobi and Tel Aviv, booked the passage. The foreign student unit at Tel Aviv University located an Israeli family with whom Kassujja could stay during his convalescence after treatment at the Tel Hashomer military hospital in Ramat-Gan.

With sparkling eyes, Kassujja tells visitors of his days in Israel—the surgery necessary to fit the prosthetic limb, the training in its use, the cordiality of the Orthodox Jewish family with whom he lived and in whose company he was always careful to wear the *yarmelke* or skullcap. Seeing him walk now, the unsuspecting are not likely to know of his impairment. And he is confident that he will once again have the opportunity to fly.

A PSYCHIATRIC SERVICE

Dr. Wilson Acuda is a Ugandan. Judged by his build, he looks like a professional football player; judged by the sadness in his eyes, he is the intellectual perplexed by the idiocies of human behavior. Dr. Acuda is one of five psychiatrists in all of Kenya. He welcomes the visitor cordially and is eager to talk about the psychiatric problems of the refugees he treats in the IRC clinic. A professor of psychiatry at the University of Nairobi Medical School, his principal affiliation is at the Mathari Mental Hospital, the only such hospital in Kenya. Possessed of the energy of an athlete, he is able to spend two afternoons a week at the IRC surgery. The more serious cases he transfers to the Mathari Hospital, but he continues to see patients at the IRC clinic after their discharge from Mathari.

Because he was already in the midst of a special study of psychological problems of refugees, Dr. Acuda volunteered his services to IRC. At the clinic, he says, there are two groups of patients: those who were mentally ill before they left home and those who suffered breakdown as a result of their flight. Counseling, he concludes, is adequate for some 30 percent; the rest have to be helped, in view of their situation, primarily with "organic therapy" — drug treatments.

To a large extent, he points out, the problem of the patients stems from situational factors. The precipitant may be unemployment experienced by people who have always worked before. (Parenthetically, he notes that Ugandan teachers have no difficulty getting jobs in Kenya since there is a shortage of schoolteachers; so too with other professionals and the highly skilled. But the government is imposing restraints on Ugandan doctors, several hundred of whom have fled to Kenya and insist on staying in the cities where the practice is lucrative.) Financial pressures and lack of housing are the major causes of the psychological breakdowns.

Discussing his work at the clinic, he says that IRC has the best pharmacy for therapeutic drugs in Kenya. Both because of the availability of medication and the staff's attitude toward patients, he is convinced that the clinic is achieving better results than any other institution dealing with such problems. Most of the patients are male. The handful of women who seek treatment are victims of separation, having been cut off from their men by the misadventures of the escape. With a life expectancy in this part of Africa averaging forty-five to fifty years, he is struck by the fact that most of his patients range between twenty and thirty.

Dr. Acuda's research may well be the first formal effort to investigate the psychological problems of African refugees. Important studies have been made of the victims of persecution, as in the case of concentration camp victims and prisoners of war. Sociologists and anthropologists have been devoting increasing attention to the impact of uprootedness on immigrant populations, but such studies are primarily academic, not therapeutic; they deal with the behavior of groups, not with the treatment of the individual. In the course of his work at the IRC clinic in Nairobi, Dr. Acuda has identified a number of unique characteristics in the population he treats.

He finds that the depressive reaction is different for Africans than among the people of developed countries. Well into the 1960s, he says, it was generally believed that Africans simply did not suffer from depression. By the end of the decade, however, the illness had become clearly visible among educated Africans. In 1975, the African Psychiatric Association officially confirmed that depression does strike the black population even though the victims do not seem to be aware of what is happening inside of them. Africans are much more likely to act out their feelings instead of internalizing them as Westerners do. They resort to expressive dancing, talking a great deal and singing, and thus dispel much of the emotion that would otherwise be repressed.

Church attendance, which is extraordinarily high in Kenya, is another outlet, says Dr. Acuda, adding that it is less common in Uganda. The religious history of the area confirms the psychiatrist's assumption about his own country. Amin persecuted the Christians from the time he himself adopted Islam. In doing so, he could rely on a history of violence that goes back to the 1880s when the Kabaka (or king) Mwanga massacred the English missionaries who had been welcomed, mistakenly, as protectors against marauding Egyptians. Yet, at the time of independence, it was estimated that Uganda had 2 million Christians, almost evenly divided between Catholics and Anglicans, with several hundred thousand Moslems and the rest pagans. Amin tried, even to the point of assassinating churchmen, to transform Uganda into a Moslem state. Hence his collusion with the Arab hijackers of the Air France plane in 1976 that culminated in the dramatic Israeli rescue operation at Entebbe. On every possible occasion he showed his contempt for the Church: when the Catholic Martyrs' Shrine was dedicated in 1975, he made an appearance caparisoned in the full robes of an Arab sheik; shortly thereafter he deported twenty Catholic missionaries.[3] Perhaps because of the hardships suffered on behalf of their religious faith, the African churches, together with their Western affiliations, have been vigorous in providing assistance to the refugees.

It may well be that the African feels his homelessness even more intensely, if that is possible, than members of other racial and national groups. The pressures that have led him into exile include a complex of issues that are at once political, economic, religious and tribal. Psychological studies of concentration camp survivors have shown that where the victims can clearly discern a reason for their plight — for example, Orthodox Jews whose theodicy explains the diaspora — the likelihood of suicide is much reduced. Where the events seem to have no rationale, emotional difficulties tend to multiply.

In the case of the Africans, or at least the population that made its way to Nairobi, Dr. Acuda found that in most cases the victims had no concept of depression. The IRC doctors, attempting to treat the physical symptoms, recognized that they were dealing with psychosomatic illness in many cases. Dr. Acuda therefore decided that the basic method of treatment would have to be drug therapy. The evidence of the patient's psychological state could be deduced from multiple physical changes — loss of appetite, weight, and libido — and an inability to sleep for more than two or three hours a night. Because the symptoms were somatic, patients at the IRC clinic always kept their appointments and readily accepted medication for their condition.

Among Africans generally, according to Dr. Acuda, the kind of traumas that might set off psychosis include an enemy's threat to bewitch; among young women, the breakup of a love affair; among students, the pressure of examinations. Indeed, there is a high degree of breakdown among African students abroad. They tend to become paranoid, due largely to the intense pressure created by their parents' aspirations and the knowledge that the family's fortune has been invested in them. The highest percentage of mental breakdown is among African students in the Soviet Union and Eastern Europe. Dr. Acuda suggests two reasons: these youngsters tend to be among the less qualified, since the better ones are likely to be accepted in the West, which is the most popular choice; and those in Communist countries find themselves subjected to heavier restrictions and remain more isolated from the rest of the community.

Whether at home or abroad, the symptoms found among such students, especially those between the ages of sixteen and twenty, are inability to see words when reading, difficulty in hearing the teacher, somnolence during the day and wakefulness at night. Sometimes the cause is poor study technique, but the victim is frequently the good student too. The trauma may be due to the wide gap in education between the student and the educational and social level of the rest of the class. In such cases, also, the parents may be putting too much pressure on the student, and treatment may have to include a change in parental attitudes.

African psychiatrists have coined the term "brain fag" for the anxiety symptoms of the students — distorted vision, headaches, sleepiness in class. These signs of mental fatigue often disappear after examinations, regardless of the student's passing or failing. In treating brain fag, Dr. Acuda sometimes shows students a diagram of the brain and discusses how mental processes occur.

In normal times African patients who suffer a psychotic attack usually go back to their native village for treatment. The pattern seems to be that two or three days after a trauma the individual begins to act aberrantly, for example, going about naked or becoming incontinent. Since refugees cannot go home, the usual treatment is to hospitalize the patient and administer chlorpromazine, which eliminates the symptoms. Dr. Acuda believes that the major factor in effecting recovery may be merely changing the environment, for instance, by hospitalization.

To a great extent, however, as he sees it, the most important element in caring for the refugees psychologically is to provide counseling on how to get jobs. At the time he was interviewed by the author he complained that there were only two trained social workers in the whole country, and that one of them, at the moment, was in London. He himself had left Uganda in 1972 to study at the Institute of Psychiatry in London under a scholarship grant, but he had decided to move to Kenya in 1976 rather than return to Amin's Uganda. Now he saw his long-range goal as training more psychiatrists. In addition he was meeting with the five counselors employed by

JRSK and giving them some rudimentary instruction while working up a full university course of training for psychiatric social workers.

At the IRC clinic, he had laid out a procedure for the treatment of disturbed patients. Referrals were made to him by staff physicians who recognized psychosomatic conditions. The refugees were then screened by Miriam Lukwago, who took time from her office duties for this purpose. Generally Dr. Acuda saw four patients a day, though sometimes the figure was as high as eight.

THE INDIVIDUAL PERSON

Nairobi did not have refugee camps as such. Under the prodding of the UNHCR representative the government had built a receiving center at Thika. Located some thirty miles out of the city, it was capable of housing 200 persons. All refugees, even those already admitted, had to go there to be processed and formally registered if they were to qualify for a food stipend from UNHCR and become eligible for the services of JRSK. Presumably those seeking resettlement would eventually get some acreage on which they could farm, which would relieve the pressure in the labor market. Despite the high unemployment at the time in Kenya, the government was showing itself to be hospitable to the fellow-Africans who were being drawn toward Nairobi as a shelter. And this at a time when Edward Hoagland was writing in *Harper's* magazine:

Kenya. Fourteen million people. Per capita income, $169; no compulsory education (a fee of some sort is generally charged). City laborers in Nairobi earn about a dollar a day, those in agriculture half a dollar. More than a quarter of the children in the nation suffer from some form of malnutrition, according to a World Bank report, and the population is expected to double in the next twenty-five years. Less than 10 percent of the rural people have available an adequate water supply. . . . To a drastic degree the country is blowing away through deforestation — charcoal burning, slash-and-burn farming, and even the hungry foraging of the elephants, which since the recent drought find their grass gone.[4]

Usually as the number of refugees mounts it becomes increasingly difficult to deal with people as individuals. Bureaucratization, always a function of size, makes it necessary to adopt general rules, methods of procedure, forms to be filled out, dossiers to be set up, and so on interminably. The humanitarian impulse is bound to be offended by the depersonalization that ultimately becomes dehumanization. Kierkegaard once said, "Every human being is an exception." However difficult the implications of this precept, each refugee is entitled to be viewed as a separate human being, with feelings and needs that are unique to him and that deserve particularized respect.

As one sits in the waiting room, the offices or the treatment rooms of the

IRC surgery, it is clear that every effort is made to ascertain the individual need. Formal questionnaires are not overlooked as a tool for this purpose; the responses from the patients reveal difficulties of transportation, location, the need for bare necessities. A sampling of the replies reveals the reactions of those who have been served: "Very nice treatment. Good smiles for patients."

Whatever the circumstances, and they are varied, the personal touch is always present. The very existence of such a clinic provides a morale boost because it is a resource that is always available—whether for the woman arriving already in labor; or the girl running into the clinic, pursued by two Ugandan men who think she is a spy for Amin because she was asking people where they came from; or the heart attack patient who is being given oxygen while the clinic driver is readying an automobile to take him directly to the hospital; or the placement of an order for dapsone by telephone to provide treatment for a patient diagnosed as a leper; or the twenty-year-old widow who has come for care because she is in her eighth month and who was denied certification as a refugee because she failed to offer *chai* to a government clerk, and whose status as a refugee must be clarified even though she has just arrived on foot from distant Ethiopia; or the woman, accompanied by an eight-year-old child, who has not slept in a bed for three months and for whom an IRC representative is now shopping to buy a mattress.

In a quiet corner of the clinic on Ngong Road one could see every day a tall young Ethiopian pounding away vigorously at an old beat-up typewriter. To remake his life and ultimately to find employment, he was learning to type and had received permission to practice whenever he had time. His story is illuminating. He had been acting headmaster in a school. Early one morning the soldiers had come and demanded that he deliver up several of his pupils. He refused. Beaten into unconsciousness with rifle butts, his face a mass of pulp and blood, he was left for dead. Teachers arriving later found him still breathing but dared not arrange for medical care. They concealed him for months until nature helped him recover, leaving him with one blind eye and half of his face paralyzed. He set out on foot and finally reached Nairobi where now the International Rescue Committee was helping him to sew up his life again. And when it appeared that special treatment was available for his condition in West Germany, IRC arranged for him to go to Munich.

Few of these Africans sought to be resettled elsewhere. Most of them assumed that they would either go home some day or would simply remain indefinitely in the country to which they had escaped. Unlike most of the European refugees and later the Southeast Asians, the United States was the last country in which they expected to come to rest. The Ugandans were unique in that they had good reason to believe Amin would be overthrown, as indeed he was in 1979 with the aid of an invading Tanzanian army that remained thereafter to engage in looting on its own. The Ethiopians, for the most part, assumed that return was unlikely. For them the challenge was to find a new life in their immediate surroundings, in contrast to the East Europeans and Indochinese who looked to IRC for resettlement elsewhere.

THE MAJOR CONCERNS

Believing that everything humanly possible must be done to help the professionals survive so they may continue to serve the needs of their people, IRC has always been especially concerned with medical personnel — physicians, nurses, technicians and ancillary workers — and with the educators, carriers of the national culture. In addition to maintaining the clinic, IRC became involved in the effort to place Ugandan teachers in the Kenya schools. Fortunately, language was no barrier since the *lingua franca* of the three countries in the former East African community is English; teachers are therefore interchangeable. In India it had been feasible to set up schools directly under IRC auspices in the heavily populated camps. The refugees in Nairobi, however, were scattered in various neighborhoods. In the western part of the country near the Ugandan border or along the northeastern shores of Lake Victoria they were intermingled with local populations. Kisumu, Kenya's principal lake port, the commercial center of a rich farm area still noted for its wild African bird life, is the fourth largest city in the country, doubly significant because it is the largest city close to Uganda. Here refugees paused to catch their breath, and sometimes to stay. Among these were the widow and family of Archbishop Luwum.

First conversations between IRC and the Kisumu district commissioner had not been hopeful. The latter was concerned about having so many refugees close to the border, the usual worry of the government in the receiving country. As he saw it, their presence posed a security problem. "If any of them are really wanted by Amin," he said, "they can easily be snatched, which would be a great embarrassment." Such fears are real. Nairobi newspapers carried constant warnings about Amin spies who might have slipped in disguised as escapees. At a time when there were 10,000 Ugandan refugees in Kenya, only 4,000 had registered with the UNHCR. A large number were willing to forego assistance and seek work on their own, many of them because they feared Amin's agents might gain access to the official rolls, with serious consequences for relatives back home.

That spies were on the scene was not a matter of surmise. A Ugandan nurse working in the IRC program could so testify. Her husband had been a member of Amin's electrical board, comparable to one of our public service commissions. During an awful night in Kampala, when a military tattoo was being held to celebrate the anniversary of Amin's accession to power, the stadium was suddenly blacked out by a power failure. Amin ordered all the members of the board arrested. For weeks she heard nothing of her husband, but one day he was brought home and exhibited to her so that she might know how he had been tortured. Then he was removed, never to be seen again. She gathered up her children and crossed the border into Kenya. One day in Nairobi while performing her nursing duties, she went to her superior. Pointing to a patient, she said, "I will never treat that man again. I know him. He is the number 3 torturer in Nakasero prison."

In the confused skein of refugee life, strange strands intermesh. An Ethiopian, telling his story to IRC representatives, recounts how he had escaped to the Sudan. The camp to which he was first sent was being run by Eritreans — from whom he had just fled. Kinga Wamwendia, predicting that new waves of Ugandan refugees would seek shelter in Kenya, told the author: "The torturers will become the tortured!" — the ultimate fate of many among Amin's henchmen. So too in the Far East, at Aranyaprathet in Thailand, the authorities found that they had to keep apart the Cambodians who had run from Pol Pot and those who had been their tormentors but were now fleeing in their turn from the invading Vietnamese.

THE LEDGER OF NEED

At Kisumu, IRC set in motion a policy of providing assistance through other organizations already on the scene. Bishop Okullo of the Anglican Church had designated Rev. David Kola to be in charge of refugee affairs, but with little available resources. IRC agreed to fund a social worker. The needs, as outlined in Kisumu, covered at least ten areas of concern. The list provides a pattern confronted by refugees everywhere:

1. *Settlement.* For this purpose, loans have to be provided so that the individual may acquire a bit of land or suitable quarters for setting up a little business.

2. *Income supplements.* The immediate requirement is sustenance. At this time in Kenya, UNHCR was giving to certified refugees a monthly subsistence as follows: for a single person, 150 Kenya shillings, approximately $20; for a whole family, regardless of the number of children, 350 shillings, or $45.

3. *Scholarships.* It is generally acknowledged that advanced students should not have their studies terminated. The refugees in Kisumu complained that scholarships were few, and there was a feeling of inequity about their distribution.

4. *Material assistance.* Blankets and clothing are second only to food among refugee needs. Even in normally hot climates the nights can be cold. Kenya, though it sits astride the Equator, is temperate in many areas because of the altitude.

5. *Medical treatment.* In Kisumu arrangements were made with two local physicians, both Asians, to provide care for refugees, with reimbursement from IRC. In many cases, IRC has favored placing doctors, nurses, technicians, pharmacists and paramedics in existing hospitals and clinics.

6. *Primary school admission.* For refugee children schooling is especially important because they would otherwise rot in inactivity. The fact that they are being educated means they will have a future even though they have lost the past. In Kenya the problem was complicated by the fact that both the government schools and the local *harambee* schools required tuition; moreover, some 30 percent of the native Kenyan children could not be admitted to the already overcrowded schools. IRC agreed to pay the salaries of additional teachers, and to provide scholarships for some of the children.

7. *Transport.* Particularly in the developing countries, communication becomes a major hurdle. Public carriers are unreliable. Much time is lost in shipping food, medical supplies, school equipment, and so on. The people in Kisumu asked that a JRSK office be set up locally so that they would not be dependent on distant Nairobi.

8. *Immigration clearance and identification.* Theoretically, a refugee who arrives in a foreign country without proper authorization is an illegal immigrant. Here the UNHCR performs the major function of arranging for legalized status. In Kenya, the first step taken by the government was to issue a formal "Prohibited Immigrant Notice." Nominally, the document instructs the individual that he must leave within three months, but it is renewable at the end of that period. Once registered as a P.I., the refugee may proceed to the UNHCR which helps him fill out the necessary papers for the Ministry of Home Affairs. Inevitably delays occur — a serious matter if allowances are not to be paid until the paper work is done.

9. *Special provisions for children.* In some places, special funds are granted. The relief workers in Kisumu, however, were particularly concerned about the needs of malnourished youngsters who required special diets.

10. *Jobs.* Almost invariably the arrival of refugees generates fears of unemployment among the local population. In one respect Kenya's situation was different from that found in other host countries. Trained personnel — physicians, nurses, teachers, accountants, engineers — were in short supply. Qualified professionals had little difficulty finding work, and immediately went off the refugee rolls. Among the unskilled workers in Kenya, however, there was large-scale unemployment, and refugees were forbidden to compete with them.

Such, then, were the concerns encountered in virtually every area receiving refugees. In Kisumu, one did not hear about another item that is often among the most difficult — housing. In Nairobi shelter was critical, and the Ugandans were often left to fend for themselves. Single men, each with his monthly allowance from the UNHCR, would band together to rent a hovel in the slum neighborhoods.

No one organization could pretend to handle this large variety of problems. IRC's primary concern was with medical care; next, with the educational needs of the children. In connection with the latter, generous grants from the Ford Foundation proved of great value. But in each of the above areas some tasks needed doing as individual refugees confronted personal crises. Whether it was as simple a matter as finding a bed for a pregnant woman or arranging to transport a one-legged air pilot for treatment in Israel, IRC staff was available.

In the end, it is the individual and his personal needs that count. On one occasion, seeking supplies for IRC/Nairobi, Charles Sternberg, IRC's executive director, corresponded with a Belgian who, like himself, had been a refugee decades before. "We were both formed by the same forces and events," wrote Sternberg, "and it is indeed an accident of sorts that we are still alive. That's why it is important that we continue in *der Kleinarbeit*. In the long run it may count for more than the big schemes."

Kleinarbeit — little works, indeed!

XII

Hong Kong — "Bloody Frightening"

*To the tourist, this little island is a paradise of local color and inex-*pensive products. By day the streets seethe with enterprising humanity. The roar of commerce rises in a throbbing crescendo. Arched above the traffic, the shopkeepers' signboards compete, as if to push each other aside; the visual profusion vies to catch the shopper's eye. By night, a pervasive neon glow discolors the faces of the crowd that swirls sleeplessly along the sidewalks.

This is as modern a city as you can find anywhere in the world. Its skyscrapers and high-rise apartments perch stolidly at the base and on the sides of the hills while Hollywood-style mansions checker the landscape. A few years ago the shuffling passers-by wore the black pajamas of old China; today only a few aged men and women remain immune to the sartorial imperialism of the West.

The tourist is not likely to realize that every other person he brushes against in the street is either a refugee or the offspring of refugees who left the mainland after the Communist victory in 1949. In that year and the following one, a population of 600,000 was rapidly outnumbered by the arrival of three-quarters of a million Chinese, principally from Kwantung province, Shanghai and other major urban communities. Today, this last remaining Crown Colony of Britain, measuring 1,050 square miles, swarms with more than 4.5 million human beings. And a new stream of refugees has been coming—ethnic Chinese from Vietnam. Hong Kong has the highest population density of any community in the world, 4,210 persons per square kilometer, as compared with Bangladesh's 1,600 and the United States's 23. "It's bloody frightening," said a British government official in Hong Kong, preparing to enforce a futile ban on the inpouring of refugees.

BY RETURN MAIL

In 1949 the government hoped to hold the number of new arrivals to 50,000 annually. For reasons of domestic policy, Red China, like Vietnam some fifteen years later, decided to open the border periodically like a steam valve venting the boiler to keep it from exploding. Unable to absorb the influx, the Hong Kong authorities often responded by deporting the new arrivals, returning them to face the fury of the tyrannical regime they had vainly escaped. Such was the situation in May 1962. The world was given a glimpse of the tragedy when a cameraman turned his lens on Li Ying, her hand covering her mouth as if to stifle a shriek of despair. She had just been told she was being sent back to the mainland. Li Ying was only one person; 60,000 others shared her fate. "It's bloody frightening."

In June, when the flood-tide abated and after the deportations had been carried out, the conscience-stricken authorities asked the remaining illegals to register, promising they would not be penalized. More than 40,000 came forward and were officially granted sanctuary. Until that ghastly month of May, the world had paid little attention to the Chinese exodus.

But even before Li Ying's terrified face caught the eyes of Western newspaper readers, the International Rescue Committee was on the scene. In January 1961 it had launched a program that, at this writing, has continued for the better part of two decades; in all likelihood it will have to extend well into the future even though Mao Zedong's regime has now been superseded by a more pragmatic leadership. In later years IRC leaders have viewed their arrival on the scene as belated. Their first response to Asian needs came in 1954 when Vietnam was partitioned and almost a million refugees fled southward to escape Hanoi's rule. Though Hong Kong's trials had begun in 1949 when the Communists defeated Chiang Kai Shek, the world paid little attention to the plight of those rushing for the exits that were still open. Organizations like IRC, in the first half of the 1950s, were wrestling with the aftermath of World War II. IRC itself was under a constant cloud of momentary bankruptcy, and could not undertake to serve on distant continents.

THE CLOSED DOOR

Throughout the 1950s and most of the '60s, Hong Kong had little support from foreign governments as it struggled to keep afloat in the human sea inundating the island. Not until 1972 did the U.S. Congress enact legislation liberalizing the immigration laws to permit a substantial number of Orientals to enter this country. Despite their own origins as an immigrant population, Americans have been frequently seized by xenophobia and exclusionary moods, especially in periods of economic stress. Sometimes it was hard to say which was the true America—the one that in 1886 had inscribed on the base of the Statue of Liberty Emma Lazarus's, "Give me your huddled masses," or the one reflected in the poem, "The Unguarded Gates," written in 1892 by Thomas Bailey Aldrich, the distinguished editor of the *Atlantic Monthly*:

Wide open and unguarded stand our gates,
And through them presses a wild, motley throng—
Men from the Volga and the Tartar steppes,
Featureless faces from the Hoang-Ho,
Malayan, Scythian, Teuton, Kelt and Slav,
Flying the Old World's poverty and scorn;
These, bringing with them unknown gods and rites,
Those, tiger passions, here to stretch their claws.
In street and alley what strange tongues are these,
Accents of menace alien to our air,
Voices that once the Tower of Babel knew!
O Liberty, white Goddess! Is it well
To leave the gates unguarded?[1]

Perhaps it is significant that Emma Lazarus's poem has proved to be, in Horace's phrase, *aere perennius*, or at least as lasting as the bronze on the base of the Statue, while those of the famous editor have only an antiquarian interest.

American policy, under the impact of the refugees' flight, was bound to undergo change. For decades, immigration had been limited to 357,000 under the National Origins Act of 1924, reduced further in 1929 to 150,000 on the basis of strict quotas keyed to country of origin. Under the impact of World War II, exceptions were made. In the 1952 Immigration and Nationality Act, Congress reasserted the quota concept despite President Truman's disapproval; he said it was based on the idea, "to put it boldly, that Americans with English or Irish names were better people and better citizens than Americans with Italian or Greek or Polish names."[2] President Kennedy tried again, arguing that until 1921 America had indeed followed the tradition embodied in the words, "Give me your tired, your poor, your huddled masses yearning to breathe free," but under existing legislation, it was necessary to add: "as long as they come from Northern Europe, are not too tired or too poor or slightly ill, never stole a loaf of bread, never joined any questionable organization and can document their activities for the past two years."[3]

In 1965, however, in a revulsion against racism, the country-of-origin quota system was liberalized, and then finally dropped in 1968. The changed attitude toward Orientals was reflected in these figures: the number of Philippine immigrants in 1971 was nine times larger than in 1965; the number of Chinese, four times; Koreans, seven times, and Indians, twenty-five times. Immigration figures show that in the period 1960-70, some 3,300,000 persons were admitted to the United States, of whom nearly 14 percent were nonwhites.

EMERGENCY MEASURES

Thereafter, each new refugee exodus from the Far East, especially of the Indochinese, would renew the question of America's immigration policy.

The influx into Hong Kong raised such a challenge, and IRC found itself involved not only in providing first aid for a population that had come to rest on a tiny island but for those in transit, some of whom could be helped to gain permanent residence in the United States.

Governments are notoriously slow to act. The spectacle of the British in Hong Kong, left virtually unassisted and therefore turning back the refugees to their former masters, brought a sense of shame to humanitarians in the countries that called themselves "the free world." The inability of the West to meet the situation with little more than expressions of consternation stirred a sense of guilt. This was not the first time nor the last when men and women who had made the break for freedom were being remanded to the hell from which they thought they had finally escaped. This had happened to the German Jews on the ship *St. Louis* who were sent back to die in Hitler's hands. It had happened after World War II when the British and Americans capitulated to Stalin's demand for the surrender of Russians who refused to go home. It was dramatized again in 1970 when a Russian seaman jumped to the deck of an American vessel at sea and was handed back as a matter of course, as if an international Fugitive Slave Act had been upheld by a world court in a new Dred Scott decision.

As IRC saw it, a pang of conscience was hardly an adequate answer to a crisis that called for more than words. In 1960, Leo Cherne had surveyed the situation. But it was not until May 1962, as larger numbers succeeded in breaching the Bamboo Curtain, that IRC sent its president, William J. vanden Heuvel, to plan a program. He found the British administration wrestling with incredible obstacles. To begin with, only 19 percent of Hong Kong's land is actually habitable. One-third of the island's water supply was being purchased from Red China and piped in; at any moment, the turn of a valve on Communist territory could have made Hong Kong a desert. Most of the food supply, too, was being imported from the mainland.

The first task was to speed material aid to the May refugees who had survived the deportations. At least half of the estimated 130,000 escapees were still in the colony. IRC hastened to distribute food, supplied by CARE, and clothing for people who had arrived with nothing more than the rags on their backs. To provide temporary shelter, a hostel program was initiated for those without friends or families in Hong Kong. So many refugees were helped that it became impossible to record each case. At least 2,000 were assisted in the first month alone. By the end of the following year, some 1,600 had been resettled in the United States. But the greater task was to integrate the refugees permanently into the economy of Hong Kong. If they had a skill or trade that was in short supply, IRC had little difficulty in helping them find jobs. If not, they were placed in vocational programs and, where desirable, were enrolled for intensive instruction in English.

SETTLING IN

In many cases refugees flee to the border zones, hoping the day will come soon when they will be able to return home. Such expectations were realized by many in the period following World War II. The Bangladeshis did indeed go back in 1972, led by a triumphant government-in-exile that had been based in Calcutta; more recently, Ugandans made their way home in the wake of Nyerere's Tanzanian troops who drove Idi Amin into exile. Those who came to Hong Kong, however, had no such dreams. Their destiny was to build a new life among kinsmen in Hong Kong who speak their language and share a common culture.

To meet the challenge coming out of China, IRC again looked to retired U.S. foreign service officers. Travis Fletcher and Halleck Rose took over. By 1963, IRC's caseload numbered about 8,000. Only a few were eligible for emigration to other ares. Many needed material aid in the form of food, clothing and housing; some wanted help in achieving reunion with their families in other Asian lands. But the greatest need was for vocational training, in line with the old maxim that teaching a man how to fish is more valuable than giving him a fish to eat. To make the refugees self-supporting became the basic objective in Hong Kong.

With the island experiencing a boom in tourism and an expansion in hotel construction, IRC decided to set up a Hotel Training School. At a nominal rental of $32 a month the authorities turned over the Royal Navy Mess Hall and Mess Kitchen in an old naval base. The Hong Kong Hotel Association cooperated in the administration of the school and provided jobs for its graduates. Before the end of the year, a hundred of them were at work in hotels. At first only fifty students could be accommodated at one time, but the facility was expanded. By the spring of 1965, however, the industry had peaked and hotel jobs were no longer available. At its closing, the Training School could boast that it had placed 500 refugees in permanent careers. Its certificate was so valuable in obtaining employment that forged copies began to circulate, and IRC's Hong Kong office was frequently called upon to verify the genuineness of papers presented by job applicants to hotels and clubs.

At the other end of the social scale, IRC maintained its interest in the professionals who had found it necessary to abandon their practice and flee to countries where their skills were not accredited. During 1963, with the assistance of the Far Eastern Refugee Program of the American Consulate General, some fifteen refugee doctors were sent to England for postgraduate study. Twelve of them successfully passed their examinations and in fulfillment of their agreement with IRC, returned to Hong Kong to work for three years in the Medical and Health Department of the colony or in a clinic approved by it. IRC's cost for each individual consisted of round-trip fare and a monthly allowance for a six-month period. As a result of this investment, the refugees were enabled to continue their professional careers and the local community received much-needed medical services.

THE DAY-NURSERY PROGRAM

Hong Kong is famous for its large supply of cheap, disciplined labor, principally because of the enormous refugee population. Many American firms have set up shop on the island, producing an infinite variety of products that compete in the home market. The daily wage for unskilled labor in Hong Kong ranges between three and seven U.S. dollars. As a result, both parents, and even older children, have to work if the family is to be maintained. The victims, of course, are the younger children; they are left with no supervision in a community that has all the hazards of urban crowding. Hong Kong officials estimate that drug addicts may number as many as 100,000 and that they spend at least $130,000,000 (U.S.) on hard drugs. The traditional method of taking heroin by fume-inhalation or "chasing the dragon," as it is called, still persists. Against such a background, the child-care centers have become a matter of great importance to the society. And especially in need of attention are the children whose families had been uprooted.

With the encouragement of the Hong Kong Department of Social Welfare, IRC embarked on a new type of venture – the operation of day-care centers. By the end of its first year the program had a capacity enrollment of sixty; by the end of 1964, a second nursery was caring for seventy-nine children, forty-five of them boys and thirty-four girls. Ranging in ages from two to seven, the youngsters are checked daily by refugee physicians and given appropriate nutritional and medical care. On admission, the children are immunized against diphtheria and polio, and food intake includes supplements like cod liver oil, calcium and vitamins.

Under the volunteer supervision of Mrs. Edward A. Martin, wife of the U.S. Consul General in Hong Kong, the program proved successful. The Department of Social Welfare urged IRC to set up additional facilities. In 1965 a third day nursery was established on Aplichau Island, a fishing community near Hong Kong, notorious as one of the colony's worst slums. The installation, named after the W. Clement and Jessie V. Stone Foundation which had contributed generously, brought the number of children under IRC's care to more than 300. An international appeal for individuals to "adopt" children, and the assistance of volunteers who kept the "foster parents" apprised of the children's progress, brought a considerable response, particularly from the United Kingdom and Belgium as well as the United States. The contributions covered the per-capita expenses of each child in the nurseries and made possible the opening of two additional installations on Cheung Chau Island.

In the years that followed, IRC's Board of Directors has periodically reviewed the day-care program with a view to determining whether it should be continued. The original objectives had been twofold: to give the young children of poor refugee families a balanced diet, health services, recreational facilities, and basic preschool education; and to enable refugee

mothers to seek work. But in the middle 1960s it became difficult to distin-
guish between local population and refugees, so great was the proportion of
escapees. Indeed, it could no longer be determined whether the children
now being cared for were of refugee origin or simply youngsters coming
from the general population living in the vicinity of the nurseries. Before
any child was admitted, however, an IRC worker visited the home. It was
determined, in statistical social service style, that the average family consisted of 5.02 persons and that family income amounted to a little more than
$50 (U.S.) per month. The type of community being served was always
working class, since the nurseries had been located in areas where refugees
were concentrated.

The Board has voted consistently to maintain the day-care program, in
part because of the strong urging of the Hong Kong authorities who feel that
IRC's program is helping the welfare administration to meet the general
problem created by the continuing influx of refugees. Individual Board
members who have visited the day-care centers that now number six, with a
population approaching a thousand, could not help but be moved by the
happy faces and vibrant health of the youngsters. The determination to
keep the program going was strengthened by reports like that of Dr. Ruby
Van, a refugee-physician, who describes the transformation that had been
made in the young lives entrusted to IRC's hands in the Aplichau nursery:

Most children's parents are laborers or vendors with very small family income. With
the fact that they have a number of brothers and sisters, these children were ignored
in their families, particularly during the daytime when their parents are working. As
a result, they were dull, and suffered from malnutrition. There are many such children in this area and they are the type of children for whom this Nursery is established.

Measurements on height and weight were taken monthly for every child. To date,
the average increases are two inches in height and four pounds in weight. On their
admission, the children were not able to write and some of them were not able to
talk. According to their ages, they were divided into two groups, namely the Junior
and Middle groups. All children under four years old are in the junior group and the
others in the middle group.

Children in the middle group were taught to write, to read, to count and to sing. To
date, they are capable of writing ten Chinese characters, numbering from one to
twelve and singing fifteen songs. In the Junior group, the children can now sit on the
chairs and listen to story telling by the child attendants. They react, however,
slowly. Many children in the Junior group wouldn't talk on admission to the Nursery; but now all, except two or three, are capable of answering simple questions.

A visitor to the island of Cheung Chau, an hour's boat ride from Hong
Kong island, finds himself in old China as he descends from the ferry to the
dock. Old women in black pajamas peddle dried fish, meat, vegetables,
housewares, under a hot sun that seems to bake exotic smells into the air.

There are no automobiles—the streets are too narrow and the roads that lead up the hillsides are mere paths that wind round and round the mountain until one reaches the summit where a new refugee camp has been opened for boat people from Vietnam, mostly ethnic Chinese, who are housed in the building of the Wah Kiu College. The climb begins with a series of steep steps and then becomes a country lane that spirals around the island, periodically affording a sweeping view of the sea and the huddled huts of the townspeople below, in the midst of which are the two IRC day-care centers.

The more recent one, opened in 1968, is an impressive structure, painted a light bluish green, that bears the name Chan En Mei-IRC Day Nursery, after a local Chinese lady-philanthropist who had donated substantial funds. Large lettering also identifies the German Metal Workers Union as a major contributor. The presence of this modern building in the midst of ancient shops and houses is the result of a broad cooperative effort. IRC had purchased the land, the Cheung Chau Rural District Committee erected the structure, IRC supplied electric fixtures and the plumbing—which includes long rows of diminutive toilets and washbasins—with funds contributed by the U.S. Refugee Program. Much of the equipment came from UNICEF through the Hong Kong Social Welfare Department. Putting it all together so that it added up to a bright, airy facility was the work of a prominent Chinese architect who gave his services without charge as a labor of love.

Standing at the door to meet the visitor is Choi Kwan Ying, the supervisor, whom her colleagues call Jessica. She introduces her professional staff of young Chinese women—fourteen child-care attendants and seven *amahs*—and proudly announces that 186 children are enrolled, of whom 163 are present today. She leads the way through six large classrooms in some of which, at the moment, the children are napping. Gradually they wake and, rubbing their eyes with tiny fists, take their places at child-sized tables where they are given refreshments. Meticulously, with a cleanliness to be envied by parents in the West, they put away the empty cups, almost strutting with self-consciousness, pride and achievement. Some of them cluster around a basket containing a live duckling that one of the *amahs* has brought in. Others work alone with clay, or daub at wall easels, or play with a profusion of toys and creative materials made accessible on open, low-standing shelves. Organized activity, led by the professional staff, begins in the classrooms: the children sit in their small chairs and sing for the visitor; they play games that call for rhythmic clapping of the hands; they try to coordinate with each other in special dances for which head-bands provide the only costume; they beat or shake tambourines. Some groups wander out into the open courtyard, shielded from the hot sun by latticed woodwork. In the outdoor playground they climb the jungle gym, or take turns on the slides, or ride about spiritedly on tricycles. And everywhere cleanliness, order and joy prevail.

Other facilities, caring for smaller numbers of children, are not as expansive but are equally well maintained even though they are located in the poor and overcrowded neighborhoods of Kowloon. One of them, serving about fifty children, is strangely serene even though it is in the throbbing business section of the city. Another, which has twice the capacity, is on the street floor of a public housing project at the foot of Lion Rock Hill. (Almost half of Hong Kong's population lives in such government-subsidized housing.) The funding of this nursery was also supplemented by the West German Metal Workers Union. To approach it one passes a cluster of shanties clinging perilously on one of those barren hillsides that obtrude throughout Hong Kong; the stolid occupants show no sign that a sudden fire or a heavy rainstorm may leave them totally homeless or dead.

FOR THE ADULTS

Events had forced IRC to put substantial efforts into caring for the children. But the needs of the adults were by no means ignored. The IRC hostel in Kowloon, providing temporary quarters for new arrivals, is maintained in an upper story of an apartment building, with access provided by a ponderous, creaking elevator. The United Nations High Commissioner pays room and board, and IRC meets the custodial costs. Here the capacity is forty-two persons at any one time.

On entering, the visitor finds himself in a small community room. A handful of youngsters, Vietnamese and Chinese, are so absorbed in watching a television set that they do not even notice the presence of foreigners; only one of them, a pretty girl of about twelve, raises her head to smile, looking up from her copybook, performing the feat of simultaneously watching television, doing her homework and acknowledging strangers. Two dormitories segregate the sexes. In a single room about ten by eleven feet, eighteen bunks arranged in three tiers fill the space. There is no effort at luxury; the rooms are bare and few personal possessions are in evidence. But the atmosphere is antiseptic, and one marvels that the cleanliness can be maintained despite the crowding. Besides the noise emanating from the television set and the occasional laughing comments exchanged by the children as they react to the program, there is quiet. Most of the residents are out, either working or looking for jobs.

A major project maintained over the years has been the China Refugee Development Organization, sponsored by IRC. It provides gainful employment for some 500 craftsmen and artists whose output includes small wooden carvings, painted scrolls and even ivory sculptures. Its retail outlet, called the Rice Bowl, sells to tourists and exports to the United States, the United Kingdom, West Germany and the Scandinavian countries. From the start in 1966, it has continued to operate in the black while providing both employment and training to refugees. In 1967, despite a chaotic period of

Communist-inspired disorders in Hong Kong that hurt sales, the CRDO successfully merchandised more than a million Hong Kong dollars worth of goods, equivalent to $170,000 in U.S. dollars.

Throughout the years IRC has continued to resettle as many people as possible and, to whatever extent possible, reduce the population pressure in Hong Kong. The first task, of course, was to assure that escapees were permitted to remain on the island until they could be moved elsewhere. Internal policies of the People's Republic of China, zigzagging between varying degrees of brutal repression and temporary lifting of the Bamboo Curtain, have resulted in peaks and valleys on the graph of flight. In 1956 Mao proclaimed: "Let a hundred flowers blossom, a hundred schools of thought contend." But by June of the following year every stalk that had sprouted fell under the sickle or was bludgeoned by the hammer of the Communist Party. The period of the Great Leap Forward, beginning in 1958, did not last long. The 1959 meeting of the party's Central Committee heard devastating economic news, ranging from the misadventures of poor harvests to industrial errors caused by falsified statistics. Critics of the absurd program of creating backyard steel furnaces, presumably to release the mystic productive powers of the masses, became the targets of a purge, a bitter foretaste of what was to come in the Cultural Revolution launched seven years later by Mao. China's domestic problems multiplied as three successive crop failures, from 1959 to 1961, led to serious food shortages, disasters that were accentuated by the Soviet Union's withdrawal of economic aid in 1960. The ensuing storms sent new waves of refugees toward Hong Kong.

THE CULTURAL REVOLUTION

Few events in recent political history can match the upheaval unleashed by Mao Zedong in anticipation of his own approaching death. In the rhetoric of Chinese polemics, it was called The Great Proletarian Cultural Revolution, and lasted from 1965 until 1968 when its chief sorcerer finally recaptured control over the Red apprentices he had released.

Preceded by months of behind-the-scenes maneuvering in the fall of 1965, the Cultural Revolution burst into the open with extravagant denunciations of and by people in the highest places, accompanied by Aesopian statements of doctrine that dramatized ideological differences without ever identifying them. The struggle was formalized in May 1966 by a circular message from the Central Committee to party units and to local governments announcing that all must "repudiate those representatives of the bourgeoisie who have sneaked into the party, the government, the army, and all spheres of culture."

Young people by the millions were brought into Peking to demonstrate against the establishment that had arisen since 1949. Their activities, orchestrated by the most deeply entrenched leaders of the establishment, soon spread. A recentralization of power was effected by turning the youthful Red Guards into human missiles aimed at the educational and cultural leadership of the country—university administrators and professors, writers and artists—as well as managers of enterprises, government bureaucrats, and various professionals. Some observers wondered whether a revolution within a revolution was not a counterrevolution, but the net result was a retention of power by Mao and a small group around him after the purge of some of his closest associates. The cannibal appetite of revolution again devoured its own children. The violence took countless lives and led to the desecration or destruction of historic treasures, including the putative grave of Confucius, that had survived millennia only to fall victim to the depravity of political man in the twentieth century. "Mindless enthusiasm and vicious vandalism," to use Robert Elegant's phrase, were unleashed under the slogan, "Let the masses manage the great affairs of the state!"[4]

But if youth was the weapon used by Mao, it was also the major victim. A program of internal deportations was initiated. Students were sent into the countryside, never to recapture the lost years and aspirations. Universities and schools were shut down; professors, teachers and community leaders were paraded through the streets in dunce caps, among them Zhao Ziyang, who was destined to become prime minister in 1980. A new bonfire of the books took place as the dominant Communist faction sought to erase the ancient wisdom and literature of Confucianism. The setback to science would not be retrievable and would prove to be the greatest of the losses imposed on China by the Cultural Revolution, as Mao's successors would ultimately concede in their program of "the four modernizations"—of the economy, the educational system, the army and science.

The immediate results of this medieval obscurantism were particularly burdensome to the young, even though they had been given the heady experience of running unbridled through the streets and permitted to torment their teachers, if they were students, or their managers if they were workers. Richard Harris, the deputy foreign editor and Asian specialist of the London *Times*, has described the mood that followed Mao's death as one of "skepticism, cynicism, and disillusion on the part of the young who were caught up in the Cultural Revolution and for a brief moment saw themselves as an idealistic advance guard. Millions were later sent to the countryside; thousands more escaped to Hong Kong. All of them felt their future to be insecure and their political ideas confused."

The early years of the Cultural Revolution had seemed to offer the young people freedom from the conventional disciplines of education, like examinations for admission and for advancement to higher levels. On June 18, 1966, the *People's Daily* in Peking announced the new educational policy:

The Central Committee of the Chinese Communist Party and the State Council took the decision to abolish the existing entrance examination method of enrolling students in institutes of higher learning in accordance with Chairman Mao's instructions and the demand of the masses. . . .

Again and again the Central Committee of the Party and Chairman Mao have pointed out that the old bourgeois educational system, including the enrolling of students by examination, must be thoroughly transformed. This old examination system of enrolling students is most dangerous and harmful to our socialist cause. It places not proletarian but bourgeois politics in command, it places school marks in command. . . . Chairman Mao has put forward the policy that education must serve proletarian politics and must be combined with productive labor. . . . It is not only the system of enrollment that requires transforming, all the arrangements for schooling, for testing, for going up or not going up to the higher class, and so on, must be transformed, and so must the content of education.[5]

The attack on the textbooks took the principal form of substituting "Mao Zedong Thought," as it was called, for traditional learning. The Little Red Book, flourished ritualistically in the air by huge crowds of young and old, became a common spectacle caught in the camera's eye for current consumption and historical preservation. The *People's Daily* formally announced the substitution of Mao's writings for the accumulated intellectual heritage of China and indeed the world:

New teaching material must be compiled under the guidance of Mao Zedong's Thought and the principle of putting proletarian politics first. The junior classes in primary schools can study some extracts from Chairman Mao's works and the senior classes can study more of them and also some of the articles including "Serve the People," "In Memory of Norman Bethune," and "The Foolish Old Man Who Removed the Mountains." Middle-school students can study *Selected Readings from Mao Zedong's Works* and articles related to these readings. College students can study *Selected Works of Mao Zedong.*[6]

In 1972 Barbara W. Tuchman, historian and expert on the Far East, visited the mainland at the invitation of the Mao government. Despite the good will she brought with her in the glow of the new Sino-American relationship, she could not help but note that many of the Buddhist temples listed in the guidebooks were "not to be seen, perhaps because of vandalism suffered during the ravages of the Cultural Revolution."[7] Her visit to the universities was particularly depressing. Courses were largely vocational, aimed at furthering only production purposes. The University of Peita (Peking) had only a thousand students though its capacity was originally 10,000. So, too, at Sian University the student body now numbered about half of the erstwhile size of the faculty. She asked to meet with members of a Writer's Union; she was told there were "no writers in Peking." Even municipal libraries, she found, were off limits, suggesting that they were no longer in operation. In her *Notes from China* she wrote:

Mao is probably the first chief of state to . . . uproot and dismember his own power structure in order to restart the revolution and keep it moving toward its goals.

This was the purpose and meaning of that mysterious frenzy — as it came through to the West in bewildering flashes — which swept China in 1966-69 and is now sanctified as the great Proletarian Cultural Revolution. Deliberately set in motion by Mao and at least some like-thinking colleagues, it was an act of extraordinary risk that could have wrecked the system. It activated the fanaticism of youth, which can be activated to anything, and set it rampaging through society, beating, persecuting, shaming, and leaving a wake of violence, ruin, and suicides.[8]

But this was not the fate of all youth. Many sought flight from the menace of intellectual imprisonment and physical exile to rural areas. Escape involved not only the hazards of making one's way secretly to the border or the coast but, for many, a three-hour swim in shark-infested waters from Po On across Mirs Bay. Another route, Deep Bay, was less formidable but also less likely to be successful because more thoroughly policed by human sharks. Still another popular avenue to freedom was to swim the Shum Chun River.

CAMPAIGN OF DISRUPTION

One might have expected the launching of the Cultural Revolution to step up the flow of refugees. It did not happen — at first. A series of events manipulated by the Communists reduced the figures. The tensions created by the Red Guard activities led to much tighter border control on both sides of the frontier and on the shores. IRC staff on the scene reported that only 6,500 refugees had made it to Hong Kong that year.

At the same time, Communist agents whose presence in Hong Kong had long been known but who were relatively quiescent were ordered into action. Heretofore, Peking had shrewdly kept hands off Hong Kong, preferring to leave it British so that it could serve as China's outlet to the Western world. Hong Kong's economic viability has depended on the New Territories, an area on the mainland north of Kowloon extending to the Shum Chun River, plus 235 small islands. The region was leased from China for ninety-nine years by a treaty not officially recognized by the Red regime but that is due to expire in 1997. Citizens of Hong Kong and refugees who have established themselves there know that their children are destined by the end of the century to become Chinese subjects unless they move on. They watch with morbid absorption the process of Communist investment in Hong Kong — the establishment of trade outlets, department stores, banks, and so on — that is paving the way for the takeover to come in two decades. They foresee a day when they, and certainly their children, will face the need to relocate somewhere in the free world.

Hong Kong's ability to live in the shadow of the Communist giant of Asia and to prosper despite the burden of a huge refugee population has been a remarkable feat. But in the days of the Cultural Revolution it seemed that the anarchic militancy on the mainland was about to spill over into the British colony. This had been foreshadowed in 1966 by events in the nearby Portuguese colony of Macao, located at the mouth of the Pearl River sixty-five miles south of Canton. With a total population of 250,000, more than half of them Chinese from the mainland, it too has served China as a gateway for exports although imports from Macao have been barred. In comparison with its Hong Kong policy, Peking has been less correct in dealing with this Portuguese colony, first visited by Vasco da Gama five years after Columbus set foot in America. During the years of the Cultural Revolution, Macao was subjected to intense pressure, beginning with riots on the island of Taipa, that ended with capitulation to China's demand that the colony be closed to refugees from the mainland and that anti-Communist activity cease. Since then a Peking veto has hung over all of Macao's political decisions.

Similar efforts in Hong Kong, however, failed. The British took Communist-inspired disruption in their stride; the policy of firmness had popular support. But the disturbances of 1967, the incitement of labor unrest, terrorist bombings and mob violence aimed at the Governor's residence, and riots in the Wong Tai Sin area where many refugees had been resettled and where IRC had one of its large day-care centers, made many would-be refugees conclude that Hong Kong was no longer a safe haven and that there was no hiding place from Communist fury.

At the beginning of the year, the refugee rate had increased to about 500 a month but then dropped off during the disturbances. By September, however, the Hong Kong authorities had matters well in hand, and by year's end there were no further incidents. The flow increased again, reaching 1,000 in December alone. By February of the next year, 2,000 Chinese fleeing from the Cultural Revolution arrived safely. In that wave were 120 refugees who arrived in three junks. Of these, twenty had been literally snatched from the sea by a Norwegian vessel after their leaky craft had capsized eleven miles southwest of Kowloon. In 1969, such an event still made headlines in the press; it had not yet become a commonplace in the South China Sea.

FLIGHT FROM THE BRAIN-WASHERS

The increase in the number of successful escapes brought a sharp reaction from the Communists. The Kwantung Revolutionary Committee, in charge of the Canton province, issued instructions to the police and military officials to increase their vigilance and to impose the most severe penalties on those apprehended, including incarceration in the notorious Labor Reform Camps operated in the spirit of *Lao Dong Gai Zao*. The words say little more than "reform through manual labor," but the reality has been described by Bao Ruo-Wang, who made his way to Hong Kong after seven years of such reformation. The son of a Corsican father and a Chinese mother, actually a French citizen, Bao had been sent off to learn the virtues of such labor principally because he "was a very rare animal—a foreigner born in China, speaking the language like a native, with the face of a Chinese." He had earned the designation "snake in the grass" because he had worked for the U.S. Marines during and immediately after World War II. In his ironic and at times even dispassionate book, *Prisoner of Mao*, he pays tribute to the logic of the Chinese, in contrast to that of the Russians:

> In our fair and pleasant world there is no shortage of countries that have built their modern civilizations on a foundation of deportation areas, concentration camps and prison farms. The Soviets have been especially notable achievers in this line. Their complex of forced labor camps was impressively vast in its prime, but it was brutally cruel, unsophisticated—and inefficient—compared to what the Chinese developed after the victory of the revolution in 1949. What the Russians never understood, and what the Chinese Communists knew all along, is that convict labor can never be productive or profitable if it is extracted only by coercion or torture. The Chinese were the first to grasp the art of motivating prisoners. That's what *Lao Gai* is all about.

> Those seven years I lived—often in abject, despairing misery, sometimes literally starving and always haunted by hunger, in perpetual submission to the authority not only of guards and warders but even more so to the "mutual surveillance" of my fellow prisoners and even to my own zealous self-denunciations and confessions— constitute my own story, of course, but far more important, they are the story of the millions upon millions of Chinese who endured the camps with me and are still in them today.[9]

It is forgotten now that the Chinese Communists, with their linguistic skill in making visual the most abstract doctrinal concepts, devised the term "brainwashing." Some people even think the phrase is an invention of anti-Communist rhetoric. What it involves is a technique of combining brutalization with indoctrination. Its practice first became known to the Western world because it was used in the prison camps during the Korean War. After the Indochina war it became the curriculum of the so-called reeducation camps of Vietnam, Cambodia and Laos.

As the Cultural Revolution picked up speed in the late 1960s, Hong Kong was again inundated. Each increase in pressure on the Chinese people brought a refugee outflow like blood spurting from fresh-cut wounds. As was to be the case with the Vietnamese a decade later, the easiest way out was on fishing boats. In its effort to batten down the escape hatches, the Kwantung Revolutionary Committee ordered that every fishing vessel manned by ten people must be accompanied by two members of the Committee; if the crew numbered more than ten, by at least four members of the Committee. But despite the stepped-up patrols on land and sea and the dire punishment meted out to the unfortunates who were caught, more than 17,000 got out in 1968.

News items in the Hong Kong *Standard* in 1969 recited episodes like the following: "An illegal immigrant was shot in the face by Chinese border guards while crossing to British territory. His companion was machine-gunned to death."[10] Describing the arrival of five "junk-loads" consisting of fifty-nine people, the newspaper said: "The refugees, all dressed in rags, told police they belonged to five related families of Kai Tau village. They said they left their village on fishing missions and sailed toward Hong Kong by night to avoid Chinese gunboats."[11] The safe entry into harbor of 500 fishermen and their families marked the first such mass escape since 1963. They were among the 3,320 new refugees who were assisted in 1968 by IRC. Fishermen were helped to build huts and acquire boats so that they might ply their trade again. Many were guided toward new types of employment.

UNDER PENALTY OF DEATH

In June 1970, a *New York Times* correspondent reported that the Chinese authorities were using mass executions in the effort to curb the exodus. He wrote: "Many hundreds have been publicly executed in Kwantung province [which borders Hong Kong's New Territories]. . . . In Kwantung it is a major offense to attempt to flee to Hong Kong and recent events have underlined the danger faced by refugees or those who attempt to aid them. The border town of Shum Chun was the scene of public executions in April and May within sight of observers on the Hong Kong side. On both occasions the charges against the victims included helping refugees escape to Hong Kong."[12]

But still they came, bringing with them stories of hardship suffered on the journey, perils more welcome than remaining with the cruel stability of life in Communist China. A university student from Shanghai who had been ordered to leave his studies and work as a farmhand told how he escaped after seven years in hiding and after being captured twice. He swam for eight hours before he reached the haven of Hong Kong where he collapsed from fatigue and hunger. Two other youths told of going into training for a year, practicing for their escape, swimming upstream against strong currents to build their strength. One of them said, "We decided we would rather risk death than be sent with a labor battalion to the Hainan commune."

The official policy of the British authorities continued to be a rejection of the refugees. In practice, if the individual was not caught at the point of entry but succeeded in reaching Victoria City on Hong Kong island or Kowloon, he would be allowed to register and remain. Still, bureaucratic snares awaited him. Eventually the officials began to demand that the refugees prove their provenance from the mainland by presenting tangible evidence in the form of Communist identity cards, ration cards or similar documentation. There was a sound reason for this: ethnic Chinese from Taiwan or other areas in Asia were pretending to be refugees in order to settle in the colony. Refugees, however, do not ordinarily carry briefcases with documents as they swim rivers, traverse jungles or slip by checkpoints surreptitiously. With the backing of the local representatives of the United Nations High Commissioner, IRC staff intervened successfully in many critical situations, since its bona fides was widely respected and it was known to be thorough in its own investigations. Without the appropriate registration, the undocumented refugee could not have gained employment.

OPENING THE DOOR

An even more important function was that of effectuating emigration for those who could qualify. President Kennedy had established a special program for Chinese refugees in Hong Kong under the "parole" power granted by law to the Attorney General. Liberalization of immigration controls had long been overdue. Continuing prejudice against Orientals had resulted in an exclusion policy that kept many families separated. In the days when coolie labor was needed in the West to build the railroads and perform the physical labor considered to be beneath the white man's dignity, the United States had received 400,000 Chinese. Viewed as an inferior race, they were the target of a powerful hate movement in the late nineteenth century. The bigots insisted that the country could no longer absorb immigration, that certain peoples were undesirable aliens, and that foreigners in general constituted a threat to wage and living standards in this country. In 1882 Congress passed the Chinese Exclusion Act, which denied entry to Chinese laborers for a period of ten years, a ban that was renewed in 1892 and then made permanent in 1902. World War II, in which China had been an ally, wrought a significant change in the racial attitudes of Americans. The emergence of a strong civil-rights consciousness, though addressed primarily to the status of blacks, inevitably affected attitudes toward the Chinese.

Obviously, it was impossible to empty Hong Kong of its refugee population and resettle them elsewhere. But the lives of thousands could be directly affected and at least some families reunited. IRC provided guidance to the few who could now be resettled in the United States. The Emergency Parole Program instituted by President Kennedy was severely limited: applicants could be accepted only if their petitions had been approved by January 1, 1963. All told, IRC was able initially to assist 1,600 to take advantage of the dispensations. Successive governmental actions have made it possible to bring about further admissions, thus rectifying long-standing injustices that had kept wives from their husbands, and children from their parents. In 1965, IRC brought in 57; in 1966, the figure rose to 1,303; in 1967, it was down to 656; up again in 1968 to 1,207. In 1969, charter flights organized by the Intergovernmental Committee for European Migration (ICEM) carried 1,097 Chinese refugees to the United States under IRC auspices. In more recent years, American immigration authorities have continued to approve the relocation from Hong Kong of IRC-sponsored refugees in numbers ranging from 1,500 to 2,000.

THE EFFECT OF RAPPROCHEMENT

The American accommodation with China in 1972, an event that was historic from many angles, did not reduce the number of Chinese who wanted to escape. Two years after President Nixon and Foreign Minister Chou En-lai, with an ailing Mao Zedong in the background, toasted each other in the great hall of Peking's People's Palace, the Hong Kong *Morning Post* was still reporting items like the following:

Refugees are fleeing from China to Hong Kong at the rate of more than 100 a week, and many of them are dying in the cold waters of Mirs Bay. The seasonal influx is being watched with concern by government officials. Last month, about 120 swam to Hong Kong across Mirs Bay or Deep Bay. Another 370 arrived here by sea, mostly in a collection of unseaworthy sampans, homemade rubber boats, bamboo rafts and practically anything that would float. Some of the refugees paddled for miles down the Chinese coast from villages on the Pearl River. The number attempting to swim is unheard of. A large number of refugees have drowned — more than 40 bodies were spotted in Mirs Bay alone, and overturned and swamped vessels have been seen.

In 1974 an estimated 21,000 made their escape, 3,000 more than the previous year. An astounding 14,000 of the refugees were young "freedom swimmers" who survived the treacherous waters. How many drowned is unknown but it is estimated that the figure is at least in the hundreds. Again the Hong Kong government decided to close the sluice gates; in December alone, 238 refugees were caught and 223 of them were sent back to China. That policy continued into 1975, when 1,233 were arrested on arrival and all but a hundred were forcibly returned to Red China. Cold numbers never tell the story. IRC's Annual Report for 1975 quotes this account in the Hong Kong *Morning Post* to convey the reality of one human decimal in the gruesome statistics:

A 26-year-old woman who swam for 12 hours to Hong Kong was sent back to China immediately after a full court turned down her application for an order of habeas corpus. Her mother, a construction site worker, broke down and fell on her knees to beg for mercy. As the weeping mother left the Supreme Court with her three sons, she said: "I was not permitted to meet my daughter after she arrived in Hong Kong. Can you tell me what is going to happen to her after she returns to China?"

"Bloody frightening," a government official had said years before.

Nor did the death of Mao in 1976 and the advent of the Hua regime staunch the flow. Despite the *realpolitik* that pushes Peking to more open relations with the West, China remains a totalitarian country, denying its people the elements of freedom. The wars of the wall posters were ultimately ended by a formal constitutional prohibition. And Hua Guofeng, at the 1978 National People's Congress, told his countrymen and the world that "Marxism-Leninism-Mao Zedong Thought" remains the ideology of China and that there is no room for the "bourgeois liberalism dreamt of by reactionaries inside the country and outside."

Reading him aright, free spirits on the mainland still eye Hong Kong as their gateway to freedom. In 1978, two years after Mao's death, more than 8,000 Chinese refugees who reached Hong Kong were dumped back across the border, but those who managed to elude the police were not pursued. The authorities estimate that the people who thus succeeded in winning their freedom numbered 25,000 to 30,000, far greater than the estimated 5,000 successful escapees in 1977.

The upward trend continues. Data, as of October 1979, revealed that the number of "illegal immigrants" caught each day averaged 180. In May alone, 14,400 were arrested. The *Washington Post* quotes the Hong Kong authorities as acknowledging that at least 28,000 avoided capture on arrival in the first three months of 1979 and were therefore allowed to remain. But the tragedy of the individuals who fall into the hands of the police and who are surrendered to Mao's successors continues to plague the conscience of the Crown Colony. That tragedy is illustrated by an item in the *Post*:

Shum Mei-ying, 22, had gone through a seven-day hike during a typhoon and a one-mile swim across shark-infested waters to escape China and join her husband in Hong Kong. She was semiconscious, paddling desperately with the help of fellow female-escapees when, just in sight of Hong Kong's shore, all hope vanished. The marine police, under orders to send all refugees back to China, chugged up in a launch and picked the two women out of the water.[13]

That was the same year in which some 6,000 others, from across the South China Sea, had anchored in Hong Kong harbor after a sea voyage of a thousand miles. The island was facing a refugee crisis more "bloody frightening" than any it had known before.

XIII

Land of Dragons: Southeast Asia

Throughout most of the nineteenth and twentieth centuries the vast reaches of Asia were dominated by Western colonialism. Here and there small groups of patriots had resisted, but with little success. Forced into exile, they left no mass movements behind. Large-scale flight was unheard of; where could one go to escape Western imperialism? But in the 1930s, in the Far East as in Europe, the earth began to tremble under the pounding feet of men, women and children seeking to escape from mortal danger. From Mukden to the Bay of Bengal, millions have since been in motion — Asians fleeing from Asians.

The end of World War II saw the sun set on the empires of the West and on the mainland over which the Japanese flag had waved for a few bitter years. The collapse of British, French and Dutch colonialism has been described by Gunnar Myrdal in his three-volume study, *Asian Drama*. Of the American role, he writes:

It was during and immediately after the Second World War that all the forces and pressures that had been gradually weakening the European colonial power system came together to effect its final collapse. Of crucial importance was the position taken by the United States. Once brought out of its isolation, it immediately began to exert pressure against the continuation of European colonialism. The Atlantic Charter drafted by Churchill and Roosevelt in 1941 as a declaration of Allied war aims stated that the Allies "respected the right of all peoples to choose the form of government under which they will live and they wish to see sovereign rights and self-government restored to those who had been forcibly deprived of them." The American leaders made it plain that they expected this principle to be applied to the European colonial dependencies. Thus Roosevelt favored an international trusteeship for Indo-China and pressed Britain to take immediate steps to grant India independence.[1]

Of Indochina Roosevelt had written to Secretary of State Cordell Hull in January 1944: "France has had the country — thirty million inhabitants — for nearly one hundred years, and the people are worse off than they were at the beginning.... France has milked it for one hundred years. The people of

Indochina are entitled to something better than that."[2] Even in the tradition-bound chambers of the State Department there was an awareness, bluntly expressed by Sumner Welles in 1942: "The age of imperialism is ended."[3] That these conclusions constituted the basis of American policy has been ignored by critics in the heat of passions engendered by the events of the 1960s and '70s.

Asia's modern ordeal by fire began well before World War II. The massive migrations got under way when the Japanese set up their puppet government in Manchuria in 1931, then invaded China in 1937, and finally swept through Southeast Asia in the 1940s. After World War II, the victorious occidentals thought to pack their bags for a return to the Orient, only to be confronted by strong resistance. Endemic nationalist movements were joined by Communist cadres who, with Stalin's support, sought to implement Lenin's strategy: "The road to Paris lies through Asia." That ultimate destination was never quite reached—at least not yet. But Communist revolution, breeding a new imperialism made more powerful by the techniques of totalitarianism, descended on the continent with all the fury of a Pacific typhoon. In less than three decades, millions of Chinese, Vietnamese, Laotians and Cambodians have been sent into flight like autumn leaves before the wind.

The irony is that World War II and its aftermath liberated Asia from the grip of Western imperialism but brought new tyrannies in its place. The European empires, struggling for survival against the Axis powers, had hoped, despite American pressure, to perpetuate their rule, perhaps in some modified form. But the totalitarians, both Fascist and Communist, had other expectations. The captured archives of the Reich's foreign office laid bare the postwar hopes of the Nazis and the Russians in an official summary of Hitler's conversation with Soviet foreign minister Molotov during the days of the Nazi-Soviet pact:

After the conquest of England [the Fuehrer said] the British Empire would be apportioned as a gigantic world-wide estate in bankruptcy of 40,000,000 square kilometers. . . . All the countries which could possibly be interested in the bankrupt estate would have to stop all controversies among themselves and concern themselves exclusively with the partition of the British Empire. This applied to Germany, France, Italy, Russia and Japan.[4]

Neither of the participants in that discussion envisioned the possibility that the peoples of Africa and Asia might try to take command of their own destinies.

THE LIQUIDATION OF EMPIRE

With the coming of peace in 1945, historical inevitability joined forces with the United States to prod London into a recognition of the new realities. The British electorate took the wheel from the hands of Churchill, once First Lord of the Admiralty, and banished him from the deck. The self-liquidation of the empire began. In 1947, after decades of Gandhi's *satyagraha* movement, India was partitioned into two independent countries. Next Burma and Ceylon were set free. The Dutch, after a military effort, decided in 1949 to surrender Indonesia. But the French, clinging to Indochina, found themselves enmeshed in a war that lasted from 1946 to 1954. It was the prelude to a drama that eventually would entangle the United States in one of the most traumatic chapters of its history.

For the Asians, the latter half of the 1940s opened the era of emancipation from the Europeans. Particularly significant was the year 1949: the eyes of the Western powers were fixed on Berlin, then under blockade, but the Communists were active on many fronts simultaneously; in that year Mao took control of mainland China.

In Indochina, 1954 was the turning point as the Moscow-trained Ho Chi Minh defeated the French at Dien Bien Phu. The Vietminh, dominated by the Communists, were fighting on two fronts—a war of independence against the French and a civil war against their own anti-Communist countrymen. At Geneva that year an agreement was signed under which France withdrew completely. The country was divided at the 17th parallel, with Hanoi to be the capital of a Communist North Vietnam and Saigon the capital of a South Vietnam oriented to the West. Reunification was to await the outcome of a free election.

IMMEDIATE NEEDS IN VIETNAM

The government in Saigon was given little chance of survival, certainly not for two decades. Among its most urgent problems was the tremendous influx of refugees from the North. Article 14(d) of the Geneva agreement had provided that the population would be able to choose which zone they wanted to live in. During a period of 300 days there was to be freedom of movement for civilians who wished to resettle. In this the treaty-makers were following the precedent established in the partition of India and Korea where, it can be said, the solution had at least a more enduring effect. It is estimated that 120,000 Vietnamese went to the North, many of them to return to the South as guerrillas a few years later. Some 900,000 Northerners, most of them Catholics, pulled up stakes and headed south. South Vietnam alone could not carry the resulting burden of absorption.

The ink was hardly dry on the Geneva agreement when IRC's chairman Leo Cherne arrived in Saigon to appraise the situation and take first steps to develop a relief program for the Vietnamese refugees. He conferred with the new Premier, Ngo Dinh Diem. With almost a million refugees coming from the North it was hoped that their ranks would add to the reservoir of leadership and administrative skills sorely needed by the new government. It became clear that two approaches would have to be used: one, a program for alleviating the mass refugee problem, and the other a specialized program to give intellectuals and students an opportunity to use their talents.

Cherne reported his findings to IRC's Board of Directors, which requested its vice chairman Joseph Buttinger to proceed to Saigon and organize refugee assistance. Buttinger was a particularly wise choice for the task because of his own record as an underground socialist fighter against totalitarianism in his native country, Austria, where he had opposed the reactionary Dolfuss regime in the 1930s as well as the Nazi occupation after *Anschluss*. His activities as a refugee himself in France and then in the United States during the war years had equipped him with unique insights, enabling him to move sure-footed through the swamps of Vietnamese politics. His discernment and analytical powers are evidenced by his three-volume history of Vietnam which was inspired by his IRC mission. In 1958 *The Smaller Dragon* appeared, followed in 1967 by the two-volume *Vietnam: A Dragon Embattled*; in 1968 a one-volume condensation containing new material on the war appeared under the title, *Vietnam: A Political History*.[5]

In that last volume Buttinger records what he saw on arriving in Saigon during the exodus from the North. "The number of those who lost everything was staggering," he wrote. His immediate challenge was to provide the essentials for survival without delay, and then to lay the foundations for a longer-range program of self-help looking to resettlement and incorporation into the economic and social life of the South. The first objective was met by rushing food, clothing and medicines into the refugee camps set up by the government, the second by a series of separate projects designed to encourage education and vocational training.

For example, financial and technical assistance was given to the Popular Cultural Association, a nonprofit private educational organization, originally established by a group of Vietnamese who had studied abroad. One of its major activities was the Popular Technical Institute, which offered night classes in vocational subjects, languages, the social sciences and Vietnamese literature. It conducted classes in the major towns of South Vietnam, with some 10,000 Vietnamese from all walks of life participating. The Popular Cultural Association is credited with having taught more than 100,000 Vietnamese to read and write. Its seminal role is illustrated also by the Freedom Centers it established in the larger cities. With libraries, auditoriums and meeting rooms, these centers attracted intellectuals and students, many of whom helped to implement a national literacy program.

It is safe to assume that the subsequent defeat of South Vietnam by the North has not erased the effects of such education. But it is not accidental that dictatorships, on taking power or at other times of crisis, turn their full fury on the educated and the professionals. This has happened repeatedly — for instance, in East Pakistan and more recently in Cambodia where Pol Pot's Khmer Rouge made school-teaching a capital offense.

Even during the war years South Vietnam, with a population of 14 million, had about 1,500,000 students in its primary schools and somewhat more than 160,000 in secondary schools. Some 10,000 students were matriculated in the universities of Saigon and Hué alone. Many of the teachers and students were products of the Popular Cultural Association, along with refugee scholars from the north. At Hué, for example, a large number of the instructors were transplants from the University of Hanoi, whose faculty had fled south as a body.

IRC and sister American voluntary agencies on the scene were soon joined by other organizations. The Philippine Junior Chamber of Commerce launched "Operation Brotherhood," sending teams of doctors and nurses to provide medical care for the refugees. In February 1955, IRC together with the U.S. Junior Chamber of Commerce rallied support in this country for "Operation Brotherhood." Through such efforts, emergency medical aid and public sanitation were brought to hundreds of thousands of refugees in the villages, and dreaded epidemics were avoided.

THE FIRST PHASE

These initial activities were conducted under relatively peaceful circumstances. To be sure, guerrilla warfare was already under way, with South Vietnamese Communists probing for soft spots in a regime that was all too vulnerable to the charge of maintaining its own lesser brand of dictatorship. The North had not yet launched its open invasion of the South to compel unification under Hanoi's rule. Many who hoped that Ngo Dinh Diem would stave off a Communist takeover and move in democratic directions were later to lose faith in him, in his successors, and in the entire effort of the United States to keep Indochina out of the Soviet orbit.

At this juncture, the South Vietnamese government, eager for assistance from abroad, was particularly interested in the International Rescue Committee because of its standing in the world community. In his book, *The Lost Crusade: America in Vietnam*, published in 1970, Chester L. Cooper, who represented the United States at the 1954 Conference on Indochina and who was in charge of Asian affairs for the White House in later years, presents this account of IRC's early role:

The American International Rescue Committee (IRC) — a group organized during World War II to assist the escape and resettlement of intellectuals from Nazi Germany and later from Soviet occupied areas — was soon seized with the question of whether it should launch a program to assist the refugees from North Vietnam. This was not an easy decision in view of the numbers and kinds of people involved. The Committee had traditionally been Europe-oriented, and it was primarily interested in scholars and professionals rather than rank and file farmers and urban workers. The IRC had remained aloof in two earlier refugee crises in Asia — the flight of anti-Communists from Mainland China to Hong Kong and from North Korea to the

South — and perhaps many of the Committee members had some feeling of guilt.* In any case, when the refugees from North Vietnam began streaming south in August, 1954, the IRC decided to participate by helping to resettle the intellectuals among them. But Committee representatives found little interest in Washington in either the refugees or in American voluntary assistance programs. The Administration felt it was doing everything necessary by providing Navy transport for the refugee movement. However, the flow from the North increased to such proportions — approximately 40,000 to 50,000 per day at its peak — that it was soon evident Diem's new government would be incapable of handling this vast problem without immediate outside help.[6]

Cooper records that on arriving in Saigon Cherne conferred with Ambassador Donald Heath to discuss a relief program but found him "distinctly discouraging." On other hand, "Diem attached great importance to Cherne's visit. The IRC concern about the refugee problem was the first evidence Diem had had of any American interest in Vietnam since he had taken office." At this time, in 1954, Cooper notes, Cherne sent a cable to the members of the Research Institute of America, of which he was executive director, summarizing his assessment of the situation. Cooper comments that "although the cable was heavily censored by the French who still controlled the post and telegraph service, the thrust of Cherne's perceptive assessment got through."

Unfortunately the full text of the uncensored message has been lost, but the following content did reach New York:

According to armistice, Communists supposed to evacuate southern Vietnam. But Communists are retaining complete control of important pockets south of Saigon. Elsewhere government suspects much Red strength, had no way of finding out how much.... Success of effort to hold Vietnam from Communists depends on whether all non-Communist Vietnamese can unite for struggle.... One point most Vietnamese agree on: Don't want French. Political and financial instability must follow unless Vietnamese government can organize important forces and U.S. continues pouring in substantial help and money.... All recognize huge stakes riding on gamble that Vietnam can survive further Communist penetration and win election supposed to be held twenty months from now. If free elections held today, all agree privately Communists would win. Reason: effect of Communist military victory plus Indochinese hatred of previous colonial status. Situation not hopeless. There is danger, but not paralysis. Future depends on organizing all resources to resettle refugees, sustain near bankrupt government, give people something to fight for and unite them to resist Communism.

---

*Note that Cooper is referring to events in 1954. IRC did not begin its Hong Kong program until 1961.

Joseph Buttinger's interest in the Vietnamese grew more intense as his contact with the people increased. He returned on many occasions, primarily to further refugee assistance, but also to express concern about the failure of the government to pursue democratic methods. Having observed Diem receive an obviously fraudulent 99 percent vote of endorsement, typical of the mandates that dictators give themselves, Buttinger wrote later: "The one-sided 'election campaign' and the methods employed to assure an almost unanimous vote for Diem were quite outrageous. . . . The use of these methods to secure the victory of a good cause boded ill for the future of a regime whose leader liked to advertise his acts as morally inspired."[7]

The fact that at this time North Vietnam was perpetrating large-scale executions among opposition peasants — Vietnamese scholars estimate the figure at 50,000, with perhaps twice as many imprisoned in forced labor camps — was no justification, in Buttinger's view, for nondemocratic methods in the South. On numerous occasions when IRC responsibilities and his own research brought him back to Saigon, he compiled lists of imprisoned oppositionists who rejected all forms of dictatorship, Communist and non-Communist alike. His interceding with the authorities for their release did achieve success in many cases.

DEPARTURE AND RETURN

By 1960 the primary task to which IRC had set its hand in Vietnam — the resettlement and assimilation of the refugees from the North — had been completed. The emergency aid program was phased out, and most of the projects were handed over to indigenous agencies and to the Asia Foundation. IRC left the country, considering it necessary to focus on more pressing crises — the resettlement of Hungarians, Cubans and assorted Latin Americans; relocating the displaced stragglers of World War II; providing help for East Europeans and Yugoslavs fleeing from Communist dictatorships; and meeting the refugee safari in Africa. South Vietnam appeared to be stable enough at this time to hold out a hand to others; from their limited resources, the Vietnamese forwarded to IRC a sum of $70,000 to help the Hungarians — perhaps the first time in history that Asians had come to the aid of a suffering Western people.

Before closing its books on the Vietnam crisis of the 1950s, IRC initiated a program that has since taken on independent existence and has constituted another chapter in the history of American humanitarianism. In July 1954, a young American Navy doctor had been working in a refugee camp in North Vietnam. His mission: to give medical aid to the refugees who were heading south to escape life under the hammer and sickle. His name: Dr. Thomas A. Dooley.

After his discharge from the Navy's Medical Corps he did not want to return to the comfortable life of an American practitioner. In Vietnam he had seen a vision of medicine serving not only the individual but linking free peoples in bonds of unity. As a result, under the auspices of the International Rescue Committee, he decided to maintain a clinic for two years in Laos, five miles south of the Red Chinese border.

Similar work had been done by Dr. Albert Schweitzer in French Equatorial Africa and by Dr. Gordon Seagrave in Burma. Out of the experiences of such men was born the idea for an international medical service that would help to bring modern medicine into regions that had never seen Western doctors. The International Rescue Committee became the catalyst for those interested in such a program. Cherne journeyed to Lambaréné and met with Dr. Schweitzer, who endorsed the plans "with all my heart." (Cherne, a gifted sculptor as well as public affairs activist, used the occasion to complete a heroic-size bust of the great humanitarian, which now stands in the Smithsonian Institution in Washington.) In February 1958 MEDICO (Medical International Cooperation) was established. Today, as an integrated service of CARE, the organization that began with Dr. Dooley's clinic in Laos and Dr. Seagrave's hospital in Burma supports activities and facilities in Africa, Latin America, South Asia and the Middle East.

In 1964, seven years after its departure from Vietnam, IRC's return became necessary. The heavy artillery had begun to provide the beat for a new march of Indochinese refugees. As the war escalated and public opinion in America divided more passionately on the issue of military involvement, members of IRC could be heard to reflect the variety of opinions surfacing in the political debate. Nationally the division was between three major groups: those who believed that the bloodshed could be stopped by a military victory for Saigon; those who argued that only a forthright withdrawal could end an increasingly intolerable situation; and those who hoped that negotiation and compromise would be the outcome. There were none in the IRC, though there was a minority in the United States, who favored outright victory for the Communists. Whatever the disagreements among IRC members, there was absolute unanimity on one issue: those who were being rendered homeless by the escalating war were entitled to the fullest measure of help that Americans could provide.

SIZING UP THE PROBLEM

By 1965 more refugees were clogging the highways than had descended from the North in 1954. Half a million were poorly housed in refugee camps, with virtually no medical facilities. Calling for top priority was the plight of more than a hundred thousand orphaned children, cared for in some cases by surviving relatives or lodged temporarily in some seventy overcrowded and understaffed institutions.

IRC workers went into action. The government had authorized the establishment of 234 classrooms for refugee children; IRC underwrote the cost of maintenance, transportation and instructional materials for 234 teachers in training. Two nurse/social workers were sent into the orphanages of Saigon, Cholon and Binh Hoa to immunize the children and the staff against diphtheria, tetanus, small pox, cholera, plague, typhoid and polio. IRC set up a program of training for female health technicians in the district dispensaries of the Mekong Delta; the curriculum included basic first aid, the administering of simple medications, elementary patient care and child hygiene.

In cooperation with the U.S. Agency for International Development, IRC undertook to find doctors and nurses willing to commit themselves to at least eighteen months of service among the displaced Vietnamese. The health situation generally was desperate: South Vietnam had no more than a thousand doctors in all, and 60 percent of them were already serving with the armed forces. According to official estimates, the civilian population of 15 million was being cared for by only 350 doctors, a ratio of one doctor to every 43,000 persons. IRC rushed a dozen teams, each consisting of a physician and a nurse, into the field. They suffered many frustrations because of lack of facilities and supplies. Not atypical was this letter from one of IRC's medical outposts:

As you can see, I have not waited for the typewriter to write to you again. I want to tell you about this morning in Tung Uyen. When we arrived there were no patients. But 15 minutes later more than 200 surrounded us, showing in their faces their illnesses as well as their desire to be cured. A sick mother with a dying child in her arms and three other feverish children hanging on to her skirt impressed me most. I could do nothing for the dying child. I did not have the proper medicine. We worked in a small room, three feet square. We almost suffocated, and through the window and door all we could see were the anxious faces of sick people. But we had neither enough nor the right medicines, and this is the greatest difficulty a doctor in Vietnam has to cope with.

IRC staff in the United States fanned out among the pharmaceutical houses. Virtually all responded promptly, and in the first year of the program 80,000 pounds of medicines were collected and shipped to Vietnam to be distributed in remote hamlets with the cooperation of medical teams of the Special Forces. In succeeding years, such contributions rose in volume, estimated at one point to be almost a million dollars in wholesale value. Not everything, of course, was available at the point of need, and IRC personnel in their field dispensaries were compelled to rely on improvisation much of the time. But despite the difficulties, many of those who had agreed to serve for eighteen months stayed on for a double tour of duty.

In line with its traditional policy, IRC turned its attention to strengthening the existing social institutions, rather than starting from scratch with its own facilities. It provided food, clothing, equipment, and personnel to orphanages. Mindful of the Vietnamese culture which stresses the preservation of family ties, IRC funded the building or expansion of day-care centers where single parents of half-orphaned children could place their youngsters while going off to work. The experience acquired in IRC's Hong Kong nurseries was adapted to local conditions so that children were properly fed and given appropriate medical attention under the supervision of a trained staff of teachers.

For these purposes, IRC linked hands with the eleemosynary institutions of the country. In Gia Dinh, it helped to fund a new wing for the Buddhist day nursery. In cooperation with the Vietnamese Women's Association it opened another center in one of Saigon's worst slums. In Bui Mon, where 600 new refugees had arrived from the rubber plantations to join 3,000 others, IRC set up a day-care center with the help of the half-million-member Vietnamese labor movement, the *Confédération Vietnamienne du Travail*, and with contributions from the West German trade unions. Later, during the Tet offensive of 1968, Bui Mon was overrun by North Vietnamese troops and the refugees had to be evacuated temporarily in a second flight. In Saigon, assistance was given to the Caritas Malnutrition Center for children and to the Buddhist Social Welfare Organization.

By the end of 1966, it was estimated that IRC teams were treating 10,000 patients a month for a variety of endemic illnesses — tuberculosis, plague, trachoma, polio, malaria and cholera — in addition to a surprisingly high incidence of congenital deformities like harelip and cleft palate. The whole catalog of misfortune was to be found, including children crippled in traffic and home accidents, and victims of the cognate diseases of malnutrition and those that developed out of unsanitary living conditons. Many of the injuries, of course, were the direct result of military action from both sides.

War correspondents paused to refresh their spirits by observing IRC's humanitarian activities, standing out starkly against the brutalities of Armageddon. The Sunday mass circulation magazine *Parade* described the team at Quang Ngai in these terms: "They volunteered for Vietnam service with the International Rescue Committee medical program. This is a crew of doctors and nurses, more than half ex-refugees, who bring mercy and medicine under great difficulty to refugees and villagers in rural Vietnam. That they are often under the guns of the Viet Cong is only one problem as the I.R.C. team cares for long lines of ill-clad and barefoot patients, many with war wounds, including napalm burns."[8] The *National Observer* quoted officials of the Agency for International Development to this effect: "For Christianity in action it would be hard to beat the teams of doctors and nurses now in Vietnam under the auspices of the International Rescue Committee. Most of the team members are themselves refugees from Castro's Cuba who at grave personal risk minister to Vietnamese refugees."[9]

IRC administrative staff were frequently confronted by those living in what Dante would have considered the lowest circle of hell. Occupying the worst status were the Montagnards or hill folk, held in contempt by the

Vietnamese as primitives and belittled as "Meos." These people had rarely received the benefits of medical care. To meet their needs, IRC inaugurated a project to train sixteen health workers to function in the Central Highlands. Discovering that leprosy was even more widespread than in most underdeveloped countries and that treatment rarely considered the psychological problem of the patients, IRC contributed the services of a social worker to the Salve Leprosy Clinic in Gia Dinh.

COOPERATIVE SELF-HELP

Important as were the immediate requirements of survival, it was clear as early as 1965 that the plight of the 1,500,000 "internal refugees" could not be handled as a temporary problem. IRC concluded that the shelters then being provided — the palm houses, shacks and straw hovels at the edge of the hamlets — must be considered only as temporary stopping places on the way to ultimate rehabilitation and permanent absorption.

Because of the vagaries of battle one could not anticipate where a new refugee camp would suddenly appear. In the summer of 1965, the author visited a refugee center in Cai Be, located in the Mekong Delta. Events at the southern edge of the Plain of Reeds had sent 2,527 families into flight; of these, 1,024 were children under the age of three. They had started in Hau My, "21 clicks to the north" — Army talk for kilometers. The villagers explained that they had fled because they were being heavily taxed by Viet Cong guerrillas who controlled the area; their sons had been abducted for conscription into the Communist forces; and their rice had been seized. They decided to migrate in a body and to seek the protection of the government. Since there are few roads, they traveled by sampan down the winding canals that crisscross the countryside. As they came southward, the population in other hamlets, hearing their story, decided to join them.

Some of them were now being sheltered in a large barnlike structure, with a few square feet of living space allocated to each family. Privacy consisted of a tattered sheet or blanket stretched on a strand of rope. Learning of their presence, USOM (the United States Operations Mission) had sent in 560 bags of wheat, each weighing 30 kilos. An oddity in this backwoods area was the sight of the children to whom USOM had given T-shirts, made up in the yellow-striped colors of South Vietnam. Aside from the food, according to the camp commandant, the Saigon government was giving each refugee seven piastres a day (ten cents) for one month, after which a lump sum payment of about 2,000 to 3,000 piastres would be provided, depending on family size, for the building of a palm house. Already the foundations had been prepared for forty-three houses and eleven others were in process. More than 50 percent of the refugees had received medical examinations from government health workers, whose training consisted of two years of health education. Some 1,200 cholera and a similar number of scarlet fever shots had been administered. A significant figure was the number of persons who had received medicines since their arrival — 2,516. Even a casual inspection underscored the composition of the refugee population: women, old men and young children.

If these people and their fellows were to be given a chance for a decent life, a program of economic integration into the surrounding environment was essential. IRC planners working with leaders among the refugees concluded that a network of handicraft cooperatives and village industries would be the most productive form of assistance. Thus supplies were furnished to the Montagnard Weaving Cooperative in Darlac, assuring a livelihood to a hundred families. In the same province a handicraft school for handicapped refugees was opened; during the Tet offensive its activities were interrupted, but then resumed. At Dong Xoai, tools were bought for the refugees so that they could construct dwellings; thereafter the tools were used to create a camp lumbering industry, providing income for the refugees and the learning of a new trade. A Sea Grass Weaving Cooperative in Gia Dinh province was equipped with table top looms, expanding its productivity. Nor were agricultural needs overlooked: improved varieties of soy bean seed and high-quality rice seed were made available for demonstration projects. To maintain morale, community centers in thirty refugee camps were provided with radio receivers.

Increasingly, IRC promoted the concept of rural development teams as the most promising avenue of refugee assistance. Self-help was indeed the most effective antidote to the apathy and demoralization that are endemic to refugee life. This approach required the use of properly balanced teams.

Typical was the group assembled by IRC to serve at Ap Doi Mon (New Life Hamlet) in Binh Duong province, where efforts were being made to build a refugee village for 6,000 persons who had been displaced by the fighting in the Iron Triangle. The core included a nurse from Denmark, an American health worker, a farm expert who had been with the Peace Corps in India, a Yale student specializing in Southeast Asia studies, and a British "generalist." Their first step was to open a dispensary, obtain medical supplies and work out a sanitation plan for the community. Next, land was assigned for garden plots adjacent to each dwelling, and fertilizer was brought in to assure a substantial yield. In accordance with Asian tradition, and to provide a ready supply of protein, a fish pond was dug and stocked. A chicken-breeding expert was imported, and with the aid of a young American woman from a Midwest farm who had been trained by the Peace Corps, a highly successful business was developed. Soon a school for the children followed. A community center was completed. And though the guns of war could be heard frequently, the sense of human dignity and personal worth still flourished.

An important part of IRC's concept was to leave the scene once a self-sufficient community had been established. After about two years, Ap Doi

Mon had obviously proved itself. IRC's farewell is stated in a valedictory report that reveals not only the achievement of its own group but a side of the Vietnamese war that has been rarely noticed:

How much progress has been made in Binh Hoa can be judged by the fact that the time has come for the IRC team to phase out its activities here. The present population of the village is now basically capable of maintaining itself economically as well as socially. Other voluntary agencies have provided their share of support. There is a functioning school, a community center and a medical dispensary in what two years ago was nothing but a barren plot of land. The chicken project and fish pond are now run by cooperatives of hamlet residents, housing has been improved and local elections have been held. One project will be maintained for some time to come —a training class in carpentry, a much needed skill in the area. The initiator, organizer and teacher of this course is a young Seabee who served in Lai Thieu and who became so committed to helping the Binh Hoa refugees that he returned as a civilian to work with them.

The success of the pilot project led to the setting up of similar teams in several locations—on the outskirts of Danang; in Montagnard territory near the Cambodian border; and in the city of Quang Ngai. Skills represented in the groups included agricultural specialists, vocational technicians, welfare and recreation workers, construction experts, and "generalists" who filled the role of jack-of-all-trades. Their initial interests were sanitation, road building, instruction (especially in sewing), employment counseling, demonstration farming, and youth activities.

Letters home reflected the hardships involved in implementing the program. An IRC nurse/instructor/midwife assigned to the Quang Ngai provincial hospital wrote about her experiences in 1969 during a Communist attack when "we had to hide in the bunker; the American house beside us was destroyed with rockets larger than last year's; and a very nice American man was shot three times and killed." She then described the "normal" course of events: "You can see now why my report is so short. I am running from the operating room to maternity and back. I have made many friends in maternity, and my twenty students are doing well. You would be very proud of some of these women. I have one very good Vietnamese doctor who wants maternity in Quang Ngai to be one of the best in the country. He will not tolerate any foolishness. I believe I am the only midwife teaching students in South Vietnam, so I'd better try and make a good job of it."

The brave men and women who volunteered for service with IRC in Vietnam were aware of the risks. No area was safe from possible attack or terrorist activity. One of the first casualties suffered by IRC came in 1969 when Miss Pham Nguyet Anh, a young Vietnamese social worker, was killed by a plastic bomb blast in Saigon's main post office. A memorial plaque was placed at the entrance to the Vinh Hoi Day-Care Center which she directed for IRC. Another worker, Charlie Cowden, IRC's community development team leader at Song Be, was more fortunate; he was wounded twice but suffered no permanent disability. He had volunteered to accompany a convoy taking food supplies to refugees at Don Xoai. In the ambush a number of Vietnamese and Americans were killed. On another occasion, a young German, serving as a community development team leader, was seized by the Viet Cong but was released two-and-a-half months later when he succeeded in convincing his captors that his mission was purely humanitarian.

For the most part, compensation received by these volunteers was nominal, and in many cases little more than travel and living expenses. Leo Cherne has expressed IRC's gratitude in these words:

I want to pay special tribute to a remarkable group of people who have given so much to the cause of refugees and human freedom: the volunteer leaders and workers of IRC.

It is these dedicated people who have made IRC a voluntary agency in the finest American tradition. They have devoted their time and unique talents to IRC in the United States and in many other countries. They are mostly Americans, but also British, Chinese, Germans, Bengalis, Cubans, Vietnamese, Latin Americans, West and East Europeans of many nationalities. Some are refugees themselves who want to help others who are seeking to rebuild their lives.

Often the volunteers work, as in Vietnam, at a real risk to their personal safety, and often on sudden notice they travel halfway around the world to help IRC respond to a refugee emergency. The volunteers serve without pay, and many of them personally contribute funds to IRC and in other ways assist in our fund raising efforts. The members of our Board of Directors constitute the core of the basic volunteerism of IRC.

The tradition of helping victims of tyranny and war — wherever they may search for asylum — is deeply rooted in the consciousness of the American people. The work of the International Rescue Committee is woven into the fabric of this American heritage, and we are deeply indebted to all the volunteers who have made this possible.

INTERNATIONAL SUPPORT

In providing assistance in Vietnam, IRC of course was not alone. Many American agencies were on the scene, supplementing each other's activities and extending cooperation to each other and to the Vietnamese social service groups so that the sum proved to be greater than the parts. Many European organizations came forward with financial support for IRC in addition to maintaining their own projects. Most notable were the French, who had long-established ties with the Vietnamese and who had not withdrawn their service organizations after the Geneva agreement. IRC's German affiliate, the *Deutsche Internazionale Fluechtlingshilfe*, sent vocational training personnel to aid the Quang Ngai operation, and the German Ministry for Expellees and Refugees, mindful of its own experience, helped with necessary funding. Among the benefits they provided were instruction and facilities for a metal workshop and an electrical shop.

With international support it became possible to expand the self-help program. At Lai Thieu, a woodworking school provided a three-month course that graduated in its first year a group of fifty-five students ranging from fourteen to fifty-two years of age, including ten Vietnamese Boy Scouts. Backed up by a staff of five, the director not only furnished instruction but instituted a marketing operation for a catalog of products that included chairs, desks, tables, louvered doors and bookcases. By year's end, the sales paid for the staff's salaries and the cost of new materials, and the school was a going concern.

In the Hoa Khanh complex of hamlets in the Hoa Vang district northwest of Danang, IRC found some 6,000 families and a population of 38,000 refugees. This group of Buddhists, Confucians and Catholics was soon organized in a self-help program by a team that consisted of a coordinator, an agricultural expert, a construction specialist, a medical corpsman, a vocational training counselor, a social worker, a recreational worker, and a generalist.

Their first target was the improvement of living conditions: litter cleanup, garbage disposal, construction of wells and latrines, improvement of houses and drainage, planting of grass and trees. Longer-range projects were launched — the production of cinvaram bricks, setting up sewing classes, raising chickens, constructing a recreation area, and helping to secure jobs for the unemployed. Particularly successful was the work of the team's agriculturist, a young Taiwanese, who gave leadership to more than 700 families in a farm program that included crop diversification and the introduction of "IR 8," often referred to as the "miracle rice." He also gave guidance on the use of fertilizers and insecticides, the planting of vegetables and watermelons, and the raising of ducks. It has been said, "If the Talmudic blessing is given to the father who teaches his son a trade, how much greater must be the reward to him who teaches a trade to the stranger."

An observer of the scene in Hoa Khanh summarized the results in these terms: "Where only sand had been, without a bush or tree, the whole area has become green and productive."

SPECIAL SERVICES

As the war raged on, the number of refugees grew astronomically. Even before the Tet offensive of 1968 that caused huge casualties on both sides, the U.S. Senate Subcommittee on Civilian Casualties and Refugee Problems estimated that some 4 million uprooted Vietnamese required material assistance. While this figure probably did not take account of turnover—people returning home or settling down for a new life with relatives in another part of the country—IRC's analysts concluded that there were at least 2,500,000 still needing shelter. "The staggering implication of this number," said an IRC report, "can be indicated by projecting a comparison with the United States, and arriving at a corresponding figure of 35,000,000 displaced Americans."

To meet the needs of this growing population of refugees required professional staff that was truly international in its composition. In 1969, for example, the twenty-two medical practitioners representing IRC came from fourteen different countries, as diverse as Austria and Australia, Turkey and the Philippines. They included five general surgeons, four hand surgeons, two public health physicians, one anaesthesiologist, one hospital administrator, five general nurses, and four nurse/midwives.

In October of the previous year, IRC had opened its 120-bed Reception and Convalescent Center in Saigon to provide twenty-four-hour pre- and postoperative care for children. This facility supplemented the work of the Cho-ray Hospital Unit of the Children's Medical Relief International (CMRI), the only children's institution in Vietnam for reconstructive and plastic surgery. The total staff in IRC's Reception Center numbered forty-eight persons—including a Canadian hospital administrator, his Vietnamese deputy administrator, four Western nurses and a Vietnamese staff supervised by CMRI's surgeons and pediatricians. Throughout the war hand surgery for civilians, and especially the children, became a major medical preoccupation. In 1969 alone the Reception and Convalescent Center cared for 1,447 admissions; in 1974 it admitted 2,500 patients. In 1975 it was turned over to CMRI, which had enlarged its hospital.

While these special services were multiplying, IRC assumed responsibility for food distribution in a number of areas. The U.S. Food for Peace Program provided the commodities: flour, dry milk, bulgar wheat, rolled wheat, rolled oats and cornmeal.

Unexpected problems had to be met—for example, teaching the recipients to prepare the foods in ways pleasing to the Vietnamese palate. IRC's chief Vietnamese social worker came up with a resource who developed a set of recipes for soups, main courses and even cookies. IRC also engaged in direct distribution of hot lunches and milk to schools and other children's institutions in an intensified war against malnutrition made necessary by the fact that the military conflict had reduced food production. A "Food for Work" program was introduced to stimulate self-help activities. It rewarded participation in projects for the improvement of school buildings and the construction of dispensaries and reading rooms. Through this program alone, it is estimated that in one year 25,500 persons received additional commodities for themselves and their families.

BEYOND TRADITIONAL PATTERNS

None of the traditional methods of assistance were ignored, but the exigencies of a prolonged war called for innovative approaches. Orphanages were being filled to overflowing by the 1970s, and the human resources needed to care for the children were proving inadequate. Called upon by Vietnamese and American officials to provide some solution, IRC evolved a new concept: a training program in "home day care." With IRC guidance Vietnamese social workers, child-care professionals and nursing specialists implemented a three-month curriculum under which refugee women were equipped to run mini-day-care centers in their own homes for the children of mothers with jobs. The instruction included information on proper feeding and hygiene. When the course had been completed and the home facilities were in operation, IRC remained responsible for supervising the home centers in which the women, many of them war widows, cared for four to eight children.

By 1973, the year of the American troop pullout, the program was in full operation. At this time it was estimated there were as many as 700,000 war orphans in the country. In the refugee camps, children constituted 50 percent of the census. Hardly surprising, since children under the age of fifteen were 48 percent of the country's 20 million people. Their behavior, remarked on by journalists and other visitors, evidenced a family solidarity that has been the basis of a hardiness the world has come to respect, most recently in the exodus of the boat people. An IRC report summarizes this moving aspect of the Vietnamese culture:

That the children are generally lively, alert and curious is due largely to the traditional fabric of family life in Vietnam; one's existence, even one's personal identity, is submerged by the family. Hence the resilience of the children. It is a common sight to observe a girl of four walking hand-in-hand with two younger siblings; a boy of five carrying a younger sister on his back while he keeps his eye on a still younger brother. A sick child is rarely "left" at a hospital or dispensary by a mother; she will spend the night on a chair beside her child, or more often on the floor, rather than deprive the young one of her presence and personal care.

American observers can only marvel at the behavior of children (generally between the ages of two to six) at day-care centers. They are absorbed in their play and educational activities. The simple but nourishing food has given them back much of their mental and physical health. Good hygienic training has helped in this process of restoration. The mutual respect that exists between adults and children — a way of life built into the people's culture — requires no harsh words or discipline.

A typical example was the IRC Kieu Mau center in Nha Trang, maintained for three- to six-year-olds. School hours for the one hundred children were from early morning to late afternoon. The day was divided between educational and recreational activities, with time given to exercise, meals, a shower, a nap, general hygiene care and training. The IRC staff consisted of a supervisor, three teachers, three caretakers, two cooks and one laborer. In some instances, for example at the Petrus-Ky center near Saigon, there was even a baby-care section for some thirty infants of poor working mothers.

WHEN THE GUNS WERE STILLED

In April 1973, the United States completed its troop withdrawal from Vietnam. One immediate result was a sharp rise in the number of internal refugees. The cease-fire agreement reached in January was theoretically to be policed by an international control commission consisting of Indonesia, Iran, Hungary and Poland. Its presence could hardly be noticed and had no effect on the continuing swath of war. In this period, it is estimated, South Vietnamese casualties mounted to the highest levels yet reached in the war; the government conceded that about 1,300 troops a month were dying in battle.

The plight of the people deepened. Along with the departure of the troops, American aid had shrunk. President Nixon asked Congress to provide $1.6 billion in military aid to South Vietnam and another $750 million in economic assistance. Congress, responding to the war-weariness of the American people, reduced the first figure to $700 million and the second to $400 million. A request for a supplemental appropriation of $300 million was rejected. At the same time, Soviet Russia and Communist China were providing economic assistance to North Vietnam estimated at $1.2 billion. As a kind of climax to the misfortunes of the Saigon regime, Peking determined to resolve an age-old dispute with Vietnam and occupied the Hsisha or Paracel Islands, some 200 miles equidistant from both countries. The archipelago continues in dispute between the devotees of Sino-Communism and Soviet Communism. More than ideology is at stake: in 1974 offshore oil and gas deposits were found in the general area.

A last-minute campaign by the Thieu government against corruption was of no avail in attempting to shore up morale. By 1975, it was estimated that 20,000 soldiers a month were deserting. They could be seen fighting with the civilian refugees in a scramble to escape on the jammed highways. Saigon surrendered. The war was over, leaving wounds that seemed unlikely ever to heal. The statisticians calculated the toll: 50,000 American dead; 400,000 South Vietnamese; 900,000 North Vietnamese and Viet Cong. But the consequences of the dread arbitrament were still to run their course. The uprooted, in swelling numbers, would be seeking asylum from the continuing torment.

With the American withdrawal, it was clear that the refugee problem would grow even more severe. IRC determined to remain as long as possible and even to increase its areas of service. In April 1973, Leonard Marks, who was later to become president of IRC, and Angier Biddle Duke led a mission of volunteer leaders to Vietnam to study the escalating needs. The mission included IRC board members David Sher, New York lawyer and American Jewish Committee activist; Cecil Lyon, former foreign service officer; IRC leader Joseph Buttinger; Isadore M. Scott, of the Rosenwald Fund; and Anthony D. Duke, founder and president of Boys Harbor which serves disadvantaged children. They were accompanied by Robin Duke as rapporteur, and IRC Deputy Director Alton Kastner. After an extensive trip throughout South Vietnam they recommended in detail where current projects should be expanded and new ones launched.

Again the emphasis was on the children. The mission pointed out that, with the restoration of the health of the war orphans, some could be adopted by American families. One immediate result was the opening in December of a new facility, a pilot seventy-bed medical rehabilitation center in Saigon. In its first year of operation, 4,000 orphans were treated at the unit and one-fourth of them were sent to permanent homes abroad through accredited American adoption agencies. Staffed with a pediatrician as head, four American nurses and a group of 35 Vietnamese nurses, technicians and aides, the unit provided access to laboratory and X-ray services, plus a nutrition station for the preparation of infant feeding formulas. Two satellite units were soon planned for Danang and Qui-Nhon.

Concurrently attention was refocussed on the ethnic minority that had long been and continues to be abused—the hill people known as the Montagnards. Some 11,000 of the Stieng tribe were being housed in Tan Rai village. IRC built a day-care center. The simple structure consisted of a cement slab floor, a wooden frame, a sheet metal roof, and wooden siding. It opened in February 1974, and received 115 Montagnard children. Under IRC supervision, the center functioned with the cooperation of the An Quang Buddhists, the largest Buddhist sect in Vietnam.

AN END AND A BEGINNING

But such activities were doomed to end under circumstances that would demand an even greater effort by American voluntary agencies like IRC. On April 30, 1975, Saigon fell to the Communists. Now the task became a unique resettlement effort, carried out in the space of a few months, and unparalleled by any previous movement of peoples. IRC personnel, including doctors and nurses, remained even after the evacuation until ordered to leave. But it was apparent that a new phase had begun.

In that same month of 1973 when the last of the U.S. forces were returning home, IRC was observing its fortieth anniversary. To mark the occasion, a seven-week exhibition was presented in the Hammarskjold Plaza Sculpture Garden, near the United Nations complex in New York. A photographic display summarized IRC activities from the days of Hitler through the Vietnamese war. Towering above the Plaza scene was William

King's "Rescue," a twenty-by-thirty foot sculpture. Shaped from half-inch aluminum, it portrayed two united figures, one in chains, with drooping arms, the other with welcoming arms extended.

But IRC was to have little time for retrospection. A troubled America had watched films of the frantic scramble of would-be escapees climbing the walls of the American embassy compound in Saigon, pleading for evacuation, attempting vainly to board overloaded helicopters taking off from the roof of the building. In those final moments, some 100,000 did succeed in reaching American ships anchored off the coast, followed almost immediately by another 50,000. In the next ten weeks, 135,000 Vietnamese were processed for resettlement in the United States and were admitted to this country; 20,000 were temporarily in Guam and other Pacific islands; and about 8,000 had found refuge elsewhere, half of them in already overcrowded Hong Kong. With the Phnom Penh domino falling to the Khmer Rouge forces who were literally to bathe their country in blood, 5,000 Cambodian refugees managed to join the Vietnamese contingent entering the United States.

IRC's director in Saigon had received explicit and unqualified instructions from Charles Sternberg in New York: "This is authorization to sign affidavits of support for Vietnamese fearing persecution. IRC assumes full responsibility against their becoming public charges in the United States. We place no numerical limitation on the number of affidavits you can sign. However, we expect first priority will be given to IRC [Vietnamese] staff wishing to leave."

FIRST ARRIVALS

From the start, IRC's activities in resettling refugees in the United States were marked by a spirit of interethnic solidarity. America's welcoming committee has had representatives from every preceding migration.

The exodus from South Vietnam had begun even before the actual fall of the capital. The day before the formal surrender a small group arrived in New York under IRC auspices — two brothers, their wives and eight children. Forty-eight hours later they were under the wings of a community group in New Hartford, Connecticut, who called themselves "Stepping Stones." They had been organized by a former Hungarian refugee who had come under IRC auspices after the 1956 uprising. Three days later another IRC-sponsored group of thirty-one Vietnamese en route to the resettlement camp at Travis Air Force Base were greeted by the Cuban refugee community in Miami. A similar service was performed by Cubans in New Orleans.

Such examples led the *New York Times* to say editorially: "Government, civic and religious leaders at all levels of society have an urgent obligation to assert their role of leadership, to dampen irrational fears. Already there are touching instances of Hungarian, Cuban and other refugees from earlier crises offering their services as individuals to help the Vietnamese people through the painful orientation that they themselves had experienced."[10]

Such activities, of course, merited special recognition. But in a sense all Americans owed a duty to newcomers arriving on these shores. This thought had frequently been expressed by President John F. Kennedy, who was intensely conscious of the immigrant antecedents of his own family. As a United States senator he had participated in IRC activities. He had sponsored the Displaced Persons Act and the Refugee Relief Act and had been an ardent advocate of immigration law reform. In 1958 he had written a book, *A Nation of Immigrants*. At the time of his death in 1963, he was completing a revised edition which was published posthumously with an introduction by his brother Robert. In the first chapter, "A Nation of Nations," President Kennedy quoted Alexis de Tocqueville on our origins: "The happy and powerful do not go into exile." Contemplating a revision of the immigration laws, the President noted that "every American who ever lived, with the exception of one group, was either an immigrant himself or a descendant of immigrants. The exception? Will Rogers, part Cherokee Indian, said that his ancestors were at the dock to meet the *Mayflower*. And some anthropologists believe that the Indians themselves were immigrants from another continent who displaced the original Americans — the aborigines." With considerable pleasure, Kennedy recalled Franklin D. Roosevelt baiting a convention of the Daughters of the American Revolution: "Remember, remember always, that all of us, and you and I especially, are descended from immigrants and revolutionists."[11]

WOULD THE DOORS OPEN?

At first the willingness of the American people to open their doors to the Indochinese seemed problematic. The economic scene was unpromising. A worldwide recession had followed the Arab oil embargo of 1973-74 and the subsequent price increases imposed by the OPEC countries. In such circumstances, the first impulse of economic strategists in Europe had been to batten down the hatches by shutting off immigration.

Until this time there had been a steady flow of workers across national boundaries. To them the sociologists had applied the term "guestworkers," people who are accepted on a temporary basis to fill the manpower needs of the host country. As of 1979 their number was estimated to be 14 to 20 million, a figure that must be added to the estimated 17 million refugees on the move across the surface of the globe. That they represent a problem to themselves and social problems to the country of residence is inevitable. Subjectively they experience the clash of cultures; in their homes they cling to their old values as they remain poised for a return to their native lands. In their children, however, they confront a quandary, for the younger generation adopts the local culture and must eventually become aliens in the ancestral country to which they too must return. Yet, in economic terms, these millions of workers and their families represent one of the most valuable resources flowing in the bloodstream of world commerce.

In the mid-1970s, countries that had welcomed foreign manpower as an answer to labor shortages began to impose stricter controls. Reacting to an influx of Asians and Africans from Commonwealth countries, Britain had revised its immigration policy and had already been denounced for it by the European Commission on Human Rights. It responded with some relaxation of its laws to permit the reuniting of families and to legalize the status particularly of Pakistanis who had flocked to the United Kingdom. France, yielding to a popular outburst against its 900,000 Algerian workers, also tightened its immigration policy. The Netherlands, embroiled in ethnic conflicts with immigrants from Turkey and the Dutch West Indies, even offered bonuses to foreign workers who were willing to go home after three years. In Switzerland, a referendum aimed at an eventual 50 percent reduction of the number of foreigners allowed in the country was barely defeated. Denmark and Norway imposed tighter restrictions on the entry of non-Scandinavians. West Germany, which had imported 3,500,000 workers from Italy, Spain, Yugoslavia and Turkey, decided it had enough and virtually prohibited immigration. An epidemic of xenophobia was spreading.

By contrast, the United States in the year ending June 1974 admitted the largest number of immigrants since World War II except for 1963 and significantly 1973. The largest national groups among the 400,000 persons allowed to resettle here were Asians and Mexicans, 130,000 of the former, 71,000 of the latter. And this was occurring at a time when concern was growing over the number of illegal aliens in the country: according to a formal statement by the Attorney General in 1974, their number was in the vicinity of 12 million. Other sources estimated the number at half that amount, but even they conceded that each year another half million were being added. In 1974 there were as yet few refugees from Vietnam; the total was a mere 3,100. Another 5,000 had arrived from Thailand. Of the Asians coming in the largest group was Philippino, followed by South Koreans, then by Chinese, trailed by Indians. The great surge of Indochinese was yet to come.

And when it did come after the collapse of Saigon, there was general recognition that it could not be a simple replay of previous migrations. America was different now, in some ways more sophisticated and therefore more receptive, in other ways haunted by its own role in Vietnam and loath to be reminded of the trauma by a living presence.

In the nineteenth century it had been easier to swing open the gates. There had been grumbling, but no effective resistance to the influx of Irish whose migration had started well before 1847, the year some 500,000 had died of starvation in the old country. In the two decades from 1820 to 1840, the emigration from the Emerald Isle had averaged 35,000 a year, reaching its highest level in 1851 and numbering about a quarter of a million.

Even before the revolution of 1848, the inflow of Germans into the United States had begun. In 1846 an Edinburgh journal in an article on German emigration reported that "the dread of destitution is a motive to emigrate in Germany as in England; but not a principal motive. . . . The one great cause of this almost national movement is the desire for absolute, political, and religious freedom; the absence of all restrictions upon the development of society; and the publication of opinions which cannot be realised at home." But after reciting the trend in the United States and noting that in Pennsylvania the German population "already balances the Anglo-Saxon," and that in several states "the debates in the houses of representatives and the laws are printed alike in German and English," it concluded with a typical xenophobic warning: "If this emigration continues in its present extent and direction, and in the course of time — what is sufficiently probable — a disruption of the great American confederacy should take place, a second Germany will have arisen beyond the Atlantic, and monopolised, along the head waters of the Delaware and Ohio, the possessions of the children of Penn."[12] All this on the *eve* of the German post-1848 exodus! In 1848 alone some 60,000 Germans arrived, and thereafter the figure was to rise from year to year until it peaked in 1854 at 215,000.

But in 1975, the American consensus was clear: those fleeing from Vietnam were entitled to a haven. Many factors contributed: the new consciousness of racial equality resulting from the Supreme Court's desegregation decision in 1954 and the Civil Rights Act ten years later; the success with which minorities had been pressing their demands; and the self-doubts about American virtue created by the war. So it was that in fiscal 1979 alone the United States opened its doors to 530,000 newcomers. That was twice the number of "legal" immigrants accepted by the rest of the world.

Clearly, factors that might have led to an exclusionary policy in other times played little role in recent years even though the new arrivals seemed doubly alien to the American culture. They brought a different cast of features and an almond-shape of eye. Psychologically their presence could have been expected to be painful: they would be a constant reminder of a lost war that had torn the nation apart. More substantial was the economic pressure resulting from the need to absorb them in the space of a few short weeks, in numbers that exceeded the annual intake of Germans in the post-revolutionary years and that threatened to match the annual intake of the Irish after the potato famine. With the nation suffering from energy shortage, inflation and unemployment, one might have expected a loud outcry that the newcomers could not be assimilated either culturally or economically.

Of course there was no unanimity, but the opposition constituted only a minuscule minority, and even its objections were voiced with a certain degree of shamefacedness. They would remain a minority, but somewhat bolder, in later years when the consequences of Communist rule in Indochina would bring another human torrent into bordering countries while the world watched the American response.

THE ABSORPTION PROGRAM

As loaded American vessels steamed eastward from Indochina in 1975, the President's Interagency Task Force on Indochina Refugees opened relocation centers across the United States: first at Camp Pendleton in California; then at Fort Chaffee in Arkansas and at the Eglin Air Force Base in Florida; and finally at Fort Indiantown Gap in Pennsylvania. Within three months IRC had placed thirty full-time resettlement workers in the four camps. The objective was no longer the distribution of food and medical services—that was now the responsibility of the government—but the administrative work of finding sponsors for individuals and their families throughout the country, helping them to obtain jobs and orienting them to a new way of life. A particularly essential task was the reuniting of families that had been separated by the war. So urgent was the challenge that several members of the IRC Board of Directors put aside their own business and family responsibilities to go to work in the camps during the initial months. Within a matter of weeks, they and other IRC personnel had succeeded in registering and processing 18,000 refugees for permanent resettlement.

By the end of 1975 the basic job had been done. Some 7,000 of the Indochinese refugees went to Canada and France and, according to official figures, about 1,500 had gone back to Vietnam to rejoin their families and to suffer whatever fate awaited a returnee. In the United States the most hospitable areas, receiving 40 percent of the 135,000, were California, Texas, Florida, Pennsylvania and Washington, D.C. By December 1975 the government camps were closed, though IRC offices continued to operate in San Francisco, Los Angeles, San Diego, Orange County (California), Seattle, Houston, Dallas, Miami, Washington, D.C., and New York. To meet the continuing needs of the resettled refugees, IRC stationed additional case workers in other areas where, together with the local affiliates of cooperating voluntary agencies, further assistance could be rendered as needed. All this was considered temporary, but the time was not far distant when this network would once again have to bear the brunt of an Indochinese exodus.

As in previous migrations, the first to seek escape were the better educated, the community leaders, members of the middle class. These were people who had cooperated visibly with the United States during the war. By the end of June, the President's Task Force published a summary of data on the refugee population. Almost 90 percent of the heads of households had high school, college or postgraduate education; one-third had studied at the university or postgraduate level. As many as 30 percent of the heads of households had professional, technical or managerial backgrounds—

doctors, teachers, engineers, scholars and writers — but would not be able to pursue their careers without considerable retraining.

A REMARKABLE EFFORT

In a revulsion against past patterns of self-glorification, it has become almost a convention that Americans must engage in public breast-beating and avoid any references to their own humanitarian achievements. There has been much written about the last days in Saigon and the frightful scene of desperate Vietnamese trying to fight their way into already overcrowded helicopters and climbing aboard transports whose helicopters finally had to be pushed over the sides to make room for additional passengers. But there has been little said of the speed and efficiency with which the U.S. government and the voluntary agencies completed the transportation and resettlement of almost 150,000 persons in a few short months. Few rescue missions in history can match that achievement.

In the past, there have been many dark spots on this country's immigration record. President Kennedy wrote critically of "the basic ambiguity which older Americans have often shown toward newcomers. In 1797 a member of Congress argued that, while a liberal immigration policy was fine when the country was new and unsettled, now that America had reached its maturity and was fully populated, immigration should stop — an argument which has been repeated at regular intervals throughout American history."[13] In the mid-nineteenth century, Lincoln had found it necessary to denounce the bigotry of Know-Nothingism. A country that had hired coolie labor to build its railroads enacted Chinese exclusion acts. At the beginning of the twentieth century, restrictive legislation clanged shut the gates while the Ku Klux Klan provided a drum-beat for opposition to "foreigners," Jews, Catholics and blacks.

In the 1970s, as the nation sought to retreat from the memories of Vietnam, one might have expected a general resurgence of xenophobia. It did not happen. At most, there were only isolated episodes of reaction, a certain amount of muttering, and scattered incidents of picketing. A year after the opening of the Fort Chaffee refugee camp, when all of its guests had already departed, newspapers throughout the country carried this U.P.I. dispatch from Fort Smith, Arkansas:

Outside the main gate of the local Army base, a three-sided marker says in Vietnamese, Cambodian and English: "In search of new lives, 50,809 refugees from Indochina passed through Fort Chaffee, May 2-December 20, 1975."

One year after the first of the refugees arrived in their new homeland, all that's left of their first camp is the marker, a lot of memories and some Vietnamese names scratched on the white barracks. There is also pride among Arkansans.

Few residents believed government officials who promised the camp would be closed in a year. Some picketed the inactive Army camp before the arrival of the refugees. One woman said publicly she hoped the refugees would "get pneumonia and die."

Governor David Pryor heard that and was so shocked that he swiftly mustered a welcoming party at the airport. More than 500 Arkansans and Fort Smith officials turned out to greet the first plane carrying seventy-one weary refugees. Fort Smith residents then began collecting toys and clothes for the Vietnamese and volunteering to help the camp.

Chaffee eventually became the largest of four resettlement camps that processed 130,000 Indochina refugees. Governor Pryor called the refugee project "one of the greatest humanitarian acts of all times."[14]

So widespread was American acceptance of this new wave of immigrants from the Far East that nobody paused to recall that only twenty years before, the then governor of that same state of Arkansas had blockaded the doorway to the schoolhouse so that American soldiers had to be sent into Little Rock to protect black pupils.

Nor, as the marker was being set up at Fort Chaffee, could anybody predict that in 1980 another wave, this time from across the Florida straits, would bring a new flood of refugees to reactivate the site as a way-station toward a better life in America. This time there would be greater resistance, to be sure. But whatever the fears, the doors would never be completely sealed. As long as tyrannies hold power in the world, America will continue to beckon.

XIV

Exodus from Indochina

Each historic spasm of flight has produced its own neologisms:
"DP's" in World War II; in more recent years, "boat people . . . land people
. . . freedom flotilla."

If you are Vietnamese, your route to freedom would probably make you
a boat person. It would take you through the waters of the South China Sea
or the Gulf of Siam, once romanticized by the Rudyard Kiplings of the
Anglo-Saxon world.

A Cambodian? Then your desire to escape the most brutal of the societies
called Communist or its successor regime installed by the Vietnamese would
send you trudging through the jungles on the western and northern borders
that separate your country from Thailand.

If you are a Laotian and love liberty, then you must know how to swim
or row a boat or find some method of flotation. You have to cross the
Mekong River, the southern and western border of your homeland, now
under Hanoi's hegemony. And though you come by water, you too will
have earned the honorific, "land person."

If a boat person, you might very well be directed by the Thai authorities
to turn your course to Song Khla or to a somewhat better place of temporary refuge, Laem Sing. Song Khla is in the southernmost portion of Thailand, a kingdom on the map of Southeast Asia that looks like a knotted fist
with its index finger extended and pointing south to Malaysia. Laem Sing is
on the northern shore of the Gulf of Siam, less than an hour's drive from
Chantaburi. There, of a weekend, diamond merchants congregate to trans-
act business and seek entertainment in the hotel dining room as a slender-
bodied, dark-skinned transvestite renders the Thai words of a rock-and-roll
duet in baritone and soprano.

HARBOR FOR THE SHIPWRECKED

The western visitor, free to come and go, approaches Laem Sing by passing through the paradoxes that mark developing nations in many parts of
the globe. The highway out of Bangkok is well paved, and the traffic at first

is appalling. In the city proper, it is as dense as you can find anywhere in the world. You may sit for ten minutes in the midst of the carbon monoxide without budging an inch. As you leave the capital, the traffic thins, and soon you are speeding along a good road between the rice paddies. Some time after the bustle of Bangkok recedes, the rice paddies also disappear. Now mile after mile you are surrounded on either side by a green spread of jungle. The villages grow smaller and drowsier. The noodle shop that sells you lunch is quiet as the diners concentrate on their food.

Eventually you leave the paved road. The motor struggles up a steep grade across a narrow track whose ruts left by the rains threaten to snap the axles. The climb takes you through a small fishing village that consists of one ragged street of hovels. The air conditioning that has protected you against the Thai temperature must now be turned off to husband the engine's energies for the long climb. Triumphantly it carries you to the summit where a large open square awaits you. On one side is a *wat* or Buddhist temple, encased in modern iron-piped scaffolding to ease the work of renovation. Across the length of the square itself, a team of men are at work winding steel cable. Opposite the temple is a smaller building with an open verandah on which a group of saffron-robed monks with shaven heads are seated, classroom style, reciting their answers in unison to the master. They pay no attention to your intrusion.

Later you are told that the temple actually owns the land on which the huddled boat people live. But there is resentment against the Buddhist priests. You hear that they make little contact with the strangers whose ramshackle, improvised huts cling to the hillside that stretches down to the sea. On occasion, you are told, one or two individuals from among the refugees may be accepted for monastic study.

You begin the descent along a treacherous rocky path, and cling to a neighbor for support. Breathless, you arrive at a level that contains a well-built cement pavilion at the end of which is a large oven with a high stack. It is the crematorium for the local dead. A wall separates you from the continuing drop of the land. Cement benches provide a gathering place for refugees who come up from the lower reaches to be interviewed by representatives of the International Rescue Committee. The data will be taken to Bangkok and will facilitate compliance with immigration regulations and resettlement arrangements for those who are eligible.

From this point you look down on the sprawl of shelters occupied by the refugees. The cluster of huts cuts a cleft in the stretch of forest, extending to the water's edge. Some of the ancient hulks are still afloat; others are drawn up on the rocky shore and are being used as dwellings. Still others have lost much of their timber, though some of the beams continue to keep their skeletal, rib-like patterns. Looking at what remains of the boats, you marvel that so many of them are able to make port. And then you are reminded of those that did not. You are told by a refugee that his wife and son left in another boat and never arrived.

At the bottom of the path you are swallowed in a congestion of palm huts. The crowding in this limited area is as bad as any you have seen — even in West Bengal during the Bangladesh crisis. One misplaced match could transform this camp into a roaring blaze. An IRC representative notes with satisfaction that the local authorities have finally responded to her insistence and have affixed at two separate places a fire extinguisher no larger than the kind you use in your kitchen back home.

You ask for the census, and learn that as many as 1,300 refugees have been housed here at one time. They have no permanent medical facilities; the only health care is provided by occasional visits from a doctor. As a general rule, the refugees may not leave the camp. The government is afraid they may melt into the surrounding population. Exceptions are made for those who are ill; they may be sent to local hospitals, or, if their condition is serious, they may actually be moved to Bangkok for treatment.

But Laem Sing is unique to your experience of refugees: you hear the laughter of children, and even the adults banter with you. This is no West Bengal, where the Bangladeshis' camps were blanketed in a silence of resignation. Here among the boat people one is made aware of a continuing sense of pride, indeed, a feeling of accomplishment. Perhaps the explanation lies in the fact that they have triumphed not only over their Communist government but over the hazards of the sea, in a journey that had to take at least five days if they were fortunate — or as much as two weeks if the engine failed — while the sun beat down mercilessly and the supply of food and water dwindled.

There is pride, too, in being able to point out the community achievements — the structure with a simple crucifix that the Catholics among them have designated as their church, and side by side an equally simple building reserved by the Baptists for their services. A tiny Buddhist shrine, a miniature temple, holds a central spot in the open area or common. Ubiquitous children follow the visitors along the paths and narrow alleys that separate the open-sided huts. Inside, sad-eyed, aged men and women, squatting Asian style on their heels, peer at the passersby. They know they will never again see their homeland, nor will they be able to worship again at the semicircular white tombs of their ancestors that still glisten, at least in memory, under the Vietnamese sun.

DEVIL'S ISLAND

Those who reached Laem Sing in Thailand were the fortunate ones. They might have landed farther south in Malaysia and been sent off to what has surely been the most crowded and barren spot on the surface of the earth — the island of Pulau Bidong.

There, in 1979, some 42,000 refugees found themselves confined to the only habitable space the island permitted, an area that would be the equivalent of two city blocks. Water and supplies had to be ferried in from the mainland to keep the new inhabitants alive. So forbidding is the terrain that even in the poverty-stricken, land-hungry world of Southeast Asia no settlers have been willing to wrestle with these parched wastes. In July 1979 *Newsweek*'s Barry Came described what he found on a visit: "Every inch of level ground on the rocky island is covered with makeshift shacks of cardboard, plywood, palm fronds and blue plastic sheeting. Some of the huts are two and three stories high. The stench of human feces pervades the atmosphere, and garbage floats on the lagoon."[1]

Rations provided by the UN and the Malaysian Red Crescent Society consisted "of 24 ounces of rice, a can of baked beans, a tin of sardines, 8 ounces of chicken stew, and some dry crackers," and were intended to last for three days. Gastrointestinal problems abounded, primarily because of the lack of sanitation and sewage disposal. But again, with the resiliency characteristic of the Southeast Asians, self-organization and a high sense of community had become the major defense against epidemics. According to the camp's outstanding leader, Father Le Ngoc Trieu, a Catholic priest educated in the United States, a large number of the refugees had received some medical training, counting among their ranks 80 doctors, more than 100 nurses and some 400 paramedics.

But these conditions, as reported by *Newsweek*, represented a substantial advance over the situation observed in December 1978 by Leo Cherne and the Citizens Commission on Indochinese Refugees, which had been set up with the help of the International Rescue Committee. Indeed the Commission itself was in great part responsible for the improvement. Writing in the *New York Times*, Cherne noted that the island's refugee population at that time consisted of 26,000 men, women and children. He made these observations: "As I left Pulau Bidong, an island about two and a half hours by fishing boat from the Malaysian resort town of Trenggenau, a Vietnamese refugee said to me: 'Please don't pity us in spite of what you saw here. We're alive, unlike our people who drowned trying to reach land, any land. But when you return to America, please try to make your people understand. . . .'"[2]

Here is Cherne's description of life as he and his associates saw it being lived by thousands of human beings, who for the moment had no immediate prospect of resettlement:

We examined their food "stocks." Their skimpy food ration would last about a day, with no assurance that more would get through the choppy seas tomorrow. Medicines and drugs in short supply. A meager and polluted water supply, with the dry season a month or so away. Sanitation? Imagine 16 toilets for 26,000 people. In one week, the number of infectious-hepatitis cases — 108 of them — had almost doubled. New arrivals sleep on the open beaches under heavy monsoon rains. Yet, "Please don't pity us."

And how can one pity such extraordinarily brave and spirited people who are pooling their skills to make their lives, and the lives of their thousands of children, more bearable on this hellish island? Besides, does pity help? The only thing that will help is concrete action to rescue Indochinese refugees from desolate camps—there are close to 200,000 in Thailand and Malaysia alone—and resettle them in countries that will have them.[3]

Fearsome as was this Malaysian island in the Pacific, there were few among the refugees who evidenced any regret at having left the more dreadful Devil's Island into which their country had been transformed. The apologists for the totalitarians were heard to argue that those who turn their backs on Communism and accept the uncertain life of exile are only the rich. When the numbers of the expatriates mount as they have in Indochina, one can only marvel that these countries, so long exploited by European imperialists, should have produced so many wealthy natives, numbering in the hundred of thousands.

"RE-EDUCATION"

What they fled from has now been documented, at least partially, in the reasons given by the refugees for their willingness to risk as much as 500 miles of open sea in waters often roiled by violent storms, in leaky boats whose owners were obviously ready to part with them permanently. The first wave, the ethnic Vietnamese as distinguished from the ethnic Chinese who had lived for generations in Vietnam and who fled or were expelled later, had been traumatized by the horrors of life under Communism. Five years after the victory of the North Vietnamese, the "re-education" camps were still in full session. Or if "re-education" was not deemed necessary, there were always the malaria-ridden New Economic Zones in the rain forests waiting to receive former city dwellers condemned to hew out rice paddies in the jungle or build canals in accordance with the plans laid down by the leaders of a faltering economy. Or, if one were considered more than ordinarily recalcitrant, there was always prison.

Those who dared an illegal escape knew the penalties. The government press served constant notice that the "Regulations Punishing Counterrevolutionary Crimes" called for prison sentences of three to fifteen years for fleeing the country or helping others to flee. In August 1979, more than four years after the fall of Saigon, the *Los Angeles Times* reported: "Deputy Foreign Minister Hoan Bich Son said that 4,000 people have been arrested while trying to leave or organizing escapes, and that some have been executed, as part of tough new measures to stop the flow of 'boat people' which has filled refugee camps throughout Southeast Asia." This frank statement was offered by way of justification, a response to the protests of neighboring countries suffering under the burden of caring for the refugees.

What Vietnam was unwilling to do, however, was to change the conditions that caused the exodus—to end, for example, the notorious re-education camps and the practice of sending people into servitude in the jungles euphemistically called New Economic Zones. Stephen B. Young, an assistant dean and East Asian Legal Studies Research Associate at Harvard Law School, who has served on the IRC-sponsored Citizens Commission on Indochinese Refugees, has written a detailed analysis, "The Legality of Vietnamese Re-education Camps," in the *Harvard International Law Journal.* He summarizes the process that Communist Vietnam called re-education:

Although the daily regimen varied, life in the camps was essentially penal in nature, generally consisting of hard work, harsh conditions, and self-denunciation. Some information about camp life has become available from interviews with Vietnamese refugees. One refugee described the Lam Son camp in Khanh Duong district of Khanh Hoa province, where 100 North Vietnamese guards and twenty instructors for political education managed the re-education of 5,000 nationalist army officers. In this camp, according to the refugee, there was neither medicine nor medical care; at least twenty men at one point died of malaria. Each resident received 500 grams (two bowls) of rice each day, and, on occasion, thin soup and pieces of pork. Dietary supplements, such as vegetables, had to be grown by the residents, and residents who did not provide the camp kitchens with fifteen kilograms of vegetables per month were placed in solitary confinement. Beating and solitary confinement for infraction of other camp rules were frequent. Only occasional visits by relatives and receipt of two kilogram packages were allowed. Clothes were not provided.

The daily regimen in this camp consisted primarily of labor. The residents cut wood from 6:00 A.M. until noon and performed other hard labor from 1:00 P.M. until 5:30 P.M. Political seminars were held after dinner. Autobiographies had to be written every few months, and camp residents were encouraged to implicate their fellow residents in these autobiographies.[4]

The pattern, according to Dean Young, had been set originally by Nguyen Ngoc Giao. Writing in the magazine of the North Vietnamese Army, he described how re-education was to be conducted: "Management must be tight, continuous, comprehensive and specific.... We must manage each person. We must manage their thoughts and actions, words and deeds, philosophy of life and ways of livelihood, social relationships and travel. Close management will avoid loopholes. We must closely combine management and education with interrogations. The management process is a process of continuing interrogation."[5]

Journalists who had denounced the politics of the United States, who had supported the North Vietnamese and the National Liberation Front, now expressed shock at what was taking place in the so-called re-education camps. Jean Lacouture, returning from one of them, described it as a "prefabricated hell."[6] Another French journalist, after interviewing former "students," wrote that "camp inmates commonly suffer from limb paralysis, vision loss, and infectious skin diseases like scabies caused by long-term, closely-packed, dark living conditions." The number of those incarcerated at any given moment has been variously estimated: in 1976 one Vietnamese official put it at 200,000, though outside analysts have estimated as many as half a million.

NEW PHENOMENON – OR OLD?

Little attention has been given to the fact that Communist totalitarianism has recently picked up an old technique of dictators: when the flow of refugees mounts, use it as a cover for expelling all who may become adversaries or who are deemed to be untrustworthy for ethnic, political or religious reasons. This tactic became one of the earmarks of the 1970s. Idi Amin's expulsion of Indian families who had lived for generations in Uganda took place in 1972 and was accompanied by overt looting of their property. It was carried over into the 1980s by Fidel Castro when 10,000 Cubans stormed into the Peruvian embassy in Havana; he opened an escape hatch for 120,000 others for reasons previously discussed here. Ever since Lenin exiled the Mensheviks and Stalin expelled Trotsky from the Soviet Union, the Communist leaders have picked off dissidents like Solzhenitsyn and deported them from their homeland.

The exodus from Vietnam has consisted of both escape and expulsion. In the first, which began in 1975 and has continued since, the refugees were originally people who had supported their former government against the Communist takeover. These were joined by many who had fought the Thieu government in the belief that it could be replaced by some kind of democracy, and then by people who had actively worked for a Communist victory, only to be disillusioned when it came.

More than half of the expellees consisted primarily of the ethnic Chinese who were driven out for a variety of reasons. They had been successful merchants and now their businesses were to be expropriated. Besides, the historic Vietnamese hatred of the Chinese still persisted, even though Red China had contributed materially to the armies of Ho Chi Minh. Now this virulence was being fed by Moscow because of the widening Sino-Soviet rift. Some 200,000 North Vietnamese Chinese, it is said, crossed the border and were received by a reluctant Peking that eventually declared no more would be accepted and then initiated a temporary invasion of Vietnam's borders.

From the South, the ethnic Chinese could escape only by boat. An elaborate government machinery was created to extort money from them. In July 1979, Charles Freeman, Deputy U.S. Coordinator for Refugee Affairs, estimated that Vietnamese were paying to officials and boatbuilders as much as a quarter of a billion dollars a month in gold. There was little originality in Hanoi's scheme: the technique had been devised in Hitler's Germany during the mid-1930s when Jews were forced to buy their way out. After Khrushchev's masons put up the Berlin Wall, the same method of extortion was used. The Bonn government, in secret but formal arrangements, literally bought freedom for thousands of East Germans at $15,000 a head.

The Vietnamese version of such trafficking in human flesh was recounted on the "MacNeil-Lehrer Report" by Miss Banh Kiet Nhan some months after she had arrived safely in the United States. This dialogue, seen and heard on television by millions, tells the details:

Jim Lehrer: Miss Nhan, first, why did you decide to leave Vietnam?
Banh Kiet Nhan: Well, because there's no freedom in Vietnam, life is so hard. And we may be arrested at any time.
Lehrer: Is that because you are Chinese, of Chinese origin?
Nhan: Yes. Because we are (unintelligible) people, and the Communist doesn't like us. Doesn't trust us.
Lehrer: I see. Did you have to pay to get on that boat?
Nhan: Yes, I have to pay to board the boat and prepare the other things. And we have to give some to the district officer to let us go.
Lehrer: You mean the government officer, of the government of Vietnam. You had to pay him, then you had to pay the boat captain . . .
Nhan: Yeah. We pay the district officer at the seashore, yes.
Lehrer: How much money was involved? How much money did you have to pay?
Nhan: I pay eight tael.
Lehrer: I beg your pardon?
Nhan: Eight tael, in gold.
Lehrer: I see. It's about two thousand dollars, is that what that is?
Nhan: Yes, about two thousand.
Lehrer: Two thousand American dollars. Where did you get the money? How did you raise the money?
Nhan: Some we left there before the eruption of Vietnam, and my relatives helped me with some. We get that sum in order to leave Vietnam.

*   *   *

Lehrer: Had you heard the stories of what had happened to Vietnamese refugees before, the sinking boats, being unwelcome in other places, and living in these crowded camps — had you heard those stories before you came . . .
Nhan: I know those before. Heard so many, many people die in the sea. But I decide to go.
Lehrer: It was worth the risk.
Nhan: Yes.
Lehrer: Rather than to stay, you'd just as soon take the risk.
Nhan: Rather than stay in Vietnam, yes.
Lehrer: I see. Now, how crowded was that boat? What were the conditions like on this small fishing boat?
Nhan: It was very crowded. We could only sit there.
Lehrer: You could just stay in one place?
Nhan: Just stay in the same place, we cannot move, even.
Lehrer: And you were seated the whole time?
Nhan: Yes. Only sit there. You cannot move, it was so crowded.
Lehrer: What about food and sanitation and that sort of thing?

Nhan: Yes. Of course we don't have enough food. We can only eat the *gam ja*, and drink very little of water.

Lehrer: Your boat was also, as I understand it, attacked by pirates out in the sea. How many times?

Nhan: We were attacked about ten times.

Lehrer: What did they do when they came aboard the ship?

Nhan: Yes, they would jump aboard to our ship and they order some to jump to their ship. Then they began to rob us. They search for our treasure and turn over our things to find whatever thing they like.

Lehrer: You mean money and jewelry, and. . . .

Nhan: Money, jewels, golden ring, and so on.

Lehrer: Did they abuse any of the people physically? I mean, did they hit anybody or hurt anybody?

Nhan: They hold knives, therefore we dare not to refuse.

Lehrer: I see. Your boat was finally rescued, you and the people on the boat were finally rescued by an American ship, is that correct?

Nhan: Yes. But after ten times robbed, one boat rob us and the boat disappear, another boat appear at once. For two days we only stay in the Thailand Gulf and rob one by one.

Lehrer: I see.

Nhan: And at nighttime they took several girls off, they took away for the whole night. And you know what happened to them.

Lehrer: Sure. Were they Thais? Were they from Thailand, is that the way you understand it, the pirates?

Nhan: Yes, surely they are Thailand fishing boats.

Lehrer: I see. Then you were rescued by an American ship. Was it a military ship, a U.S. Navy ship?

Nhan: Yes, Navy ship.[7]

The story of human suffering on the sea lanes leading from Vietnam will probably never be fully told. The agony had been going on for months before the world began to awaken to the horror. If any one man is responsible for alerting the civilized nations to what was happening, the credit must be given to Henry Kamm, the *New York Times*'s Asian correspondent. In 1978 he received the Pulitzer Prize for his meticulous work in describing the ragged caravans on the jungle paths, the foundering flotilla on the sea lanes, and the fate of those who reached the refugee camps and those who did not. His interviews with both the victims and the victimizers, his ability to talk to peasants and high government officials, have produced reportage and analysis for which history will be grateful.

Not least among his services in presenting the whole truth has been the documentation he provided on the failure of Western society to meet its responsibilities. Rationalizations and bureaucratic evasions have blocked efforts to achieve speedy resettlement. Domestic economic stringencies have stood in the way of needed appropriations for refugee relief. In addition, a general fear in the United States of getting involved again in Southeast Asia made Congress and the President reluctant to take action.

LAW OF THE SEA

Among the most shocking facts revealed by Kamm was the ease with which "advanced" commercial nations abandoned the ancient law of the sea that any vessel in distress must be given full assistance. Citing chapter and verse, Kamm proved that freighters in the South China Sea were steaming away from sinking fishing boats loaded to the gunwales with refugees. Ship captains watched through the lenses of the telescope as men, women and children drowned.

Reporting an interview with the captain of the freighter *Tomoco*, which flies the Panamanian flag but is operated by Japanese owners, Kamm wrote: "Capt. Edgar A. Silverio has just saved the lives of 31 people, but in view of the fact that a year ago he rescued 18 others, he is worried whether he will be allowed to keep his job."[8] Once taken aboard from their fast-sinking boat, the refugees told him that his was the fifteenth ship to come near but it was the only one willing to make a rescue. Kamm pointed out why the skippers of fourteen vessels decided to violate both their conscience and the law of the sea: their shipowners were more concerned about the financial loss occasioned by resulting delays, by the need to off-load the refugees at unscheduled ports, and by the refusal of Asian countries in many cases to let the boat people ashore. Malaysia, for example, at one time threatened to bar vessels with such a human cargo from entering harbor even to land their regular freight. One Greek ship had to make the long voyage around the Cape before it could disembark a catch of refugees in Mombasa. In another instance, an Israeli captain found no port willing to receive the people he had plucked from the sea. Ultimately, they had to be flown to Tel Aviv for resettlement. Another vessel that had taken on thirty-one boat people traveled two months and more than 1,600 miles before its passengers could be put ashore.

The journals of the shipping industry were replete with items on the additional expenses incurred by vessels that picked up refugees. For example, *Lloyd's List* reported on July 2, 1979, that the British ship *Sibonga* was applying for reimbursement from its insurer for the feeding and clothing of almost a thousand extra passengers and for the increased running expenses caused by the delay. Similarly, the ship *Roachbank* was seeking compensation for the cost of remaining anchored off Taiwan for about a month while the captain negotiated with the authorities to admit 300 refugees. In Britain, P and I (profit and indemnity) shipping clubs finally began to add to their rules provisions for insuring against losses resulting from rescues at sea. But the masters of many ships, rather than undergo the inconvenience, the time loss, the additional fuel expense and port charges incurred by entering unscheduled harbors, preferred to close their eyes to the distress signals coming from the fishing boats.

Against this background one can understand the dilemma of decent men like the master of the *Tomoco*. It was no easy decision for Captain Silverio to bring aboard the fourteen men, eight women, and nine children of whom the youngest was only ten months, who were nine days out of Vung Tau located near Ho Chi Minh City, and who were running into seas that he described as "rough to very rough." Having made the choice dictated by conscience, he told Henry Kamm that he feared for his job because he had obeyed the law of the sea before and had been reprimanded. "Of the twelve ships that sail for my company," he said, "I am the only one who picks up refugees."

Kamm's dispatch to the *New York Times*, which casually mentioned the shipowner, the Daiichi Chuo Kisen Company, Tokyo, was read by hundreds of thousands of readers in the United States. One of them, Leo Cherne, promptly dispatched a message to the company on the letterhead of the International Rescue Committee urging that instead of being penalized Captain Silverio deserved a commendation. A few weeks later, a reply from Tokyo indicated that henceforth the company's vessels would follow the law of the sea.

Aware of the pressures now building up on sea captains, IRC instructed its Southeast Asian staff to give priority to refugees who needed off-loading from rescue ships at ports of call. One example of the impact came in the form of a letter addressed to Charles Sternberg by the president of a shipping company flying the Panamanian flag. He wrote:

On behalf of *Lydia Compania Maritima S.A.* I wish to express our most sincere appreciation and profound, earnest gratitude for the concern, interest and unremitting help you tendered to the fifty-one Vietnamese boat refugees that the *Lydia* rescued on the South China Sea, and to our ship.

We sincerely hope and believe that the prompt and successful conclusion to this episode in which the *Lydia* was involved, and in which you rendered us such invaluable assistance, will encourage other ships' captains to take the same humane initiatives and somehow help solve this desperate international quandary.[9]

While intervening to help rescued boat people gain individual approval for admission to countries of first asylum, IRC, in conjunction with its Citizens Commission on Indochinese Refugees, sought enforcement of what had come to be civilized society's rules for safety at sea. The psychologists write of a phenomenon called cognitive dissonance—a process by which we change our perceptions to suit our momentary need. Even well-informed people had begun to accept the notion that international law did not mandate assistance to boats in distress, that, at most, this was only part of a romantic tradition of the sea but was not really binding on ships' captains. Eventually, however, outraged admiralty lawyers assembled the unequivocal texts of the appropriate international conventions and treaties. Law review articles traced "duty to rescue" back to its formulation in the Brussels International and Salvage at Sea Convention, adopted in 1910, which read in part: "Every master is bound, so far as he can do so without serious danger to his vessel, her crew and her passengers, to render assistance to everybody, even though an enemy, found at sea in danger of being lost. . . ."

This mandate had been accepted through the years by sixty-three nations in formal ratification. They included the United States, the United Kingdom, Japan and the Soviet Union. To be sure, two countries, Liberia and Panama, whose flags of convenience fly over many American-owned ships, have never put their signatures to the Brussels Convention. Nevertheless, successive international agreements by which they are indeed bound have reiterated the principle. Following the enormous death toll of the Titanic disaster, the rule was again under consideration at a 1914 conference in London which was adjourned by the outbreak of war. Today, seagoing nations are committed to the provisions of the 1958 Convention on the High Seas and the 1960 London International Convention for the Safety of Life at Sea, frequently cited as SOLAS.[10]

According to Prince Sadruddin Aga Khan, for many years the United Nations High Commissioner for Refugees, available data from the end of 1975 to September 1977 showed that 2,652 Indochinese refugees had been rescued at sea. But so widespread had become the news of ships turning their stern to imperiled boat people that the High Commissioner, in October 1977, found it necessary to address a letter to the International Chamber of Shipping, asking it to remind its members that "the need of persons in distress at sea is of such obvious urgency as to impose a clear humanitarian duty on the masters of passing ships to go to their rescue" and that international SOLAS regulations should be respected.[11]

President Carter instructed the U.S. Maritime Commission to inform American-flag vessels that they were under a legal duty to take aboard foundering or endangered refugees. But in testimony before the U.S. Senate Subcommittee on Refugees, Leo Cherne noted that most American-owned ships now sail under foreign registry, and he urged the government to explore the possibility of expanding President Carter's order "to all U.S.-owned vessels."

The news of men, women, and children being left to the mercy of the waves continued to assail the conscience of the world, but meanwhile the shores of neighboring countries were being barred to the boat people. Public opinion in the United States began to respond to the pressure created by foreign correspondents like Henry Kamm and by organizations like the Citizens Commission, IRC and the other voluntary agencies. For all their desire to forget Vietnam, Americans applauded in overwhelming numbers when President Carter ordered the Pacific fleet to scour the waters off Indochina and take aboard all in need of help.

Even more important was obtaining the cooperation of the much more numerous ships of the merchant marine traveling those lanes. The most influential figure in achieving their compliance with the law of the sea was the American Secretary of State Cyrus R. Vance. During the course of a conference with Cherne and other members of the Citizens Commission, he came up with the most important contribution made to the life-saving effort at sea. As he himself pointed out, the principal obstacle to picking up the boat people was the sea captains' fear that they would not be permitted to off-load their unexpected passengers at the next port of arrival; in some cases they were being refused permission to enter the harbor. Vance suggested that a practical solution would be to authorize American consuls in those ports to accept such off-loaded refugees for immediate admission to the United States, but this required the approval of the Immigration and Naturalization Service, a branch of the Department of Justice. An hour later Cherne was in the office of INS Director Leonel J. Castillo who promptly consented to the Secretary of State's proposal.

LEDGER OF AGONY

Some day the historians and scholars of a free Vietnam will attempt the enormous task of auditing the books on the boat people, just as Jews since the Holocaust have sought to record every detail of the anguish visited on the captives of the concentration camps. Present accounts of the ordeal on the high seas must remain incomplete. The statistics can only be estimated, but many of those who have attempted to calculate the magnitude of the misery floating in the South China Sea have concluded that fully 50 percent of the boats that put out never reached shore.

Nor is there any device that can plumb the depths of their suffering. An Associated Press dispatch in 1979 describes a boat stranded on a coral island off the Philippines: "A teenage girl watched helplessly for 140 days as the 49 persons who fled Communist Vietnam with her starved to death in the rotting hull of an abandoned ship. She survived on seagulls, oysters and a little rainwater." By what factor must this be multiplied so that one can understand the arithmetic of human agony? A *New York Times* article datelined Kuala Lumpur reported: "More than 100 Vietnamese refugees drowned off Malaysia's east coast when their boat capsized while being towed out to sea. It was carrying 227 refugees and the bodies of ten others who had died on the trip from Vietnam. The refugees had sought permission to land at Mersing in Malaysia's southernmost state of Johore, but authorities refused to let them come ashore and towed the boat to sea."

On television, millions of Americans watched as Bill Bradley, forgetting that he was an NBC correspondent and remembering only that he was a human being, waded into the sea in front of his own cameras to help snatch drowning refugees from the water while jeering local inhabitants refused to lend a hand.

From Bangkok, Henry Kamm wrote in the lead paragraph of a story filed in November 1979: "Seventeen Vietnamese refugees, including four young children, were murdered by Thai fishermen at sea and most of the thirty-seven women aboard four refugee boats raped many times by about 500 fishermen during a period of twenty-two days in which the survivors were held prisoner on an uninhabited island off southern Thailand." The local police acknowledged that fifty-seven boats had made visits to the scene to participate in the robbery, rapes and beatings. A pilot flying over the island spotted bodies floating in the water while fishing boats stood by; the pirates had thrown children into the sea in order to force their parents to jump after them. Representatives of the UN High Commissioner for Refugees who came to provide aid were themselves threatened with violence. "So frequent are the attacks," Kamm concluded, "that a refugee worker said few women between the ages of ten and fifty in the southern Thai camp of Songkla had not been raped, and even fewer refugees had not been robbed before arrival."[12]

LAND PEOPLE FROM LAOS

During the war in Southeast Asia, the kingdom of Laos, once a French protectorate, also became a battleground. By 1970 the Communist Pathet Lao had been reinforced by a North Vietnamese army numbering 67,000. With the collapse of Saigon the government in Vientiane passed under Hanoi's hegemony. As in every country taken over by the Communists, an exodus got under way.

Refugees who managed to escape the Laotian border patrols and reach northern Thailand brought word of how the transition into Communism was being achieved. Everybody over the age of fifteen had been ordered to report to nightly "samminas" — a corruption of the French word *séminaires* — where physical endurance was taxed by lectures running as long as four hours, dissipating the energy that would be needed next day for the nation's *three-year* plan. (In a small country, things must be done on a smaller scale.)

But no amount of lecturing could counteract the propaganda of reality — the deterioration that had invaded Laos along with the 30-40,000 Vietnamese troops who remained after the war. In an effort to tighten the bamboo curtain, Laos broke off diplomatic relations with France in 1978. Fleeing Laotians brought news of increasing hardship. The situation was so bad that the Communist regime even had to accept 10,000 tons of rice, worth $5 million, from the capitalist enemy, the United States. At best, this was a token in view of the UN's estimate of a 113,000-ton shortfall.

The worsening of the economy multiplied the pressure on the people. Prince Souvanna Phouma, who had been prime minister of Laos before the Communist conquest and who had been kept on in Vientiane as an "advisor" to the new regime, told Henry Kamm in 1979 that 10-15,000 of his former followers had been banished to "rigorous" work in the countryside. In some of the camps the prisoners were forced to labor with no shade in hundred-degree temperatures. Such people would not be permitted to return to the cities, said Souvanna Phouma. "We cannot let them come too close to the Mekong. They would be tempted to cross the river." And besides, "It is the West that attracts them, Europe and America. That is their dream."[13]

The majority, of course, could have no hope of escape. Dr. Didier Sicard, a French physician who had just completed four years working and teaching in Laos, told a leftist Parisian journal of the psychological consequences wrought by the new regime: "The country is drained of its force. At the hospital, more and more, I diagnosed psychosomatic illnesses, ulcers—in short, the typical pathology of a state of being under constraint. Around us, all who had kept some courage were fleeing. The young ones above all, the vital force. In the void, the Vietnamese are settling, almost without conflict. Some years yet, and Laos will be a Vietnamese province."[14]

This is how Laos looked from the inside. And yet, as late as 1977, a strong resistance movement continued to operate, especially in the hills inhabited by the Hmongs, or "free people" as they call themselves. Before the war they had lived placid lives, governed by their own kings or tribal chieftains. In their mountain locations they had maintained subsistence economies, growing swidden rice and tending livestock while their women worked patiently in needlepoint, embroidery and appliqué. Preferring to live in isolation, they proudly passed along to their children the cultural heritage their forebears had brought with them from China in the 1850s.

Like the Montagnards of Vietnam, they were considered enemies of the new regime. Indeed, during the war they had formed an army of their own, equipped by the U.S. Central Intelligence Agency. Despite their lack of sophistication, they won the admiration of their allies because of their courage and intelligence. But their cooperation with the Americans, coupled with the historic race prejudice of the Laotians, made them a special target for genocidal persecution. Mass flight was their only hope.

Even the majority population, the lowland Laotians, bitterly resented the hegemony of Vietnam. Not only were thousands of civilians pressed into service to dig irrigation canals near Vientiane, but even the Communist premier Kaysone Phomvihan was required by his masters to wield pick and shovel in a demonstration of proletarian solidarity. Soon the stream of refugees flowing into Thailand included high-ranking party officials who had found themselves subordinated to Vietnamese authority. To end local resistance the regime had set up a network of village and neighborhood "supervisors"; if they failed to keep order they were themselves arrested.

As the Communists consolidated their control, the flight across the Mekong accelerated. Out of a total population of 3 million, almost a quarter of a million people had left the country by the end of 1978. In the drama of the boat people, it is often overlooked that the land people—Laotian and

Cambodian — outnumbered the Vietnamese, at least until the mass expulsion of the ethnic Chinese began in earnest in the last years of the 1970s.

THE THAI BURDEN

In 1975 alone Thailand received more than 70,000 refugees. From March 1975 to April 1977, some 40,000 had been resettled abroad. But Thailand found that it still had 77,000 on its hands, huddled together in some fifteen dilapidated camp sites. It turned to the United Nations High Commissioner for Refugees and to the international voluntary agencies which undertook to provide, as itemized by the Thai government, "soap, mosquito nets, blankets, food supplements, vitamins, medicines, educational materials, hygienic supplies, sports equipment, musical instruments, water pumps, tools, etc. Their technicians, working side by side with Thai authorities, are providing advice for such self-help projects as family centered gardening, animal raising, and the development of handicrafts or cottage industries designed to bring about economic self-sufficiency and to improve day by day living conditions within the camps."

IRC had arrived in Thailand in February 1976. Its first medical team was staffed by people who had worked for IRC in South Vietnam. From the start, the doctors, nurses and support personnel emphasized medical and nutritional assistance to the refugees from Vietnam, Laos and Cambodia. The greatest immediate needs were at Nong Khai in the Northeast, Sikhiu in the interior, and Aranyaprathet, the major crossing from Cambodia. Soon several hundred refugees had been recruited or trained as paramedics and lab technicians.

At the time the author visited the Nong Khai camp in 1978, some 40,000 Laotians and Hmongs were being sheltered. In reality, there were two separate camps, maintained by the Thai government along ethnic lines. In each IRC was operating a hospital equipped for physical examinations and treatment, including an obstetrics unit, a pharmacy and a laboratory. Much, of course, was rudimentary, and improvisation was at a premium. A Y-shaped wooden delivery table had been constructed and covered with oilcloth. A newly acquired barber's chair replaced the kitchen stool that had been used formerly by the dentist. Delivery of a microscope was the occasion for a community party. The addition of a milk distribution shed brought long lines of children throughout the day, along with smiling parents. Maternity and child-care services were supplemented by counseling on family planning.

In a typical month, the hospital for Laotian refugees reported that 1,960 patients were treated and 163 hospitalized. The rolls showed twenty-one births and two deaths. In the Hmong hospital, the comparable figures were 4,217 patients examined and treated, with 252 admitted. On the average, eighteen deaths a month could be expected. Among the Hmong outpatients, many were new arrivals who had come with wounds that needed cleansing. The statistics alone demonstrate the special hardships visited on the Hmongs, whose care was rendered even more difficult because they first had to be educated to accept modern medicine. IRC's doctors found that the morbidity or sickness rate among these hill people was about 25 percent.

Directing the medical work was an extraordinary physician from the Philippine Islands, Dr. Dominica P. Garcia, a slight figure of a woman whose bearing nevertheless commanded instant authority. She had originally wanted a career as a journalist, but her father considered such a role unbecoming and the family compromise had been medical school, a result for which thousands of refugees in Thailand would ultimately be grateful. Associated with her, and carrying major responsibility for IRC's Hmong Hospital, was Dr. Levi Roque, also a Philippino.

The reputation of both physicians extended not only throughout the refugee camps of the Northeast but far to the south, reaching the Cambodian border. In the detention centers to which the refugees were first sent as "illegal immigrants," the field visits of the IRC medics were awaited—for example, in Phon Phisni where most of the arrivals were Hmongs and the local governor or his deputy provided prompt notice to IRC of emergency needs; in Bungkarn where the arriving Hmongs were generally "in worse shape than ever," as Dr. Garcia described them; in the detention centers of Bo and Sri Ching Mai, where the refugees were mostly Laotians who arrived in somewhat better condition, principally because they had had more assistance on the way.

"THE YELLOW RAIN"

At Nong Khai IRC staff first learned that Hmong villages and farms had not only been bombed from the air but that poison gas had been dropped on the villagers. In the Phou Bia region, artillery had pounded their homes into rubble. The area had been a major Hmong center, with almost a third of Laos' Hmong population of 350,000. Reaching the Thai frontier was a sixteen-day journey through forests and areas mined by the Pathet Lao. IRC's Dr. Roque found that some 80 percent of those who finally arrived were suffering various degrees of malnutrition. Many of the children had experienced irreparable brain damage from extreme malnutrition, their only sustenance having been bamboo shoots and roots.

Received in Nong Khai, they were crowded into small quarters—five persons to a hut measuring two by four meters. Their allotment of food, funded out of the overtaxed resources of the UN High Commissioner, came to a daily ration of 500 grams of rice, with children under twelve receiving half that amount. But even this was preferable to remaining behind in villages whose wells had been destroyed, whose thatched houses had been set afire by ground troops, and whose crops had been poisoned by "the yellow rain" spread from the planes of the Pathet Lao.

As Hitler had once made Spain a testing ground for new weaponry, a Soviet team of chemical warfare experts had taken up posts in Laos to supervise poison gas arsenals in the cities of Pakse and Seno. During a visit to Nong Khai, members of the Citizens Commission on Indochinese Refugees heard eyewitness accounts of what had happened under the skies of Phou Bia. "Not one of the refugees interviewed," says Cherne, "failed to know at firsthand of the yellow and green powders and liquids which had been dropped. . . . Not in one instance did we learn of the dropping of these chemicals which was not accompanied by the most severe illness during the hours which followed, and, in almost all cases, the consequences involved death."[15]

During the month of February 1978, similar reports emanated from various sections of the hill country. From Xiangkohang and the juncture of the Nam Theng and Nam Ka rivers in south central Laos came word of gas attacks delivered by rockets fired from aircraft. Two poisons apparently were being tested. William Safire in the *New York Times* quoted this report of the consequences: "Both agents made the victims feel as if their bodies were going to blow up, severe coughing yielded blood. The throat felt hot and it hurt to swallow. These symptoms followed by eyes turning yellow as if the victim had jaundice, the vision becoming blurred, and the nose tingling as if hot pepper had been inhaled. Breathing caused a sharp pain, teeth felt loose and gums smelled rotten. . . . Five thousand people in the area of attack, two hundred known to be affected. . . . Anyone whose bare skin was touched by a droplet suffered severe necrosis of the affected area, high fever, skin red turning bruise-dark. Took about two weeks to die."[16]

A year later, Washington was to address formal inquiries to the Soviet Union about reports that a thousand persons had died in Sverdlovsk as a result of an explosion in a germ warfare plant. According to underground Russian sources, the blast had released a microorganism called the "I-21 strain." Moscow contended that the situation was merely an outbreak of anthrax. Beyond question in the ensuing controversy was the fact that the Kremlin, in four years of arms reduction negotiations, had consistently refused to permit on-site inspection of chemical and biological warfare facilities. Later, in 1980, according to Safire, photos from Afghanistan showed that the Red Army had brought with it the easily recognizable TMS-65, a military accessory used to decontaminate vehicles exposed to poison gas.

By 1981 the issue had become an international *cause célèbre*. Were the Soviets manufacturing, distributing and encouraging the testing of these weapons on people in Asia and Afghanistan? Sterling Seagrave, a former reporter for the *Washington Post* and son of the noted "Burma Surgeon" Gordon Seagrave, assembled the evidence in a book called *Yellow Rain: A Journey Through the Terror of Chemical Warfare.*[17] He estimated that, by 1979, the possible number of victims might have reached 15-20,000 persons. United States government figures put the deaths at 6,000 Laotians, 1,000

Cambodians and 3,000 Afghans. Dr. Richard Harruff, of the New York University Medical Center, testified that he had seen and treated hundreds of yellow-rain victims while in Thailand. Dr. Amos Townsend, of the IRC medical staff on the Cambodian border, reported conversations with Vietnamese defectors who told him that Hanoi's invading troops had suffered self-inflicted casualties as a result of their chemical warfare.[18]

The American Broadcasting Company produced a documentary based on the findings of a group of scientists it had assembled to examine yellow rain samples.[19] Their analyses confirmed the reports and revealed that the chemical attack consisted of trichothecenes and concentrations of T-2 toxin produced from certain strains of fungus, in combination with certain irritants, incapacitants and nerve agents. The *Wall Street Journal*, more consistently than any other publication, maintained a steady drumfire of articles presenting the evidence. The *New York Times*, as late as March 1982, expressed doubts about the charges,[20] but its own columnist Tom Wicker, a severe critic of U.S. policies, was already writing in January 1982 about the "solid evidence that they [the Russians] have developed and used toxic substances for lethal purposes ('yellow rain') in Asia."[21] Four days after its editorial criticizing the evidence so far adduced, the *Times* devoted more than a page and a half to excerpts from a detailed report to Congress by the State Department on Communist use of chemical weapons.[22] The United States formally charged the Russians with responsibility for "chemical warfare activities in Laos, Kampuchea and Afghanistan," in violation of the Geneva Protocol of 1925 that banned chemical and bacterial weapons, and the Convention on Biological and Toxin Weapons of 1972.

THE ROAD TO SAFETY

In November 1978 the *New York Times* published excerpts from a report by Dr. Garcia to the IRC office in New York. Reflected is not only the plight of the refugees but the sensitivity with which they were being cared for by a dedicated medical team. Dr. Garcia's summary of the situation cannot be surpassed for eloquence and simplicity. She wrote:

Reports from Hmong newcomers are truly distressing. With their little crops destroyed by poison gas, they leave their villages with no food provisions. For weeks they hide in mountain jungles avoiding Vietnamese and Pathet Lao patrols. They eat roots and leaves, sometimes poisonous mushrooms. Nobody dares beg for rice from Lao settlements. Many contract malaria; whiplashes from brambles and bushes get infected and become festering ulcers; their feet terribly swollen. When enemy troops sight them, they are fired upon and a number sustain gunshot wounds which, too, get readily infected.

Out of the thousands who leave the villages only a few hundred reach the river where more are decimated by drowning. Women with babies strapped to their backs are so faint with hunger, pain and fear that they lose consciousness while being towed by the "stronger" members of the family. When they regain consciousness, the babies at their backs have died by drowning.

The Mekong River at this time is quite swollen and debris swirls wildly in the current. Being mountain people, the Hmongs are helpless in water and cannot swim. They grab on any number of floating objects, banana stalks, dead limbs of trees. A few manage to bring empty plastic gallon containers, still others inflate ordinary grocery plastic bags. It is not unusual to find these survivors clinging to their make-shift "life-savers" even long after they have been in the detention centers. They carry them up to the hospital wards where they finally get proper treatment.

The horror and misery of their flight to safety is etched in their blank, tear-stained faces. Men and women weep readily at the nightmarish memory of their ordeal. Husbands, wives, children, parents have been lost in the process. Gone is the familiar look of initial elation found among newcomers. One is ready to assume that they know very little the difference between communism and freedom. Their main concern is to escape oppression and annihilation of their tribes. . . .

The IRC Medical Team is almost always on the spot to render first aid to the new arrivals. No one knows for sure when they come, but the need to follow up treatment and change wound dressings of previous cases almost daily prepares the team for any new ones coming. Antibiotics, vitamins, fever pills are literally dropped into the mouths of semi-conscious patients. Abscesses are incised, drained and dressed, ulcers debrided, gunshot wounds cleaned and stitched, recent abrasions painted with disinfectant. Bandage, gauze, cotton and plaster are used by the kilograms. Cleaning salves and tinctures flow. God, they deserve every little help we can give them.[23]

Not mentioned in her report to the New York office of IRC was the personal refuge she was providing for two children. One was a two-week-old girl whose mother, recently widowed during the river crossing, simply could not care for the baby. The other was an eleven-year-old boy named Bi Xiong who had arrived alone at the camp, the sole survivor of some fifty Hmongs, the total population of his village, who had attempted to make their way to the Mekong. En route they had been intercepted by Pathet Lao patrols and only a handful finally reached the river bank. The group included Bi Xiong, his parents and his sister. All plunged into the water, using four-foot lengths of bamboo under their arms to give them buoyancy. The boy saw his family struck by bullets. His last remembrance of them is bamboo poles floating downstream. Bi Xiong alone reached Nong Khai. Wretched and emaciated, more dead than alive, he was turned over to the IRC staff.

Now he could talk again of the life he had known. Interviewed through an interpreter and recorded on a cassette, he could even smile as he listened to a playback of his voice. Weekends he lived in Dr. Garcia's house outside the refugee camp; weekdays he would return to the camp so that he might attend classes set up for the refugee children and become, like them, a child with a future.

CARNAGE IN CAMBODIA

From the north and the east, the Laotians continued to flood into Thailand, filling the camps of the land people. In the south, the boats chugged into the coves in numbers that soon revealed a serious economic fact about Vietnam—the loss of a third of its fishing fleet with consequent deprivation of its major source of protein. But the most lurid of all the Indochinese frontiers was the escarpment that separates the high ground of Thailand from the land to the south and east, the country of the Khmers, once Cambodia, since renamed "Democratic Kampuchea." For here the most wretched of the earth were staggering out of the forests, driven by the worst sadistic government yet to emerge out of Communist revolution.

In the first interval after the Communist victory in Vietnam, Laos and Cambodia, a sigh of relief was heard around the world. The war was over at last. Where was the predicted bloodbath? At first there was unwillingness to admit that a new reign of terror had started. Many in the West distrusted the reports of their own governments, even when the allegations were confirmed by the living evidence of hundreds of thousands of refugees, and, in the case of Cambodia, the silent testimony of dead millions. Nevertheless, the Asian will to freedom found expression and could finally be heard in the sound of shuffling feet.

Barred from the scene by the Khmer Rouge, Western analysts reported developments with extreme caution. The evidence came in gradually. One can trace the process of reluctant acceptance of the truth by reading in sequence the sections on Cambodia to be found in the authoritative yearbooks of the *Encyclopaedia Britannica*. Describing the events of 1975, when the shock of the mass deportations from Phnom Penh was still too recent to have been absorbed, the 1976 *Book of the Year* reported:

> It was peace and friendliness as the new order began. Khmer Rouge soldiers asked people to stay calm while ministers and officials of the fallen regime were summoned to "help formulate measures to restore order." Seven days of celebration were ordered, coinciding with the Cambodian New Year on April 13. After the celebration came *what looked like a crackdown*. U.S. sources, *quoting themselves*, reported a bloodbath and widespread revenge killings. While these remained unconfirmed by other sources, all were agreed that the new authorities in Phnom Penh were enforcing a harder discipline than their counterparts in other Indochinese states. . . .

> The entire population of Phnom Penh was forcibly evacuated from the city, soldiers pushing the old and the sick along with the others into the countryside. It was described as a purificatory drive with the promise that the city would be repeopled in due course. The *outside world inferred* that the food situation in the ravaged country was so desperate that the whole populace had to be put to work in agriculture. (Emphasis added.)[24]

As in the case of Hitler's concentration camps, the world could not bring itself to recognize the frightful truth until long after the event. In April 1975

Deputy Premier Ieng Sary addressed a conference of nonaligned nations in Lima, Peru. As summarized by the *Book of the Year*: "He justified the mass evacuation of Phnom Penh on the twin grounds that it was impossible to ensure food supplies in the capital and that a secret political-military plan drawn up by 'traitors' like Long Boret to retake power at the end of six months had been uncovered. He said that the crop situation held out the promise of Cambodia's becoming self-sufficient in food by the end of the year."[25] A peasant's paradise was in process of being built.

The next *Book of the Year* (1977) reports the creation of a "legislature with farmers holding 150 seats, workers 50, and soldiers 50."[26] As for the kind of government the people were receiving, a grim note was now sounded in a single sentence: "The trickle of news that came out of Cambodia during 1976 helped confirm the postwar regime's reputation as a harshly different entity from its brother victors in neighbouring Vietnam and Laos."

But details were still lacking. For any real suggestion that horror had been unleashed in the tightly-sealed country, one must wait until the 1978 *Book of the Year*. Summarizing the events of the preceding year, it reveals that the Angkar Leou (Organization on High), the secret body of unidentified leaders, is now admitted to be "the 17-year old Communist Party of Cambodia."[27] Says the *Book of the Year*: "The timing suggested that Cambodia's formal entry into the ranks of the world's Communist states was intended to appease China, its main supplier of material aid and technical expertise. Some observers thought it was also a move to give Cambodia a new face untainted by the Angkar Leou's two-year reign of terror."[28]

Thus, by 1978, the existence of the terror had come to be known. But the Western perception was still unfocussed; the general public did not know that refugees were straining to break out of the country. The *Book of the Year* refers to continuing border clashes between Cambodian troops and their neighbors in Thailand and *Vietnam*!

Not until the 1979 *Book of the Year* does one begin to get the full sense of the gruesome realities. Now Cambodia is "dogged by a continuing reputation for excessive cruelty at home."[29] President Carter's denunciation of the government as the worst offender against human rights is reported. Britain has demanded that the UN Human Rights Commission conduct an investigation—a suggestion that is not supported by the UN majority. For the first time statistics begin to appear: "Western sources" are quoted as claiming "that one million-two million of Cambodia's claimed population of eight million have died of hunger and disease or in purges since the Communist takeover."[30] And now the shape of things becomes more discernible as the *Book of the Year* account takes note of the portents:

Impressions of excessive harshness were only strengthened when Premier Pol Pot gave what amounted to the first exposition of Cambodia's state philosophy. In an unprecedented interview in March [1978], he told visiting Yugoslav journalists that his country was developing a new kind of socialism for which there was no model.

To achieve its objective, the leadership was abolishing all vestiges of the past, such as educational institutions, money, cities, and the family.[31]

Among the losses suffered by the people of Cambodia were their schools, the means of exchange, the right to choose an urban dwelling, and the opportunity to enjoy the most sacred personal relationship the human race has contrived since it appeared on earth — the family.

The 1980 *Book of the Year*, reporting the events of the preceding year, provides the final touch. Now the Vietnamese army is in occupation of the country, an event described as follows: "On January 7, 1979, rebel guerrillas backed by Vietnam seized power in Phnom Penh and set up a People's Revolutionary Council headed by Heng Samrin. . . . Heng Samrin lost no time in announcing an eight-point program that pledged restoration of freedom to the people. This liberalization and the end of the Pol Pot regime, which had become known as one of the cruelest in modern times, seemed to mark a turn for the better in Cambodia. But political realities pointed otherwise. The fact that Pol Pot's ouster was the result of a Vietnamese invasion raised fears in Southeast Asia of an expansionist Hanoi."[32]

But the most significant fact, left like a corpse in the graveyard of Cambodian history, with no epitaph for comment, is in the statistical paragraph that opens each annual review. It reads: "Pop. (1979 est.): between 4.5 million and 5 million *according to official figures.*" (Emphasis added.) In 1975 the *Book of the Year* had reported the figure 7,190,000.

OUT OF THE SILENCE

It had taken years to penetrate the almost hermetic seal wrapped around Cambodia by the Communists. In 1975, Sydney Schanberg of the *New York Times* had seen the mass deportation of a million people from the city of Phnom Penh. He had watched men, women and children being marched through the streets after only minutes in which to prepare for the journey. In the last report out of Cambodia before the silence descended, he noted that no arrangements had been made to provision this second "long march" in the annals of Asian communism. There was no water, food, medication or shelter. He had faithfully reported the spectacle of hospital beds being pushed along the rutted highways by relatives who still clung to the outmoded "bourgeois" notions of family loyalty. That scene was replayed in every major city. Along the route, laggards were beaten back into line by the soldiers. Those too weary to continue were left to die at the roadside or, more mercifully, were shot in the presence of their relatives.

Schanberg's dispatches won him the Pulitzer Prize for international reporting in 1976. During the next few years he busied himself with an effort — which ultimately proved successful — to find a Cambodian aide named Dith Pran who had risked his own life to save Schanberg from Khmer

Rouge killers. But for months following the original *New York Times* revelation it was as if a hospital curtain had been drawn around the dying nation so that no one might see.

Like all efforts at genocide, this one too was irrational, but as Raymond Aron has said, while the goal may be irrational the madmen unfortunately practice an "instrumental rationality" that proves altogether too efficient. In Cambodia, the new regime moved directly towards massive physical geno-cide — the destruction of body and flesh — by methods that started with the annihilation of the health care professionals. Similarly, cultural genocide was perpetrated by closing the schools and condemning all educators, indeed all educated, to death in remote work-camps. The rationale was simple: to have healed the sick was evidence of service to the overthrown ruling class; to have taught in the school system was *ex post facto* a capital offense.

Nevertheless a few people in the Western world refused to remain silent. Leo Cherne, because of his work with Indochinese refugees, had come to know the facts fairly early in the postwar period. Together with a handful of others he attempted to arouse public opinion. Involved in public debates with apologists for the new regimes in Indochina, he found himself at first in a small minority. His letters to international agencies like the UN Commission on Human Rights brought no response other than an acknowledgment of their receipt. His articles, for example in the *Washington Star*, brought sharp rejoinders that a progressive revolution was being slandered or, in more subdued tones, that the writer was being misled by refugees who had a stake in misrepresenting the truth.

Outstanding among the critics was the well-known scholar in linguistics, Noam Chomsky of Massachusetts Institute of Technology. A long-standing critic of U.S. policy, he could see no evil in the behavior of those whose cause he had espoused in the Indochinese war. Sneering at Cherne's earlier predictions of a "bloody purge of the non-Communist leaders and intel-lectuals," Chomsky asserted that "executions numbered at most in thousands"[33] — thus raising the question: How many deaths make a blood-bath? In reality the deliberately planned deaths reached the millions. Not until after the Communist armies of Vietnam invaded Pol Pot's Communist Cambodia in January 1979 did the Khmer Rouge leader Khieu Samphan acknowledge that 2 million Cambodians were "missing," though he attrib-uted this to the Vietnamese while they credited him and his Pol Pot col-leagues with the deaths of 3 million compatriots. (Jack Anderson, the American columnist, has written that "Khieu Samphan, the titular head of state" in the Pol Pot regime, was "the reigning intellectual of the collective leadership." Says Anderson: "Vicious and violent, Khieu Samphan probably provided the ideological rationale for the slaughter of the inno-cents.")[34] Of Westerners like Cherne who wrote about the death toll, the M.I.T. expert in linguistics used these words: "To determine the credibility of those who transmit reports is a critical matter for anyone concerned to discover the truth, either about Cambodia or about the current phase of imperial ideology."35 As late as 1979 he was still seeing an imperialist plot in accounts of the Cambodian genocide: "The success of the Free Press in reconstructing the imperial ideology since the U.S. withdrawal from Indochina has been spectacular. . . . The system of brainwashing under freedom with mass media voluntary self-censorship in accord with the larger interest of the state, has worked brilliantly. The new propaganda line has been established by endless repetition of the Big Distortions."36

Leopold Labedz, the editor of the British publication *Survey*, has documented the activities of critics like Chomsky as part of a new *trahison des clercs*, a betrayal by intellectuals of the values that are the most precious possession of civilized societies.37 On the other hand, he also cites a long list of former sympathizers of the Southeast Asian revolution who have recoiled from the consequences of the Communist success in Cambodia. He reviews the evidence that became available as one result of the internecine warfare between the Vietnamese and Khmer Rouge Communists. He quotes Chris Mullin, reporting in the British left-wing journal *Tribune* on his visit to Cambodia:

Visitors to Phnom Penh these days [after the Vietnamese occupation] are taken on a gruesome little ritual tour of Khmer Rouge handiwork. The highlight is the Tuol Sleng prison (a converted high school) which has records listing over 16,000 inmates, of whom only five are said to have survived. . . . Of course, there is no need for the visitor to believe any of this — though it is graphic enough. Instead he or she can take a car along any of the roads out of Phnom Penh. Choose any road, no one will prevent you. Drive until you want to stop at a village, any village, and ask what happened in the Pol Pot time.

I drove one day to Kros, a village 19 kilometres along the road to Battambang. The village I chose at random had a population of around 2,000 before the coming of the Khmer Rouge. Today there are just 853, mostly women.38

All over the country similar relics of Khmer Rouge savagery were found. At Toule Bati, twelve miles from Phnom Penh, 129 mass graves were found containing a golgotha of 1,643 skulls. This had been the site of a teacher-training school in the days before the Communist victory.

Eventually writers who had themselves been eloquent opponents of the *ancien régime* began gradually to recognize that Cambodia had simply exchanged new monsters for old masters. For example, there was Jean Lacouture, who early in the Vietnam war had predicted that the Diem regime and its successors, even with U.S. support, could not survive if they failed to establish a united democratic society in South Vietnam. His sharp pen had stung military briefing officers relaying body counts; for example, he said the Americans considered any dead Vietnamese a Viet Cong. William

Shawcross, who had written a scathing book denouncing American policy in Cambodia during the war, declared in March 1980 that the country, five years after the Communist victory, was now "a society whose very sinews had been ripped out."[39] The French priest, Father François Ponchaud, who had come to Cambodia at age twenty-six and who was expelled by the Communists thirteen years later, also spoke up. He had denounced the American incursion into Cambodia during the war, pinning his hopes, albeit reluctantly, on the Khmer Rouge as the only answer to what he considered the exploitation by the Sihanouks and the Lon Nols.

Such observers were now chilled to the marrow by the massacre. They had been loath to believe that the ultimate fruit of the bloody war and the revolution they had sincerely tried to help could have the bitter taste of poison in the aftermath. At first there was disbelief by men like Father Ponchaud. In his book, *Cambodia: Year Zero*, he writes of a letter he received from a Cambodian friend in Paris recounting dread events. He told himself that he must try to understand before reaching any judgment: "There were two pitfalls to avoid: excessive mistrust and systematic criticism of the new regime, and blind infatuation with a revolution which many, like myself, had longed to see."[40] In his personal investigation of the facts recited by refugees he decided that he would disregard the reports of those who spoke French and therefore could be deemed to have been associated with the wealthier classes. Instead, "I was mainly interested in ordinary people, army privates, peasants and laborers, who could neither read nor write nor analyze what they had seen but whose illiterate memories could supply exact details."[41]

On every hand, however, the accounts were the same. Father Ponchaud was compelled to write:

In the beginning I was not opposed to the Khmer revolution: having lived with the Cambodian peasants from 1965 to 1970, I was painfully aware of their exploitation at the hands of the administration under the corrupt Sihanouk regime. From 1970 to 1975 I shared the lives of the poor in the suburbs of Phnom Penh under the Lon Nol regime. From the tens of thousands of refugees who fled the "liberated" zones in 1973, I learned of a harshness of the revolutionary regime, but I regarded it as a transitory necessity imposed by the war. So I welcomed the revolutionaries' victory as the only possible means of bringing Cambodia out of its misery. But after making a careful and full study of the broadcasts of Radio Phnom Penh and the refugees' testimony relating to 1975 and 1976, I was compelled to conclude, against my will, that the Khmer revolution is irrefutably the bloodiest of our century.[42]

In addition, he disposed of the argument that points to French colonialism and the role of America in Indochina as justification for the cruelty of the Cambodian Communists toward their own people. "But accusing foreigners," he writes, "cannot acquit the present leaders of Kampuchea: their inflexible ideology has led them to invent a radically new kind of man in a radically new society. A fastinating revolution for all who aspire to a new social order. A terrifying one for all who have any respect for human beings."[43]

ESCAPE HATCH INTO THAILAND

A major listening post from which one could hear the cry of the Cambodians was the border town of Aranyaprathet in Thailand. The city itself is little more than two main streets, with ancillary alleys. At eight in the morning a loudspeaker summons all the king's subjects to stand at attention as the national anthem is played. The Buddhist monks, with cups extended, are soon begging for their daily ration of rice. The marketplace comes alive as the slender women in multicolored sarongs begin their shopping. Scarcely two miles away, across a small bridge, is Poipet, the nearest Cambodian town. But few of the refugees who ultimately arrive in Aranya come across the bridge. The highways are patrolled by menacing men, and often children in their early teens bearing arms. The surrounding jungles provide safer passage.

The visitor finds the refugee camps here, like others throughout the world, a scene of utter congestion. Along with the huts whose exterior walls are woven of palm fronds are several long wooden buildings with roofs of corrugated iron. Each family has its "cell" in these structures and enjoys some sense of privacy. In front are wooden pallets, narrow decks on which the residents squat, some of them already preparing their evening meal, cooking on small charcoal braziers a portion of rice, fish, or frogs. (Wherever there is a pond in a refugee camp, you can see women and children frog-hunting.)

Walking down a half-mile of narrow lane transformed by the monsoon season into a river of mud that sucks at your feet, you come to a longhouse inhabited exclusively by young men. Some of them are naked to the waist, casually displaying ornate tattooing on their brown skins. You are told that these are "freedom fighters" who cross the border after dark to harass the Pol Pot government (that has not yet been attacked by the Vietnamese). Your informant explains that such guerrilla activities are tolerated by the Bangkok government which finds that they provide useful intelligence — particularly in view of the frequent Khmer Rouge raids on Thai villages and the kidnapping of villagers who are resisting local Communist insurgents.

But most of the refugee population remain aloof from insurgent activities. They have had enough of violence. Here, as at Nong Khai, the visitor is struck by the entrepreneurial self-help spirit of the people. Little businesses are in operation. Fruit, vegetables, cooked foods and sundries are hawked. A group of craftsmen have picked a likely spot for their workshops and are carving *apsaras*, the undulant figures of temple dancing-girls, out of soapstone. A fairly large building, at one point, carries a sign in English that reads "Technical Center"—a facility for the teaching of new skills that the refugees will take with them to whatever place of resettlement awaits them. A former officer in the Lon Nol army and another refugee took the initiative and set up the center to provide training in electronic communications, welding, weaving and so on. Blackboards in some rooms display French and English writing that indicates language study.

In one of these instruction rooms, you sit down with a man named Span On, a former teacher in Cambodia. It is hard for the inexperienced occidental to guess the age of Asians, but despite his youthfulness you can assume that he is middle-aged. During the war, he had had no contact with the American forces; nevertheless he was condemned by the Khmer Rouge because, as a schoolteacher, he had been employed by the state and was therefore automatically an *ancien fonctionnaire*. All of the schools had been closed immediately after the Communist victory; education was the enemy that stood in the way of creating the new man on which the state was to be built. Immediately after the Khmer Rouge troops arrived, he was deported from his home to a place twenty or thirty kilometres away. His wife was sent elsewhere, in line with the new policy of separating families. He never saw her again. Years later, here in the Aranyaprathet camp, he received word that his wife and children had all been executed.

In the "new economic zone" to which he had been transported, he was set to work clearing a place in the forest. Since no housing had been provided, he and his comrades had to construct their own crude huts out of jungle detritus. Traditionally, the work of cutting and hauling away trees has been done by water buffalo; none were available here, and each man, as he put it, had to be his own buffalo. As had become the standard in Cambodia, he worked from six in the morning until dark, and sometimes, along with the others, he was forced to continue working until well into the night.

This servitude was accompanied by frequent beatings for the slightest infraction of rules, and often for no reason other than the desire to keep the victims cowed. Consistently refugees have reported a policy of murder by bludgeoning in order to save ammunition. The rationale for this irrational plague of killing is provided in Sydney Schanberg's description of the experiences of his aide Dith Pran in these words: "Life was totally controlled and the Khmer Rouge did not need a good reason to kill someone; the slightest excuse would do, —a boy and girl holding hands, an unauthorized break from work. 'Anyone they didn't like, they would accuse of being a teacher or a student or a former Lon Nol soldier, and that was the end.'"[44]

The compensation for forced labor was a starvation diet. Even before famine spread like a disease across the nation, the deportees were being systematically starved. Eventually, the whole productive system of the country collapsed under the impact of the economic disruption and the human destruction wrought by the regime. The population that still remained in the villages suffered stark hunger. To avoid identification as an "intellectual," with its inevitable consequence, Dith Pran had fled to the village of Dam Dek, where he remained for two and a half years before he made his escape to Thailand. Schanberg writes: "In Dam Dek, the rice ration was eventually reduced to one spoonful per person per day. The villagers, desperate, ate snails, snakes, insects, rats, scorpions, tree bark, leaves, flower blossoms, the trunk of banana plants; sometimes they sucked the skin of a water buffalo. Reports reached Pran's village that to the west the famine was even more severe and that some people were digging up the bodies of the newly executed and cooking the flesh."[45]

MEDICAL CARE

Refugees who reached the safety of Thailand gave the same accounts no matter what region of Kampuchea they had fled. Many bore the marks left by years of suffering. The visitor could readily see the additional scars left by the jungle route to freedom. One stands at the door of the hospital in Aranyaprathet, funded in part by the International Rescue Committee and staffed with personnel provided by the French organization, *Médecins sans Frontières*. Greeting new arrivals are Dr. Pascal Griletti-Bosviel and his wife, Yvonne, a nurse, who head the team. Working with them is IRC's Marthe Arsenault, a nurse originally from Quebec who has spent many years of her life in Indochina. Her home, in one of the dusty streets of Aranya, is a veritable warehouse storing medications and hospital supplies. She speaks not of her patients but of her "children."

Eighty percent of those in the hospital, says Dr. Griletti-Bosviel, or Dr. Pascal as you soon begin to address him, have been smitten by a new and especially dangerous strain of malaria that attacks the brain. As you walk between the cots and stop to talk with the patients, you learn that at least a dozen have crossed the border within the past week and some are still recovering from bullet wounds. One of them had been shot in the cheek, as he ran gasping from the Khmer Rouge patrol; the bullet emerged through his open mouth. Asked about the problems confronting the hospital, Dr. Pascal responds that there is a serious insufficiency of laboratory equipment and facilities.

Increasingly IRC took on the responsibility among American agencies for filling the void in refugee health care. Its medical activity in Thailand had begun in 1976. By December 1979 it was maintaining a staff of sixty-five doctors, nurses and paramedics, supported by an even larger number of refugees trained on the job, to serve the Cambodians. By April 1980 the number of IRC medical personnel had risen to 105.

This was accomplished in part through an ingenious program worked out with the New York Hospital-Cornell Medical Center which provided "released time" to personnel willing to serve in Thailand. Based on the use of rotating teams expected to stay two to six months in the camps and on the borders, the volunteers would staff field hospitals, train the refugees in first aid and medical support activities, and on returning would help orient the next group. The first team consisted of seventeen volunteers—two faculty members in Cornell's Departments of International Medicine and Public Health, four senior residents, five fourth-year medical students, and six nurses. The Medical Center had agreed to continue the compensation of the faculty members and residents; since the nurses had to take leaves of absence, they received stipends of $1,000 per month. Supplies were contributed by two American pharmaceutical houses.

Such groups were bolstered by young American medical students who, at their own expense and on their own time, went to the Cambodian border where they offered their services to IRC teams. By now some 300,000 Cambodians were believed to be in the area. Some of the volunteers even crossed the boundary line to provide assistance to the sick and wounded, often at personal risk from the Khmer Rouge, Vietnamese troops and the freebooters who infested the area. Typical of the situations encountered in the refugee hospitals was this letter from a volunteer serving with IRC in the Khao I Dang pediatric ward:

The cases come every day. Most get better but too many die. For those who get well, there is great joy all around, playing and joking and happy scenes of departure when they leave. You hope it will be those that will stay in your memory, but it is the ones that break your heart that stay the most vivid. Like the grandfather who buried all but one of his children and grandchildren in Cambodia, and brought in his last sick grandson. A day later, the little child just faded away. Then a teenage girl carried in her little brother stricken with meningitis. As we tried to save him through the night, she stood close by, touching him, sponging him off and weeping. When he died, she quietly left, leaving her brother on the floor wrapped in an old blanket.

XV

In Search of Shelter

The Indochinese disaster following the Communist victory in Vietnam, Laos and Cambodia was soon compounded by the struggle between Soviet and Sino-Communism. Historians will need years, perhaps decades, to unravel all of the threads woven into the shroud that now envelops much of Southeast Asia. The falling out among the self-styled Marxist nations led the pro-Russian Vietnamese to cross the borders of Cambodia. For its own esoteric reasons, the Khmer Rouge had identified with Red China. Ironically, the latter had already begun to make overtures, even before Mao's death, toward the United States, demonstrating that geopolitics and tribal interest are more powerful than ideology. And as the storms of politics and nationalism roared through Asia, the smaller nations shivered in the wind.

Among the tragic evidences of man's continuing inhumanity to man was the ambivalent response of the neighboring non-Communist countries. Thailand and Malaysia, in particular, soon found themselves bearing a disproportionate share of the refugee burden. Most unenviable was the position of Thailand, whose common borders with the new Communist countries stretch across more than 1,500 miles. After January 1979, Bangkok's fears mounted as Vietnamese troops took Phnom Penh. An army of occupation numbering 200,000 now faced a Thai army that could hardly match the strongest military power in Southeast Asia, a country that had already defeated the United States in a protracted war and then had followed up by repulsing an attack from Red China in 1978.

Malaysia too, separated by less than 600 miles of water, could feel the hot breath of Vietnamese expansionism. Indeed, all the members of the Association of Southeast Asian Nations (ASEAN), including also Indonesia, the Philippines and Singapore, watched with consternation as the refugees became their problem. Thailand and Malaysia found themselves carrying the heaviest load. Tenuous economic structures were being asked to provide refuge. Local poverty-stricken populations, against a centuries-old background of racial disdain, met the newcomers with hostility. While the world clucked over the fate of the homeless, few nations flung open their doors. Thailand and Malaysia soon became convinced that they would be permanently saddled with an alien population they could not support and did not like. More than half a million Indochinese were on the move. The West, while denouncing the brutality of the Communist regimes that had driven these people onto the high seas and into the border jungles, was apparently unwilling or unable to relieve the pressure on the countries of first asylum. *The Economist*, looking on from London, had summarized the picture in these terms:

Shares have been conspicuously unequal up to now. Some countries with wide open spaces and mixed populations have refused to take a single refugee. The worst examples include Brazil, Venezuela, Colombia, Argentina and Uruguay. Canada and New Zealand have helped, but not enough. Germany's contribution is out of line with its resources. Sweden and Japan have given money, but closed their doors. As judges even of their own self-interest, these countries are foolish to be so uncharitable; most people enterprising and determined enough to risk their lives on the high seas are likely to make good citizens. Britain can testify that refugees from tyrannies tend to enrich, not impoverish, their host societies. The argument that Vietnam is America's problem or China's or Russia's will not wash. It is every decent human's problem, and it will not be wished away.[1]

Fairly early after the tidal wave had struck the shores of Thailand and Malaysia it became clear that the breaking point was near. Observers on the scene, in touch with public opinion and officialdom in these countries, feared that the time would come when the refugees would be pushed back across the border if they were land people like the Cambodians and Laotians or pushed out to sea if they were boat people like the Vietnamese. Organizations concerned about refugees knew that a determined effort would have to be made to head off, if possible, or to postpone if it was not, the day when another stain would blot the history of the twentieth century. If that time came, the onus would fall on all who had stood idly by—not just on the overburdened Thais and Malays.

THE "PROCESSING" PROCEDURE

The challenge was to move as many of the refugees as possible to permanent places of resettlement. In this respect, it was reasonable for the world to place a major responsibility on the United States both because of its recent and continuing role as a Pacific power and because of its greater resources. In addition to providing help on the scene, Americans had a duty to speed up the process of resettlement.

The International Rescue Committee and the other American voluntary agencies recognized that this was a top priority item. In line with their policy of dividing responsibilities to avoid waste and duplication of effort,

it was agreed that IRC would provide the manpower to facilitate the processing of immigration papers on behalf of the refugees in the boat and land
camps. Some seventy IRC staff members, operating out of Bangkok, moved
into the camps, sometimes staying for weeks at a time, to help the refugees
register and qualify for resettlement in the United States and other countries
of ultimate asylum.

Under the regulations of the Immigration and Naturalization Service of
the U.S. Department of Justice, a point system of priorities determined who
would be permitted to enter the country.[2] Four categories, in order of their
priority, had been set up:

Category I — applicants seeking reunification with family members in the
United States.

Category II — refugees who had been employed by the United States
during the war.

Category III — those who had given military service for their own government during the war.

Category IV — general humanitarian reasons.

To be in "Cat I" is the most desirable status since the fact that close relatives are already in the United States is the surest ticket to admission. But
one consequence of this system of priorities is that the criteria are not
always consistent with human need. To be sure, there is logic and moral
validity in furthering family reunification and in favoring those who
worked with the United States during the war. But Cambodians complain
that sharp inequities have resulted simply because few of them have
relatives in America. One survey shows that of the Indochinese admitted to
this country, 78 percent are Vietnamese, 17 percent Laotians, and only 5
percent Cambodians.[3] American presidents, confronted with other inequities that they have not been able to resolve, have been heard to say that "life
is unfair." Nowhere is this more evident than in the fate of the people swept
from their homes by the political storms of the twentieth century.

Those who are fortunate enough ultimately to find refuge in the United
States are likely to have been in touch, somewhere along the line, with an
IRC representative. On first arriving in Thailand, for example, the refugee
would be considered an "illegal immigrant" and would be taken into custody
by the Thai police. Since the nearest jail was usually filled to overflowing
with refugees, he would be sent to a detention center to be certified as a
refugee.

In 1978 the author visited the police station at Sri Chiang Mai in the north
of Thailand where two large cells were packed with squatting men, their
haunches pressed against each other. They stared expressionlessly from
behind the bars. One of the refugees was pointed out as having come the
greatest distance — from Kwantung in China — but the others could not con-
verse with him because of the language barrier. Even though they were
being held as prisoners they were not being treated unkindly: one of them

returned to the cell from taking a shower, and it was evident that the door was not even locked. On the story above, whole families were being lodged, each assigned a section on the open floor of the large room or a few square feet in a corridor. Here, IRC's Dr. Garcia, on a field visit, was putting her stethoscope to the chest of a Laotian suffering from pneumonia. A pregnant woman in her eighth month was also being questioned about her health and was reassured that when her time came she would be removed to the local hospital.

But a grimmer picture could be seen in other parts of the country. Word had reached Bangkok that some 400 Cambodians had arrived through the jungles, singly and in small groups, and that the jail in Thapraya was not large enough to hold them. They had been put out in a field near the police station, with no shelter whatsoever, even though the rainy season was on. So far, even representatives of the United Nations High Commissioner for Refugees had been denied permission to visit, but a small team of IRC staff led by Nancy McLaren, then head of IRC's medical program in Thailand, had already wheedled their entry. A supply of blankets was on the way, but at the time of our visit some of the refugees were huddling on the wet ground under the few available trees. Fortunately, the porch of the police station was built on stilts, and the ten women and children in this group of 400 had been given shelter under it. Nearby a few vehicles were parked; lying under them were men who thus found meager protection from the pelting rain. Mounted on poles some 200 yards from the building was a corrugated roof, under which several score of the refugees squatted. The wind beat in on them from the open sides, drenching the remnants of clothing still left on their backs after the hike through the jungle. That corrugated roof, said the police chief pressuring for assistance, had been lent by nearby villagers but would have to be returned soon. He even asked for rolls of barbed wire — "to protect the Cambodians from any who might want to attack them."

The refugees were easily recognized: all of them — men, women and children — had had their heads completely shaved, ostensibly a matter of hygiene but also, as some suggested, an ingenious indicia of their status. If they attempted to slip by the police and lose themselves among the people, they could be readily spotted. But another method of identification was at hand — the gray, hollow faces. "The look of Auschwitz," said one of the IRC workers.

In the detention phase of the processing, the purpose of the Thai government was to establish that the individuals were genuine refugees and not Communist infiltrators planted by their governments. Once their bona fides had been established they could be registered officially as refugees and could then be transferred to one of the more than fifteen camps in Thailand. There the UN High Commissioner would provide sustenance, as IRC staff undertook the laborious work of interviewing each individual or family group to ascertain the appropriate category. If there were reasonable hopes of resettlement in the United States, IRC would then prepare the papers for submission to the Immigration and Naturalization Service.

Since escape from their homeland was hazardous at best, the refugees rarely possessed all of the papers they were likely to need to establish eligibility. Indeed, the mere possession of the kind of documentation that proved the holder had kinsmen in the United States, or had cooperated with the Americans or his own government in fighting the Communists, was itself a hazard. In many cases those who had survived pirate raids on the high seas or who had scrambled past patrols in the forests had lost their possessions. Nevertheless, by using trustworthy Vietnamese, Laotian and Cambodian experts it was possible to confirm or disprove allegations made during the interviews. A large volume of data had been assembled against which assertions could be checked.

At the outset, in a procedure that IRC staff called "card writing," essential personal information was recorded: the family tree; the names of all living relatives and their whereabouts if known; whether any had died; and the names and addresses, if available, of relatives already in the United States. Frequently, there were "add-ons" — the inclusion in the family processing of relatives who arrived later at the camp. If the refugee claimed military service or employment with a U.S. agency during the war, he would be subjected to a second interview. As word of the criteria spread among the refugees, they did not hesitate to exaggerate their own identification with the Americans or their service with their own army. In the interest of assuring that those with major claims did receive priority, interviewers frequently pressed hard in virtual cross-examinations, demanding, for example, the name of the American under whom the refugee claimed to have worked. Subsequent checking would then determine whether there had indeed been such an American officer or official at the stated place and time.

A typical case, as recounted by a refugee in the Nong Khai camp, elicits the simple facts that summarize the life of a Laotian family caught in the grip of history. The interviewee is a fifty-seven-year-old woman, occupation housewife. Her husband is dead. She has had six children. Two daughters accompany her, aged twenty-four and seventeen. She knows that two of the children are dead. The whereabouts of the other two are unknown. Of the two daughters with her, one is married but the husband is in a Laotian prison because he had supported the anti-Communist government. Three of her children have reached Thailand.

ADDRESSING PUBLIC OPINION

Once the Immigration and Naturalization Service of the United States approved an individual or family for resettlement, sponsors had to be found. Every voluntary agency engaged in refugee assistance worked feverishly to locate groups—frequently churches and synagogues, often local community leaders who rallied others—that would take responsibility for individuals or families. By the end of 1977, IRC alone had committed itself to resettle 24,000 Indochinese, and in 1978, an additional 4,000. Depending on government policy in increasing the number of paroles granted to refugees to permit their entry outside of immigration quotas, IRC prepared in 1979 to handle another 8,000.

But the pace of admissions was altogether too slow to give Thailand and Malaysia a sense that the refugees would be moving on to other places of refuge better able to receive them. Under then existing regulations, American policy permitted the entry of only 17,000 a year. That just about equaled the number of refugees who were arriving in Thailand in *one month* during 1978. Increasingly, there was talk that Thailand and Malaysia would shut the gates. Even without action by the authorities in Bangkok and Kuala Lumpur, local communities were already taking matters into their own hands. Leaky boats about to land were being pushed back into the surf, and in a number of horrifying scenes caught by newspaper photographers and television cameramen the resulting drownings were recorded visually for the archives of inhumanity.

The International Rescue Committee undertook to awaken American public opinion to the urgency of immediate assistance and prompt liberalization of the country's immigration policy. In December 1977, IRC leaders organized the Citizens Commission on Indochinese Refugees, headed by Leo Cherne and William J. Casey. The latter had worked with General Donovan in the Office of Strategic Services during World War II, had been chairman of the Securities and Exchange Commission, and later, in the Reagan administration, head of the Central Intelligence Agency. Since the 1950s, he had been an active member of IRC's Board of Directors. After serving as chairman of its executive committee, he was elected president of IRC, but his term of office was interrupted by his call to Washington to assume the post of Under Secretary of State for Economic Affairs.

In the Citizens Commission, Cherne and Casey as cochairmen presided over a cross-section of the major political, cultural and religious leaders of the nations concerned with the fate of the Indochinese. Their impact on government and the media was due in great part to the breadth of representation: Monsignor John Ahern, Director of Social Development of the Catholic Archdiocese of New York; Professor Kenneth Cauthen of the Colgate Rochester Divinity School; Rabbi Marc H. Tanenbaum, Director of Interreligious Affairs of the American Jewish Committee; James Michener, the author; John Richardson, Jr., President of Freedom House and former Assistant Secretary of State for Educational and Cultural Affairs; Thelma Richardson, who had led a notable battle for civil rights; Bayard Rustin, a leader in the black community, president of the A. Philip Randolph Institute and chairman of Social Democrats, U.S.A.; Cecil B. Lyon, former diplomat, who for many years had directed IRC planning and programs in critical situations; Stephen Young, a member of the New York Bar Association's Commission on International Human Rights, subsequently a dean in the Harvard Law School, fluent in Vietnamese and Thai; and Louis A. Wiesner and Robert De Vecchi of the IRC staff, both former foreign service officers. Because of other pressing commitments, Albert Shanker, president of the American Federation of Teachers, Mrs. Lawrence Copley Thaw of the IRC Board of Directors and a veteran worker in many refugee camps, Warren Meeker of the Research Institute of America and IRC Deputy Director Alton Kastner, were unable to join the mission on its initial journey in 1978 but participated in the planning, follow-up activities and later missions. Shanker, on his own, made a subsequent visit to the camps and played an important part in rallying the continuing support of the American Federation of Labor-Congress of Industrial Organizations.

In the fact-gathering phase, the Commission split up into two groups. One, led by Cherne, headed for the camps in Thailand; the other, under Casey's leadership, left for the "islands" — Indonesia, the Philippines, and Taiwan. The latter team was to visit Malaysia too, but at the last moment the government announced that as a Moslem country it would receive the delegation only if Rabbi Tanenbaum were not included. The members voted unanimously not to accept the terms and went on to Indonesia, also a Moslem country, which welcomed them without raising any religious issue. Elsewhere the Commission encountered religion in another form, an experience that Cherne has described in these words:

The most moving episode for a number of us in the course of the trip took place in the largest of these camps at Nong Khai. Several thousand of the Laotian refugees and their Buddhist leader conducted a large ceremony in the community hall which had been constructed for all of their group purposes. A huge offering symbolizing life in the form of a cluster of fruits, vegetables, flowers and religious amulets was the centerpiece. The members of the Commission were asked to gather in front of the offering as the Buddhist priest conferred upon us the honor reserved for "holy men." It is nearly impossible to describe the reverence on the faces of these people who were dressed in their native costumes, in ages ranging from childhood to the most elderly, taking their turn to tie a white string made of hand-woven pure cotton around our wrists. After the knot was tied, they would rub a hand over our arm or face. It was explained to us that the knot symbolized their reverence and the touching was for the purpose of deriving from the contact some of our "holiness."*

---

*John Everingham, an Australian journalist who swam the Mekong from Nong Khai with scuba gear to rescue a young woman, Keo, now his wife, offers a different version of the significance that the Hmongs attribute to the strings. Describing the farewells as one such family leaves the refugee camp for the United States, he writes: "Before the family departs, the incantations of a shaman entice spirits (the Hmongs believe each person has three) to return and protect the travelers. Friends crowd round to tie strings around the ... wrists, symbolically confining those protective spirits inside their bodies." (John Everingham, "One Family's Odyssey to America," *National Geographic* 157 (May 1980): 649.)

Tradition required that except as the strings fell off by themselves, we were not to remove them for 72 hours. I believe Bob DeVecchi is still wearing a couple of his. I finally cut mine off in Washington a week later when in the succession of conferences with Brzezinski, Mondale, Vance, and the three hours of testimony before the House Subcommittee on Immigration, Citizenship and International Law, it became apparent that my wrists appeared to be wrapped in bandages which had now become quite dirty and might even suggest that I had slit my wrists. Frankly, I think I would have if our mission had failed.[4]

The ceremony described by Cherne was brought to an intensely emotional conclusion when Bayard Rustin "got up and said simply that he would like to sing two not very well-known freedom songs which were sung by his people in their darker times. Bayard has a magnificent voice. He once sang with the Paul Robeson group when both were young. I can assure you that his songs are still reverberating in Nong Khai. There were no ethnic distinctions among the tears they produced."[5]

The mission proved to be an extraordinary success — in two ways. Of immediate significance was the reaction of the Thai government. Some months after the Commission's visit the author of this book was told by public officials in Bangkok that the coming of the Commission gave the authorities the first substantial reason for believing that Thailand would not be left alone to carry the burden. The mere knowledge that American public opinion would now hear powerful voices calling for assistance to the beleaguered countries of first asylum had given reassurance that the borders would not be closed by decree.

Commission members Casey, Lyon and Wiesner had visited the Philippines, Taiwan, Macao and Korea in the hope that temporary holding centers could be established in those countries to relieve the pressure on Thailand and Malaysia. These efforts were to bear some fruit later, especially in the Philippines. Warren Meeker, on a follow-up mission to Taipei a few weeks later, succeeded in getting the Republic of China to take some steps. Here 17 million people, many of them refugees from the mainland, were already crowded into 36,000 square miles, resulting in a population density of 464 persons per square kilometre, second only to Bangladesh among nations and, of course, Hong Kong. Taiwan nevertheless agreed to set up a special reception center for a thousand Indochinese in addition to the 10,000 it had taken previously, and to contribute half a million dollars to IRC's Asian activities.

Now world opinion was beginning to respond. Back home in the United States the Commission found a receptive audience for its recommendations. Before any of its members had a chance to recover from jet lag and from their strenuous travel to the refugee camps, they were already at work reaching the nation's centers of influence. Rustin and Cherne plunged immediately into a session with the leaders of the AFL-CIO, who happened to be holding an executive committee meeting in Florida. At the insistence of government officials, the whole Commission was convened in Washington for discussions with State Department representatives, congressmen, senators, Vice-President Mondale, National Security Adviser Zbigniew Brzezinski, and the newly designated United Nations High Commissioner for Refugees, former Prime Minister Poul Hartling of Denmark, whose fortuitous visit made it possible for the Commission to give a working luncheon in his honor with the cooperation of the State Department.

QUESTIONS AND ANSWERS

The full Commission appeared before the House Judiciary Committee, which has jurisdiction over immigration. There a striking exchange took place that deserves a better fate than to be buried in the minutes of a congressional hearing. Accurately reflecting the feelings of their constituents, the congressmen were asking the questions that troubled thoughtful people across the country: Hasn't the United States done enough already? What are other countries doing? If we admit these refugees, will we not encourage even more to come? If we open the gates wider, will not other countries feel they can afford to do less? How can we admit Southeast Asians when we are rejecting wetbacks from Mexico? Repeatedly, the members of the Commission were pressed by committee members: What assurances can you give that other countries will accept a proportionate share of the resettlement burden?

Monsignor John Ahern, usually a reserved and quiet man, suddenly raised his hand and asked Chairman Joshua Eilberg for permission to speak. The effect of the ensuing dialogue, joined later by Bayard Rustin, was like a discharge of lightning that clears the air. Reproduced from the stenographic record, this was the exchange:

Msgr. Ahern. I find that the question which has been raised a number of times, what other countries will do, is acutely embarrassing, first because the Commission as such can offer hopes, not guarantees.

Secondly, it ignores a substantial current history. On Monday I interviewed a gentleman who is a Ugandan refugee in Kenya, one of 60,000. I am not aware that Kenya asked us how many we would take before they took any.

Finally, the measure of what we do is not what others do, but what we are able to do. If we get into the situation in which we are waiting for others, it is almost the Kitty Genovese syndrome: who is going to call the police first, and the lady dies anyway.

There was silence. Then:

Mr. Rustin. Mr. Chairman, I would like to say a word on this, if I may.

Mr. Eilberg. Mr. Rustin, of course.

Mr. Rustin. One of the fundamental political questions I hope will not be obscured in this debate is: if there are any people who should not want more refugees in this country it is, on the one hand, the trade union movement and, on the other hand, minority groups in this country which have in our ghettos — and I am not speaking merely of blacks, but poor whites, Mexican-Americans, and others, 30, 40, 50 percent, and some experts say 60 percent, unemployment.

I would like to point out three simple facts and have done.

It is not the trade union movement which is raising these questions. On the one hand, George Meany has adopted through his executive council our recommendations.

On the fourth of this month blacks — the 15 so-called outstanding spokesmen for the black community — are meeting in Atlanta. A statement has been prepared for them which essentially says, Let us not obscure the issue of American humanity.

There are those in our community — the black community I speak of exclusively, now — who are arguing we must not have another refugee come. We have such unemployment. The fact of the matter I submit to you, Mr. Chairman: if America can be cruel enough not to admit into this country people who, if they are sent elsewhere will be shot, that same cruelty will make it impossible for . . . us Americans to deal with the problems in our ghettos and for our poor.

This is a moral question in which we cannot turn our backs on the only thing I have been able to defend in America — despite segregation, mistreatment. . . .

One final point: if anybody in this room thinks that by letting any of these people in they are taking jobs away from Americans who need them, they have not come to grips with one of the most serious problems we face in unemployment, and that is the tremendous distance between the aspirations of American poor, blacks first, and their ability to perform. Most Americans here will not, who need it, take the ill-paying jobs and dirty work that many of these refugees will take as they start the upward path to mobility, as all of us in the past, wherever we came from, had to take.

I am addressing myself only to the political and moral question that if blacks and workers are taking this affectionate attitude, what ought not other Americans do?

Mr. Eilberg. Thank you, Mr. Rustin. Mr. [Hamilton] Fish?

Mr. Fish. Father Ahern and Mr. Rustin, you have done a great service to this Committee.

I think the Father alluded to the fact that the question had come up numerous times but we were waiting for the answer that we finally got from you two, and this will be of enormous help as a matter of the public record and in the course of any debate on legislation of the House.[6]

Rustin did not content himself with words spoken before a congressional committee. He promptly secured the signatures of eighty-five leading American blacks in support of the Commission's recommendations. They included Vernon Jordan of the Urban League; Benjamin Hooks of the National Association for the Advancement of Colored People; Julian Bond of Georgia; Rev. Ralph Abernathy, who succeeded Martin Luther King as head of the Southern Christian Leadership Conference; Lionel Hampton, the musician; Jesse Jackson of PUSH; Clarence Mitchell of the NAACP; A. Philip Randolph, the pioneer black unionist; Roy Wilkins, former executive director of the NAACP; Percy Sutton, former president of the City Council of New York; Coretta Scott King; Dr. Martin Luther King, Sr. – and virtually every black mayor in the United States.

Major civic organizations hastened to support the Commission's recommendations. The Anti-Defamation League of B'nai B'rith, the National Council of Jewish Women, and the National Council of Voluntary Agencies joined with other national groups in approving the findings of the Commission. Columnists added their voices. Individuals like James Michener sent personal appeals to the President. George Meany, in the closing year of his presidency of the AFL-CIO and virtually on the eve of his death, sent hand-delivered messages to both the President and the Secretary of State urging that the Commission's recommendations be implemented as national policy.

A PROGRAM FOR AMERICA

It would be difficult to find another occasion when a group of private citizens had so profound and prompt an effect on national policy. Within a month after the Commission had brought back its findings to America the White House began to take steps to effectuate a new refugee program for the United States. Despite the domestic problems in a period of inflation and unemployment, there was general agreement in the country that the government could do more than it had already done, and that Americans as individuals could contribute more to relief agencies working in the field.

This was the initial success of the Commission. But its most significant contribution was its impact on permanent policy. The specifics of its program proved eminently practical and were speedily initiated by President Carter with no opposition from any quarter. The Commission had called for the adoption of "a coherent and generous policy for the admission of Indochinese refugees over the long range." Previously, a top limit of 17,000 had been set on refugee admissions per year; now the number was raised to 25,000, with 20,000 to come from Thailand. Later the figure was increased to 40,000, and then to 50,000. Emergency provisions in existing legislation permitted the government to admit additional numbers under the "parole" powers given to the Attorney General. Though there had been controversy over whether this provision permitted action only in behalf of individual hardship cases or was applicable to whole groups, both Republican and Democratic administrations in the White House had interpreted it to allow en masse admissions.

In May 1978, two months after the Commission's return, Vice-President Mondale went to Bangkok where he announced that the United States was providing $2 million to work up a plan for resettlement and would lead an effort among the industrialized Western nations and their allies to raise "tens of millions of dollars" to fund the resettlement process. The long-range objective was described by President Carter in a "town meeting" in Bardstown, Kentucky, when he recalled his answer to a young woman who "said she didn't think we should take in any refugees because it was too much of a burden on the American people." President Carter, in answering a question on the same subject, said: "But let me repeat very briefly what I told her: There is a total of about 220,000 Vietnam refugees that we're going to take into our country. These were our allies and friends during the war. They fought alongside us; their lives were in danger. That's one refugee for every thousand Americans. It's not too heavy a burden for America to bear. In addition to that, this is a nation of refugees."[7]

In June 1979, while Congress studied new legislation introduced by Senator Edward M. Kennedy, the President announced that the monthly quota of 7,000 Indochinese would be doubled. In addition, he revealed that the current expenditure on the refugee program, about $200 million, would be increased by another $150 million. Joining with the chief executives of Japan, Canada, Italy, France, West Germany and Britain, he called upon Secretary General Kurt Waldheim of the United Nations to assemble an international conference on the events in Indochina.

The prime result was the enactment of the Refugee Act of 1980, which authorized the routine admission of 50,000 refugees a year—a sizable increase from the previous figure of 17,000. In addition, the President was given authority to meet special contingencies by admitting an additional number after consultation with Congress. The effort of the Citizens Commission on Indochinese Refugees to achieve a more "coherent and generous policy" had borne fruit.

The legislation also reflected a concern expressed by the Commission in its recommendations—the importance of broadening the definition of the term refugee. The Commission report had argued:

The suggested distinction between "economic" and "political" refugees from Indochina is spurious, invidious, and often used quite consciously to relieve any who would normally assist political refugees from feeling any obligation toward the assorted "economic refugees." The ability to make such a classification has even, in violation of the Universal Declaration on Human Rights, been used as justification of forcible repatriation of refugees in some instances.

Reorganization of economic life in all three of the Indochinese countries has been massive and harsh. The consequences have been nearly universal. These governmental measures can be understood only as part of an integrated effort to reorient the entire life, culture and politics of those peoples. By identifying as enemies of the State all whose lives have been based on private property, freedom of expression, or a different allegiance of philosophy, these regimes endanger a multitude if not most of their subjects. The very act of fleeing seals the fate of any who might otherwise have escaped persecution. Few if any would run the terrible risks of escaping to face possible indefinite stay in refugee camps or rejection by country after country, merely because their balance sheets were unsatisfactory.[8]

As Cherne hastened to point out on releasing the recommendations, this concern went beyond the issues in the Far East. "While the Commission's work sharply focused its urgency and efforts on the refugees from Indochina," he said, "the results already brighten the prospects for continued haven in the U.S. for those who flee dictatorships in Latin America, the Soviet Union and wherever else the most elemental human rights remain denied."[9] His organization, the IRC, had long been involved in the effort to win sanctuary for Haitians fleeing the oppression of the Duvalier regime. The Refugee Act of 1980, which was introduced as S. 2751 a month after the return of the Commission from its investigation, took cognizance of the problem. Addressing the Senate, Edward Kennedy, one of the bill's sponsors, said: "In contrast to the definition in the present law, which only recognizes the plight of homeless people from Communist areas and certain countries in the Middle East, the proposed definition recognizes the plight of homeless people in all parts of the world."[10]

Throughout its report the Commission emphasized that the example of the United States would be decisive in influencing the behavior of other nations — those bordering on Vietnam, Laos and Cambodia, as well as those on other continents. Having taken a more generous stance itself, as urged by the Commission, the U.S. could now take the lead in worldwide discussions. The meeting convened by the UN in Geneva resulted in other nations increasing their commitments and provided a forum in which pressure could be exerted on Vietnam to allow for a more orderly exodus. Indeed, a paradoxical effort was made: on the one hand, there was sympathy for those who had succeeded in escaping from tyranny; on the other, Hanoi was being implored to reduce the outflow and spare its neighbors. The irony drew little comment from the pundits who oversimplify the contradiction of currents that sweep the rough seas of twentieth century politics.

The melange of escape and expulsion is a new device to which Communism in these latter decades has turned. In Soviet Russia and the East European countries, the purpose has been to rid themselves of dissidents and groups like the Jews and Armenians who adamantly preserve an ethnic identity and ideology. Vietnam has been wary of its Chinese community for generations and now fears the presence of potential followers of Peking.

Cuba has sought to compensate for its economic debility and the failure of its internal propaganda by diluting a refugee population with elements it considers undesirable. In all such cases there was a systematic program of extortion by which the regime enriched its treasury, and individuals in positions of power, on their own behalf, sought profit.

At Geneva, Hanoi did agree to abate the flow. By now, the country's fleet of fishing boats was depleted and the departures by sea were much reduced. (Yet the figures for Indochinese entering the United States in 1981 still reached 16,000). But a new route opened up. Increasingly escapees turned westward, slipping across the borders of Cambodia, traversing that unhappy country to arrive as "land people" in the Thai camps. That they were still being received was due in great part to the fact that the Citizens Commission had made the refugees' plight the world's business. A letter from the White House to Leo Cherne saluted "the enviable record of the Citizens Commission's work in meeting a grave humanitarian challenge," and added: "I was aware of the important fact-finding role which the Commission has played over the last two years; however, I had not understood the extent to which the Commission had served as a catalyst in building a positive consensus on Indochinese refugee policy."

FAMINE

By 1979 the spotlight of world attention was riveted again on Cambodia. With the Soviet-backed Vietnamese in Phnom Penh and spreading through the countryside toward the Thai border, the first impulse among observers was relief that the vicious Pol Pot had been defeated. Though he continued to wage a fanatical guerrilla war, it was expected that some degree of normalcy would be achieved for the moribund people of Cambodia.

It was not to be. The destruction of the economy had gone so far that it was virtually impossible to restore rice production. Around the globe the message was flashed that the survivors were now facing extinction under the hammer and sickle of the grim reaper, famine. Preparations went forward among Western countries to send in large quantities of food and trucks with which to distribute the supplies; the Khmer Rouge had deliberately destroyed the public transport system as part of its plan to limit internal communications. Planting had virtually ceased as a result of the successive misfortunes of Pol Pot tyranny and Vietnamese invasion. Now it was expected that Hanoi, which had finally joined in the worldwide denunciations of the Khmer Rouge, would use its occupation to demonstrate a humanitarian concern by beginning to feed the starving population. Instead, politics as usual proved paramount. After all, was it not Lenin himself who said that "bread is a political weapon"?

In the summer of 1979, more than six months after the Vietnamese invasion of Cambodia, officials of the United Nations Children's Fund and the International Committee of the Red Cross met with government representatives in Hanoi and Ho Chi Minh City to ascertain the facts. It was agreed that 2,250,000 Cambodians out of an already decimated population were facing imminent starvation. Oxfam/America, the famine relief organization, reported that "eighty percent of Cambodia's children are suffering from the worst forms of malnutrition; the rest are severely hungry. Most of the population subsists on a rice ration of 4.5 ounces per person per day, a level below that needed to survive. Less than five percent of the country's rice lands are under cultivation; people have eaten the seedlings to stay alive."[11]

In addition, the conferees reported that the whole infrastructure of the nation had been destroyed. No health or welfare machinery existed. Hospitals had been officially vandalized. To demonstrate hatred for Western bourgeois values, all equipment, laboratory facilities, typewriters, books, medical journals, had been mangled beyond recovery. Later, when the medical school in Phnom Penh was finally reopened by the Vietnamese, all that remained of the faculty was several corpses preserved in formaldehyde. One doctor who was able to go into hiding explained that he had survived because for four years he did not wear his eyeglasses lest they betray him as an "intellectual."

A horror-stricken world organized to send in food. Warehouses in Phnom Penh and the seaport city of Kompong Som began to fill up with supplies. But the channels of distribution that even the worst of pre-Communist governments had managed to maintain were no longer available. Their restoration had no place on the Vietnamese agenda. Indeed, according to General Prem Tinsulanond, the Thai Defense Minister, Hanoi's troops in the last three months of 1979 had killed 20,000 civilians in northeast Cambodia in a drive to disrupt the delivery of food supplies lest they pass into the hands of the Pol Pot guerrillas.

By mid-1980 the United States alone had spent or committed $78,700,000 to Cambodian relief, and then pledged an additional $8 million. It provided more than $35 million through the United Nations World Food Program alone. Other sums were directed to funding relief activities by voluntary agencies. Two American religious organizations—the World Vision Relief Organization and the American Friends Service Committee—won the permission of the Vietnamese occupiers to enter the country. Most, however, were barred. Like the International Rescue Committee, they were compelled to do their work on the Thai-Cambodian border to which thousands were flocking, many to escape altogether, others to seek provisions for their families, going home with sacks of rice on their backs or pedaling their supplies on bicycles. Many brought to the border stories of unfortunate returnees waylaid by Pol Pot guerrillas, Vietnamese troops or nonideological brigands. Bread was not only the weapon, it was also the prize.

A few journalists admitted to Cambodia sought to track down the ultimate fate of the rice and rice seed. They reported that dilapidated wharfs made unloading a matter of weeks, while other ships idled at the river docks in Phnom Penh or in the harbor of Kampong Som waiting their turn. Meticulously Henry Kamm recorded the data on individual vessels: the Vietnamese ship *Eastern Rise*, delivering 4,000 tons of rice for the occupation troops, stood at anchor for twenty days without a kilo being moved; in fact it ran out of water for its own crew before it could be berthed. The first mate of a Soviet ship said that his vessel, in from Vladivostok, had to wait thirty days before it could begin to discharge its load of 2,600 tons of rice. Though international contributions had provided 1,100 trucks, few showed up at dockside to take deliveries.[12]

A period of confusion set in. Conflicting versions of life in Cambodia began to circulate. As in the days of Hitler, there was an unwillingness to recognize that cruelty could cut as deep as evidence long after the event would show. A four-column headline in the *New York Times* on the third day of the new year 1980 read: "Relief Officials Report They Saw No Famine in Cambodia." A cursory reader might have turned away with a sense of relief, but those who reached the lead paragraph learned: "Representatives of international relief agencies report that they saw hunger, malnutrition and sickness but not outright famine in Cambodia in mid-December, during the most extensive trip through the country they have thus far been permitted to take." The next paragraph quoted their warning that "within two months Cambodia's 1979 rice harvest, estimated at only 10 percent its normal volume, would be used up." And in the third paragraph: "They also reported that nearly all the aid brought into Cambodia so far by the joint operation of the International Committee of the Red Cross and two United Nations agencies 'remains in warehouses' in Phnom Penh and Kompong Som." As the story proceeds, the *Times* quotes its sources as emphasizing that they were confined to "main roads and did not see the situation in remoter areas," the reasons given by the authorities being "security problems and lack of time."

Even if political considerations — especially the desire of the regime to starve the Pol Pot opposition into surrender — had been put aside, incoming supplies once landed could filter only slowly into the countryside. Those familiar with the geography were convinced that the fastest route would have been by convoys of trucks from Bangkok, but this would have meant admitting relief agencies into the areas where Hanoi's hold was weakest. From Phnom Penh the supply route was beset by difficulty. Roads and bridges had fallen into decay during the four years of Pol Pot's rule. Whatever was passable was being used for the movement of Vietnamese troops.

The semantic specters that haunt international relationships also barred the movement of food. Theoretically, the only effective instrument for transporting supplies was the military machine now occupying the country; to hand over international contributions to the Vietnamese army would have been tantamount to recognizing the occupation as lawful. Indeed, Hanoi was deliberately trying to use the famine to win a stamp of legitimacy. The United Nations had continued to recognize the Pol Pot regime — not to do so, it was argued, would violate the principles of the UN Charter. To send in food without the consent of the "lawful" government recognized by the UN would clearly be a breach. Despite the willingness of Western nations and some aid sent by the Soviet Union, hunger took hold. The effects were to be seen in the faces of those who suceeded in reaching Thailand. Some arrived so debilitated that, falling on the rain-soaked ground, they drowned in a few inches of water because they had no strength to lift their heads out of the ruts.

HUMANITY RESPONDS

The shocked conscience of the world was not silent. If food could not get through to the heartland, at the very least something could be done for those who reached the Thai border. In New York Joseph Papp, head of the New York Shakespeare Festival, organized the theaters to appeal for contributions between the acts. Until this event, which set an example for theaters throughout the country, the only such collections ever made were on behalf of the actors' welfare fund. Thus the American theater demonstrated its willingness to help Cambodians in the same way it helps its very own. IRC's call for people to assist with the collection brought more than 250 volunteers to the Broadway and off-Broadway theaters. Members of the cast stood before the curtain and either spoke their own words, or read this brief statement:

"In Cambodia, the world is witnessing a tragedy which may have no parallel in history," U.N. General Secretary Kurt Waldheim said recently. Since 1975, as many as 3½ million of the country's population of 7 million have died, Waldheim said, and "up to 90 percent of the surviving children are suffering appalling malnutrition."

One hundred thousand Indochinese refugees will die in the next four weeks, most of them children and the elderly, unless something is done to change this unspeakable horror in Southeast Asia. We of the theatre community — actors, writers, composers, producers, designers, directors, stage managers, stagehands, ushers — all of us are appealing to our audiences in every Broadway theater, each night this week, to join us to help save the lives of these innocent victims. Your money will be converted into medical supplies, doctors, nurses and paramedics, through the offices of the International Rescue Committee already operating in Thailand, and shipped without delay. Each day, each hour, each minute that passes, a starved child is dying. The ushers will pass baskets among you for your donation, and please give generously. Save someone's life tonight.

The goal set by Papp and his committee had been $100,000. When the collection bags were emptied and combined with individual gifts from theater folk, the total reached twice that amount. At ceremonies in New

York's famed Shubert Alley the theater committee turned over a check for $200,000 to IRC's chairman.

By the end of the year, public contributions to IRC had reached the $5 million mark, making it possible to send additional medical teams to Thailand and Malaysia. Other voluntary agencies reported similar responses from their contributors. In one week alone CARE collected $600,000 towards its announced goal of $5 million for Cambodian relief.

Ad hoc groups sprang up to raise funds for transmission through the voluntary agencies. Established organizations such as the International Arts Center assembled entertainers and athletes to perform in an event called "The Day of the Child." The day-long program included a chorus numbering hundreds who sang Beethoven's Ninth Symphony, with Schiller's stirring "*Alle Menschen wirden Brueder sein.*" The Arts Center, whose trustees include diplomatic representatives of eighty-eight governments, turned over the proceeds to the Red Cross, CARE and IRC. Fund-raisers for the various voluntary agencies reported uniformly that the response of the American people was "unprecedented," exceeding even the contributions in the Hungarian crisis of 1956. "People have been waiting for this opportunity to do something for the Cambodians," said one observer. "They welcome the chance to give."

"CAMBODIA – MARCH FOR SURVIVAL"

Nevertheless, in the early months of 1980, public attention began to wane. The media, fearful that repetitive stories would only bore their audiences, turned to emphasize other sensations such as the upheavals in Iran and the Soviet invasion of Afghanistan. The Citizens Commission and the IRC began to search for a new approach that would restore the Cambodian crisis to public attention. Discussions in New York focused on methods of dramatizing the situation. Simultaneously in Paris the leaders of *Médecins sans Frontières* were wrestling with the same problem and thinking of the same solution – a "March for Survival" on behalf of the Cambodian people. Telephone conversations between New York and Paris, followed by quick plane flights and an immediate weekend conference, led to a specific program. The plan was to assemble a convoy of trucks in Thailand laden with food and medications, to be accompanied by doctors and relief workers and escorted by prominent citizens from all over the world to plead for entry into Cambodia. If, as was feared, permission were denied, the supplies could be turned over to the Cambodian refugees already on the Thai border.

Among those who played a prominent role in building support was Joan Baez, a charismatic leader of young people, who in song and speech had organized pacifist resistance to American policy in Indochina. Now she called upon her old associates to demonstrate their sincerity by coming to the aid of the still-suffering population of Southeast Asia. Many responded affirmatively, but there were some, like Jane Fonda, who showered her with abuse. No amount of vilification, however, could lead Baez to abandon her dedication to the people she had set out to befriend in war and peace.

Even before the March was in contemplation, she had hoped that Hanoi might be influenced by a public appeal from the peace activists of the 1960s and '70s. She assembled a group that raised more than $50,000 for advertisements in the nation's leading newspapers, signed by herself, Daniel Berrigan, Allen Ginsberg and other such figures.[13] Her invitation to join the effort was met with stony silence from many who had been her close associates. Of 350 invitations sent out, less than a hundred responded. Philip Berrigan signed but then withdrew his name. A telephone call to Daniel Ellsberg, the man who had leaked the Pentagon Papers to the press, elicited a reply that all he was interested in now was "my future in the antinuclear movement."[14]

Baez's group addressed a message to the Communist government of Vietnam, condemning "your brutal disregard of human rights." It charged that the regime had rounded up more than 150,000 political prisoners and had used torture on its own citizens. It expressed sorrow that "instead of bringing hope and reconciliation to war-torn Vietnam, your government has created a painful nightmare that overshadows significant progress achieved in many areas of Vietnamese society."

The ensuing controversy among the former associates rarely dealt with the assertions put forward by Baez. The apologists made no real attempt to rebut the record based on a testimony of sheer numbers — the hundreds of thousands of witnesses whose very presence in the refugee camps was proof of the brutality they had experienced. Tepid denials that Cambodia was now in a state of starvation after five years of Communist control led Baez to write in a letter to the editor of the *New York Times*:

I do not wish to detract from the tremendous efforts of the numerous relief organizations that have done a superhuman job on behalf of the Cambodian refugees. However, there is a general attitude promoted by a few of these groups of adopting a highly diplomatic, if not fawning, public manner toward the puppet government of Phenom Penh. This attitude is that the less the public knows about food distribution, the better.

When our "March for Survival" made an appeal at the Thai/Cambodian border to allow doctors, medicine and food into the outlying provinces and rural areas of Cambodia, we were accused of "kicking down the back door when the front door is already open." I am sure the front door is open. I am sure that the foyer is well polished. And I am equally sure that visitors are well screened.[15]

Those who were eager to turn the spotlight off a starving Cambodia, now in the grip of 200,000 Vietnamese troops, shook their heads sadly over Joan Baez's activities. One type of comment emanating from the reluctant dragons of the old antiwar movement was the deprecating statement, "Joan is involving herself perhaps a little beyond where she may want to go." Her reply was direct: "I want to go to the *root* of the problem, which is *no longer* what the United States, or France, or Japan, or floods and famine, or Pol Pot are doing in Vietnam, Laos and Cambodia. It is 1980 and the root of the problem is a totalitarian government in Hanoi, which runs one of the smoothest public relations operations since the Russian Politburo of the '30s." Painfully she recalled "the sentiments of a friend of mine, a French journalist and one-time staunch supporter of Hanoi, with whom I spent many hours in a bomb shelter in 1972. He argued furiously with me then because I would not toast the shooting down of a B-52. His words today about the leadership in Hanoi: 'They really had us, didn't they?'"[16]

In typical Communist polemical style, the Soviet press set the theme for denunciation by designing a tendentious amalgam, describing her statements as a "lampoon lavishly paid for by the American organization Amnesty International, which is famous for its hatred for socialist countries." (Amnesty International, which won the Nobel Peace Prize in 1977, is based in London.) Under a heading, "The Degradation of Joan Baez," *Sovietskaya Kultura* wrote: "Recently she sang in Seattle. Around the building where the concert was held, there was a stormy crowd of people holding up signs which said, 'The CIA likes Joan Baez and Joan Baez likes the CIA!'"[17] Moscow did not have to take lessons in Joe McCarthy's notorious technique of guilt by association. In the 1930s Trotsky had identified it as the Stalinist "amalgam."

AT THE POIPET BRIDGE

As one of the leaders of the March for Survival, Baez hoped that the boundaries crossed by the Vietnamese army the year before could now be crossed by a small band of world citizens bringing sustenance. But the Vietnamese soldiers stood grimly silent at the Poipet bridge, barring the way. An international group of about 200—many with famous names, others anonymous young people who had decided to add their presence—pleaded through bullhorns that they be permitted to deliver their truckloads to those in need. The voices of civilization, speaking in English, French and Khmer, brought only expressionless stares from the occupation troops only a few yards away.

For weeks Radio Phnom Penh had told the soldiers and border guards that the March was the beginning of an imperialist invasion. What they saw was a vanguard representing the civilized world, armed only with gifts of food and medicines, who had come to this dusty road at Aranyaprathet and the Poipet bridge to bring help to their fellow-creatures. And when they were turned away they sat down in the dust for five solemn minutes to meditate and pray in silence, and to give thought to what was in their hearts.

In her letter to the *Times* Miss Baez noted how deep was the need and how tragic the rejection. "Hundreds of doctors from around the world (including France, Cuba, Czechoslovakia, East Germany, Canada, Scandinavia and Russia) have applied for visas," she wrote. "To date, only a small team of Russian doctors has been allowed into Cambodia. Right now 400 doctors work in Thailand round the clock with 150,000 refugees to aid in combating malaria, tuberculosis, malnutrition, dysentery, pulmonary pneumonia, intestinal parasites and countless other illnesses and diseases."

Beside her at the border, in addition to the members of the Citizens Commission and *Médecins sans Frontières* were world-famous writers like Elie Wiesel, the historian of the Hitler holocaust, who explained to correspondents, "I had to be here because when I was there no one came for me"; Winston Churchill III, bringing with him a great name and tradition; two-score members of the British, French and Italian parliaments; trade unionists from Denmark and West Germany. Persons from every walk of life marched along under a hot Southeast Asian sky, carefully keeping off the shoulders of the road which the Thai military warned had been mined against the possibility of Vietnamese invasion out of Cambodia. These men and women represented some forty organizations whose members number 50 million of the world's people. The European press alone had sent seventy journalists to cover this effort to redeem the good name of humankind in an age of atrocities.

Among the marchers were many "celebrities" — one of the reasons for the attention then being focused on this remote border station. A news conference in Bangkok, held in a steaming room on the eve of the March, heard the objectives and the hopes that had led writers, legislators, clergymen, political analysts and other personages to put aside their private and professional business for a journey into an area where death by disease and human destructiveness were imminent realities. A cynical press corps, with long-standing grievances of their own, belabored the spokespersons for the group with critical questions, commenting particularly on the presence of people from the theatrical world.

This attitude brought forth a response from one of the marchers, the distinguished Swedish actress and author in her own right, Liv Ullmann. "I left the celebrity behind me," she said in words that were fortunately preserved on tape, "and I'm here as a human being, a woman in her forties, a mother. I am here because I don't believe anymore in all the nice words and petitions. I believe what my heart and my conscience are telling me: Something is very wrong and unfair in our world."

To the critics in her audience who felt that the March, at best, could be no more than a gesture and at worst might plug the trickle of aid that was getting through, she said:

Haven't there been other marches for freedom where the marchers were asked to be silent because things would eventually be worked out if one at the moment were only a little careful and diplomatic? Thank you, Martin Luther King, for not listening to those warnings. Has there not been a smell from the pipes of certain ovens in Poland that some people wondered about, and did not those who "knew" and even inspected the camps of these ovens, for some diplomatic reason, keep quiet about them? Was not our great excuse, when we finally found out, that we did not know, we did not see? Don't we have an obligation to those who entered the gas chambers with a lifted head because they felt in their hearts that maybe there was a *why* to this, that the world would get to know and never let it happen again? . . .

I will be quiet no more. I want to do this march. I want to go to the border and see myself if it is really true that they will not let us in with food and medicine. I want to go that road tomorrow because it is the same road as the road to the gas chambers; and I will not be the one later to say I did not know, I did not see, I did not hear.

She sat down. There was a hush, and then her electrified audience, having endured two long steaming hours, burst into applause.

The marchers did indeed go home with a sense of frustration. They had not fulfilled their major purpose, though they had finally delivered the medicines and food to the refugees on the Thai side. Nor did they escape the continuing barbs of the cynical. Indeed some journalists, in the comfort of their editorial offices, derided the March. For example, *Time* magazine published an article headed "Cambodia: The Fancies and the Facts," with a subheading "A march is foiled, but the omens are encouraging."[18] It coupled concession with criticism by saying that the "march helped renew the world's interest in the country, at a time when its situation — at least for now — seemed to be improving." Then stacking up what it called "fancy" against "fact," *Time* offered this piece of analysis:

FANCY: The Cambodians are in imminent danger of being wiped out as a race.

FACT: There are now about 150,000 Cambodians in refugee camps well inside Thailand. An estimated 740,000 Cambodians, mostly civilians, are within a short distance of the border on the Cambodian side; it takes a considerable amount of imagination to speculate that they will all die of starvation or be killed.

Presumably, genocide has failed if 890,000 Cambodians out of an original population of 7,000,000 have saved their lives by fleeing to a neighboring country. But even such arithmetic cannot mitigate the brutal reality. By an irony of editorial happenstance, the back of the page in the same issue of *Time* carried an essay by Alexander Solzhenitsyn that opened with the sentence, "The West began its perilous miscalculation of Communism in 1918: from the very beginning the Western powers failed to see the deadly threat that it represented."[19]

It did not require great political discernment to recognize that an elemental respect for life, in this tragic historic moment, could not be left wholly to the vagaries of journalism or the decisions made in government ministries. It could be implemented by personal actions based on personal values. Individual victims of the fanatical doctrinaires and power-hungry ideologists could be rescued. The Citizens Commission, on one level, had proved that private persons could arrest the attention of the world and influence the attitudes and policies of governments. On another level, all across the United States men and women on their own—in churches and synagogues, service organizations, fraternal orders, trade unions—showed they could band together and serve as hosts for refugee families in need of resettlement.

But the most constructive consequence of the March was that its dramatization of the events in Cambodia compelled the countries of first asylum to keep their borders open. Until then, the internal pressure to seal all entrances against the Indochinese had been intensifying. The countries of first asylum, rebelling against the disproportionate share of the burden, had been stiffening their posture. In the light of the increasing pressure, the behavior was as understandable as it was unacceptable. The deputy prime minister of Malaysia in an unguarded moment told correspondents that his government would order the shooting of any more boat people who tried to land. Of course this attitude did not become policy, but its effect could be seen in an alleged decision that led to the towing out to sea of 40,459 Vietnamese boat people, according to Malaysia's Home Affairs minister, and in the beating and robbing of refugees by local residents who resented their presence.[20]

NEW FEARS

For Thailand the problem was compounded by the proximity of the Vietnamese soldiers. Following Hanoi's invasion of Cambodia in January 1979, the Thai government was presented with a new refugee population—Pol Pot's followers who obviously could not be housed with the people who had been their victims. In some of the camps warfare broke out as the Khmer Rouge sought domination, sometimes to the point of opening fire with the weapons they had brought. To swell their own ranks they often terrorized refugees into remaining even after they had been offered a chance to move out. As potential bases for guerrilla operations against the puppet government imposed by the Vietnamese, the camps frequently came under artillery barrages from across the border.

When the Bangkok government sought to encourage refugees to return to Cambodia, an effort denounced by Hanoi as support for Pol Pot's guerrillas, Vietnamese troops crossed the border to engage Thai troops in combat. At the same time Laotian soldiers attacked a Thai gunboat in the Mekong River, leading to a temporary halt in trade relations between the two countries. Increasingly Thailand feared that its future as the only non-Communist nation in the area was in jeopardy.

As early as 1977 some foreign observers on the scene had predicted that the time would come when the refugees would simply be herded back into their own countries of origin. In one of the darkest moments in present refugee history Thai officials, pretending that people were merely being moved to a new site, loaded thousands into buses and transported them across the border. At gunpoint they were ordered to descend to the jungle floor on the Cambodian side. Some 42,000 were thus stranded without any supplies in a ravine that had been mined by Vietnamese troops. Shattering explosions followed. A few weeks later only 7,000 were still alive. Eventually, after remonstrances from around the globe, they were readmitted to the safety of Thailand.

In the interim, one of the survivors, a former schoolteacher named Chey Rith, had made his way back from what the refugees called the Valley of Hell, only to be captured by the Thais and expelled again. Once more he returned; this time he reached Bangkok. Deciding to entrust his fate to any foreigner he chanced to meet, he approached a woman in the street. "Excuse me, Miss," he said in halting English, "I am a Khmer refugee, and I would like to find a Christian church." She helped him make contact with Roman Catholic missionaries who led him to American Embassy personnel, who then turned him over to IRC under whose sponsorship he was admitted to the United States.[21]

The possibility of forced return is always present in the mind of the refugee. It is difficult to appreciate the emotions of men and women who, having lost freedom in their native land, give up everything in order to be free — even in poverty — in a new land. But how can one understand the emotions of the refugee who flees with pounding heart, fearing discovery; who crosses over to freedom after a hazardous journey; who kisses the soil of deliverance — only to be seized and sent back into the hands of his tormentor? He crosses a chasm on a tightrope, but on reaching the solid ground is flung into the abyss.

The refugee is not likely to know the terminology of international politics that has contrived a word for such forced repatriation. It is a French word, *refoulement*, which in the original means simply the act of pushing back. The verb from which it is drawn, *refouler*, was used in the Middle Ages to describe the ramming of powder and ball into a cannon. The explosive connotations are still appropriate, for twentieth-century *refoulement* is an act deemed so destructive that it has been formally outlawed among the nations who have signed the Convention Relating to the Status of Refugees. Article 33 declares in straightforward language: "No Contracting State shall expel or return a refugee to the frontiers of territories where his life or freedom would be threatened."

Nevertheless, there have been tragic moments when the signatories have disregarded this commitment. In 1974, the Danish government, despite a long and honorable record of service to the oppressed, was preparing to send back twelve Polish tourists who had defected from the cruise ship *Stefan Batory* in Copenhagen. In that case, IRC succeeded in preventing the expulsion by arranging for transfers to West Germany and other countries.

Less happy was the outcome in the case of the Lithuanian seaman, Simas Kudirka, who leaped from a Russian fishing boat at sea onto the deck of a U.S. Coast Guard cutter in an attempt to defect. After radio communications with headquarters, the Americans permitted Soviet crewmen to board their ship and forcibly remove the would-be defector. Both the rear admiral in command of the Coast Guard district and his immediate subordinate were later subjected to disciplinary proceedings and were permitted to retire after a formal reprimand. After three years of imprisonment Kudirka was permitted to leave the Soviet Union and was admitted to the United States.

In Southeast Asia, the ultimate answer to *refoulement* could only be resettlement, and the United States, though not alone in bearing responsibility, was expected to play the leading role. In identifying those eligible for admission to this country, the International Rescue Committee became the major processing organization—interviewing, evaluating, recommending and transmitting the findings to the Immigration and Naturalization Service.

From the moment of incarceration on crossing the Thai border to the day of departure from the transit center in Bangkok, the refugees looked to IRC representatives to provide services and guidance. The last phase before departure was removal to the transit center—a large building in Bangkok, its "rooms" improvised by sheets hung from the ceilings. A large courtyard, filled with long tables, provided an outdoor mess hall. To the visitor the setting seems all confusion, but, as if drawn by a magnet, knots of refugees throughout the day cluster around a metal post near the entrance. Here the names of those scheduled to depart are listed daily, and one can glean the news, or lack of it, in the faces of the readers. Nearby a group ready to leave by bus for the airport take count of their children and the few belongings they can carry in hand. Off to one side, seated at a table, is an IRC interviewer talking with a refugee whose departure has been held up because his medical examination showed traces of opium in his urine. Thorough questioning reveals that the man had been given a cough medicine a few days earlier, and that he is not disqualified.

To the casual eye, much of the legal procedure seemed to be conducted by persons without official standing. Actually, what had happened was that the U.S. State Department, overwhelmed by the sheer volume of work, asked the voluntary agencies on the scene to help with its emergency staffing. The VOLAGS had agreed that IRC, among its other responsibilities, would serve as the recruiting agency for the government's refugee service.

DEPARTURE AND ARRIVAL

It is a long flight from Bangkok to Los Angeles or San Francisco, especially for passengers who have never before been in a plane. Everything is new and startling. There was a time when many of the refugees, particularly the Hmongs, did not understand that there were lavatories available, or that the meals served to them were free. They leave the plane with dazed, weary, solemn, even frightened expressions. They wear tags labeled ICEM — the Intergovernmental Committee on European Migration (recently renamed to delete "European") — which is the organization that arranges the transportation. Having passed through Customs and Immigration in Honolulu, their reception by representatives of the voluntary agencies is much simplified. They do not have to go to the baggage claim area since they already have their few possessions with them. It is strange to see which piece of home they decided to bring with them. An old woman clings to a dented and tarnished aluminum teapot. A little girl has a small wicker basket strapped to her back; it is filled with clothing. Mothers carry a more precious cargo — babies tied to their backs. A Hmong boy sits on an airport bench clutching a crossbow, probably of his own manufacture. Readily identifiable are the Hmongs by their colorful appliquéd and embroidered handbags.

Several agencies are on hand to greet them. Each sponsoring group seeks out the families for which they are responsible, not a very difficult task because the names are crayoned in bold letters on shopping bags that ICEM provided in Bangkok. An IRC worker, a pretty Vietnamese volunteer, scurries about among the refugees, pressing an adhesive IRC tag on the coat or dress of each person she finds on her list. Now the anxious faces are more relaxed as each VOLAG leads its group aside for briefing through interpreters. Those scheduled for resettlement in other cities are accompanied to their connecting planes and the agency worker waits to see them board; the others are taken to hostels or more permanent housing already arranged for them.

Now begins the unglamorous but creative task of integrating the newcomers into a culture that is as alien to them as they are to their new neighbors. Housing is the most immediate need, and in most large American cities it is a difficult problem. Work must be found, but despite the ups and downs in the economy the lower-level jobs are usually available and are taken with alacrity by the refugees who are confident they can work their way up. The visitor to IRC's office in Los Angeles is gratified when a young man bursts in to announce proudly that he has just been promoted and has become the first Vietnamese manager of a McDonald's. But he is realistic, and expresses concern that some of his black fellow-workers may resent becoming his subordinates. And there is also the depressing story of the Vietnamese doctor, in his middle forties, who says it is too late to study for a medical license and who is now washing floors in a hospital in order to be near the work he loves.

INTEGRATION IN A NEW CULTURE

The best way to understand what resettlement means is to visit the homes of recent arrivals. Uch Nath is a young Cambodian who has a job as a mechanic. He lives with his wife and three children in a small, one-bedroom house in a poor Los Angeles neighborhood. Proudly he takes his guests to the small adjoining garage where he has built himself a press on which he embosses his own prints of Angkor Wat, painting the product in garish colors. Their sale provides him with additional income. His conversation is one continuing paean of joy.

The visitor finds similar satisfaction in the home of Lo Eng, a Hmong who escaped from Laos with his family. His wife, shyly and worshipfully, greets Virginia Callahan of the IRC staff. Just a week before, the couple had been reunited with a mother, brother and sister newly arrived from Thailand. A one-month-old baby, the first of the family to be an American, was born by Caesarian, with IRC as virtual midwife. While working in the Nong Khai refugee camp, Mrs. Callahan had learned how the Hmongs distrusted Western medicine; at the request of the obstetrician, she had spent hours explaining the procedure to the pregnant woman. Mrs. Eng finally agreed to the operation on condition that Mrs. Callahan would remain with her in the delivery room. The living quarters of the family, including the baby and two other children, are dingy rooms on the ground floor of an old apartment house very much in need of repairs. Once again Virginia Callahan tries her powers of persuasion, this time urging the parents to encourage the children to spend time out of doors. But so far the reluctance cannot be overcome.

The tour continues, again in areas of low-income housing, frequently in Chicano neighborhoods. The next visit becomes a condolence call occasioned by the death of the mother. The father too is absent; he is in a prison in Saigon. Six children, ranging in age from six to twenty years, have been orphaned. An "adopted sister," aged twenty-eight, appears to be the most woebegone of all, but it is explained in an aside that her status in Vietnamese society would really be that of an indentured servant. Two uncles have arrived—one from Texas who is planning to stay and take care of the children; the other a professional photographer who will soon be on his way to Michigan.

The most dramatic interview is in the home of a twenty-three-year-old Cambodian woman named Li Lin. On our arrival, she throws her arms around Virginia Callahan and greets her as *"ma mère."* Li is attractive, her almond eyes set off in smooth rounded features. Speaking in French she relives the events of life in Phnom Penh and in "the new economic zone." She describes the dreadful day when the civilian population was exiled from the capital. A soldier—a fourteen-year-old boy with a rifle whose military status was indicated by his red *foulard*—came to the door with orders that all must leave their homes in twenty minutes. For three days she, her husband and her four-year-old son, along with the total population of Phnom Penh, marched on foot into the countryside. She saw men, women and children die at the roadside. Never before had there been the sight of relatives pushing the beds of patients whom they had retrieved from the hospitals,

intravenous bottles bobbing from racks. Those without beds limped until
they dropped.

Thereafter, her life became a kaleidoscope of pain, designed in every
color of inhumanity: separation from her husband, each being sent to work
in different locations; labor as a beast of burden clearing the trees from the
forestland; her arms covered with sores as a result of her assignment to
gather human excrement and spread it as fertilizer; her daily ration of rice,
the equivalent of an eight-ounce can dented so that it could hold only about
four ounces, into which the food distributor would insert his thumb to
further decrease the portion; her need to tie up her son lest he stray into the
jungle while she was working; news that her husband had been executed
because someone had discovered a picture of him with a group of Americans; her escape by bribing the camp commandant's wife to get permission
for her to visit her parents; her flight in the jungle and her chance meeting
with ethnic Vietnamese-Cambodians heading for Vietnam; arrival at the
border, only to find that she and her son would not be admitted with the
others; her pleading for three hours with the Vietnamese soldiers not to send
her back, and her insistence that they shoot her son first so that she might
ensure that his sufferings were over; her persuasiveness in pleading for entry
and her arrival in Saigon where she located her dead husband's thirteen-
year-old son by a previous marriage; her getting on a boat with the two
youngsters; and finally, their arrival in Song Khla. There, at the height of
exhaustion and the depth of depression, she met Virginia Callahan whose
ministrations helped restore her to health and eventual refuge in the United
States. Now she was learning English and preparing to find work.

Such was the outcome for some of the individuals who had decided to
take the long route to freedom and a chance to raise their families in dignity.
As of December 1979, the figures showed that 280,000 Indochinese had
been admitted to the United States, with IRC resettling more than 35,000 of
these. As the number of monthly admissions increased, new IRC resettlement offices had to be opened in Atlanta, Boston and San Jose, bringing the
total in that year to fourteen. In California, where almost a third of the
Indochinese are now living, five offices had to be maintained. At the beginning of 1980, IRC was girding itself to receive 15,000 to 18,000 Vietnamese,
Cambodian and Laotian refugees, in addition to an already overwhelming
number of Cubans. Moreover, it continued to carry responsibility for
processing the emigration of the refugees in Thailand on behalf of all the
American resettlement agencies.

NOT WITHOUT PAIN

At best, resettlement means difficulties — hardship for the refugee, inconvenience at the very least for the host community. No matter how rewarding the refugee may find his new-found freedom and no matter how cordial

the community, his situation remains precarious. Some measure of local resistance is bound to exist. Fortunately, America has been undergoing a change in the direction of greater tolerance. Even in the increasingly paranoid atmosphere of recent years, with America losing friends around the world, its embassies being assaulted in Moslem countries and its diplomats being taken hostage in one of them, there might have been grave danger that a new xenophobia would spread across the land. Overt racism has gone out of style, and the nation's preoccupation with civil rights issues has discouraged blatant prejudice. But problems remain, and sentiment oscillates. Paradoxically, the assertion of black identity has stimulated a new ethnic consciousness among other groups, partly as backlash, partly as rebellion against the disparities of class and social status. The "melting pot," once a major image in American mythology, has all but disappeared.

The term had been conceived by Israel Zangwill, the English-Jewish author, as the title for a play first produced in 1909. In the climactic scene the protagonist declaims: "America is God's Crucible, the great Melting Pot where all the races of Europe are melting and reforming." Zangwill's figure of speech is powerful: "Here you stand in your fifty groups with your fifty languages and histories, and your fifty blood hatreds and rivalries, but you won't be like that for long, brothers, for these are the fires of God you've come to — these are the fires of God. A fig for your feuds and vendettas. German and Frenchman, Irishman and Englishman, Jews and Russians — into the Crucible with you all! God is making the American." Though the critics showed little but scorn for the drama at its opening in Washington, one member of the audience shouted across the auditorium, "That's a great play, Mr. Zangwill!" It was Theodore Roosevelt. His judgment was echoed by throngs that filled a Broadway theater for months.

Though "Americanization" became the leitmotif, integration did not come easily. Even powerful international religious organizations like the Roman Catholic Church found it difficult to seat Polish immigrants next to Irishmen in the pews, Germans next to Italians, Lithuanians next to French-Canadians. German Jews, no matter how philanthropic, kept their social distance from the Jews of the Lower East Side in New York. For a time, even the Reform Jewish synagogue, organized as the Union of American Hebrew Congregations, abandoned efforts to help Jews fleeing Russian pogroms and announced that it "no longer assumes any charge of the subject of material aid for the emigrants arriving in the United States." Irving Howe, in *World of Our Fathers*, quotes Louis Marshall, himself one of their number, as writing that the German Jews "held themselves aloof from the people. . . . They acted as Lords and Ladies Bountiful bringing gifts to people who did not seek for gifts. . . . The work [of the Educational Alliance they founded] was done in such a manner as not only to give offense, but to arouse suspicion of the motives."[22]

Nevertheless, if practice often subverted theory, many institutions did undertake steps to meld a common culture. Labor unions, struggling against the powerful industrial and political interests, strove for a unity of workers that would transcend ethnic origins. But even while trying to prevent one group from being pitted against another as strikebreakers, their federation leaders were pleading for a ban on new immigration. The public school system undertook to provide a pattern of shared American values. After more than a century of educational effort — the fight for free public education began in the United States even before the Civil War — American pluralism continued to exist in a state of tension. Despite the tradition of individualism fathered by the New England transcendentalists, the pressures toward conformity have always been evident in the drive towards Americanization. The immigrant is an obvious target for those who cannot tolerate difference. In recent years, however, there has been a tendency in the United States towards a reassertion of ethnic identity, one of the by-products of the civil rights and feminist movements.

In any case, there were always some xenophobes who saw in immigrants and refugees a danger that the "national character" was about to be diluted. Under the impact of World War I, Theodore Roosevelt, who had shouted "bully" for Zangwill's melting pot, hawked the slogan, "America for Americans." Because immigrants were associated with radicalism, the foreign-born were often viewed automatically as un-American. For example, a popular novelist, Kenneth Roberts, author of *Northwest Passage*, wrote a series of articles on immigration in the widely read *Saturday Evening Post*. Revised and published in 1922 in book form, his diatribes singled out various groups by name. He denounced those who "work all day by the side of other people of their own race.... Their first love is for their mother country. They have no hesitation in pursuing an emphatically un-American course.... [The Slavs] have been brought up to break the laws.... The Jews are most difficult to handle because of their ruthless concentration on self-interest." He condemned the newcomers as "paupers by circumstances, and parasites by training and inclination." He warned: "Races cannot be cross-bred without mongrelization.... Unrestricted immigration has made a mongrel race out of the south Italians [and] out of the Greeks. Unrestricted immigration will do the same thing to Americans."[23]

Depression in the 1930s provided a strong impetus for reducing immigration to a minimum. Laura Fermi, in *Illustrious Immigrants*, illustrates the virulence of xenophobia at that time:

When it became known in 1932 that Albert Einstein planned to come to the United States, the Women's Patriotic Corporation tried to prevent his entry, claiming that he was a member of Communist organizations. On December 4, 1932, the *New York Times* published testimony of the board of the National Patriotic Council calling Einstein a German Bolshevist and stating that his theory "was of no scientific value or purpose, not understandable because there was nothing to understand."[24]

In the years preceding America's entry into World War II, antisemitism seemed to be growing, but as isolationism began to lose its gloss, social attitudes once more shifted in liberal directions. However inchoate the country's policies have been, the tendency has always been to maintain a tradition of asylum. Even when seen in its worst light, American attitudes have moved a long way from such nineteenth century editorial rhetoric as the following: "The floodgates are open. The bars are down. The sally-ports are unguarded. The dam is washed away. The sewer is choked. . . . The scum of immigration is viscerating upon our shores. The horde of $9.90 steerage slime is being siphoned upon us from Continental mud tanks." Not even in the days when Castro was said to be spewing criminals and "undesirables" into the refugee pipeline in 1980 did any newspaper descend to this primordial level.

REGIONAL PROBLEMS

The relative calmness with which the Southeast Asians were received in most local communities in the 1970s and '80s is indeed extraordinary. That the nation was able to reach this high moral level was not a contradiction of, but a development out of, America's past. For though there have been some strident advocates of divisiveness, there have always been strong voices that speak in the accents of human brotherhood.

To be sure, there were isolated instances where media sensationalism made headlines out of atypical episodes. In one situation a handful of Vietnamese lost in a big city were pictured as hordes of homeless refugees wandering the streets. California, Texas and Louisiana are the country's three leading settlement areas because their climate is most congenial to Asians; some scare stories have circulated in those states. In California, public fears have been expressed about the danger of disease. It is true that a higher incidence of tuberculosis develops among refugees than among native Americans, but the invidious statistics should be tempered by the realization that tuberculosis has been all but eliminated in the United States. A 10 percent increase in the number of cases looks terrifying in a headline, but it is insignificant when the base figure is practically zero. A rise in the incidence of esoteric diseases such as salmonella, shigella, amoebic disorders and parasitic infections, usually encountered only in Third-World countries, provided grist for sensational articles. One newspaper reported a "nearly tenfold increase in leprosy" in the period from 1964, a strangely chosen base year, to 1978.[25] Sober observers like the chief of the communicable disease branch of the San Francisco Public Health Department offered reassurance that "tuberculosis responded quickly to antibiotics, that leprosy was 'very difficult to transmit despite its biblical image' and that parasites responded to a combination of medication and improved sanitary conditions."[26]

There were isolated stories of conflict from different sections of the country. Friction between Vietnamese refugee fishermen and local boatmen, in one case, exploded into murder. Chicanos in Denver complained that housing authorities were bending the rules to favor refugees. Vandals attacked refugee property and administered beatings in Augusta, Maine. Blacks feared that their communities, already victimized by unemployment, would suffer from the new competition. Exposure to culture shock brought hostilities. *Newsweek* reported: "In New Orleans itself, Vietnamese newcomers in the Algiers section have antagonized locals by handling each loaf of bread and piece of fruit in grocery stores, by irrigating their gardens and thus boosting local water bills and by wearing pajama sleepware that is the closest approximation of their native clothing."[27]

By and large, however, such frictions were successfully contained by methods learned in negotiations to end ghetto strife. Fortunately, the language used by the participants in such controversies was less than confrontational. In the New Orleans situation, some 8,000 Vietnamese had been resettled. Community problems had already been multiplying, with local unemployment reaching 7.7 percent and the list of people waiting for public housing numbering 10,000. This background led to a clash between the local chapter of the Urban League and the Associated Catholic Charities which was deeply involved in the effort to aid Vietnamese families. The level of discourse could be seen in the comments of Clarence Barney of the Urban League: "We subscribe to the notion that America ought to provide opportunities to the refugees. But it is absolutely wrong to say that the government should bring in Vietnamese where there's already too many people competing. It's like taking two starving babies in a crib and throwing in one bottle." Father Michael Haddad replied: "Certainly this is a depressed area and jobs and housing are tight. But how can we justify picking out the Vietnamese and saying that they cannot come?" Ultimately, a meeting of the two leaders in the presence of the city's black mayor led to a joint proposal for Federal funds to meet the needs of both the refugees and the community.[28]

THE UNEMPLOYMENT ISSUE

The assumption that the newcomers represent a major threat to the jobs of native Americans is a familiar refrain in every period. In 1975, when the country was in recession and unemployment was reckoned at 9.1 percent, a huge number of Vietnamese refugees arrived. According to a Gallup poll, 54 percent of the American people opposed their resettlement in this country. When the economy turned upward again, it was discovered that the 170,000 Indochinese had not become new recruits in the army of the unemployed or competitors for the jobs of those already employed. Darrel Montero and Judith McDowell of the University of Maryland have tracked their progress, reporting in early 1979 that "fully 94 percent of those who sought jobs are employed, and income among the refugees has increased steadily since 1975. A majority (51 percent) of households report a combined monthly income of $800 or more, with fewer than 3 percent reporting less than $200." But their findings also showed that most of the refugees had accepted lower-status positions than they had held at home. Montero and McDowell emphasized that "over 90 percent of the Vietnamese refugees' income is from wages and salaries, not public assistance."[29] Fears that they might become a charge on society have not materialized.

This has been due to two reasons: the resiliency of the refugees who have taken it for granted that they must begin their new life with a lower status than they had enjoyed at home, and the effectiveness of the resettlement agencies in winning the support of the American people, even in areas that once were considered provincial and ethnocentric. Iowa, for example, has taken a generous mix adding up to about 3,000 — not bad when compared with New York State's 6,000, which is not too good when compared with California's 70,000 and even Louisiana's 8,000. The new Iowan population consists of 1,300 Thai immigrants, not refugees; 1,050 Vietnamese, 200 Lowland Laos, 400 Hmongs, and 50 Cambodians. The program was formally adopted by the state government, which placed its official seal of approval on such activities by establishing a state-funded Refugee Service Center. Governor Robert Ray, with widespread approval, thereafter announced that the state would welcome 1,500 boat people. The director of the program, who also has responsibility for finding jobs for the refugees, says: "We tell our refugees this country only gives you two things: entry into the country and an opportunity to live in a free society."[30]

The problems of adjustment are illustrated by the Iowa experience. The refugees had been brought into the state because most of them were said to be farmers. But there are no rice paddies in Iowa, and these farmers had never seen, much less operated, a John Deere tractor. The solution, however, was found by providing vocational training so that the refugees could be placed in light industry.

SUCCESSFUL TRANSPLANTS

A uniquely successful refugee community, involving the most exotic population, has been built in what might have appeared to be the least likely place in America — Missoula, Montana. Here, because the terrain provides "geographical compatibility," a group of 800 Hmongs are thriving under conditions that allow them to maintain much of their culture while enjoying the good will of the local community. Missoula, though a university town, is a small Western ranching city which had never had more than a 1 percent minority population. In 1976, when the first refugees arrived, there were some unpleasant incidents of verbal and physical abuse, cli-

maxed by a fracas over public health and sanitation issues. But the aftermath has been a demonstration of what can be achieved when the leaders of
two cultures teach mutual respect. Nan Borton of IRC's national staff, who
supervised the Missoula project, says: "That the town has received its refugees with as little overt backlash as it has is due initially to the dedication
and hard work of a group of American sponsors in the town – work which
the IRC office has followed up and extended."

Of considerable importance in Missoula has been the self-organization of
the Hmongs as the Lao Family Community, whose Council of Elders pre-
sides over internal affairs. Under the leadership of Moua Cha, who was a
student at the University of Montana when Laos fell to the Communists, the
LFC has devoted a great deal of time to orienting Missoulan sponsors and
volunteers, a substantial number of local citizens whom IRC has interested
in assisting the refugees. It provides instruction in English and serves as a
communications link and lubricant in relations with the schools, public
health authorities and employment services. Pam Roberts, IRC's local
representative, organized an Indochinese Support Group in the town, consisting of some seventy volunteers who belong to one or more of seven
working subcommittees: publicity – which makes available press releases,
slide shows, public service announcements about the refugees; home tutor-
ing – a highly successful program for which IRC paid 50 percent of the cost,
with the other half paid by the volunteers, so that tutors could be trained in
the latest methods of language instruction; health and medical needs – a
program directed by a volunteer public health nurse, using student nurses
whose work with refugees counts toward their academic practicum; drives
for household goods and clothing; gardening assistance; transportation;
and housing. Contributing significantly to the success of the community
effort has been the fact that state officials have cooperated actively.

In other parts of the country similar results have been achieved because
private entrepreneurs have recognized that the refugee population is an
invaluable resource. One observer has been led to comment that Americans
may be reassured by noting that the Protestant work ethic is alive and well
among the Buddhist refugees. An example of synergistic success through the
cooperation of businessmen and sponsoring agencies is the case of Showell
Farms in Maryland, which mass-produces and packages chickens. The
refugees work hard and earn $4 per hour, with fringe benefits that include
insurance, health and dental plans, a paid one-week vacation and even
pensions if they remain long enough. The employer, however, is reconciled
to high turnover, knowing that after accumulating sufficient savings the
workers are likely to seek other jobs in warmer areas of the United States.
Something of IRC's approach to placement is discernible in a memorandum
sent by Charles Sternberg to the resettlement offices around the country.
Discussing the Showell Farms experience, he wrote:

I have often expressed my bias against resettlement of refugees in very small communities or company towns since, I have felt, this creates isolation and dependence on one employer. That's why I think little of agricultural placements. If Showell Farms refutes my prejudice, this is, in part, due to the fact that it is not a farm but a chicken factory and, much more important, because our Washington office has remained in close touch with the refugees and there have always been enough of them to counteract a feeling of loneliness.

The advantage of Showell is that the hourly wage is not less but rather more than the first wage in most other jobs we can find for unskilled Indochinese; that housing is very cheap by city standards; and that the employer does not expect the refugees to stay on forever but seems to be rather resigned to their leaving after a few months, one suspects, often in their own cars.

Thus, in the last analysis, the issue for the Indochinese, as it has been for their predecessors who fled from Europe to the New World, becomes a matter of finding jobs, housing and education so that their aspirations for liberty and security can be fulfilled.

Poul Hartling, the United Nations High Commissioner for Refugees, has said: "I sometimes fear that it is relatively easy for the world to be reconciled to the tragedy of an unknown refugee who drowns, or otherwise perishes, for he makes no demand on any nation. It is far more difficult to be reconciled to resolving the problems of those who live." That indeed has been one of the truths perceived by the founders of the International Rescue Committee in the 1930s; it is a truth that will be very much with us in the remaining decades of this century.

XVI

The Balance Sheet

For the victim, not a hair's breadth separates the Goering Reflex ("When I hear the word Culture I reach for my gun") from the Mao Reaction ("Political power grows from the barrel of a gun"). To the eye of the social scientist, there are indeed differences, but to the men and women who dissent, the doctrines mean the same: the dungeon, the torture chamber, the bullet of the executioner. When brute force is the juridical premise of a society, the best of its citizens will look for every crevice that allows escape.

In our lifetime, countless millions have been plunged into slavery and death by ideologues of all shades and shirts—black, brown or red. Still other millions, however, have dared to make the voyage to freedom. To be sure, wherever they have gone they have found neither perfect freedom nor perfect contentment. For some, the attempt has ended in disillusionment, but for most, it has meant the one thing that makes life worth living—a chance to hope. Though they have left behind their valued possessions and lifelong associations, they can believe in their future because they still carry with them their psychological and spiritual resources. Those who do make it to safety survive in their new surroundings because they have hearts and feet that don't wear out.

Sometimes they flee *en masse*, like the 10 million East Pakistanis, the 2 million Indochinese, the near-million Cubans, the three-quarter million Ethiopians, the half-million Angolans. Sometimes they are a mere handful crashing through a border checkpoint or groping their way at night along a mountain path. Or they may be lone figures who once knew power and have lost it. Or they may be ex-Communists, idealists who traveled into Utopia but did not have the foresight to buy a round-trip ticket. Or they may be those stubborn devotees of freedom whose love of country condemns them to separation from it, like the dissident who, on his arrival in the United States is asked by a television interviewer, "Why do you, Vladimir Bukovsky, decide that you can stand up against your government?" and who replies, "If not I—who?"

In the twentieth century, as in previous ages, it can be said that one way to measure the evil in a society is the degree to which it extrudes its population as if between the rollers of a giant press. When refugees pour out of a country like water through a ruptured dam, they are bursting the boundaries of a land that is no longer theirs but that they hope some day to reclaim.

The multinational character of the refugee migrations is testimony to the desire for freedom that is fundamental to human nature. Apologists for dictatorial regimes, themselves enjoying the freedoms of democratic societies, suggest cynically that other peoples — Africans, Asians, Russians — do not really want liberty because they have much more urgent needs, like bread. A typical example is the statement of David Lattimore writing in the *New York Times Book Review* in 1979: "Group orientation being ancient, Communist China cannot be blamed for depriving her people of rights they had not previously enjoyed."[1] But apparently there are Chinese who do blame their regime so intensely that they are ready to risk their lives in shark-infested waters to escape the ancient "group orientation" so acceptable to an American book reviewer exercising his right to freedom of the press.

THE CONTINUING TASK

It is estimated that 17 million refugees now roam the world. As this is written, the International Rescue Committee finds itself confronting challenges on new fronts. The Russian invasion has sent nearly a million Afghans across the border into Pakistan. In the first year of the 1980s, IRC's President John C. Whitehead, accompanied by staffer Lou Wiesner and Edwin J. Wesely, a Board member, was at the Pakistani frontier developing a program of assistance for the men and women fleeing the Russian troops. Because Islamabad feared Soviet retaliatory moves, it hesitated to approve the presence of IRC medical teams, but months of negotiations finally proved fruitful. As the Indochinese and Cuban crises continued, Communist expansionism and tribal war in the Horn of Africa required an IRC presence in Sudanese refugee centers. Martial law in Poland, the Communist weapon against the working class, has brought defections among foreign service officers; Sweden and Vienna are providing asylum to those who have fled, and IRC is on hand to sustain and resettle. There is little hope that the flow of refugees around the world will abate in the years ahead.

Fortunately, IRC has not stood alone and has allies in the other voluntary agencies. But it has served a unique function: nonsectarian, it has filled the gaps that might otherwise have existed in the humanitarian pattern woven by the religious relief agencies. The magnitude of the work done by Catholic, Protestant and Jewish welfare groups is beyond measurement, and IRC's officers have cooperated with them through the American Council of

Voluntary Agencies. There has been a moving display of unity among the spiritual and humanitarian leaders of the free world.

Committed to an ethic rooted in its democratic credo, IRC has been able to act in areas where governments could not move. In Hungary, when the Western nations were paralyzed by fear of unleashing global war, rescue work could still be carried out on the edges of the Iron Curtain and a message of solidarity communicated to a heroic people. Twenty-five years earlier, in Vichy France, the United States government could not contravene the laws of a regime that it recognized for purposes of maintaining a listening post on the Hitler-occupied continent; but private American citizens could maintain an underground railway for anti-Nazi politicals and intellectuals. In Africa, American public opinion could support anticolonialism by giving aid to refugees long before governmental policy expressed itself. In the Western hemisphere, refugees from regimes like that of Trujillo could be assisted by IRC while Washington was still attempting to extricate itself from policy dilemmas. When the United States, negotiating with Mao's government through the good offices of Islamabad, "tilted towards Pakistan," American citizens could take their stand alongside the victims of the Bangladesh crisis. In Southeast Asia, during both the Indochina war and its aftermath, Americans addressed themselves to humanitarian needs by functioning through agencies like IRC.

At the same time, though a private organization, IRC has had the opportunity to work with governmental and intergovernmental programs. During World War II it participated in the National War Fund, and after the fighting implemented numerous contracts with the federal government's United States Escapee Program. It has worked with the State Department's Office of Refugee and Migration Affairs and with the recently established U.S. Coordinator for Refugee Affairs. Its resettlement activities have led to close cooperation with the Department of Health, Education and Welfare and its successor. Throughout the years it has been the recipient of operational grants from the United Nations High Commissioner for Refugees and has maintained a close working relationship with the Intergovernmental Committee for Migration, as it is now called. The record has been one of mutual cooperation.

Perhaps the most remarkable aspect of IRC's history has been its success in raising a common banner to which every freedom-loving element in the nation has been able to rally. The whole spectrum of America's pluralism has been represented in IRC's councils. Businessmen have contributed funds and material supplies for the refugees. In its most critical period following World War II, it attracted leaders like General William Donovan, who recognized the importance of American support for all democratic forces in Europe, including the democratic socialist governments struggling against Communist subversion. Trade union leaders and industrialists have worked side by side in a joint effort to help the opponents of tyranny, regardless of class, creed, race, nationality, or political identification. This was the case in the days of Hitler; it was also true in the early 1950s when, for example, David Dubinsky of the International Ladies Garment Workers Union, and Lessing Rosenwald (who had already arranged for a contribution of $100,000 from the Rosenwald Fund) jointly and successfully appealed to the Ford Foundation to contribute $500,000 to IRC's Resettlement Campaign for Exiled Professionals. Virtually every group loyal to the American tradition of freedom and asylum has contributed to IRC's work. Presidents of the United States, whether Democratic or Republican, have applauded IRC; congressmen and senators from both parties, conservatives and liberals, and democratic socialists such as Norman Thomas have participated in IRC's campaigns.

What has unified them behind IRC's work has been a shared belief in the sanctity of the human being. No matter how astronomical the numbers of refugees may become in any given crisis, the ultimate reality is the suffering borne by the individual person. All carry the same burdens, but each feels the anguish in his own way. The uniqueness of the human person is visible even when one looks out at thousands huddled on the grounds of the Peruvian embassy or under the open skies of West Bengal. For each the pain is distinctive. It was Kierkegaard who said that "every human being is an exception" — and none are so exceptional as those who are homeless. Perhaps it has been best said by Bulgarian-born Elias Canetti, who fled to England in 1938 and won the Nobel Prize for Literature in 1981: "One can touch the unhappiness of the whole world in a single man, and as long as we don't give him up then nothing is given up."

Whether they come in hordes or handfuls, bereft of home and possessions, they bring with them a capacity for tears, but also for laughter. They mourn what they have given up and grieve for those who were lost at sea or who fell victim to the jungle path or who were impaled on the barbed wire. They long for the relatives left behind and dream of landmarks in the homeland. But they also know how to joke, as witness the sign in Spanish raised by Cubans landing in Key West: "Will the last to leave Cuba please turn out the lights." Indeed, the lights were turned out many years ago, but there is always hope that they will be turned on again.

"NOTHING HUMAN IS ALIEN. . . ."

In serving the need of the refugee as an individual, IRC believes that nothing is more inimical than standardization of policy and routinization of practice. As his person is unique, so too are his requirements.

To summarize the unlimited variety and scope of IRC's activities means virtually to sample the range of human experiences. IRC has set up schools and nurseries; provided psychiatric services for refugees; clothed and fed and housed the homeless; trained apprentices; transformed actresses into fashion designers; equipped workers and professionals with vocational tools — a sewing machine for a dressmaker, a violin for a musician, a typewriter for a journalist, an evening gown for an entertainer; paid laboratory fees for researchers and work permit fees for laborers; taught English to people speaking many languages; bought textbooks and slates for students; given toys to children; helped an agronomist decide whether he would have better opportunities in Australia or the United States; paid the costs of emigration — fees for visas, medical examinations, photo-copies of documents.

IRC has set up art shows for painters; bought equipment for a Yugoslav refugee football team in Italy; financed a concert tour by refugee musicians; counseled Hitler victims on how to file indemnity claims; sent polio vaccine to relatives of refugees still behind the Curtain; shipped a Ruddock Peritoneoscope to a Polish doctor ("I lack words to express my gratitude... first instrument of its kind in Poland... a milestone in the development of the science and practice of hepatology"); purchased prosthetic limbs; helped groups defect *en masse* at the Rome Olympics, the Brussels World's Fair, and youth rallies in Berlin and Vienna; sponsored special commissions, such as that led by Harold Zellerbach in 1957, to induce world action correcting substandard conditions in refugee camps, and more recently the Citizens Commission on Indochinese Refugees; arranged for a dentist to fill a cavity; paid "key money" so that a refugee could take possession of an apartment; fed another while he finished his novel. The list is inexhaustible.

During these many years, IRC has trained specialists in immigration law. Gisele Birnbaum, a full-time volunteer, is IRC's chief immigration counselor. She has a law degree from the University of Brussels, and came to the United States in 1940 after escaping from the Nazi occupation of her native Belgium. Working with her as an advisor on immigration regulations is another full-time volunteer, Jacques Rapoport, also a Belgian. IRC studies have provided background data for the formulation of emergency governmental directives and the enactment of legislation like the Displaced Persons Act, the Refugee Relief Act, Public Law 85-316 (passed during the Hungarian crisis), the 1960 Public Law 86-648 (known as the "fair share" law), President Kennedy's action on Chinese refugees, and the Refugee Act of 1980. Helping the refugee through the maze of legalism has been an IRC responsibility, albeit at times a heartbreaking one. For the laws are such that the man who decides to be free on Monday may find refuge in the United States while the one who makes his decision on Tuesday may not. Long hours of research have often proved fruitful: a refugee ineligible under one country's immigration quota may prove to be eligible by birth under another quota, because the accidents of history and the tides of war have so juggled the map of continents.

In one year alone, 1978, IRC helped refugees from thirty-six countries, ranging literally from A to Z: Afghanistan, Albania, Angola, Bulgaria, Burma, Cambodia, Chile, China, Cuba, Czechoslovakia, Ethiopia, Ghana, Guinea, Haiti, Hungary, Iran, Iraq (Armenians and Kurds), Laos, Lebanon,

Morocco, Mozambique, Namibia, Nicaragua, Nigeria, Poland, Rumania, Somalia, the Soviet Union (Russians, Ukrainians, Armenians, Jews), South Africa, Syria, Tunis, Uganda, Uruguay, Vietnam, Yugoslavia, Zimbabwe-Rhodesia.

All this has been done with remarkable cost-effectiveness. A study of various charitable and public service organizations reported by *Forbes* magazine showed IRC expending only six percent of its total income on fundraising.[2] Its achievements in the field are due to an important facet of IRC's unique character—its mobility. Its quick-reaction capability is due primarily to its sensitivity to the political realities of our times and to its ability to summon a wide range of volunteers to take on assignments, even in distant places like Calcutta, Peshawar, Aranyaprathet, Khartoum or Kisumu. Whenever a crisis develops, its doors are besieged by specialists who know the culture and idiom of the refugees and the neighboring host countries, experts in logistics and commodity distribution, physicians and nurses, who are eager to serve. In the resettlement work its field offices around the world—in Bangkok, Brussels, Buenos Aires, Geneva, Hong Kong, Khartoum, Kinshasa, Kuala Lumpur, Madrid, Mexico City, Munich, Paris, Peshawar, Rome, Trieste and Vienna—are linked to its key offices in the United States and Canada—Atlanta, Boston, Dallas, Houston, Los Angeles, Miami, Missoula, Montreal, New York (its headquarters), Portland, San Jose, San Diego, San Francisco, Santa Ana, Seattle, Washington, D.C. and West New York (N.J.).

In great part, this facility to respond to new challenges coming from different directions and often simultaneously is due to the impact of the guiding spirits who have led the organization through its four decades. The list of its chairmen in the order of their service is imposing: publicist Amos Pinchot; journalist Oswald Garrison Villard; historian Charles A. Beard; philosopher John Dewey; lawyer Hollingsworth Wood; educator Frank Kingdon; theologian Reinhold Niebuhr; economist Leo Cherne. They have presided over an organization of volunteers who sustain a professional staff that literally encircles the globe. And despite its earth-spanning structure, IRC has established a remarkable record for internal managerial performance: its cost control makes it one of the most fiscally responsible nonprofit institutions in the United States. At the same time its officers and Board of Directors recognize that a single organization, no matter how impressive and efficient, cannot possibly cope with more than a fraction of the problem. But in the darkness created by totalitarianism and dictatorship, every ray of light takes on special luster and is visible across vast distances, like a match in the midst of a wartime blackout.

Though events and circumstances bring shifts in emphasis to IRC's work, the multiplying numbers of refugees have made resettlement a primary task. From its headquarters in New York the officers and Board members not only provide policy and direction but accept on-site and foreign service assignments. Charles Sternberg, as head of the staff, is recognized as one of the world's leading authorities on refugee assistance and resettlement; his career of service to refugees stretches in time and geography from Vichy's Marseilles to Indochina in the 1980s. On the other side of his desk have sat refugees from every corner of the earth, and he has heard virtually every accent in which freedom is spoken — German, Yiddish, Czech, Spanish, Russian, Hungarian, Rumanian, Croatian and Serbian, French, Dutch, Chinese, Bengali, Annamese, Tibetan. Indeed, the decision to be free is articulated in every tongue. Sternberg's art is the application of a political therapy made necessary by the pathology of the twentieth century.

HEALING THE WOUNDS

Refugees who have been able to bring themselves to speak of their experiences tell of the trauma they encounter, sometimes long after the initial break. Apparently the fact of homelessness seems to penetrate consciousness only with the ultimate realization, as one of them says, that "now you can take nothing for granted." The normal acts of living, no matter how trivial, can no longer be performed out of habit. Every act requires thought and conscious decision; and tomorrow the same act will require rethinking and redecision. No anchor, substantive or symbolic, is available to the refugee to give him stability in such a crisis.

At first, he may persuade himself that his exile will be short-lived — perhaps a matter of months or at most a few years. He may choose for his place of exile a site close to his native land, particularly if he is "political." He would like to remain in Vienna if he is Hungarian, in Miami if he is Cuban, in Kenya if he is Ethiopian. His orientation is to look homeward.

But the time comes when the harsh reality of totalitarianism strikes with a new terror: the battle will be long, and it may be many years, if ever, before return is possible. Even if he still thinks and plans for the eventual homecoming, he realizes he must sink roots in his new community and become a part of its life. For some, this even means a subtle change — from "refugee" to traditional "immigrant." Some plan primarily to play a role in the future life of their native land; others, while still eager to win liberation for their brethren, envision their children growing up in a new land of brighter opportunity. In most cases, the refugee, whether he is European, African, Asian or Latin-American, turns to the United States. No matter what hostile propaganda about America has been drummed in his ears — indeed, no matter what self-criticisms Americans may utter about their own country — he knows that here there is freedom to think, to speak, to make his own choices, without fear of imprisonment or torture.

But he learns also that a free country is not necessarily homogeneous. His coming will be met with debate as men and women weigh their own interests against the claims of humanity. There will be fears of economic competition and insistence on barring the doors. But he is heartened to know that there are also strong spokesmen in his behalf, such as the late President George Meany of the AFL-CIO addressing the President of the United States: "I am aware that some voices have been raised in opposition to a more liberal policy [of admitting refugees] on the grounds that it would exacerbate our unemployment problems and antagonize the trade union movement. I do not have to remind you that no one is more concerned about the problem of unemployment than the AFL-CIO, but that problem will hardly be affected by the number of Indochina refugees we are talking about.... Unemployment is not the only thing the labor movement cares about. We care about the suffering human beings everywhere."

The virtue of a moral decision is that it rises above self-interest, sometimes reaches into the area of self-sacrifice. Perhaps because almost all present-day Americans are descendants of political, religious or economic refugees, there is embedded in the national awareness a realization that the dislocations of migration may produce pathologies in individual and group behavior. Adjustment to a new culture does not come easily. As Irving Howe has pointed out, when success finally comes to an ethnic group — as it has to the Germans, the Irish, the Italians, the Jews and the other Eastern Europeans, as well as the Chinese and the Japanese — they tend to dwell on the heroic achievements and forget that "there was crime, there was wife desertion, and there were juvenile delinquency, gangsterism and prostitution during the eighties and nineties, as well as during the early decades of the twentieth century — probably more than the records show or memoirists tell."[3]

The hardships of adjustment and the frustrations aroused by assimilationism, the widening gulf between first and second generation immigrants and the irritations of lower-class identification are painful. Sometimes the tribulations of the journey itself lead to aberrations. Among the more recent arrivals, some of those reared in a totalitarian world may find the burdens of freedom too novel and too hard to bear. For the essence of a free society is the right to choose, a right that is harnessed to a duty of accountability — at the very least, an acceptance of personal responsibility for the consequences of one's choices.

These realities cannot be dismissed. No population is immune to the statistical operation of nature's bell curve, and there will always be people at the lower end. Americans who forget their own past are likely to see the undesirable minority, however small, as doubly perverse and troublesome because the offenders are "aliens" who should recognize a special obligation to behave.

ASSETS FOR THE WORLD

But the evidence is emphatic that in giving shelter to refugees the nation receives more than it gives. Simon Kuznets, Nobel Prize winner for economics and author of the concept of gross national product, has demonstrated statistically that America's growth and prosperity have correlated with its admission of immigrant populations. Winston Churchill has said: "The idea that only a limited number of people can live in a country is a profound illusion. It all depends on their cooperative and inventive power. There is no limit to the ingenuity of man if it is properly and vigorously applied under conditions of peace and justice." Since the refugees, as a group, tend to be the more venturesome and the more freedom-loving souls in their own lands, they bring with them the "inventive power" of which Churchill speaks. And the host country benefits from these human resources, even as it husbands them for a possible return to their homeland.

In the period following World War II IRC was able to help refugees return after long exile to their native lands where they carried on the fight for democratic government. Their ranks include men who have since played prominent roles in Germany, Italy, Austria and France. In the immediate postwar period, the resistance to communism was led by people who had gone back to Czechoslovakia, Poland, Hungary and other lands after Nazi exile. In Latin America, scores who found temporary shelter in the United States returned to the firing line in countries like the Dominican Republic and Nicaragua. Even Castro had found shelter from the Batista dictatorship in the United States.

Those who chose to remain permanently in the countries of resettlement have contributed richly to their adopted lands. In the United States, the roster includes some of the greatest scientific minds of the twentieth century — Einstein from Germany, Fermi from Italy, Teller and Szilard from Hungary. There are thousands whose names make no headlines but who work at lecterns in our universities; who use their engineering talents to build America; who as skilled craftsmen add to the quality and quantity of our output; who as executives expand our gross national product and our commerce, thus increasing our living standards; or who, as authors, playwrights and composers of music, enrich our culture.

At this moment in our troubled history, the nation needs more scientists, engineers and technicians to keep it in the forefront of industrial and technological programs. Whether they are "refugees" or "immigrants," the newcomers provide a reservoir of talent to help build the quality of life in America and to make the nation strong against the buffeting of international winds. In the decade from 1967, to 1976, the United States received 49,000 physicians and surgeons from abroad and more than 100,000 scientists and engineers. By 1978, American citizens who won Nobel prizes in chemistry and physics numbered sixty-seven; of these, nineteen were foreign-born. Of the fifty-eight Americans who won Nobel prizes in physiology and medicine, eighteen were foreign-born. So too our industrial plant is the beneficiary of the machinists, technicians, skilled craftsmen, tool-and-die makers admitted to our shores; our economy is stronger for the immigrants who became entrepreneurs, opened new businesses and provided more jobs. A nation that continues to be a magnet for the people of the world has not yet exhausted its potential for greatness.

Cold statistics cannot measure the value of the human treasure thus assembled in America. The International Rescue Committee, by assisting refugees to take a creative place in American society, has seen broken lives made whole again. It has given men and women an opportunity to recover from the wounds inflicted by cruel regimes. Once healed, they have been able to take up new lives as architects, journalists, teachers, lawyers, executives, economists, philologists, theologians, textile designers, shopkeepers, painters, sculptors, musicians.

The late Reinhold Niebuhr, America's outstanding theologian who for many years served as chairman of the International Rescue Committee, once said:

Never before in the 20th century has any nation been presented a greater opportunity to contribute so directly to the preservation of invaluable creative sources and to the enrichment of its own civilization.

There never was a time when America could so significantly stimulate her own culture through proper utilization of the talents which these human beings offer. These men and women are survivors of those who are responsible for the best their nations have produced. If we fail to seize this unique and pressing opportunity, we collaborate in the most grievous waste of creative talent in human history.

In its activities around the world, IRC has come to know many nationalities, races, and creeds. It has no illusions. It has watched mankind at its noblest and at its worst. It has been witness to the virtues and vices of all peoples and races. It has seen heroic men and women accepting generosity with both gratitude and dignity; it has seen others, disturbed, frantic, self-centered, making exorbitant demands. It has observed outpourings of enthusiasm and the dullness of apathy. It has seen people contribute unstintingly while others passed by without a glance for those less favored by history and geography.

From its variegated tapestry of human experience, IRC has emerged with hope for the future even though the evening of the twentieth century has brought heavy shadows. The current battles for the preservation, restoration or enlargement of freedom are desperate indeed. Powerful instruments of technology are in the hands of adventurers and fanatics. Totalitarian institutions are entrenched in a large portion of the world, and the number of democracies still continues to dwindle. Crafty dictators, dedicated to expansionism and hegemony, control the mass media of communication in their countries. The ultimate in scientific weaponry is in the hands of rulers who consider themselves the state and believe the state to be above all moral constraints.

Meanwhile the political institutions of the non-Communist world often seem unable to devise stratagems for coping with subversion from within and military pressure from without. Nor do societies in the free world know how to resolve the dilemma of avoiding internal interference in the affairs of other nations and yet at the same time pursue policies that will restrain the Brezhnevs, Pol Pots and Pinochets, the Idi Amins and the Somozas. So, too, there is lack of wisdom, if not of will, in determining how one can reject a Shah of Iran or a government of South Africa without inviting successor regimes that are even more repressive. In the interim, while the democracies seek solutions, new flows of refugees are being released into the arteries of the world.

To extricate mankind from the web of despair will remain the prime task in the remaining years of this century. Because the outcome is very much in doubt, the free world cannot allow any of its assets, physical or human, to be dissipated.

All that can be said of the future is what we know from the past. So long as people risk death to cross the mine fields, cut through the barbed wire, tunnel under the walls, beat their way through jungles, or fight wind and wave, it is clear that the desire for freedom is alive in the human spirit. Those who dare are entitled to the assurance that there will be friends waiting to receive them. Thomas Jefferson said he had sworn "eternal hostility against every form of tyranny over the mind of man." Such a vow is not easy to keep, as history has shown us. But because Americans still struggle to observe it, there is reason for hope in the world. For the story is far from its conclusion. One can end the latest chapter in the struggle only with the word: *And...*

Notes

PREFACE

1. Edward Alsworth Ross, "The Germans in America," *Century Magazine* 88 (May 1914): 104.

2. Edward Alsworth Ross, "The Scandinavians in America," *Century Magazine* 88 (June 1914): 296.

3. Edward Alsworth Ross, "Italians in America," *Century Magazine* 88 (July 1914): 444-45.

4. Edward Alsworth Ross, "The Hebrews of Eastern Europe in America," *Century Magazine* 88 (September 1914): 786.

5. Ibid., 479.

6. Thomas C. Wheeler, ed., *The Immigrant Experience* (New York: Penguin Books, 1971).

7. Czeslaw Milosz, "Biblical Heirs and Modern Evils — A Polish Poet in California," in Wheeler, *Immigrant Experience*: 198.

8. Ibid., 206.

9. Ibid., 199.

II. ESCAPE FROM HITLER

1. William L. Shirer, *The Rise and Fall of the Third Reich: A History of Nazi Germany* (New York: Simon and Schuster, 1960): 252.

2. Ibid., 185.

3. Both essays are included in Arthur Koestler, *The Yogi and the Commissar and Other Essays* (New York: The Macmillan Company, 1945).

4. The dramatic story of Fry's achievements has been recorded in the work of two participants, one of whom was Fry himself. See Varian M. Fry, *Surrender on Demand* (New York: Random House, 1945); and Mary Jane Gold, *Crossroads Marseilles 1940* (Garden City, N.Y.: Doubleday and Company, 1980).

5. Gershom Scholem, *Walter Benjamin: The Story of a Friendship*, trans. Harry Zohn (Philadelphia: Jewish Publication Society of America, 1981): 224-226.

6. Interview with Charles Sternberg, "Rescue Is Their Business," *New York Sunday News Magazine* (January 27, 1980).

7. Laura Fermi, *Illustrious Immigrants: The Intellectual Migration from Europe 1930-41*, 2d ed. (Chicago: University of Chicago Press): 87.

8. Joseph Buttinger, unpublished autobiographical notes.

9. Varian Fry, *Operation Emergency Rescue* (New York: *American Labor Conference on International Affairs*, reprint by International Rescue Committee, 1965): 3.

10. Buttinger, *Autobiographical*: idem.

11. Fry, *Surrender on Demand*, vi.

III. "AN IRON CURTAIN HAS DESCENDED"

1. Speech by Winston Churchill at Fulton, Missouri, March 5, 1946.

2. Janis Sapiets, "Conversation with Solzhenitsyn," *Encounter* 44 (March 1975): 71.

3. Nicholas Bethell, "After the Last Secret," *Encounter* 45 (November 1975): 88. This article is an epilogue to Bethell's *The Last Secret: The Delivery to Stalin of Over Two Million Russians by Britain and the United States* (New York: Basic Books, 1974).

4. Quoted in Hugo Bieber and Moses Hadas, *Heine* (Philadelphia: Jewish Publication Society of America, 1956): 389-90.

5. Claire Sterling, *The Masaryk Case* (New York: Harper and Row, Publishers, 1970): 348-49.

IV. ISLAND OUTPOST — WEST BERLIN

1. Quoted in David Martin, *Saving Freedom's Seed Corn: The First 25 Years of the International Rescue Committee* (New York: International Rescue Committee, 1958): 17.

2. During this period the American press kept a bright spotlight on the flight of refugees. A sampling of the coverage includes items like the following: "Anti-Stalinists Abroad Called Big Soviet Fear. In plea for 'Iron Curtain Refugees,' Bedell Smith Says Reds Recall Lenin." (*New York Herald Tribune*, October 26, 1949). "Byrd, Smith Urge Aid for Refugees. Admiral and General Join in Pleas for Those Who Fled Iron Curtain Areas." (*New York Times*, October 26, 1949.) "Refugees Pouring Past Iron Curtain. Agency Here Helps Genuine Foes of Totalitarianism to Relocate in Free Lands." (*New York Times*, January 22, 1950.) "Spaatz Cites Rift in Iron Curtain. Chairman of Refugee Drive Says 300,000 Have Broken Through With Vital Facts." (*New York Times*, November 3, 1950.)

3. Raymond D. Gastil, ed., *Freedom in the World: Political Rights and Civil Liberties 1980* (New York: Freedom House, 1980): 5.

V. AFTER STALIN — THE WINDS OF REVOLT

1. Quoted in David Martin, *Saving Freedom's Seed Corn — The First 25 Years of the International Rescue Committee* (New York: International Rescue Committee, 1958): 24.

2. Ibid., 25.

VI. HEROISM IN HUNGARY

1. François Bondy, "European Notebook – Budapest's 'October'," *Encounter* 48 (March 1977): 68.
2. Leo Cherne, "Thirty Days That Shook the World: An Editorial," *The Saturday Review* (December 22, 1956): 22.
3. *That Freedom May Not Perish* . . . (New York: International Rescue Committee, n.d.), unpaged.
4. Ibid.
5. Cherne, "Thirty Days," 22.
6. Paul Jonas, "Home Thoughts From Abroad," *Harper's* 254 (April 1977): 21.

VII. HOMELESS IN EUROPE

1. Two reports were issued by the *Zellerbach Commission on the European Refugee Situation*, one in 1958 and a supplementary special report entitled *European Refugee Problems 1959*. The original report included the text of basic international documents like the *Geneva Convention on Refugees*, the *Statute of the Office of the United Nations High Commissioner for Refugees*, and various provisions relating to the functioning of the Intergovernmental Commission for European Migration (ICEM).
2. Speech of Angier Biddle Duke, at Conference on Refugees, Geneva, November 20, 1958.
3. Adam B. Ulam, "Titoism," in Milorad M. Drachkovitch, ed., *Marxism in the Modern World* (Stanford, Calif.: Stanford University Press, 1970): 153.
4. Max Lerner, *America as a Civilization: Life and Thought in the United States Today* (New York: Simon and Schuster, 1957): 23.
5. *Statute of the Office of the United Nations High Commissioner for Refugees*, Chapter II, Sec. 6(A)(ii).
6. Ibid., Chapter I, Sec. 2: "The work of the High Commissioner shall be of an entirely non-political character; it shall be humanitarian and social and shall relate, as a rule, to groups and categories of refugees." The final phrase is intended to discourage activities on behalf of single individuals and to require a concentration on groups. Actually, UNHCR officials have found it essential to make judgments on particular individuals in order to determine whether they meet the definition of refugee.
7. Zellerbach Commission, *1959 Report*: 46.
8. Quoted, ibid., 49.
9. Ibid.
10. Ibid., 51.
11. Quoted, ibid., 73.
12. "$91 Million Pledged to U.N. for Palestinian Relief," *New York Times*, December 6, 1979.
13. Roy A. Medvedev, *Let History Judge – The Origins and Consequences of Stalinism* (New York: Vintage Books, a division of Random House, 1973): 476-77.
14. The rape of Czechoslovakia has been described in detail by a high-ranking Communist official who fled to Vienna in 1977. Zdenek Mlynar, *Nightfrost in Prague* (New York: Karz Publishers, 1980).

15. Memorandum of the Jewish Labor Committee, *Treatment of "The Jewish Question" by Polish Solidarity,"* February 24, 1982, listing a series of quotations from *Solidarnosc* during October and November 1981. An accompanying statement reviews the objective evidence of the government's complicity in the anti-Jewish demonstration of March 8.

16. Laraine Lippe, "From Russia With Love: One Woman's Experience in the Pre-migration Counselling of Soviet Refugees," unpublished master's thesis, School of International Living, Brattleboro, Vt., January 2, 1978: 7.

17. Ibid., 12-13.

18. "Khrushchev Scores Soviet 'Parasites'," *New York Times*, June 26, 1961.

19. Malcolm W. Browne, "Soviet Jew Delivers Challenge on Rights," *New York Times*, July 12, 1977.

20. Walter Reich, "The Case of General Grigorenko—A Second Opinion," *Encounter* 54 (April 1980): 15.

21. Walter Reich, "Soviet Psychiatry on Trial," *Commentary* 65 (January 1978): 40-48. This article recounts how the World Psychiatric Association, after a bitter debate, adopted a resolution condemning the Soviet practice of imprisoning dissidents in mental institutions. Dr. Paul Chodoff, a Washington psychiatrist who led the floor fight for the resolution, said: "It is abhorrent that people should be labeled insane solely because it suits the state for various reasons to handle them in this fashion, or because psychiatrists can be found to collaborate in this manner."

22. "An Emigré Waits for Scholarly Job," *New York Times*, December 5, 1975.

23. Simon Markish, "Passers-by: The Soviet Jew as Intellectual," *Commentary* 66 (December 1978): 34.

24. Lippe, *From Russia*, 53-54.

VIII. HURRICANE IN THE CARIBBEAN AND LATIN AMERICA

1. Herbert L. Matthews, *Revolution in Cuba—An Essay in Understanding* (New York: Charles Scribner's Sons, 1975): 382.

2. Quoted in letter to editor, from Saul Bellow, Senators Henry M. Jackson and Daniel P. Moynihan, Lane Kirkland, Arthur Schlesinger, Jr., et al., *New York Times*, October 12, 1979.

3. Huber Matos, "Letter from a Havana Prison," *New York Times*, November 17, 1975.

4. Irving Howe, "Mercy," *New York Times*, June 22, 1977.

5. "Vance Hints Better Ties If Cuba Frees Prisoners," *New York Times*, January 28, 1977.

6. "The Situation of Women in the Political Prison System of Cuba," Report of the Inter-American Commission on Human Rights, Organization of American States, June 1976, excerpted in *Of Human Rights*, Georgetown University (Fall 1977): 5.

7. President Johnson's statement was made in September 1965 at the base of the Statue of Liberty as he announced an airlift from Cuba which brought 260,000 Cubans to the United States. Castro ended the airlift in 1973.

8. Editorial, *Miami Herald*, August 4, 1968.

9. Hugh Thomas, "The Life and Times of Fidel Castro," *New York Times Book Review* (June 15, 1980): 3.

10. "Opinion Roundup," *Public Opinion* 3 (June/July 1980): 40.

11. Amitai Etzioni, "Refugee Resettlement: The Infighting in Washington," *The Public Interest*, no. 65 (Fall 1981): 27-28.

12. "Miami Sees Long-Term Benefit From New Refugees," *New York Times*, June 9, 1980.

13. "Text of State Dept. Statement on a Refugee Policy," *New York Times*, June 21, 1980.

14. "Reagan Aide Defends Detention of Haitians," *New York Times*, December 16, 1981.

15. Raymond D. Gastil, ed., *Freedom in the World: Political Rights and Civil Liberties 1980* (New York: Freedom House, 1980). For data on the individual countries, see alphabetized sections in "Part V — Country Summaries," beginning at 209.

16. Cecil Lyon, *Report to IRC*, January 28, 1974.

17. Edward M. Kennedy, *Opening Statement at the Hearing of the Senate Refugee Subcommittee on the Chile Parole Program*, October 2, 1975.

IX. BIRTH PAINS OF A NATION — BANGLADESH

1. The Steering Committee of the International Committee on the University Emergency then issued a statement, "Premeditated Massacre of Bengali Scholars," *Freedom at Issue* 7 (May-June 1971): 5.

2. Gunnar Myrdal, *Asian Drama: An Inquiry Into the Poverty of Nations* (New York: Pantheon, a division of Random House, 1967): vol. 1, 240-241.

3. Editorial, "The Sixth Capital," Calcutta *Statesman*, July 29, 1971.

4. Jon E. Rohde, Dilip Mahalanabis and Pierce Gardner, *Guideline to the Management of Common Medical Problems Among Bangladesh Refugees* (Calcutta: International Rescue Committee and All India Institute of Medical Sciences, 1971).

5. Pierce Gardner, Jon E. Rohde and M.B. Majumdar, "Health Priorities Among Bangladesh Refugees," *The Lancet* (April 15, 1972): 834-36.

6. Rochelle Girson, "International Rescue Committee: Friend to the Displaced," *The Saturday Review* (December 4, 1971): 101.

X. TWILIGHT OF EMPIRE IN AFRICA

1. George H.T. Kimble, *Society and Polity*, vol. 2 of *Tropical Africa* (New York: Twentieth Century Fund, 1960): 232.

2. Ibid.

3. From *Report of the Commission on Closer Union of the Dependencies*, London, 1929, reprinted in T. Walter Wallbank, *Contemporary Africa: Continent in Transition* (New York: D. Van Nostrand Company, 1956): 158-59.

4. Henry Kyemba, *State of Blood: The Inside Story of Idi Amin's Reign of Fear* (London: Corgi Books, a division of Transworld Publishers Ltd., 1977): 56-57.

5. Ibid., 98.

6. Will Durant, *The Reformation: A History of European Civilization from Wyclif to Calvin: 1300-1564 (Part VI, The Story of Civilization)* (New York: Simon and Schuster, 1957): 193.

7. Ibid.

8. Bayard Rustin and Carl Gershman, "Africa, Soviet Imperialism, and the Retreat of American Power," *Commentary* 64 (October 1977): 38-39.

9. Ibid., 38.

10. Ibid., 42.

11. Ibid.

12. "The Distress of the Cabindan Refugees," *Church Newsletter* (Kinshasa), January 20, 1977.

XI. ESCAPE TO KENYA

1. Patrick Kumumwe, "Escape from Nakasero," *Drum* (March 1978): 6-13.

2. Martin Marty, "The Modern Martyrs," *Britannica Book of the Year 1978* (Chicago: Encyclopaedia Britannica, Inc., 1978): 618.

3. Henry Kyemba, *State of Blood: The Inside Story of Idi Amin's Reign of Fear* (London: Corgi Books, a division of Transworld Publishers Ltd., 1977): 179-80. Chapter 8, "No One Is Sacred," details Idi Amin's attack on the Christian churches.

4. Edward Hoagland, "At Large in East Africa," *Harper's* 253 (August 1976): 64.

XII. HONG KONG – "BLOODY FRIGHTENING"

1. Aldrich's poem appeared originally in the *Atlantic Monthly* for April 1892. It is quoted in Horace M. Kallen, *Cultural Pluralism and the American Idea: An Essay in Social Philosophy* (Philadelphia: University of Pennsylvania Press, 1956): 84-85.

2. Quoted in John F. Kennedy, *A Nation of Immigrants*, rev. ed. (New York: Harper & Row, 1964): 78.

3. Ibid., 77.

4. Robert Elegant, "China's Next Phase," *Foreign Affairs* 46 (October 1967): 149.

5. Franz Schurmann and Orville Schell, eds., *Communist China: Revolutionary Reconstruction and International Confrontation*, vol. 3 of *The China Reader* (New York: Vintage Books, a division of Random House, 1967): 620.

6. Ibid., 621.

7. Barbara W. Tuchman, *Notes From China* (New York: Collier Books, 1972): 47.

8. Ibid., 49-50.

9. Bao Ruo-Wang (Jean Pasqualini) and Rudolph Chelminski, *Prisoner of Mao* (New York: Coward, McCann & Geoghegan, Inc., 1973): 10.

10. Hong Kong *Standard*, March 23, 1969.

11. Hong Kong *Standard*, August 10, 1969.

12. "Hundreds Executed in Kwantung as Drive Against Criminals and 'Counter-revolutionaries' Intensifies," *New York Times*, June 7, 1970.

13. Quoted in International Rescue Committee, *Annual Report 1978*: 9.

XIII. LAND OF DRAGONS – SOUTHEAST ASIA

1. Gunnar Myrdal, *Asian Drama: An Inquiry Into the Poverty of Nations* (New York: Pantheon, a division of Random House, 1967): vol. 1, 143.

2. Ibid.

3. Ibid.

4. Raymond James Sontag and James Stuart Beddie, eds., *Nazi-Soviet Relations 1939-1941: Documents from the Archives of the German Foreign Office* (Washington, D.C.: U.S. Department of State, 1948): 242-43.

5. All three volumes appeared under the imprint of Frederick A. Praeger, Publisher, New York.

6. Chester L. Cooper, *The Lost Crusade: America in Vietnam* (New York: Dodd, Mead and Company, 1970): 130-31.

7. Joseph Buttinger, *Vietnam: A Dragon Embattled* (New York: Frederick A. Praeger, Publisher, 1967): 890-91.

8. Quoted in International Rescue Committee, *Annual Report 1966*: 4.

9. Ibid.

10. Editorial, *New York Times*, May 2, 1975.

11. John F. Kennedy, *A Nation of Immigrants*, rev. ed. (New York: Harper & Row, 1964): 3.

12. Quoted in Stanley Feldstein and Lawrence Costello, eds., *The Ordeal of Assimilation* (Garden City, N.Y.: Anchor Press/Doubleday and Company, 1974): 11.

13. Kennedy, *A Nation of Immigrants*, 69.

14. United Press International, May 1, 1976.

XIV. EXODUS FROM INDOCHINA

1. Barry Came, "A Rocky Haven of Pulau Bidong," *Newsweek* 94 (July 2, 1979): 47.

2. Leo Cherne, "Hell Isle," *New York Times* (February 3, 1979).

3. Ibid.

4. Stephen B. Young, "The Legality of Vietnamese Re-education Camps," *Harvard International Law Review* 20 (Fall 1979): 525-26.

5. Ibid., 526n.

6. Jean Lacouture has been widely recognized as an outstanding writer on the former French colonies in Southeast Asia. He had been among the most vigorous opponents of the Vietnam war, but has become as outspoken in condemning the tyranny of the Communist victors as he was in condemning U.S. policies. The fate of Cambodia has been particularly shocking for him, as he reveals in painful detail in a book called *Survive le Peuple Cambodgien (Let the People of Cambodia Live)*, published by Seuil in Paris. Elsewhere he has written: "Shame alone would justify my writing this little book — which is, in essence, *un cri d'horreur* — the shame of having contributed — however little, however negligible the influence of the press in this case — to the establishment of one of the most repressive regimes in history." ("The Revolution That Destroyed Itself," *Encounter* 52 (May 1979): 53.)

7. "Indochinese Refugees," *The MacNeil/Lehrer Report*, July 4, 1979, transcript: 1-3.

8. Henry Kamm, "Captain Who Saved 49 Vietnamese Fears for Job," *New York Times*, June 23, 1978.

9. Letter to Charles Sternberg from D.F. Georgiadis, "Lydia" Compania Maritima, S.A., May 12, 1978.

10. An excellent analysis of the relevant admiralty laws will be found in a Report to the Admiralty Committee of the New York City Bar Association, dated January 19, 1979, prepared by Diana L. Melnick, Esq.

11. Letter from Sadruddin Aga Khan, United Nations High Commissioner for Refugees, to Chairman, International Chamber of Shipping, October 3, 1977.

12. Henry Kamm, "Refugees Raped and Murdered by Thai Fishermen," *New York Times*, November 23, 1979. Similar stories of rapes have appeared frequently. On May 7, 1980, the *Times* carried a story by Bernard D. Nossiter, datelined the United Nations in New York, indicating that one of every two boats that landed in Malaysia reported attacks and rapes by pirates. Despite a plea from Poul Hartling, the United Nations High Commissioner for Refugees, that United Nations interventions be presented, Secretary General Kurt Waldheim apparently took the position that the problem was largely one for the Malaysian and Thai governments. The United States, loath to antagonize friendly nations, made no formal representations but did deliver a patrol boat to Thailand for the purpose of countering piracy. In July, Henry Kamm was able to report that seven Thai fishermen had been sentenced to eight to twenty-four year prison terms for such attacks.

22. Henry Kamm, "10,000 Laotian Aides Reported Detained," *New York Times*, March 25, 1979.

14. Henry Kamm, "Laos Resists Newest Overlord, Hanoi," *New York Times*, February 12, 1979.

15. Quoted in William Safire, "The Other Gas Crisis," *New York Times*, January 28, 1980.

16. William Safire, "Yellow Rain," *New York Times*, December 13, 1979.

17. Sterling Seagrave, *Yellow Rain: A Journey Through the Terror of Chemical Warfare* (New York: M. Evans and Co., 1981).

18. Dr. Townsend's *Interim Report of Chemical Warfare Use Against Hmong in Laos* submitted to the International Rescue Committee covers a series of episodes from April through June 1981. A table analyzes the occurrences by: date of event; place; mode of delivery; weapon description; reporter; animal/human results; plant results; and conclusion.

19. The documentary is summarized in a lengthy editorial in the *Wall Street Journal*, December 18, 1981.

20. Editorials casting doubt on the charges were entitled "Too Quick on Yellow Rain" (November 17, 1981) and "Seeing the World in Red and Yellow" (March 19, 1982).

21. Tom Wicker, "An Unneeded Horror," *New York Times*, March 23, 1982.

22. "Excerpts from State Department Report on Chemical Warfare," *New York Times*, March 23, 1982.

23. Dominica P. Garcia, "In Thailand, Refugees' 'Horror and Misery'," *New York Times*, November 14, 1979.

24. "Cambodia," *Britannica Book of the Year 1976* (Chicago: Encyclopaedia Britannica, Inc., 1976): 178.

25. Ibid., 179.

26. "Cambodia," *Britannica Book of the Year 1977* (Chicago: Encyclopaedia Britannica, Inc., 1977): 181.

27. "Cambodia," *Britannica Book of the Year 1978* (Chicago: Encyclopaedia Britannica, Inc., 1978): 234.

28. Ibid.

29. "Cambodia," *Britannica Book of the Year 1979* (Chicago: Encyclopaedia Britannica, Inc., 1979): 232.

30. Ibid.

31. Ibid.

32. "Cambodia," *Britannica Book of the Year 1980* (Chicago: Encyclopaedia Britannica, Inc., 1980): 228-29.

33. Noam Chomsky and Edward S. Herman, *The Political Economy of Human Rights* (Boston: South End Press, 1979), vol. 2: 347.

34. Jack Anderson, "3 Million Slain in Cambodia," *Syracuse Post Standard*, November 2, 1979.

35. Chomsky and Herman, *Political Economy*, 149.

36. Ibid., 299-300.

37. Leopold Labedz, "Of Myths and Horrors," *Encounter* 54 (February 1980): 37-49. See also "Letters: Chomsky Replies," in *Encounter* 55 (July 1980): 93-94, and Labedz's response, "Chomsky Revisited": 28-35.

38. Labedz, "Chomsky Revisited," 33.

39. William Shawcross, "A Society Whose Sinews Were Ripped Out," *Washington Post*, March 17, 1980. A further account of the horrors visited on Cambodia by the Khmer Rouge is given in his article, "The End of Cambodia," *New York Review* 26 (January 24, 1980): 25-30.

40. François Ponchaud, *Cambodia: Year Zero* (New York: Holt, Rinehart & Winston, 1978): x.

41. Ibid., xv.

42. Ibid., xiv.

43. Ibid., xvi.

44. Sydney Schanberg, "The Death and Life of Dith Pran: A Story of Cambodia," *New York Times Magazine* (January 20, 1980): 39.

45. Ibid.

XV. IN SEARCH OF SHELTER

1. "Human Flotsam," *The Economist* 269 (December 16, 1978): 13.

2. A valuable summary of the regulations of the Immigration and Naturalization Service is provided in a document, dated May 22, 1978, addressed to "Indochinese Mutual Assistance Associations" by Jean Sauvageot of the Refugee Task Force of the U.S. Department of Health, Education and Welfare, Office of Family Assistance.

3. These figures were provided by Abdulgaffar Peang-Meth, former press and information officer of the Cambodian Embassy in Washington, and president of the Cambodian Moslem organization in the United States, Khmer Islam. (*New York Times*, June 21, 1980.)

4. Leo Cherne, *A Personal Recollection* (New York: International Rescue Committee, Citizens Commission on Indochinese Refugees, February-March 1978): 8.

5. Ibid., 12.

6. Ibid., 16-18.

7. "Transcript of Selected Questions and Answers at Carter's Meeting in Kentucky," *New York Times*, August 1, 1979.

8. Cherne, *A Personal Recollection*, includes the full text of the Commission's recommendations as an unpaged addendum. The recommendation on the distinction between "economic" and "political" refugees is Number 6.

9. Ibid., 28.

10. *Congressional Record* 124, March 15, 1978.

11. "Can We Save the Cambodian People?," Appeal by Oxfam-America, *New York Times*, October 7, 1979.

12. Henry Kamm, "Food for Cambodia Is Tied Up in Ports," *New York Times*, April 6, 1980.

13. "Open Letter to the Socialist Republic of Vietnam," *New York Times*, May 30, 1979.

14. Robert Lindsey, "Peace Activists Attack Vietnam on Rights," *New York Times*, June 1, 1969.

15. Joan Baez, letter to the editor, *New York Times*, March 4, 1980.

16. Letter written to a pacifist friend, dated February 28, 1980.

17. "Soviet Assails Joan Baez for Anti-Vietnam Letter," *New York Times*, August 15, 1979.

18. "Cambodia: The Fancies and the Facts," *Time* (February 18, 1980): 47.

19. Ibid., 48.

20. A dispatch from Henry Kamm in Kuala Lumpur said: "Malaysia in effect withdrew its threat today to force the 75,000 Vietnamese refugees in camps here back out to sea and to shoot on sight any newcomers nearing its shores. The threat was made Friday in informal comments to reporters by Deputy Prime Minister Mahathir Mohammad." ("Malaysia Cancels Threats to Refugees," *New York Times*, June 19, 1979.)

21. Deirdre Carmody, "Cambodian Tells of His Harrowing Escape," *New York Times*, July 1, 1979.

22. Irving Howe, *World of Our Fathers* (New York: Harcourt Brace Jovanovich, 1976): 231n.

23. Quoted in Laura Fermi, *Illustrious Immigrants: The Intellectual Migration from Europe, 1930-41* (Chicago: University of Chicago Press, 1968): 23.

24. Ibid., 30.

25. *Los Angeles Times*, July 23, 1979. The story carried a banner headline across the front page in inch-high type: "Disease Control Dilemma."

26. "Refugees a Strain on Health Services," *New York Times*, July 19, 1979.

27. "Louisiana: Vietnam Fallout," *Newsweek* (September 11, 1978): 36.

28. Ibid.

29. Darrel Montero and Judith McDowell, "Refugees: Making It," *New York Times*, March 12, 1979.

30. Many sociological studies have demonstrated the high rate of economic success achieved by immigrant populations in the United States. An article in *Forbes*, the business magazine, says: "A recent study by Barry R. Chiswick of the University of Illinois, Chicago Circle, found that earnings of foreign-born, legally admitted Americans are 9.5% lower than the native-born if they have been in the U.S. for only 5 years, but only 3.4% lower after 10 years, equal after about 13 years and 6.4% and 13% *higher* after 20 years and 30 years respectively." (Phyllis Berman, "Does the Melting Pot Still Meld?," *Forbes* 122 (October 30, 1978): 63.)

XVI. THE BALANCE SHEET

1. David Lattimore, review of *The China Difference* by Ross Terrill (New York: Harper & Row, 1979), in *New York Times Book Review* (August 12, 1979): 15.

2. "Getting and Giving," *Forbes* 123 (February 5, 1979): 50.

3. Irving Howe, *World of Our Fathers* (New York: Harcourt Brace Jovanovich, 1976): 96.

Selected Bibliography

The function of a bibliography is twofold: to provide sources to which the individual seeking further detail may turn, and to indicate the kind of material on which the author has relied. The data on the International Rescue Committee are drawn from its voluminous files, annual reports, staff memoranda, field correspondence, minutes of meetings, surveys, communications with and from government officials, supplemented by interviews with those directly involved and by personal observation. The historical background against which IRC activities have been portrayed is based on the sources indicated below.

PREFACE

Feingold, Henry L. *Zion in America: The Jewish Experience from Colonial Times to the Present.* New York: Hippocrene Books, Inc., 1974.

Glazer, Nathan and Daniel Patrick Moynihan. *Beyond the Melting Pot.* Cambridge, Mass.: The M.I.T. Press, 1963.

Kallen, Horace M. *Cultural Pluralism and the American Idea: An Essay in Social Philosophy.* Philadelphia: University of Pennsylvania Press, 1956.

Milosz, Czeslaw. "Biblical Heirs and Modern Evils: A Polish Poet in California," in Thomas C. Wheeler, ed., *The Immigrant Experience: The Anguish of Becoming American.* New York: Dial Press, 1971, pp. 193-210.

Ross, Edward Alsworth. "The Germans in America," *The Century Magazine,* Vol. 88, No. 1, May 1914, pp. 98-104.

_____. "The Scandinavians in America," *The Century Magazine,* Vol. 88, No. 2, June 1914, pp. 291-298.

_____. "Italians in America," *The Century Magazine,* Vol. 88, No. 3, July 1914, pp. 439-445.

_____. "The Hebrews of Eastern Europe in America," *The Century Magazine,* Vol. 88, No. 5, September 1914, pp. 785-792.

CHAPTER II, "ESCAPE FROM HITLER"

Arendt, Hannah. *The Origins of Totalitarianism.* New York: Harcourt Brace & World, 1966.

Benjamin, Walter. *Reflections: Essays, Aphorisms, Autobiographical Writings.* Translated by Edmund Jephcott. New York: Harcourt Brace Jovanovich, 1978.

Dawidowicz, Lucy S. *The War Against the Jews.* New York: Bantam Books, 1975.

Djilas, Milovan. *The New Class.* New York: Harcourt Brace & World, 1957.

_____. *The Unperfect Society: Beyond the New Class.* New York: Harcourt Brace & World, 1970.

Egan, Eileen and Elizabeth Clark Reiss. *Transfigured Night: The CRALOG Experience.* (Council of Relief Agencies Licensed for Operation in Germany.) Narberth, Penn.: Livingston Publishing Co., 1964.

Fermi, Laura. *Illustrious Immigrants: The Intellectual Migration from Europe 1930-41.* Second edition. Chicago: University of Chicago Press, 1968.

Fry, Varian M. *Surrender on Demand.* New York: Random House, 1945.

Gold, Mary Jane. *Crossroads Marseilles 1940.* Garden City, N.Y.: Doubleday and Company, 1980.

Grosser, Paul E. and Edwin G. Halpern. *Anti-Semitism: The Causes and Effects of a Prejudice.* Secaucus, N.J.: Citadel Press, 1979.

Grunberger, Richard. *The 12-Year Reich: A Social History of Nazi Germany 1933-1945.* New York: Holt, Rinehart and Winston, 1971.

Handlin, Oscar. *A Continuing Task: The American Jewish Joint Distribution Committee 1914-1964.* New York: Random House, 1964.

Heiden, Konrad. *Der Fuehrer: Hitler's Rise to Power.* Translated by Ralph Manheim. Boston: Houghton Mifflin Company, 1944.

Knapp, Wilfrid. *A History of War and Peace 1939-1965.* London: Royal Institute of International Affairs, Oxford University Press, 1967.

Laqueur, Walter. *The Terrible Secret: Suppression of the Truth About Hitler's "Final Solution."* Boston: Little, Brown and Co., 1981.

Lash, Joseph P. *Eleanor and Franklin: The Story of Their Relationship Based on Eleanor Roosevelt's Private Papers.* New York: W. W. Norton & Company, 1972.

Levin, Nora. *The Holocaust: The Destruction of European Jewry 1933-1945.* New York: Thomas Y. Crowell Co., 1968.

Papanek, Ernst (with Edward Linn). *Out of the Fire.* New York: William Morrow and Company, 1975.

Scholem, Gershom. *Walter Benjamin: The Story of a Friendship.* Translated from the German by Harry Zohn. Philadelphia: Jewish Publication Society of America, 1981.

Shirer, William L. *The Collapse of the Third Republic: An Inquiry into the Fall of France in 1940.* New York: Simon and Schuster, 1972.

_____. *The Rise and Fall of the Third Reich: A History of Nazi Germany.* New York: Simon and Schuster, 1960.

Toland, John. *Adolph Hitler.* New York: Ballantine Books, a division of Random House, 1976.

Truman, Harry S. *Memoirs of Harry S. Truman*. Garden City, N.Y.: Doubleday & Co., 2 volumes, 1955.

CHAPTER III, "AN IRON CURTAIN HAS DESCENDED"

Acheson, Dean. *Present at the Creation: My Years in the State Department*. New York: W. W. Norton & Company, 1969.

Bethell, Nicholas. *The Last Secret: The Delivery to Stalin of Over Two Million Russians by Britain and the United States*. Preface by H. R. Trevor-Roper. New York: Basic Books, 1974.

_____. "After the Last Secret," *Encounter*, Vol. XLV, No. 5, November 1975, pp. 82-88.

Bieber, Hugo and Moses Hadas. *Heine*. Philadelphia: Jewish Publication Society of America, 1956.

Gastil, Raymond D., ed. *Freedom in the World: Political Rights and Civil Liberties 1980*. New York: Freedom House, 1980.

Halle, Louis J. *The Cold War as History*. New York: Harper and Row, Publishers, 1967.

Harriman, W. Averell and Elie Abel. *Special Envoy to Churchill and Stalin 1941-1946*. New York: Random House, 1975.

Koestler, Arthur. *The Yogi and the Commissar*. New York: Macmillan Company, 1945.

Korbel, Josef. *The Communist Subversion of Czechoslovakia 1938-1948: The Failure of Coexistence*. Princeton, N.J.: Princeton University Press, 1959.

LaFeber, Walter, ed. *The Origins of the Cold War, 1941-1947: A Historical Problem with Interpretations and Documents*. New York: John Wiley and Sons, Inc., 1971.

Lukacs, John. *A History of the Cold War*. Garden City, N.Y.: Doubleday and Co., 1961.

Sapiets, Janis. "Conversations with Solzhenitsyn," *Encounter*, Vol. XLIV, No. 3, March 1975, pp. 67-72.

Solzhenitsyn, Alexander. *The Gulag Archipelago*. Translated from the Russian by Thomas P. Whitney. New York: Harper and Row, Publishers, 1974.

Sterling, Claire. *The Masaryk Case*. New York: Harper and Row, Publishers, 1970.

Tolstoy, Nikolai. *The Secret Betrayal*. New York: Charles Scribner's and Sons, 1978.

CHAPTER IV, "ISLAND OUTPOST — WEST BERLIN"

Gastil, Raymond D., ed. *Freedom in the World: Political Rights and Civil Liberties 1980*. New York: Freedom House, 1980.

Jacobs, Dan N., ed. *The New Communist Manifesto and Related Documents*. New York: Harper Torchbooks/The Academy Library, Harper and Row, 1961.

Lukacs, John. *A History of the Cold War*. Garden City, N.Y.: Doubleday and Co., 1961.

Mee, Charles L., Jr. *Meeting at Potsdam*. New York: M. Evans & Co., 1974.

Ulam, Adam B. *Stalin, The Man and His Era*. New York: Viking Press, 1973.

Windsor, Philip. *City on Leave: A History of Berlin, 1945-62*. London: Chatto & Windus, 1963.

CHAPTER V, "AFTER STALIN – THE WINDS OF REVOLT"

Crankshaw, Edward. *Khrushchev's Russia*. Baltimore, Md.: Penquin Books, Ltd., 1959.
_____. *The New Cold War*. Baltimore, Md.: Penguin Books, Ltd., 1963.
Fainsod, Merle. "Krushchevism," in Milorad M. Drachkovitch, ed. *Marxism in the Modern World*. Stanford, California: Stanford University Press, 1965.
Kennedy, John F. *The Strategy of Peace*. Edited by Allan Nevins. New York: Harper & Brothers, 1960.

CHAPTER VI, "HEROISM IN HUNGARY"

Bondy, François. "European Notebook – Budapest's 'October'," *Encounter*, Vol. XVIII, No. 3, March 1977, p. 68.
Bursten, Martin A. *Escape From Fear*. Syracuse, N.Y.: Syracuse University Press, 1958.
Cherne, Leo. "Thirty Days That Shook the World: An Editorial," *The Saturday Review*, December 22, 1956, pp. 22-23, 31.
Jonas, Paul. "Home Thoughts from Abroad," *Harper's*, Vol. 254, April 1977, pp. 20-21.
Life magazine, editors of. *Hungary's Fight for Freedom*. Foreword by Archibald MacLeish. New York: Time, Inc., 1956.
Michener, James A. *The Bridge at Andau*. New York: Random House, 1957.

CHAPTER VII, "HOMELESS IN EUROPE"

d'Encausse, Hélène Carrère. *Decline of an Empire: The Soviet Socialist Republics in Revolt*. Translated by Martin Sokolinsky and Henry A. La Farge. New York: Newsweek Books, 1979.
Lippe, Laraine. *From Russia With Love: One Woman's Experience in the Pre-migration Counselling of Soviet Refugees*, Master's thesis, unpublished, January 2, 1978.
Markish, Simon. "Passersby: The Soviet Jew as Intellectual," *Commentary*, Vol. 66, No. 6, December 1978, pp. 30-40.
Medvedev, Roy. *Let History Judge: The Origins and Consequences of Stalinism*. New York: Alfred A. Knopf, 1971.
Medvedev, Zhores A. *The Medvedev Papers: The Plight of Soviet Science Today*. London: Macmillan London Ltd., 1971.
Reich, Walter. "The Case of General Grigorenko: A Second Opinion" (a psychiatrist's report on his examination of General Grigorenko after his release to the West), *Encounter*, Vol. LIV, No. 4, April 1980, pp. 9-24.
Tabori, Paul. *The Anatomy of Exile: A Semantic and Historical Study*. London: Harrap, 1972.
Taylor, Telford (with Alan Dershowitz, George Fletcher, Leon Lipson and Melvin Stein). *Courts of Terror: Soviet Criminal Justice and Jewish Emigration*. New York: Alfred A. Knopf, 1976.
Ulam, Adam B. "Titoism," in Milorad M. Drachkovitch, ed., *Marxism in the*

Modern World. Stanford, California: Stanford University Press, 1970, pp. 136-163.

Vernant, Jacques. *The Refugee in the Post-War World*. New Haven: Yale Press, 1953.

Wiesel, Eli. *The Jews of Silence: A Personal Report on Soviet Jewry*. Translated from the Hebrew with an historical afterword by Neal Kozodoy. New York: Holt, Rinehart and Winston, 1967.

CHAPTER VIII, "HURRICANE IN THE CARIBBEAN AND LATIN-AMERICA"

Draper, Theodore. "Castroism," in Milorad M. Drachkovitch, ed., *Marxism in the Modern World*. Stanford, California: Stanford University Press, 1970, pp. 191-224.

_____. *Castro's Revolution: Myths and Realities*. New York: Frederick A. Praeger, Publisher, 1962.

Etzioni, Amitai. "Refugee Resettlement: The Infighting in Washington," *The Public Interest*, No. 65, Fall 1981, pp. 15-29

Gastil, Raymond D., ed. *Freedom in the World: Political Rights and Civil Liberties 1980*. New York: Freedom House, 1980.

Horowitz, Irving Louis, ed. *Cuban Communism*. New Brunswick, N.J.: Transaction Books, 1971.

Pachter, Henry M. *Collision Course: The Cuban Missile Crisis and Coexistence*. New York: Frederick A. Praeger, Publisher, 1973.

Thomas, Hugh. *Cuba: The Pursuit of Freedom*. New York: Harper & Row, Publishers, 1971.

CHAPTER IX, "BIRTHPANGS OF A NATION—BANGLADESH"

Edwardes, Michael. *History of India: From the Earliest Times to the Present Day*. London: The New English Library, Mentor Edition, 1967.

Gardner, Pierce; Jon E. Rohde; and M. B. Majumdar. "Health Priorities Among Bangladesh Refugees," *The Lancet*, April 15, 1972, pp. 834-836.

Girson, Rochelle. "International Rescue Committee: Friend to the Displaced," *The Saturday Review*, December 4, 1971.

Levenstein, Aaron. "Calcutta: A Dying City 'Out of Hand'," *Freedom at Issue*, No. 10, November-December 1971, pp. 1-2, 16-20.

Moorhouse, Geoffrey. *Calcutta*. New York: Harcourt Brace Jovanovich, 1972.

Myrdal, Gunnar. *Asian Drama: An Inquiry Into the Poverty of Nations*. 3 volumes. New York: Pantheon, a division of Random House, 1968.

Statement of Steering Committee of the International Committee on the University Emergency, "Premeditated Massacre of Bengali Scholars," *Freedom at Issue*, No. 7, May-June 1971, p. 5.

Warner, Denis. "Bangladesh: Is There Anything to Look Forward To?", *The Atlantic*, Vol. 242, No. 5, November 1978, pp. 6-13.

CHAPTERS X AND XI, "TWILIGHT OF EMPIRE IN AFRICA" AND "ESCAPE TO KENYA"

Brooks, High C. and Yassin El-Ayouty, eds. *Refugees South of the Sahara: An African Dilemma*. Westport, Conn.: Negro Universities Press, 1970.

Gann, Lewis H. and Peter Duignan. *White Settlers in Tropical Africa*. Baltimore, Md.: Penguin Books, Ltd., 1962.

Hoagland, Edward. "At Large in East Africa," *Harper's*, Vol. 253, No. 1515, August 1976, pp. 64-68.

Kimble, George H. T. *Tropical Africa: Society and Polity, Vol. II*. New York: Twentieth Century Fund, 1960.

Kyemba, Henry. *State of Blood: The Inside Story of Idi Amin's Reign of Fear*. London: Corgi Books, a division of Transworld Publishers Ltd., 1977.

Legum, Colin. *Congo Disaster*. Baltimore, Md.: Penguin Books, 1961.

Magdalany, Fred. *State of Emergency: The Full Story of Mau Mau*. Boston: Houghton Mifflin Co., 1963.

Oliver, Roland and J. D. Fage. *A Short History of Africa*. Baltimore, Md.: Penguin Books, 1962.

Rustin, Bayard and Carl Gershman. "Africa, Soviet Imperialism, and the Retreat of American Power," *Commentary*, Vol. 64, No. 4, October 1977, pp. 33-43.

Wallbank, Walter T. *Contemporary Africa*. Princeton, N.J.: D. Van Nostrand Company, Inc., 1956.

"When a State Goes Insane," Editorial, *New York Times*, May 2, 1979.

CHAPTER XII, "HONG KONG—BLOODY FRIGHTENING"

Bernstein, Richard. *From the Center of the Earth: The Search for the Truth about China*. Boston: Little, Brown & Co., 1982.

Bloodworth, Dennis. *The Chinese Looking Glass*. New York: Farrar, Straus and Giroux, 1967.

Bulletin of the Atomic Scientists. *China After the Cultural Revolution: A Selection from the Bulletin of the Atomic Scientists*. New York: Random House, 1972.

Butterfield, Fox. *China: Alive in the Bitter Sea*. New York: Times Books, 1982.

Cohen, Arthur A. "Maoism," in Milorad M. Drachkovitch, ed., *Marxism in the Modern World*. Stanford, California: Stanford University Press, 1970.

Leys, Simon. *Chinese Shadows*. New York: Viking Press, 1977.

Ruo-Wang, Bao (Jean Pasqualini) and Rudolph Chelminski. *Prisoner of Mao*. New York: Coward, McCann and Geoghegan, Inc., 1973.

Schurmann, Franz and Orville Schell, eds. *Communist China: Revolutionary Reconstruction and International Confrontation, 1949 to the Present*. New York: Vintage Books, a division of Random House, 1967.

Schwartz, Harry. *China*. New York: Atheneum, 1965.

Terrill, Ross. *The China Difference*. New York: Harper & Row, 1979.

Tuchman, Barbara W. *Notes from China*. New York: Collier Books, 1972.

Wickert, Erwin. "Journeys to the Grave of Master Confucius," *Encounter*, Vol. LIV, No. 3, March 1980, pp. 9-12.

Wood, Dianne, ed. *Hong Kong 1979*. Hong Kong: Government Publications Centre, 1980.

CHAPTER XIII, "LAND OF DRAGONS: SOUTHEAST ASIA"

Buttinger, Joseph. *The Smaller Dragon.* New York: Frederick A. Praeger, Publisher, 1958.

_____. *Vietnam: A Dragon Embattled.* 2 Volumes. New York: Frederick A. Praeger, Publisher, 1967.

_____. *Vietnam, A Political History.* (A condensation of the previous volumes with an additional chapter on the war.) New York: Frederick A. Praeger, Publisher, 1968.

Cooper, Chester L. *The Lost Crusade: America in Vietnam.* Foreword by Ambassador W. Averell Harriman. New York: Dodd, Mead & Company, 1970.

Kennedy, John F. *A Nation of Immigrants.* Rev. Ed. New York: Harper & Row, 1964.

Myrdal, Gunnar. *Asian Drama.* Volume 1. New York: Pantheon, a division of Random House, 1968.

Shaplen, Robert. *Time Out of Hand: Revolution and Reaction in Southeast Asia.* New York: Harper and Row, Publishers, 1968.

Sontag, Raymond James and James Stuart Beddie, eds. *Nazi-Soviet Relations 1939-1941: Documents from the Archives of the German Foreign Office.* Washington, D.C.: United States Department of State, 1948.

CHAPTER XIV, "EXODUS FROM INDOCHINA"

"Agony of the Boat People," *Newsweek,* July 2, 1979, pp. 42-50.

Citizens Commission on Indochinese Refugees. *Report.* New York: International Rescue Committee, 1978.

Kamm, Henry. "The Agony of Cambodia," *New York Times Magazine,* November 19, 1978, pp. 40-42, 142-152.

Labedz, Leo. "Of Myths and Horrors," *Encounter,* Vol. LIV, No. 2, February 1980, pp. 37-49.

Ponchaud, François. *Cambodia: Year Zero.* New York: Holt, Rinehart & Winston, 1978.

Schanberg, Sydney. "The Death and Life of Dith Pran," *New York Times Magazine,* January 20, 1980, pp. 16-23, 35 *et seq.*

Seagrave, Sterling. *Yellow Rain: A Journey Through the Terror of Chemical Warfare.* New York: M. Evans and Co., 1981.

Shawcross, William. "The End of Cambodia?", *New York Review of Books,* January 24, 1980.

United Nations High Commissioner for Refugees. A summary of UNHCR activities, *UNHCR,* No. 4, October-November 1980.

United States Department of State. *Chemical Warfare in Southeast Asia and Afghanistan.* Washington, D.C.: United States Department of State, 1982.

Wicker, Tom. "An Unneeded Horror," *New York Times,* January 29, 1982.

Young, Stephen B. "The Legality of Vietnamese Re-education Camps," *Harvard International Law Journal,* Vol. 20, No. 3, Fall 1979, pp. 519-538.

CHAPTER XV, "IN SEARCH OF SHELTER"

Baez, Joan. "Open Letter to the Socialist Republic of Vietnam," full-page advertisement, endorsed by other prominent citizens, *New York Times,* May 30, 1979.

Cherne, Leo. *A Personal Recollection: Citizens Commission on Indochinese Refugees*. New York: International Rescue Committee, February-March 1978.

Everingham, John. "One Family's Odyssey to America," *National Geographic*, Vol.
157, No. 5, May 1980, pp. 642-661.

Fermi, Laura. *Illustrious Immigrants: The Intellectual Migration from Europe,
1930-41*. Second edition. Chicago: University of Chicago Press, 1968.

Garrett, W. E. "Thailand: Refuge from Terror," *National Geographic*, Vol. 157, No.
5, May 1980, pp. 633-642.

Howe, Irving. *World of Our Fathers*. New York: Harcourt Brace Jovanovich, 1976.

Kelly, Gail Paradise. *From Vietnam to America: A Chronicle of the Vietnamese
Immigration to the United States*. Boulder, Colo.: Westview Press, 1977.

Stone, Scott C. S. and John E. McGowan. *Wrapped in the Wind's Shawl: Refugees
of Southeast Asia and the Western World*. San Rafael, California: Presidio
Press, 1980.

Torjesen, Hakon; Karen Olness; and Erik Torjesen. *The Gift of the Refugees: Notes
of a Volunteer Family at a Refugee Camp*. Eden Prairie, Minn.: The Garden,
1981.

Wain, Barry. *The Refused: The Agony of the Indochina Refugees*. New York: Simon
& Schuster, 1981.

Index

About the Author

AARON LEVENSTEIN is Professor Emeritus of Management at Baruch College of the City University of New York. He directed the IRC's program in India during the Bangladesh emergency. He is the author of *Labor Today and Tomorrow, Why People Work, Freedom's Advocate, The Nurse as Manager,* and has contributed articles to the *American Journal of Orthopsychiatry, Social Science, Freedom at Issue,* and *The Wall Street Journal.*